scandalous bodies

Diasporic Literature
in English Canada

Smaro Kamboureli

OXFORD
UNIVERSITY PRESS

OXFORD
UNIVERSITY PRESS

70 Wynford Drive, Don Mills, Ontario M3C 1J9
www.oupcan.com

Oxford University Press is a department of the University of Oxford.
It furthers the University's objective of excellence in research, scholarship,
and education by publishing worldwide in

Oxford New York

Athens Auckland Bangkok Bogotá Buenos Aires Calcutta
Cape Town Chennai Dar es Salaam Delhi Florence Hong Kong Istanbul
Karachi Kuala Lumpur Madrid Melbourne Mexico City Mumbai
Nairobi Paris São Paulo Singapore Taipei Tokyo Toronto Warsaw

with associated companies in Berlin Ibadan

Oxford is a trade mark of Oxford University Press
in the UK and in certain other countries

Published in Canada
by Oxford University Press

Canadian Cataloguing in Publication Data
Kamboureli, Smaro
Scandalous bodies : diasporic literature in English Canada
Includes bibliographical references and index.
ISBN 0-19-541450-0

1. Canadian literature (English) – Minority authors – History and criticism*
I. Title.

PS8089.5.M55K35 1999   C810.9'8   C99-931834-9   PR9188.2.M55K35 1999

Cover Image: Geoff Power / Photonica
Cover & Text Design: Tearney McMurtry

1 2 3 4 - 03 02 01 00
This book is printed on permanent (acid-free) paper ♾.
Printed in Canada

To my parents

Για τους γονεις μου

που εχασαν και το αλλο παιδι τους,

και την οικογενεια του, στην διασπορα

— οπου και να ειμαι εισαστε μαζι μου —

For Laura and Meg Kroetsch

Contents

Preface and Acknowledgements   vii

Critical Correspondences:
The Diasporic Critic's (Self-)Location   1

One   **Realism and the History of Reality:**
F.P. Grove's *Settlers of the Marsh*   27

Two   **Sedative Politics:**
Media, Law, Philosophy   81

Three   **Ethnic Anthologies:**
From Designated Margins
to Postmodern Multiculturalism   131

Four   **The Body in Joy Kogawa's *Obasan:***
Race, Gender, Sexuality   175

Notes   222
Works Cited   245
Index   261

Preface and Acknowledgements

This book developed out of a number of questions and experiences I began mulling over in the late 1980s. That was the time when ethnic literature in English Canada was slowly beginning to establish its own ground; it was also the time when multiculturalism, already in its second decade as an official policy, entered a 'new' stage as Canadians began vigorously to express their opinions on the merits and perils of officially sanctioning ethnicity.

Although I did not set out to write anything resembling a history of ethnic writing in Canada, in the early stages of this study I was interested in tracing the principal events and ideological forces that had made ethnic literature marginal, the better to appreciate the intricacies of recent changes in the Canadian literary tradition. My reading of ethnic literature in a systematic way began at a time when the canon ignored an entire body of works by writers whose names, more often than not, were 'hard to pronounce', or who wrote about cultural traditions beyond Canada's own.

In my attempts to trace the development of Canadian ethnic literature, I kept discovering many beginnings—each pointing to a different trajectory. Beyond the historical patterns of Canada's colonial legacy and the persistent discrimination suffered by Canadians of minority origins, ethnic literature defies a unified approach. 'Diaspora' may commonly evoke displacement, but particular communities and individuals resist being subsumed into a single narrative; instead, they demand that we address their cultural, historical, and ideological specificities.

When I committed myself to writing a book about ethnic literature, there existed very few critical studies seriously concerned with ethnic writers and their diasporic contexts. A few special issues of journals addressed the relationship between ethnicity and literature; a small number of essays sought to identify literary, psychological, or thematic patterns in this literature. There was no substantial criticism on ethnicity growing out of what we might safely call the mainstream critical tradition. This situation changed after 1985 with the publication of various books and edited collections of essays. Yet, as Enoch Padolsky observes, they 'were written by minority critics and published by minority-oriented presses' (375). There were, of course, articles and books on such authors as F.P. Grove; but those studies rarely, if ever, thematized the ways in which ethnicity is inscribed in the texts and authors they examined. While a number of small presses have been instrumental in the emergence of diasporic writing, it is only during the past few years that this literature has become, as mainstream publishers and the media keep telling us, *de rigueur*. During this same period the terms of the debates about ethnicity and multiculturalism have changed in both enabling and troubling ways.

This study is the result of my engagement both with ethnic writing in Canada and with the various contexts that have informed it. Yet *contexts* is the crucial word: contexts as the diverse political and intellectual settings within which ethnic culture is produced; contexts as the critical and personal terrains that I have traversed as a reader of that literature. For reasons that I hope will become apparent in the course of this study, my emphasis on history should not be taken to mean that I attempt to offer either a linear reading of the development of ethnic literature or a synthesis of that body of writing. Linearity pays no heed to disjunctions, and synthesis always entails ignoring or diminishing differences. Thus I have deliberately avoided discussing a wide range of the many diasporic voices that have emerged since the late eighties. If I have a single objective in this study, it is not so much to define ethnic diversity as to problematize difference. This is one of the reasons why I have refrained from joining the ongoing debate about the semantic and political differences between diaspora and ethnicity as concepts; although they are different, their genealogies overlap, and I have decided to work with their intersections rather than to offer definitions that could at best be provisional.

If plot, as Peter Brooks tells us, is 'the logic or perhaps the syntax of a certain kind of discourse, one that develops its propositions only through temporal sequence and progression' (xi), then, strictly speaking, this book lacks a cohesive syntax. Its narrative does not always unfold sequentially, nor does it present a single argument or interpretation, let alone adhere to a single method of reading. Instead of making the complex issues I am concerned with here fit a preordained theoretical model or systematic approach, I have let specific texts give shape to my readings. In fact, methodological issues, and the constant need to revisit them, become a kind of leitmotif in the book. Above all, this study does not pretend to be free of biases; if anything, what I believe—in the double sense of informed attitude and embodied knowledge—will be only too apparent in the text, even when those beliefs are not directly stated.

One of the central intentions of this study is to move beyond the inclination, fostered by multiculturalism, to mythologize and hence to idealize articulations of ethnicity. As Rey Chow says, mimicking the tenor of certain multicultural attitudes, the notion that the '"other" can say or do anything in the current climate without being considered wrong' is not just misbegotten but capable of doing more harm than good. 'As history shows,' Chow argues, 'idealism is always anchored in violence' (1998, xxiii). My intention in this study, then, is to analyze the elements of diasporic literature and official multiculturalism, rather than to construct a positivistic image of the ethnic imaginary as it is produced either by members of the diaspora or by the Canadian state and its institutions. The Us and Them paradigm, which figures prominently in many studies of ethnicity and multiculturalism in Canada, is rooted in a reality of asymmetrical relations.

Granted, many of these asymmetries are still present, but we cannot eradicate them simply by resorting to reductive relativism and the reversal of binary thinking. The answer is not to effect a perfect symmetry, and thus yield to the futile promises of a utopian project; rather, I think we need to learn how to live with contradictions, and to do so without fetishizing difference.

Hence this book's title: *Scandalous Bodies*. 'Scandal' and 'body' are equally polysemantic in this study. 'Body' refers to corporeality, but also to the body politic; it is what I focus on, more often than not, in order to examine the politics of identity. The body's desires, its traumas, its abuse are all contingent on the body politic and its various manifestations. Similarly, 'scandal' is a sign of excess and transgression, but also of violation and indignity. Neither the diasporic body nor the body politic is scandalous in itself. Although I am heedful of the many issues I was unable to explore in this study, I hope I have not lost sight of the fact that the true scandal in this case would have been to propose a single 'moral' concerning multiculturalism—to disregard the fact that contingency, be it hidden away or easily observable, holds the key to any change we may effect.

The book opens with an essay (I hesitate to call it a chapter) that records my thinking and writing process as an academic who disavows disinterest-as-objectivity. It is an essay as in *essai*: a trial, a test—in effect, my attempt to make sense of the incommensurability of ethnicity, to address the reciprocity that exists (or ought to exist) between an academic's professional discourse and her daily life. In a move that may surprise some readers, it includes my response to Wim Wenders' film *Wings of Desire*. Ostensibly irrelevant to diasporic Canadian literature, this film (and my writing about it) enabled me to take a fresh look at some of the central themes in this book, at a time when I had reached a critical impasse. It allowed me to thematize some of the consequences of the representation of diasporic subjectivity in the West, and to begin to understand some of the implications of the diasporic critic's location and her cultural and pedagogical responsibilities. 'Critical Correspondences', then, takes the place of both a formal introduction and a conclusion.

The four main chapters, although they have distinct historical and thematic foci, are all written in a manner that relies on both centrifugal and centripetal movements: I offer close readings of particular texts (some literary, some not), but also move beyond those texts to examine the ideological implications of historical contexts or events that shed light on them, their critical reception, or their cultural and political functions. If there is any single privileged approach, it is close reading: not the kind that views a text as a sovereign world, but one that opens the text in order to reveal the method of its making, the ways in which it is the product of the ongoing dialogue between various realities. Each one of the chapters—no matter how explicitly focused on a particular text—thus deals with other texts and discourses: hence the narrative detours that contribute to their length.

Chapter One, on F.P. Grove, announces one of the recurring concerns in this book, namely the ways in which the tradition of Canadian/ethnic literature relates to historical realities. Taking Grove as my case study, I test the realism of his first novel in English against such realities of his time as attitudes towards immigrants, universal values, and the construction of the nation and its cultural capital. My interest in the relation of literature to cultural and political forces turns, in Chapter Two, towards three perspectives from which we can examine multiculturalism: media, law, and philosophy. While neither a communications specialist, nor a legal expert, nor a philosopher, by training or by disposition, I am concerned here with the ways ethnic subjectivity is produced by the media, by the Canadian state, and by the philosopher Charles Taylor. The cultural politics that emerges from my examination of media representations of multiculturalism points to a tendency towards the management and commodification of ethnic subjectivity. This tendency is not unlike that manifested in the Canadian Multiculturalism Act, which legitimizes ethnic difference. Taylor's response to 'the politics of recognition', while it has very little to do with multiculturalism, at least as I understand it, raises important questions about what constitutes the modernity of the self in today's multicultural climate.

The focus on the genre of anthologies in Chapter Three continues my investigation of the contingencies that inform the representation of diasporic experience. In the first part I examine the way ethnic anthologies function as cultural archives of the varied, and often contradictory, representations of ethnic subjectivity; in the second I focus on Linda Hutcheon and Marion Richmond's anthology *Other Solitudes*, in order to examine the questions raised by Hutcheon's reading of multiculturalism, especially when considered in the light of her theory of postmodernism. In the last chapter, which centres on Joy Kogawa's *Obasan*, I examine how the female body functions as a site where the constructions of race, gender, sexuality, and nationalism are implicated in each other while retaining their distinct roles in the formation of the subject. As elsewhere in this study, I discuss the corporeality of diasporic subjectivity as both a product and a reflection of historical events, but also as a site of resistance.

What I have learned in writing this book has a provisionality that comes from the speed with which we are obliged to dispel inherited assumptions. I hope that the future will be less coercive than the history we have known until now.

The debts I have accumulated in writing this book are beyond counting. I wish to acknowledge those people who so generously and for so long supported me when I needed support. I also wish to acknowledge those who unknowingly gave me their support. Among those unsuspecting benefactors are friends, colleagues, and not a few strangers whose comments at conferences and elsewhere, whether directly addressed to me or to others, compelled me to think differently and to go on writing. The work of pioneering scholars, whose names appear too frequently in this study to require repetition, has been formative in my thinking and a constant source of inspiration; if I have been too creative in my appropriation of their work, any unfortunate results are solely my responsibility.

Students do not always realize the impact they have on their teachers, so I would like to include in this list of unsuspecting benefactors the students I have taught or supervised over the past few years at the University of Victoria. They have taught me much, and made the exchange a most rewarding and exciting experience. Special credit goes to those who participated in my undergraduate and graduate courses on diaspora, and to the committed and resistant (and for that reason all the more enthusiastic) students who took with me a graduate course on pedagogy in the fall of 1997.

My protracted project would still be in the making had I not been fortunate enough to have the invaluable help of dedicated and meticulous research assistants. Lorna Jackson's initiative and care were essential during the first three years of this project. Craig Burnett and Kurt Slauson were generous with their assistance. More recently, Karen Solie has proven both reliable and enthusiastic. And I am thankful to Carole Stewart for her assistance in proofreading and in checking bibliographical entries.

I am grateful to the Social Sciences and Humanities Research Council of Canada for a three-year research grant, and to the University of Victoria for four internal research grants that facilitated the research for and writing of this book.

I am greatly indebted to institutions in both Canada and overseas where I was given the opportunity to present early versions of parts of this book between 1991 and 1998. They include, in Canada, the University of Calgary (on three different occasions), Queen's University, University of Guelph, University of Alberta, University of British Columbia, Trent University, University of Northern British Columbia, Université de Montréal, and Simon Fraser University; and, abroad, the Free University in Brussels, the Aristotelian University in Thessaloniki, the University of Leeds, Victoria University in Wellington, the universities in Aachen, Augsburg, Munich, Giessen, and Bayreuth, the Association for Canadian Studies of the German-Speaking Countries conference in Grainau, the Nordic Association of Canadian Studies conference at the University of Aarhus, and the Canadian Studies programs at the University of New Delhi and the universities of Himachal Pradesh and in Trivandrum, Kerala. Many thanks to those who invited me and to the organizers of the conferences.

Very special thanks are due to the colleagues and students in the institutions where I was invited to teach Canadian literature and multiculturalism in India and Germany. I am particularly grateful to Shirin Kuchedkar, at the time Director of the Canadian Studies Centre at the S.N.D.T. Women's University in Bombay, and to Konrad Gross of the Canadian Studies program at the University of Kiel. They, and their families, could not have been more hospitable and generous in making me feel at home. Many of their colleagues also received me warmly; although they are too numerous to mention here, I remain grateful to them as much for their intellectual support as for the many ways in which they helped me negotiate my day-to-day living in India and Germany. I cannot overstate my appreciation of the enthusiastic reception and intellectual challenge that the students at those institutions offered me. I am particularly indebted to Christa Meyer for her friendship and selfless care, and not least for introducing me to her women friends, the 'Kieler Gang', whose hospitality, spiritedness, and infectious good cheer made my stay in Kiel an unforgettable experience.

At home, I owe deeply felt thanks to Lola Lemire Tostevin, who joined the 'Kieler Gang' briefly, and who has never waivered in her support when it was most needed. I continue to feel blessed by Phyllis Webb's friendship; her intellectual presence will continue to have an enabling impact on my life. Evelyn Cobley and David Thatcher have never failed me as friends and colleagues—their integrity and care are exemplary; I am also grateful to Evelyn for finding the time to read the final version of the manuscript. Sally Livingston was a most meticulous and patient editor. Roy Miki has been a continuing source of inspiration and encouragement. During the long time that it has taken me to complete this project, Robert Kroetsch's support was unwavering and his patience, in my times of discontent, unfailing.

Earlier versions of portions of this book appeared in *Open Letter* 8, 5-6 (Winter-Spring 1993); in *Multicultural States: Rethinking Difference and Identity*, edited by David Bennett (Routledge, 1998); in *Ariel* 25, 4 (October 1994); and in *Gramma* 6 (Spring 1999).

John Robert Colombo 'My Genealogy' from *Roman Candles: An Anthology of Poems by Seventeen Ital-Canadian Poets*, edited by Pier Giorgio Di Cicco (1978). Published by Hounslow Press. Used by permission.

'Conceiving the Stranger' by Nigel Darbasie from *Voices: Canadian Writers of African Descent*, edited by Ayanna Black. Published by HarperCollins Publishers Ltd. Copyright © 1992 Ayanna Black. Used by permission.

'Mamaetu' by Horace Goddard from *A Shapley Fire: Changing the Literary Landscape*, edited by Cyril Dabydeen (1987). Published by Mosaic Press. Used by permission.

Critical
Correspondences:
the Diasporic Critic's
(Self-)Location

There is no document of civilization which is not at the same time a document of barbarism. And just as such a document is not free of barbarism, barbarism taints also the manner in which it was transmitted from one owner to another.

Walter Benjamin (1969, 256)

Would that the gods could make all exile a birth, all dismissal childbirth.

Michel Serres (89)

'[D]iasporic consciousness' is perhaps not so much a historical accident as it is an intellectual reality—the reality of being intellectual.

Rey Chow (1993a, 15)

I

This book could be seen as the other of the manifesto on ethnicity that I wanted to write but never did. I realized this one day in the mid-nineties when I reread Robert Kroetsch's 'I Wanted to Write a Manifesto' (1995). It was not what he says in that essay that put things into perspective for me; rather, it was the Möbius effect of his title that offered momentary relief from the critical impasse I had reached: a 'political paralysis', an 'inability to make difficult critical choices' (Roman 73), and, along with that, a reluctance to commit myself to the fixity of words on the page. This was the time of the presumed certainties of political correctness, the 'politics of blame' (Said 1986, 45)[1] and vociferous advocacies, but also a period of global upheavals.

Like other Canadians at that time, I felt the excitement of social and cultural changes, yet was also discomfited by the pressures of the struggles over the politics of location and agency on the home front and, globally, those over ethnocentrism. I experienced the various events and debates of those years as if they belonged to a 'revolutionary moment', yet I also felt suffocated by the tendency of the sides involved to reduce them to 'brutal simplicities and truncated correspondences' (Stuart Hall 1996, 288). As a teacher and an immigrant who was trying to write a study I had come to call my 'ethnic project', I tried to achieve a meaningful balance between experience and political analysis. It was not easy; in fact, I found it to be virtually impossible.

I felt that my study was in search of a different author. It kept changing direction, resisting the narrative threads I was intent on following, moving in and out of Canada and its literature, conflating various temporalities—and thus revealing my historical imagination to be *other* than what I thought it was. I soon began to show signs of personal and academic weariness, the effects of the seemingly tangible gap that separates academic discourse from social reality, government and institutional policies from practice, the intricacies of academic argument from the heat and pressures of personal emotions and engagement.

I was caught in the web of what Immanuel Wallerstein calls the 'very passionate political debates [that] hinge around' the names of difference:

> Are there Palestinians? Who is a Jew? Are Macedonians Bulgarians? Are Berbers Arabs? What is the correct label: Negro, Afro-American, Black (capitalized), black (uncapitalized)? People shoot each other every day over the question of labels. And yet, the very people who do so tend to deny that the issue is complex or puzzling or indeed anything but self-evident. (Wallerstein 71)

The 'people' Wallerstein talks about, I realized, are not the only culprits in this denial of complexity, a denial that speaks of the incommensurability of identity. Even when we bear 'labels' different from theirs, we all move among them; we are them by virtue of contiguity, if not consanguinity. This realization made all the more painfully ironic the recognition—a commonplace, indeed—that people's warfare, be it cultural or military, continues despite the fact that colonialism, nationalism, diaspora, race, and ethnicity have already been analyzed rigorously, often with the cool precision that is afforded the cadavers of the past.

As academics, we have learned to tread gingerly on these paths of history. Indeed, those 'labelled', and others like them, are no longer the *objects* of our studies; they are the *subjects* of their own discourse—at least that is what many of us academics argue. But who are we? Whose interests do we represent beyond our own academic interests? Who do we write for, and why? Is it only the colonial subject that practises mimicry? And, for that matter, what is the range of states of being and mind that colonialism covers? Does self-location, that most frequently recurring and debated issue today, suffice to immunize academic discourse against the perils of representation (speaking for or about others), against the politics of the institutions that we are complicit with—however strong our avowed desire to change them? What cultural and political dynamics does the theatre of the classroom dramatize? How do we as individuals negotiate our polit-ical stance vis-à-vis the history both of ideas and of the institutions in whose contexts we teach? In other words, how do we position ourselves in relation to representation? More to the point, how do I, as an academic, as someone who teaches Canadian literature—and does so with an accent, as I am sometimes reminded by peers and students alike—fit within these debates?

I sought answers to these questions, questions that relate in a tangible way to the theories and practices of colonialism, nationalism, diaspora, and racism. I immersed myself in narratives and histories that were significant and relevant to my 'ethnic project', but that spoke as well to my own life-narrative as a Canadian citizen who is also a member of the Greek diaspora. I saw the global state of affairs in general, Canadian culture in particular, and my personal condition as part of the same continuum. This was a matter not of synchronicity, but rather of the 'kind of disjunctive temporality' that Bhabha talks about, a double recognition of 'causality' as what 'displace[s] the present' and what 'make[s] it disjunctive' (1994, 177). At the same time I wanted to affirm, in the light of threats to Canadian post-secondary education in general and the backlash against the humanities in partic-ular, that my academic and pedagogical interests were not at odds with myself as reader, with my responsibilities as a Canadian citizen, with the 'accountability' that the Canadian state demands of academics today—as if we had so far been either irrelevant to or irresponsible towards the production of our culture.

As I went about learning and unlearning, so my 'ethnic project' kept being written and unwritten continuously. I could not reconcile in a single study the two imperatives I had come to think of as my guiding principles: first, to locate my 'ethnic project' within pedagogy—pedagogy in the sense both of my own teaching practices in the classroom, and of the subtle and not so subtle ways in which the desire-machine of the state socializes us; second, to negotiate the contingencies that inform an academic's task. This was not just a matter of finding the right shape and scope for my project; it was, above all, a matter of the diffi-culty I encountered in negotiating, let alone incorporating into my study, what both personal experience and theoretical insight compelled me to confront.[2]

As theorists and critics of postcolonial and ethnic writing we have devised ingenious and eloquent tropes by which to account for such rifts: irony, inherent contradictions, distanciation, autobiography, reflexivity, ambivalence, filiation and affiliation, hybridity. All these figures pay tribute to our deliberate attempts to problematize our academic and writerly conditions, to position ourselves in the midst of our academic communities and in between the communities we write about. Still, I couldn't help recognizing the psycho-medical metaphors of, say, Tom Nairn's and Homi Bhabha's theories—the pathology of the body national, the neurosis of the state—as collapsing into their literal references. Illness was no longer a metaphor; the situation they were describing was actually diseased. Reading 'the social body as a process' (Burroughs and Ehrenreich 3) was no longer a matter of figurative speech. As Mary Douglas says, 'The human body communicates information for and from the social system in which it is a part' (83). I began to see the material signs of my body—including my whiteness (the whiteness of a southern European) and my accent—as stress signs symptomatic of the condition of the social body I was trying to understand. I had become a medium of representation. I was reminded at that stage of what Judith Butler says about bodies: that their 'materiality [must] be rethought as the effect of power, as power's most productive effect' (1993b, 2). The physical symptoms of my frustration, then, were signs of what was wrong with the social body I was trying to understand—and, closer to home, of what was wrong with me.

'Practices of representation,' Stuart Hall says, 'always implicate the positions from which we speak or write—the positions of *enunciation*' (1990, 222). Acknowledging from the start the four most frequently cited factors determining one's subjectivity—gender, race, class, and diaspora—could provide me with an 'imaginary coherence' (Hall 1990, 224): they would locate me unequivocally in a position that would be characterized as ambivalent, at best. Although my race and class would put me close to the 'centre' of things, there could be no doubt that, when combined with my gender and diasporic experience, they would also modify that 'centrality', would sway my position towards a certain 'marginality'. I could frame myself within these categories only if I assumed them to be stable and coherent, internally unvaried. But they are not. That '[i]dentity is not as transparent or unproblematic as we think', that it is a 'production' (Hall 1990, 222), has become a commonplace of many discussions of identity and ethnicity today.

At the same time, however, the insistence on positioning ourselves has assumed the force of a political imperative: only by doing so can we give our arguments credibility, only by labelling ourselves will we locate ourselves securely within history. But constructing our books as mirrors of ourselves does not do away with the persistent question of representation. The logic of self-location, it seems to me, is no less fraught with problems than the positions of alleged neutrality and liberalism are.

Positioning myself in these terms and ways did not promise to frame my study productively. If anything, it promised instead to reveal my complicity with the kind of 'ethnic absolutism' (Gilroy 1993)—once a Greek, always a Greek; once an immigrant, always an immigrant—that I have always found to be reductive. Self-fashioned authenticity can easily become a straitjacket that is not that different, either ideologically or structurally, from the social attitudes that make diasporic subjects Other to their host societies.

As Asha Varadharajan writes:

The reflection on subject positions has become unavoidable for the sympathetic Western critic who chooses to engage with the other without presumption or patronage. The danger of this timely recognition of a perhaps inescapable ethnocentrism is that it could be turned easily enough into an excuse for inaction. This conscientious refusal to speak for those whom the discourse of Empire designates as other would become a way of absolving oneself of the responsibility for the brutality of history. Since the Western critic is inevitably implicated in the history of colonization, any intervention on behalf of the other, it could be argued, will be contaminated by that history and therefore futile. The process of self-scrutiny would then translate itself into consolation for the wrongs of the past and into paralysis in the present. (xvi)

Varadharajan proceeds to show that the 'native informant is equally subjected to these problems' (xvii). And, in the case of a diasporic critic like myself, these problems are further amplified by the hybridity of my position.

The pressure I felt to position myself, instead of resolving my tensions, kept pointing to various layers of my subjectivity, revealing my identity to be unsettled, continuously disrupted, determined by different alliances on different occasions. Was this a symptom of the incommensurability of identity? Or was it a sign of my co-optation, a symptom of fickleness (capricious or not) in my politics? Whether this pressure was the result of intellectual demands originating within Western theory or of specific calls from my Canadian peers, at conferences and other social gatherings, to position myself, it took on the appearance of disciplinary action. The more I failed to see the salience of giving credibility to my critical discourse by locating myself in precise (and presumably authentic) terms, the more frustrated I felt because of the social and academic pressures to do so. For the location I was expected to inhabit seemed to suggest, on the one hand, a reification of the categories of race and ethnicity and, on the other, a withdrawal from the arena of *critical* debates that were themselves generally regarded not as discursive practices but as absolute stances.

The disciplinary, hence totalizing, intent that informs the gestures of self-location might be seen as an instance of restricted economy, a closed system of relations that articulates events in regulated ways while remaining unaware of the effects of its control.[3] Moreover, that intent points to a desire to avoid or eliminate or—at the very least—control the presumed infection of one's subjectivity by that of another. Were subjectivities unalloyed, unequivocal entities, such preventive gestures would be necessary. But if subjectivity is, as I believe it to be, irresolute, the product of filiation together with the frequently mutilating practices of nationalist warfare and coercive assimilation, then reflexivity, as Varadharajan argues, 'reveals itself as an inadequate comprehension of the functioning of ideology'. In this instance, reflexivity 'assumes that there are no chinks in the armor of the system and fails to recognize that the processes of both colonization and decolonization were and will remain incomplete' (Varadharajan xviii). Thus the implicit narrative in the politics of self-location—that we can only speak for ourselves—often leads to what Linda Alcoff calls a '"retreat" response' (17). This ranges from strategic silence, or self-inflicted silence, to other forms of retreat that renounce advocacy and hence relinquish the intention to bring about change.

In trying to understand the intricacies of the politics of self-location, I felt trapped within Vico's view of human history as a cycle of repetition—and without the optimism of his vision. There is no human history without repetition, Vico tells us in *The New Science*. But as Said writes:

> if we question the neatness of a cycle imposed by Vico on the huge variety of human history—then we are forced to confront precisely what the cycle itself circumvents, the *predicament of infinite variety and infinite senselessness*. Take history as a reported dramatic sequence of dialectical stages, enacted and fabricated by an inconsistent but persistent humanity, Vico seems to be saying, and you will equally avoid the despair of seeing history as gratuitous occurrence as well as the boredom of seeing history as realizing a foreordained blueprint. (1983, 113; my emphasis)

I wanted to write a manifesto that would circumvent that 'predicament'; to act on my desire to begin *in medias res*, in the liminal space I inhabit in the present, while turning my back on the past of the critical tradition, resisting 'the subservience that always accompan[ies] the classic pedagogical procedures of forging links, referring back to prior premises or arguments, justifying one's own trajectory, method, system' (Derrida 1985, 3).

That was how I came to want to write a manifesto that would free me from the legacy of master narratives, that would release me into the future of history, while dangling from the trembling wings of the *angelus novus*—Walter Benjamin's angel of history (1969).[4] I wanted to shatter the mirrors of repetition. At the very least, I wanted my repetition to make a *critical* difference, to interrupt, however briefly, the cycle of repetition. '[R]epetition is useful as a way of showing that history and actuality are all about human persistence, and not about divine originality' (Said 1983, 113).

As Benjamin says, 'To articulate the past historically does not mean to recognize it "the way it really was" (Ranke). It means to seize hold of a memory as it flashes up at a moment of danger' (1969, 255). I knew that this moment of danger is always located in the present. That was why I did not want to be held hostage by the past, the past as archive but also as the lived, and living, present. For I could not reconcile the disturbing realities of, say, the breakdown of Yugoslavia, or the Canadian soldiers' behaviour in Somalia, or the reactions to the Writing Thru Race conference, with the realism of the media's representation of those events. Behind those representations lurked the spectre of history as repetition. Nor could I always find an easy and unambiguous position for myself in the debates that took place in the early 1990s.

Without necessarily believing in an evolutionary vision of history, I began to despair at the thought that the old adage about history repeating itself might be, after all, the one and only true instance of determinism. I failed to see any 'forces troubling the continuity' (Said 1983, 119) that repeated history. I had not realized at the time that the problem lies not in the dichotomies of 'academy vs reality', or 'theory vs practice', but in the slippages that occur between the constructed categories of the real and realism as they facilitate and/or impede the traffic of critical discourse from one category to the other. And so I toyed with the idea of writing a manifesto as a way of moving beyond my position of retreat.

A manifesto is supposed to rise above history. It is intended to take us beyond the cultural predicament of historical repetition, to defy determinism. Its historical value is posthumous, for a manifesto wants to be judged by the future it announces. The method behind the promises it makes is not supposed to be simply additive. Its rhetoric, its pledge to deliver something new, speaks of radical breaks. It didn't take me long to realize that, if my manifesto were to have any efficacy, it would reside in the manifesto's promise to redeem me/us from the spectre of historical catastrophes. The manifesto has, in other words, a messianic message.

Still, I reminded myself, I have always found messiahs to be as dangerous as they are seductive. Their power and seductiveness reside in their absolutist vision. They have the power of a sign that is at once eschatological and apocalyptic, of the past and of the future. Redemption is always the antecedent of catastrophe. A manifesto, then, cannot help being accountable to the past. The past, as Benjamin so acutely says, 'carries with it a temporal index by which it is referred to redemption' (1969, 254).

I am thankful that my messianism was only ephemeral. I could not turn my back on the temporality of our present moment, on the disjunctiveness of the space we inhabit. Nor could I remain suspended from the wings of the angel of history. In no time I would be swept away by the violence of the storm that holds the *angelus novus* suspended between past and future. For the angel of history, Benjamin says, has his face

> turned toward the past. Where we perceive a chain of events, he sees one single catastrophe which keeps piling wreckage upon wreckage and hurls it in front of his feet. The angel would like to stay, awaken the dead, and make whole what has been smashed. But a storm is blowing from Paradise; it has got caught in his wings with such violence that the angel can no longer close them. This storm irresistibly propels him into the future to which his back is turned, while the pile of debris before him grows skyward. This storm is what we call progress. (1969, 257-8)

The angel's position was too precarious for a mere human, and an academic at that, to mimic. The *angelus novus* is, after all, the 'guardian angel of the critics of nationalism' (Bhabha[5]); Tom Nairn, Benedict Anderson, Anne McClintock—to mention just a few—all look in his direction. The *angelus novus* is the allegorical figure epitomizing the contingencies that determine the relationships between communities and individuals. He hovers, as Bhabha so aptly puts it, over 'anxious nations & nervous states'. We live in the shadow of his open wings. We may empathize with his predicament, to the extent that our fallen condition allows us to do so, but we live in the midst of the debris that he only gazes upon from afar.

II

If it was the image of the *angelus novus* that made me acknowledge defeat, the image of a different kind of angel helped me overcome my critical impasse. It was one of the angels in Wim Wenders' film *Wings of Desire* (1987),[6] those angels who gather together in the soft silence inside the walls of Berlin's public library as dark falls, whose presumed freedom is limited by their inability to intervene substantially in the affairs of humans.

These library scenes are among my favourites in *Wings of Desire*. But only on seeing the film for the third time did I hear one of the anonymous humans in the library reading a passage that refers to Paul Klee's *Angelus Novus*, a painting owned by Benjamin, and to Benjamin's flight to Paris. Since I did not know German, it was only the names that caught my attention.[7] Until then, the fluttering wings of Benjamin's *angelus novus* had struck me as the image of an entropic movement; but upon rereading 'Theses on the Philosophy of History', the essay in which he talks about the *angelus novus*, I remembered that Benjamin also says that 'the "state of emergency" in which we live is not the exception but the rule,' and that it is 'our task to bring about a real state of emergency' if we are to 'improve our position' in political struggles such as the ones against fascism (1969, 257) or racism.

Although in *Wings of Desire* this 'state of emergency' is highly aestheticized, it is what haunts the angels about the past and the present, and as a result about the future. The film's action takes place in Berlin before the collapse of the Wall. Unlike the Berliners who live on either side of the Wall, the angels effortlessly cross that borderline. But both East and West Berlin were equally ravaged by the Second World War. German nationalism, political ideologies, and the fragmented life-narratives of most of the humans for whom the angels show concern are all part of the film's address to the questions that emerge from the lived and living histories enacted by its angelic and human characters alike. Above all, the film dramatizes the politics of diaspora without pitting substantive political judgement against non-committal cosmopolitanism, individuals against communities, narcissistic authenticities against cultural pluralism. *Wings of Desire* visualizes what we cannot see, but it does not yield to the seductive illusion of transparency. It is the crisis of (total) knowledge, a resistance to the fetishization of origins, that motivates one of its angels to become an immigrant. Similarly, what has motivated me to include my response to the film in what follows is my desire to release myself from the hold that nativism has on Canadian literature (be it ethnic or not), to trace the possibilities of diaspora in a film that does not declare itself to be about ethnicity.

III

Like academics, Wenders' angels take notes, and they keep their notebooks wherever they go. The film opens with a hand writing while a voice recites, 'Als das Kind Kind war . . .' ('when a child was a child').[8] This poetic passage becomes a leitmotif in the film, repeated for the last time in the closing scene. 'Als das Kind Kind war . . . '—written, we subsequently find out, by the hand of an angel—announces the deep longing that infuses the film thematically and formally. It is a longing for what has been lost, but also for what has not yet been experienced. Yet this is not the kind of nostalgia that turns one's gaze backwards, towards some kind of originary point that might be nostalgically mythologized because it has been distanced or lost—one of the tropes through which the immigrant experience has been structured in some ethnic texts and analyzed by some critics. It is, instead, a nostalgia for what is not yet known, for the process of othering that informs subjectivity. The act of writing, a human act in itself, suspends the other-worldly nature of angels and locates them within history, and at the same time on the other side of it. They function as *angeli novi*, especially when we see them perched—their wings now visible, now invisible—on the winged shoulder of Victoria, who holds a wreath of olive branches and stands on top of the Siegessäule, a monument to war erected in 1871.

Yet the emphasis on writing in the film's opening scene does not mean that writing is the privileged enunciative mode.[9] Quite the contrary: writing is foregrounded precisely in order to counterbalance the orality that permeates the film. Most of the time, the angels are seen straining their ears in order to make out distinct utterances in the din of human voices; and they often cover their ears, seeking a few moments of quietude. Still, the dialectic relationship suggested between these signs of orality and writing is just a ruse, for orality in the film is not always synonymous with voice. More often than not, what we hear as a voice is a character's interior monologue, silence translated into language. And there are other kinds of discourses, too, that mediate written or oral language and contribute to the film's treatment of epistemological questions.

For example, when Damiel, one of the angels, picks up someone's pen in the library, he turns it this way and that, but the pen remains in its material form on the desk where he finds it. The pen he holds, then, is the double of the original pen, at once visible and immaterial. The epistemological question raised here about the materiality of objects and bodies is one of the keys to the way the film approaches the discursiveness of a subject's position. From the viewer's human perspective, Damiel and the other angels are portrayed as belonging to what Butler calls the 'domain of abject beings, those who are not yet "subjects", but who form the constitutive outside to the domain of the subject' (1993b, 3). Damiel's picking up the pen (and later a stone) dramatizes the angels' predicament: they live beyond the inquisitive domain of epistemology, since they are supposed to possess complete knowledge, but at the same time they stand outside the practice of knowledge, since they lack human experience.

Interestingly, Wenders' original script was about fallen angels, those angels who pleaded with God to change his plan to abandon humanity in 1945. God, however, angered by their interference, 'banished [them] from heaven, exiling them to the desolation of Berlin in 1945. There they were doomed only to observe the follies of human existence, unable to intervene in the course of events' (Cook 35).[10] Although concerned with history, the film's angels are not specifically tied to it; nevertheless, their perceptions of the human world across its eons of existence, together with their feelings about what they witness, are certainly an integral part of their angelic condition. Perhaps this is the reason why the angels spend their nights inside West Berlin's public library, the repository of the archive of human knowledge.[11]

The angels' notebooks mark the economy of their desire; they speak of the distance that separates them as guardian angels from the humans they so caringly, but often ineffectively, guard. Their notebooks show language to hold a position of primacy in the film. These angels register humanity through representation, their angelic scripts being sites where we can encounter meaning. We are forever booked inside textuality. And what is more important, if representation promises recognition, that recognition is 'overlaid with misrecognition' (Mulvey 17).

The beauty and the message of *Wings of Desire* lie in the paradox of the film medium. It can show the range—and the limits—of the angels' efficacy only by translating their angelic invisibility into visibility, and by doing so anthropomorphically. Filmic conventions, as Laura Mulvey says, 'focus attention on the human form. Scale, space, stories are all anthropomorphic. Here, curiosity and the wish to look intermingle with a fascination with likeness and recognition: the human face, the human body, the relationship between the human form and its surroundings, the visible presence of the person in the world' (17). The human shape of the angels, then, attests not to their reality but to their realism, to the fact that humans have constructed them in their own image. Furthermore, the viewer is a step ahead of the film's human characters in knowing that the angels are real and hovering around them, but their reality, mediated as it is by visible materiality and technology, is artifice, a matter of representation. The film's reliance on visibility is not only a sign of the constructedness of representation; it is also a reminder of the angels' voyeurism, a suggestion that the angels, despite their invisibility, have an active effect on the objects of their gaze. The viewers—who can see the angels even though they are not supposed to be able to—thus reflect the angels' spectatorship.

The writing scene that opens the film fades into a close-up image of an eye whose realism affirms the angels' omnipresence, their eternal (eternalized) gaze. It is similar to the kind of eye that adorns the domes of many Greek Orthodox churches, an eye that is supposed to remind the congregation of the vigilance of the divine I. In the film, it is children who are able to return the angels' gaze; although some humans can feel the angels' presence, a feeling invariably accompanied by feelings of happiness or relief, only children can see the angels *as* angels—a reminder of how prized innocence is, and of the price we pay for knowledge.

The implications of this complex case of invisibility and visibility came home to me when I read Chow's statement that 'visuality [determines] the nature of the social object,' that 'the production of the West's "others" depends on a logic of visuality that bifurcates "subjects" and "objects" into the incompatible positions of intellectuality and spectacularity' (1993a, 60). In this context, to be a guardian angel means to operate (within) a panoptic system within which humans are trapped. These angels may be denaturalized by the film medium, since the invisibility that determines them becomes its opposite, but that process does nothing to change the human condition of irreducible visibility. What it does accomplish points to yet another element in the film's complexity, showing us that the condition of the angels, even though they exist beyond history, is affected and subverted by the otherness of humans. The angels' eavesdropping on humans, the way the angels represent the human world through writing, the regret they express about their inability to prevent such disasters as suicide, the doubts they confess to each other as to the *raison d'être* of their existence—all these disclose that the seeds of difference and doubt are already planted in them. Eternity has its own history of angst.

From the beginning of the film, Wenders makes it clear that the very perception of angels as pure is a misrecognition. Their 'purity' is adulterated by the epistemological questions raised by the polarity of the angels' existence; a polarity, however, that is never quite reduced to the simplicity—what Foucault calls the 'Hegelian skeleton' (1980, 115)—characteristic of binary structures. To be an angel in *Wings of Desire* means to be constantly aware of the slippage between reality and realism: 'Whenever we participated [in human history],' says Damiel, 'it was only a pretence.' This condition is similar to the one the film's adult viewers experience as they become aware at once of the limitations of their gaze and of the children's ability to see the angels *as* angels. What compensates them for their limitation is their awareness of the filmic devices that Wenders employs; yet there is nothing to compensate for the fact that the paradoxical operations of visibility in the film reveal the limit of realism.

There is one angel in the film who wishes to challenge this state of affairs, who desires to forfeit what we presume to be the privileged position of power/knowledge held by angels. Damiel cannot eliminate the binary of visibility and invisibility, but he is able to subvert it by his desire to know what it feels like to be human: 'I want to end my eternity, and bind me to earth.' His is a desire inspired by limits: the limits of representation and the limits of complete knowledge. 'I've been outside long enough,' he says, expressing his desire to become human, which is also a desire to critique the panoptic position: 'I want to turn what I've learned from my timeless downward-watching into sustaining a hazy glance.' What Damiel is about to do is forsake his omniscient position, replace it with finite, and therefore flawed, human knowledge. For what he covets in humans is their ability to be uncertain, to guess, to surmise: 'finally to suspect, instead of forever knowing all,' as he says. He wants to put an end to the condition that Cassiel, his angel friend, describes in his definition of what it means 'to be alone': 'to do no more than observe, collect, testify, preserve.' Being around humans, reading their minds, watching them during their most intimate moments, witnessing all the intricacies and intrigues that comprise history—none of this gives the angels direct access to what humanity entails. Their invisibility and complete knowledge make a mockery of the Western aspiration towards totalized knowledge; their desire to know doubt and to lose absolute control is, similarly, an indictment of hegemony.

If guardian angels are an allegorical reminder that we live under the vigilant eye of a power we cannot see, let alone understand or resist—that, by implication, hegemony is a pervasive condition—then Damiel's desire to become human demonstrates the limits of that power, attests that power as imaged by the angels is nothing more than an admission of lack, a grand fiction.

The vulnerability of the power system the angels represent lies in its complex need for otherness. '[M]uch more than . . . a negative instance whose function is repression,' as Foucault says, '[w]hat makes power hold good, what makes it accepted, is simply the fact that it doesn't only weigh on us as a force that says no, but that it traverses and produces things, it induces pleasure, forms knowledge, produces discourse' (1980, 119). This function of power becomes manifest in the film every time an angelic hand laid on the shoulder of a distraught human induces change by alleviating pain or by suspending despair, however momentarily.

Having declared that he wants 'to conquer a history for' himself, Damiel announces to Cassiel that he has decided 'to take the plunge'.[12] Although Damiel is to retain some vestiges of his angelic condition, he falls hard on the face of the earth, his fall accompanied by a loud thump, the clanking sound of his angelic armour. But the sound of his crash gets lost in the noise of the city. The precise moment of his fall is marked by a shift from black-and-white to coloured cinematography. Colour as an instance of the semiotics of difference defines the film's human perspective.

Damiel's fall occurs while he is on the east side of the Berlin Wall, but when he recovers from his fall he finds himself in West Berlin. Damiel touches the blood of his head wound; he tastes the blood that colours his fingers. Its taste verifies his human condition, it affirms his act of choice. His trauma, together with his first physical experience of the winter cold, is precisely what materializes his desire to be human: that is, to be visible and vulnerable to the effects of the body's materiality. It is interesting then that, while feeling his body, he doesn't realize that he no longer wears his ponytail, one of the markers of the angelic condition that he shared with Cassiel. The visible Damiel looks the same as the invisible angel he was, but his missing ponytail, together with his thinning hair, is the first sign of the transformation that accompanies his dislocation, a token price he has to pay for his desire to cross the boundary between eternity and temporality. His wings are clipped, so to speak. He becomes a hybrid of angel and human.

Like a child who keeps asking 'What is this? What is that?', Damiel asks the first man he encounters to name the colours of the graffiti he sees on the west side of the Berlin Wall. Red, orange . . . — the man is slightly unsure, but nevertheless names them. This naming act discloses, once again, the angels' epistemological limits while at the same time revealing the instability of referentiality in the film's human habitat. The man also gives Damiel some loose change to buy a cup of coffee. It is a casual gesture made in the urban spirit of anonymous solidarity. Damiel, at this point, looks more like a street person than the angel he was only moments ago; indeed, he is a person without a fixed address. Still, the stranger's offer of change serves as a welcome to a world that is at once familiar and foreign to Damiel. More important, as the first thing he's offered after he becomes human, this money signifies both materiality and materialism, the cultural and political economy that structures diasporic experience.

Damiel carries his armour under his arm, a relic speaking of his diasporic condition in Berlin. The fallen angel can begin to articulate his desire only by coming to terms with the vestiges of his past—holding on to some parts of it, disposing of others. He carries the armour under his arm until he comes upon a junk shop. His armour is a trace of his past; it is also the capital with which he begins his new life. Although throughout the film Henri Alekan's camera 'appears to move around . . . as though walls, doors, and windows presented no obstacle' (Rogowski 401), mimicking the immateriality of angels,[13] the camera does not follow this new immigrant into the junk shop. Thus the viewer does not witness the transaction. As Damiel finds out later, he is taken in, for the price (DM200) he receives is well below the armour's value; further, it is apparent that the shopkeeper does not recognize the equipment as part of an angel's garb; perhaps the shopkeeper thinks it is a theatrical prop, a kind of folk costume—a sure sign in the film of the putative relationship between reality and realism.

By selling his armour Damiel disposes of his past, but this does not mean that his angelic condition is completely eradicated. Like the other 'fallen' and hybridized angels in the film—Peter Falk is one of them—Damiel has the privilege of a double perspective. Displacement, then, is succeeded by a certain shift, an absence that need not be synonymous with loss; or, conversely, loss might be seen as signifying an enabling, if not inevitable, condition. Wenders is careful to avoid any suggestion that Damiel's new condition is dialectically related to his former one. Instead, the transformations that Damiel experiences speak of the inevitability of translation, of acculturation, of (ex)changes. This, I think, is the reason why we see the fallen angel begin his new life through commerce. The money he makes by selling his armour buys him some second-hand clothing (a sign of his new-found visibility, the need to adapt and adopt), and a hot dog (a sign of acculturation that points to the intricacies of appetite as metaphor in diasporic writing).

Highlighting the contamination that Damiel undergoes in his new condition is the fact that one of the first things he learns how to do as a human is smoke. His first cigarette is offered to him by Peter Falk, who plays himself acting in a war film in the ruins of the Anhalter-Bahnhof. It is no coincidence that it is a visitor to Berlin, himself an angelic immigrant to the world, and an American citizen at that, who becomes Damiel's 'companiero'.[14] And, as David Caldwell and Paul W. Rea point out, 'Falk, meaning "hawk", is recognized by Berliners as "Colombo", meaning "dove" in Italian' (49)—a further indication that recognition is misrecognition, that identity is never monologically defined, that reality is always mediated by its realism, as illustrated by the metafilmic allusions via Falk/Colombo.

It is in reply to a child asking for directions outside the junk shop that Damiel first finds himself practising the usefulness he lacked as an angel—one of his first performative acts. But if he has become a human because his angelic immateriality lacked agency in human terms, then this performative act is at once humorous and ironic: although a recent arrival, Damiel knows Berlin better than any Berliner, so he proceeds to give directions that are exact but too elaborate, and he speaks so quickly that the child becomes confused; the viewer is left with the impression that he may not find his way. This brief episode announces the defining limits of Damiel's new-found hybrid subjectivity, and stresses, once more, the instability of referents and meaning. But as far as his human life is concerned he is still a babe, so to speak; oblivious to the confusion he has caused in the child, he walks away looking entirely pleased with himself.

He sets out to find the woman with whom he has fallen in love. It is the aspiration to understand the other that others Damiel. Although steeped into the debris of human history,[15] Damiel, unlike the *angelus novus*, takes the plunge. In so doing not only does he function, in more ways than one, as an allegory of the diasporic subject, but he becomes a diasporic subject himself. This is certainly a reminder that displacement is, more often than we might wish to realize, a fall into a history with which we are not quite familiar, an affirmation of desire, a gesture towards the otherness that already resides within us. It is also a reminder that the new reality is not necessarily the only cause of the trauma that accompanies displacement; that trauma may also derive from the forces that construct subjectivity, that give rise to the desire, or need, to become diasporic subjects.

More than an allegorical figure, however, Damiel is truly an immigrant. Difference and the opacity of subjectivity are not alien concepts to him. For example, before he wills himself to become a fallen angel, we follow his gaze over the anonymous face of a Turkish woman in a laundromat who is thinking in her native language, and a German widow on her way to the cemetery where her husband is buried, talking to her dog. Berlin, still divided by the Wall at the time of the film, encompasses more differences on either side of the Wall than the Wall itself signifies.

Marion, the woman with whom Damiel is in love, is also a diasporic subject. He first encounters her while he is still an angel. A trapeze artist, she dons chicken wings to perform her act in Circus Alekan, named after the film's legendary cinematographer. Ironically, when we first see her, she is complaining about her costume, afraid that she might fall during her routine rehearsal because the chicken wings are so awkward. That Marion's first appearance in the film is as an artist who protests against the tenuousness of her artistic props reinforces visually the notion that realism is a potentially dangerous enterprise, that its verisimilitude may be bought at the price of loss or death. Problematizing the medium employed, as Marion does, seems to be one way of dealing with this danger. This is not a case of practice making perfect; instead, Marion shows the importance of remaining alert, of practising reflexivity.

It is during this moment of Marion's uncertainty and danger that the black-and-white cinematography of the film changes to colour for the first time. Since everything we see is filtered through the gaze of angels or their humanized siblings, Damiel is present during this scene. Indeed, it is the range of emotions he experiences that colours the film. 'What is important here,' Rogowski says, 'is that this instance signals the emergence of human emotions in Damiel: upon seeing Marion endanger herself . . . , Damiel is shown to experience an intense human emotion that affects his outlook. It is highly significant that Damiel's first encounter with Marion is associated with compassion, with concern for the well-being of another. The angelic gaze of indifferent benevolence has, for a short moment, turned into a humanly loving gaze' (403). Rogowski is right, for Damiel is a contaminated subject before he forfeits his angelic identity. The viewer, though, is not given enough time to concentrate on what Damiel's face reveals.

Citing lack of money, the circus manager announces the end of the season's performances that very night: this financial decision seems to precipitate Damiel's fall, for this is the eve of the day that he will land on earth. As Marion exits the circus tent, still wearing her wings and followed by the invisible Damiel, she walks by her male co-workers, one of whom teases her by saying, 'an angel passes.' For the second time in this scene the camera catches Damiel reacting in a human fashion: hearing the words, he recoils in shock, fearing that the comment was made in reference to him. He forgets, for a moment, that he is invisible, beyond the human gaze. His forgetting, an antecedent of his humanized condition, is yet another sign that his angelic subjectivity is already impure.

An example of misrecognition, this incident prefigures the visibility that Damiel is about to choose. Above all, it stresses yet again the fissures present in angelic epistemology. Even as an angel Damiel is not a transcendental subject in relation to humans, but one who already bears traces of the very thing he desires, namely to surmise, to be uncertain, to fear. Thus when Damiel falls into the web of visibility, and therefore the maze of history, he knows all too well that he can never regain his privilege of invisibility, never go back to his 'homogeneous, empty time' (Benjamin 1969, 261). It is precisely the nature and consequences of his choice that validate the process leading to the alteration of his subjectivity, a process that sheds light on the diasporic experience. The displacement and defamiliarization that characterize diaspora are not, then, the exclusive result of immigrants' and ethnic subjects' being marginalized. The desire for displacement may already be present in the decision to immigrate.

Having just lost her job, Marion gives her wings to the circus's accordion player. Foreshadowing Damiel's renunciation of his own wings, Marion's gesture punctuates the end of her career as a trapeze artist, the fading of one aspect of her subjectivity into another. Yet this does not mean that she forfeits realism for an unadulterated form of reality; rather, as the film goes on to show, she is about to move closer to an understanding that reality is always realism.

In her trailer, on the last night of Damiel's angelic existence and under his panoptic eye, we see her become sad, if not despondent, and we hear her think about the meaning of her existence.[16] She feels lost. Her melancholic mood is reinforced by the record she plays and her plaintive thoughts about her past and present. Still, the nostalgia that pervades this scene is not intended to reproduce her past; rather, she sees in the difficulties of her present the possibility of starting anew, of coming to terms with alterity. As she says, 'I'll wait for a photo at the photomat, and it'll come out with another face.' She is surrounded by photographs and other mementos of her past life, but her discourse on the past points towards the future—her own as well as Damiel's. 'Here I am a foreigner,' she says, 'yet it's all so familiar.'

As is the case with the Turkish woman earlier in the film and, later, a Japanese woman in a nightclub, both of whom think in their native languages, Marion's interior monologues are in French, her mother tongue. 'Instead of homogenizing the mental discourses of the characters,' Rogowski says, 'the film accepts ethnic and other kinds of diversity' (403). Nevertheless, even though the film does not ignore Marion's ethnic difference within her German milieu, it does show both the cultural polyvalence and the polyphony of the space she inhabits. She sings in English along with Nick Cave, whose record she listens to, and often shifts in her thoughts from French to German. When, later in the evening, she comes across Peter Falk in front of a food stand, she recognizes him as Lieutenant Columbo and speaks to him in English.

Marion's and Damiel's encounter in 'reality', a matter of love conventions as well as both chance and decision, has a happy ending. But instead of following the ways in which they romance each other I would like to pause a little longer to examine how language in the film embodies the discursive complexity of cultural differences, how personal identity is intertwined with historical contingencies.

Wenders is intent on conveying a certain cultural authenticity in his characters; hence they act for the viewer as ventriloquists of sorts. The fact that the characters are unaware of being heard is significant, for it is their unawareness that lends authenticity to their voices, and thus to what they disclose about their identities. Their cultural authenticity, though, is curtailed by the fact that native tongue and garb function as references not to their sites of origins—to which their cultural authenticity might presumably be traced—but to Berlin's hybridized urbanism. Still, Wenders does not suggest that Berlin is 'populated by endangered authenticities' (Clifford 1988, 5). Berlin, one of the most visibly multicultural German cities, is instead imaged as a site of 'cultural incest, [where] a sense of runaway history pervades, drives the rush of associations' (Clifford 1988, 4). Indeed, it is the image of Berlin as 'an extremely tolerant city', a city where 'freedom . . . is limited and [the] sense of freedom is more intense and almost unlimited', the city where the German 'peace movement . . . started', that lies behind Wenders' decision to set his film there. For Wenders, who had worked in the United States for eight years before making *Wings of Desire*, living in Berlin (although not a Berliner by birth) and making a movie there was 'like coming home' (Wenders in Paneth 4).[17]

Taking a 'Bakhtinian approach to ethnicity in cinema', Robert Stam argues that the representation of ethnic difference 'emphasize[s] less a kind of one-to-one mimetic adequacy to sociological or historical truth than the interplay of voices, discourses, and perspectives' (1991, 256). *Wings of Desire* is indeed a polyphonic film in that it consists of 'a plurality of voices which do not fuse into a single consciousness, but rather exist on different registers and thus generate dialogical dynamism' (Stam 1991, 262).

The representation of Marion as a diasporic character exemplifies this discursiveness. Her random shifts from one language to another, coupled with the uncertainty that comes with the loss of her job, illustrate her hybrid identity and at the same time stress the heterogeneity of Berlin as a city. It is also important, however, that Marion is not the only character—central or minor—who embodies this kind of polyphony. From Damiel to a Turkish family in their car; from Peter Falk to the Jewish people who act as extras in a Second World War film he is making; from Homer, whose origins are no longer Greek but German, to the Australian rock star Nick Cave, whom we see giving a concert and who really did live in Berlin for a number of years—all the characters inhabit a space where they are both displaced and at home in some way or another. Significantly, this ambivalent condition is not presented as paradoxical: it is natural that not only those residing in Berlin but those passing through it are diasporic subjects, at odds with, yet steeped in history. While ethnic difference is pronounced, cultural authenticity—whether of ethnic subjects, angels, or German citizens—is curtailed, shown to be a flawed paradigm of universal or essential notions of identity.

The term 'ethnicity', Ella Shohat argues, 'reflects a peripheralizing strategy premised on an implicit contrast of "norm" and "other", much as the term *minority* often carries with it an implication of minor, lesser, or subaltern' (1991, 215). This is certainly one of the strategic ways in which hegemonic discourses have employed ethnicity, but it is not the way ethnicity is inscribed in Wenders' film. Besides lending an ear to the inner voices of minority subjects, Wenders subverts the silence often imposed on them either by the state apparatus or by their internalized inferiority complex. Inner voice is synonymous with native tongue, but it reaches the film's German- and English-speaking viewers through translation;

nevertheless, translation does not prevent the native tongue from functioning as ethnic coding.[18] Inner voice reflects the interiorization of cultural authenticity, but that interiority does not necessarily point to essentialism; it is altered, indeed amplified, by translation in an attempt to disidentify the subject's position. Orality (mother tongue) and writing (translation or a tongue foreign to the speaker) are not intended to identify ethnic origins as real and Berlin as a space that adulterates that reality. The film does not develop its characters through dependence on any foundationalist assumptions.

When Marion ventures out of her trailer—a mobile home that stresses the transience of her subjectivity, the mobility that marks the diasporic condition— she meets Peter Falk by accident, goes to a nightclub to listen to Nick Cave, and walks into the bar of the Esplanade where she meets the man she seeks but doesn't yet know: Damiel. Every movement she makes introduces yet another discourse—about ethnicity, culture and art, social and gender roles—that, although seemingly irrelevant to her French identity, brings her closer to what she desires. Her identity is produced by her complex interaction with elements differ- ent from what might be taken to be ethnically authentic about her. Indeed, it is the repetition of disparity, together with the contestation of dissimilar elements, that forecloses any binary figuration of who she is. Her identity can be figured only through images of alterity. Hence her body sways to Nick Cave's music, in a space where strangers of various backgrounds stand at once alienated from each other and united in the music's hypnotic impact on them, before she walks to the bar where she meets Damiel, yet another stranger.

The concert scene shows that Wenders does not strive to evoke Berlin as a pluralist society, one in which pluralism might induce a sense of equal standing. Nowhere in the film do I detect this kind of suspect positivism, or any unambigu- ous embracing of historical modalities. Rather, Berlin is imaged as a city that is the product of heterogeneity, a collage made up of chips of personal and national histories that create contesting correspondences—culturally, economically, and socially. If the angels' panoptic gaze operates in pluralistic terms insofar as it is focused on and absorbed by as wide a cast of characters as possible—old people fed up with life, parents frustrated with their children and vice versa, dark- skinned people and light-skinned people, gentle children and children who are bullies, rich and poor people, West and East Berliners, famous and anonymous faces, janitors and epic poets (and the list goes on)—this kind of pluralism does not bracket the various minority positions represented by the characters we see through the angels' eyes. On the contrary, it exposes Berlin as a text of varying entanglements and does so by constantly iterating the liminal space occupied by both power and marginality, realism and reality.

Had Wenders desired to give us a homogenized Berlin, a city where equilib- rium was the order of the day, he would have given us different panoramic views. Berlin as we see it in *Wings of Desire* is a mangled city, a city scarred by ideologi- cal battles, by war and genocide, and divided by the Wall.[19] If the angels exist in a time that offers a synchronic view of the world, that view alternates with the diachronic images of history permeating the film. Damiel's decision to take the plunge shows that eternity is the ultimate archive of memories; that, far from being the verification and fulfilment of the Western progressivist vision, homogeneous, empty time is a phantasm.

It is interesting that, like Rilke's angels in *Duino Elegies*, the angels are not intended to represent an exclusively Christian ideology. As Helmetag points out, Rilke makes clear in a letter that his angel 'has nothing to do with the angel of the Christian heaven (rather with the angel figures of Islam)' (254). Similarly, Damiel, who as an angel could be seen as occupying homogeneous, empty time, does not have a history as a human, and this lack is of concern to him. Nor, as a fallen angel, does he become a Lucifer figure. The same problem is dramatized by Peter Falk when he makes a casual reference to his grandmother, who must be a figment of his imagination, yet who enables him to invent a genealogy where there was none. Since as a fallen angel he cannot possibly have a biological, let alone heavenly, grandmother, this slippage speaks of the obsession with lineage that marks the conception of ethnicity both inside and outside ethnic communities. What's more, it is not a lie, for it speaks of the desire and the potential to establish new alliances. It shows the archaeology of the self to be a matter of the *critical* correspondences that shake loose the reality/realism dyad. Thus while Peter Falk's invented genealogy is an escape from ahistoricity, it is also a sign of the constructedness of history.

Hence the image of the tottering Homer who suffers at once from the burden of history and from lapses of memory. We first see him ascending with great effort the steps that lead to the upper level of the library, the Berlin angels' house. He is an old man, out of breath, having a hard time putting on his glasses. His musings reveal that he can no longer compose great epics; instead he laments that no one has yet written an 'epic for peace'. At the library he goes through a book of photographs by August Sander, *Menschen des 20.Jahrhunderts* (People of the Twentieth Century),[20] and the film's camera projects a number of these images, which show the devastation that followed a bombing attack on Berlin. Alongside destroyed buildings we see a dead baby, wounded people, and people looking for survivors. Homer does not explain why he never wrote an epic about that war, but the photographs flood him with memories.

He goes to Potsdamer Platz where, he nostalgically remembers, he used to have coffee with his friends and chat about the world at Cafe Josti. He forgets that the plaza was destroyed in the war, that beneath the fondly remembered site was Hitler's bunker. It is indeed significant, as Caldwell and Rea suggest, that 'Homer has incomplete human knowledge of history . . . [that his] otherwise good memory seems to fail for the years 1933-45' (48). It is also significant, I would add, that Wenders translates the machinations of genocide within the Nazi fascist state into the historical amnesia of a Greek poet whose Germanic identity in the film is partly a strategy exposing the implications, both imperialistic and universalizing, of German classicism. That the mnemonic devices of Wenders' Homer have gone awry undercuts the universalism that Homer has come to signify as a literary sign. It is, then, highly ironic that the Greek epic poet par excellence is cast as a post-Second-World-War German, a retired poet, a poet devoid of words. That a poet of warfare has forgotten what was possibly the most devastating war in history might suggest that Homer has read Adorno's dictum on writing poetry after Auschwitz—only he has forgotten that as well. Thus Homer exemplifies a different aspect of the diasporic condition: the exaltation of mobility in the name of emancipation, which traditionally valorizes travellers like Odysseus as cosmopolitan paradigms of the Western patriarchal self while seeing immigrants as subjects of a lower order. Wenders' Homer is the product of the false consciousness that often facilitates the traffic of literary and intellectual traditions. He may be a Greek German, but he has nothing in common with Germany's Greek 'guest workers'. While Peter Falk invents a genealogy, Homer unwrites his. He epitomizes the death of diasporic subjectivity by appropriation and assimilation.

In contrast to Homer, who laments the present and wishes to return to a past that precedes the war, Damiel falls directly into the present. Although living in time as a fallen angel is a new experience for him, the present he enters is not new: marked by repetition, especially as it is imaged in the scenes relating to Peter Falk's war movie, this is a present that quotes the past, but does so with a critical difference. Pitted against Homer's nostalgia for a past he misremembers is Damiel's nostalgia for the present as a space and time of transition. Wenders assigns Damiel the role of being 'man enough to blast open the continuum of history' (Benjamin 1969, 262). And this is where the optimism of the film lies, an optimism that is not to be confused with redemption from the spectre of history. Damiel, an already contaminated subject, merges with Marion, whose subjectivity is similarly impure. Their love and sexual union offer the lure that history might begin anew, but that beginning is not represented as one that will obliterate the past: it is not a beginning that promises salvation from the wreckage of history. Indeed, the film's sequel, *Far Away, So Close*, plunges them, along with the viewers, deep into history as it is lived in the present by Cassiel who, after falling from the sky above Berlin, eventually gets killed.

Wenders does not suggest that a return to the past is an inescapable movement that restores sameness; rather, he shows that the past is inscribed in the present yet is not its irreducible opposite, the site that always authenticates the now. The past is present only insofar as it produces and is represented by the present, but its presence does not necessarily suggest linear development, a promise of change or progress. Although time seems to stop when Marion delivers her love monologue to Damiel, I see this pause as a moment arresting 'the homogeneous course of history' (Benjamin 1969, 263). She is *woman* 'enough to blast open' its continuum.

The final scene, after Marion's and Damiel's first night of love-making, which we do not see, is structured as a triangle that both repeats and alters the past, while resisting teleological closure. Cassiel, still in ponytail, watches Damiel manoeuvre the ropes with which Marion practises her trapeze act: a fallen angel, a woman whose art defies gravity, and an angel still unsure whether to take the plunge. Damiel's interior monologue speaks of his happiness, but this happiness is defined in terms of the uncertainty that lies ahead. The story, we read, is 'To be continued.'

V

The confrontation with history in *Wings of Desire*, the film's prescient mode, its ambivalence concerning strategies of representation, its complex positioning of diasporic subjects—all these made my viewing of it an enabling experience. It became, literally, a heuristic strategy that facilitated my attempts to deal with multiculturalism in Canada. The film became relevant to my 'ethnic project' not as an allegory, a parable of the many issues involved in a study of minority subjectivities and the construction of ethnicity, but as a complex text that gave me both the distance and the proximity I needed to read Canadian multiculturalism. Its simultaneous depiction of reality and realism, its problematizing of visuality and the remembering of history, helped me to realize the importance of including in this study more than one set of articulations, of avoiding a unifying theme, a single thesis.

VI

What determines the role of the diasporic critic? How does she move inside the cultural and political syntax of the communities in which she participates? And what is her intellectual task?

Given her hybridity, the diasporic critic might function as a 'native informant' on two fronts. As a diasporic subject, she might easily claim the 'authenticity' of her ethnicity. She would thus speak with a degree of authority on what constitutes otherness as a double sign: a sign of (her) minoritization as well as a sign of (her) difference articulated in positivistic terms. As a Canadian subject, she might claim a different kind of authenticity, one encompassing the presumed cohesiveness of the dominant position. She could then use this authenticity strategically in order to critique the dominant system from within or, possibly, to embrace it with irony, even complicity.

However, both configurations of the diasporic critic as 'native informant' imply ideological contradictions. '[S]potlighting,' as Chow says, 'the speaker's own sense of alterity and political righteousness' does not automatically 'turn powerlessness into "truth"' (1993a, 13 and 12). By positing herself as ethnic, the diasporic critic practises 'self-dramatization', what Chow calls 'tak[ing] the route of self-subalternization, which has increasingly become the assured means to authority and power' (1993a, 13). Conversely, were the diasporic critic to relinquish her claim to ethnicity by adopting a seemingly neutral position, she would have little choice but to resort to a kind of liberal pluralism or relativism—and thus face further entanglement with the forces that demand she assume a stable position. In either case, the diasporic critic would suffer detrimental effects from the very act of self-location. Aligning herself with one *or* the other position, she would perform her declared identity while forgetting the incommensurability of history.

As Trent Schroyer says in his foreword to Adorno's *The Jargon of Authenticity,* 'Dialectically conceived "subjectivity" is historically formed and yet not reducible to historical determinations' (xii). There are always elements that are unassimilable, that extend beyond the binary structure within which the diasporic critic has traditionally situated herself. Thus the pressure to take a position becomes a form of intellectual swindling, of giving in to the 'jargon of authenticity' that Adorno calls 'a professional illness' (18). The authenticities of each position are complicitous with each other. As Adorno suggests, the jargon of self-location aspires to erase the distance between the two positions by representing the critics either as 'sharers in higher culture' or as 'individuals with an essence of their own' (18). The two positions are 'mediated through each other in frightful ways. And since they are synthetically prepared, that which is mediated has become the caricature of what is natural' (19).

Predictably, we can understand the diasporic critic as a Janus-faced figure. She is at once Canadian and ethnic. But this doubleness does not necessarily present her with a choice that will resolve the either/or condition of her hybridity. Like the Janus-faced figure[21] that Bhabha uses to talk about linguistic ambivalence and national discourses, the diasporic critic's twinned figure is characterized by 'prodigious doubling' (1990a, 3). There is no symmetry between the particularities of the diasporic critic's background and her present condition, no way (and for that matter no reason) to reduce once and for all the complexity that informs either position. As her ethnic background cannot be reduced to a stable and essentially 'true' past, so her national identity as Canadian resists simplification. Ethnicity is not a condition that she possesses naturally; nor is her ethnic identity fixed and stable in her birthplace or in relation to her ancestral origins. Her ethnicity is determined as much by her intellectual and life trajectories as by the Canadian state's and Canadian society's construction of the national imaginary and multiculturalism. Were the diasporic critic to speak from the dominant perspective, adopting a Canadian point of view (assuming, for a moment, that 'Canadian' is to be exclusively construed as a sign of dominance), she would at once announce her right to do so and run the risk of eliding the particularity of her diasporic perspective. The objective is neither to construct an opposition nor to effect a balance between these positions; instead, it is to produce a space where her hybridity is articulated in a manner that does not cancel out any of its particularities.

These particularities, however oppositional they may seem, are related through contextualities and historical contingencies. They are the constituent elements of the *mise en scène* of diasporic subjectivity, a scene that is constantly under revision in a *mise en abîme* fashion. Indeed, these elements apostrophize each other in the way Derrida suggests when he defines apostrophe as 'A genre and a tone. The word—apostrophizes—speaks of the words addressed to the singular one, a live interpellation (the man of discourse or writing interrupts the continuous development of the sequence, abruptly turns toward someone, that is, something, addresses himself to you), but the word also speaks of the address to be detoured' (Derrida 1987, 4). Such detours are essential if I am to remain vigilant with regard to both the diasporic critic's 'shuttling self' (Spivak 1993, 63) and the historical modalities that inform hybridity.

In the same way that hybridity must be understood not only as the distinguishing characteristic of diasporic subjects but also as a constituent element of the culture they inhabit, so apostrophe as gesture and modality addresses the diasporic critic but is also that critic's address to her culture. It is a gesture that speaks against cultural relativism—that is, against the anthropological view of culture as an organic and cohesive whole. It is also a gesture that should point, given current global developments, towards a radically revised concept of nationalism. We may live in a postcolonial era, as many insist, but globalism and certain kinds of transnationalism may well prove to be more than a political and economic phase—possibly even the antecedents of new colonialisms. If it is part of the diasporic critic's task to foreground hybridity, she should also be vigilant against constructing that hybridity as a 'closet idealism' that may 'reduce the complex givenness of material reality to its symbolic dimensions' (Cheah 302).[22] Thus an acknowledgement of hybridity does not signal a resolution of the politics and historical materiality of diaspora. It must be accompanied by the will to question the metanarratives of development and progress that assent to hybridity. Lest I be misunderstood, let me say that I am not arguing against development in the sense of efforts to, for example, improve the conditions of ethnic labourers or women immigrants, or programs addressing systemic discrimination. Rather, I am talking about the need to continue questioning the 'enlightened' reason in whose name a society, usually mobilized by the juridico-political agendas of the state, sets a course towards the future as a means of salvaging itself from history. As prosperity does not guarantee happiness, so progress does not necessarily transform history. As Rudolph Vierhaus puts it, 'The suspicion is that progress brings with it immeasurable dangers and that a stage has been reached wherein the social costs have outstripped the gains' (332). Given this state of affairs, what is the responsibility of the diasporic critic?

VII

If the problems of colonialism, nationalism, and multiculturalism have been 'forcefully articulated and thought out', as Michel de Certeau says, why 'the violence, the tensions, and ultimately the failure? Simply because history does not obey the speech that challenges it' (63).

Simply. The lucidity with which de Certeau exposes the artlessness of the beast that history is, and the teasing gap between discourse and action, was another thing that made me aware of the rift that has shaped my project. This is the rift that exists between my desire to write—'a desire . . . that is ceaseless, varied, and highly unnatural and abstract, since "to write" is a function never exhausted by the completion of a piece of writing' (Said 1983, 131)—and my desire to see this writing *translated* into a certain kind of efficacy. And I have remained conscious, throughout the process of this study, of yet another rift, one that acknowledges the contradictions between my original desire to see my writing, potentially, as translation and my belief in writing as just one more discursive practice among many.

If in expressing these contradictions I appear to shy away from the intellectual task at hand, if this discussion strikes some readers as too coy, I would point to Spivak's comments in her essay 'Responsibility' (1994). '[O]ne way of being responsible to the thinking of responsibility,' she writes, is 'that whatever is formalizable remains in a sort of intermediary stage. . . . Full formalization itself must be seen not as impossible but as an experience of the impossible, or a figure for the impossible, which may be to say the "same thing"' (22). It is through this spirit of responsibility that we can appreciate what is constructive about the irreducibly ambivalent condition of the diasporic critic. Spivak is very persuasive when she observes that '(the thinking of) responsibility is also (a thinking of) contamination' (23), that a '"responsible" thought describes "responsibility" . . . as attending to the call of that irreducible fact' (26).

There are two ways in which I understand 'that irreducible fact'. Being responsible does not mean feigning disinterestedness in the name of academic objectivity—a pretence that Spivak, among others, rightly sees as 'an unacknowledged partisanship to a sort of universalist humanism' (20); nor does being responsible entail the obligation (this, too, part of the humanist legacy) of furnishing solutions to problems, of putting into action a progressivist vision—that is, measuring our success as critics by the efficacy of our conclusions or the alternative visions we offer. This is not merely a case of the 'end' testifying to the validity of the 'means', but rather the 'end' being beyond our horizon of understanding. Envisaging a progressivist 'end' to today's cultural and social malaise may sound like a worthwhile and heroic project. Nevertheless, it is the kind of project that, I believe, attempts to transgress the coercion of historical paradigms, to exit from history instead of employing history against itself; it forfeits the reality of contamination and the perils implicit in emancipatory discourses. As Radhakrishnan writes:

> In our attempts to change the subject on the basis of what we hold to be good and desirable, and moral and politically correct, we cannot afford to forget how this very blueprint or telos that we are acting upon could be potentially wrong and repressive, even barbaric. For example, did humanity always know that racism is wrong and sexism abhorrent, that colonialism and imperialism are

illegitimate and unconscionable bodies of knowledge, that homophobia and normative heterosexuality are unacceptable? Briefly, did we always know that our norms have a flip side that is objectionable? Is not the very moment of the emancipatory critique the expression of a contradiction? (1996, 20)

Practising responsibility in the name of progress leads to teleological narratives; this is definitely not the answer to questions about self-location, diasporic identities, and accountability. While responsibility is, in part, a response to urgency, to the states of emergency that Benjamin talks about, being responsible does not promise a smooth transition from the position of witness to that of activist.

Instead, being responsible, in my understanding, means negotiating our position in relation both to the knowledge we have and to the knowledge we lack. It means practising 'negative pedagogy', 'inhabiting . . . that space where knowledge becomes the obstacle to knowing' (Johnson 1982, 166 and 182). Responsibility, then, entails the recognition that what we know may already be contaminated by what we do not know, and vice versa. Thus knowledge is no longer conceived as an object that is already valorized and therefore worthy of remaining in circulation. Rather, negative pedagogy redefines the object of knowledge as nothing other than the process leading towards ignorance. If we are responsible enough to admit that knowledge is at once what fills in gaps and itself creates gaps, what both 'enlightens' and destroys, then knowledge produces ignorance; negative predagogy is thus the exact opposite of what we may call positive pedagogy, that is, teaching as a teleological narrative.

This is what Barbara Johnson, Shoshana Felman, Barbara Freedman, Robert Con Davies, Rey Chow, Gayatri Spivak, and R. Radhakrishnan, among others, argue in their different, and often contradictory, ways. Although not all of these arguments have emerged within a diasporic context, negative pedagogy is relevant to a multicultural society because it may enable us to begin to address history and the historicity of our present moment *responsibly*—without, that is, maintaining the illusion of innocence or non-complicity. Whether we call this mode of being and learning negative pedagogy or 'oppositional pedagogy' (Freire, Con Davies) or 'teaching terminable or interminable' (Felman), or 'learned ignorance' (Freedman), or 'deconstructive', 'critical', and 'radical pedagogy' (Radhakrishnan),[23] there are some recurring elements in the way responsibility materializes in this kind of practice.

Negative pedagogy thematizes not only the object of knowledge, but also the method of learning and unlearning inherited truths. It is thus self-reflexive with regard to its methods as well as the positions of teacher and student. In fact, the purpose of its self-reflexiveness is to disturb the binary relation, and the accompanying hierarchical model, of pedagogue and student. Since one of the objectives of this method of learning is to radically question knowledge and its modes of production, the teacher can no longer occupy an axiological position: teacher and student alike become learners.

'Learner' does away with *and*, a paradoxical word signalling at once conjunction and separation, the two conditions that conventionally mark the teacher/student dyad, whose dynamics are structurally not all that different from those of the centre/margin dialectic. In its traditional usage in education and sociology, 'learner' suggests the democratization of teaching, yet it retains the stamp of elaborate and careful attempts to measure success and failure, to quantify pedagogical results. In these contexts learners are regarded, more often than not, as receptacles of knowledge-as-product; they are to be taught through devices tailored to serve knowledge, which, although not always axiomatically conceived, is carefully packaged as a 'terminable' object with transparent value and truth.

The learner I have in mind, though, is not to be considered as part of a 'teaching machine' (Spivak 1993), territorialized and therefore controlled through the desire-machine of the state (Deleuze and Guattari 1983); this learner is not a construction of the rampant empiricism that operates through various guises of benevolence. Rather, negative pedagogy creates the conditions for a learner defined not only as someone who desires to learn, but also as someone who learns how to desire. This kind of desiring is intransitive.

The primary task of this learner is to decode the guises in which knowledge is made manifest. Thus he is firmly situated within history, including the history of pedagogy as a teaching practice and as the body of disciplinary methods employed by the state apparatus. As Radhakrishnan remarks, this learner's '"subject position" in history precludes the possibility of generating ex nihilo a pedagogical method identical with her desire' (1996, 111-12). What this means for learners is that they don't simply learn knowledge as a specifically designated object: they also learn how knowledge is produced, perceiving the power relations usually concealed behind the force of knowledge. This pedagogy, then, deals with a different kind of knowledge, the kind that traces the relationship of knowledge to ideology, and vice versa. Not merely the job of the diasporic critic, practising responsibility through this pedagogical perspective is a task that all members of a given community, especially those in academe, must begin to come to terms with.

Chapter 1

Realism and the History of Reality: F.P. Grove's *Settlers of the Marsh*

[T]he poverty of the wandering exile discloses the richness of the errant subject.

Mark Taylor (206)

In *A Stranger to My Time: Essays by and about Frederick Philip Grove* (1986), edited by Paul Hjartarson, Walter Pache argues that 'It seems questionable whether "ethnicity" in Grove's case is a relevant critical category' (17). Indeed, Pache warns future readers of Grove that 'it seems *dangerous* and *misleading* either to draw conclusions from [Grove's] ethnic background or to assess his work in terms of "ethnic literatures"' (17; my emphasis).

In this opening chapter, I will proceed by resisting Pache's advice. To delve into a study of diasporic literature in Canada by way of a testy alliance—ethnicity and danger—invites reflection on important questions. To start off with some of the methodological and thematic issues raised by the problematic case of Grove, the con man par excellence of Canadian literature, provides an appropriate launch into ethnicity, an appropriate movement through which to join the cross-cultural traffic of identities.

Simply put, it is not my intention here to prove that Grove is an ethnic author; ethnicity is not an essence. Rather, I wish to begin by addressing Grove, and the ways he has been read, precisely because of the inconsistencies and concerns that surround his case. What can we learn about the discursive space and cultural politics of ethnic writing in Canada from the kinds of critical attention that Grove has received? Grove arrived in Canada at the turn of this century and published his first novel in English in the mid-1920s, a time of a great influx of settlers and immigrants as well as major debates and policies concerning immigration. Although my study is not offered as a chronological survey of Canadian ethnic literature, beginning with Grove is crucial because of the historical perspective it affords my overall argument. This does not mean that I posit Grove as *the* origin of Canadian ethnic literature. 'The term origin,' Benjamin tells us, 'is not intended to describe the process by which the existent came into being, but rather to describe that which emerges from the process of becoming and disappearance. Origin is an eddy in the stream of becoming' (1977, 45). It is through this sense of origin, of becoming and disappearing, that I would like to examine what the case of Grove can tell us about the tradition and reception of diasporic writing in Canada.

Together with Laura Goodman Salverson's *The Viking Heart* (1923) and Martha Ostenso's *Wild Geese* (1925), Grove's *Settlers of the Marsh* (1925) belongs, in our recent way of thinking, to the early stages of the tradition of ethnic fiction in Canada. This is true so long as we don't assume that tradition to be a continuum of stable paradigms, be they aesthetic or political, of what constitutes the representation of cultural difference. The tradition of ethnic writing in Canada might be best examined and appreciated if we kept in mind that this, like other literary traditions, is as much a construct of critical discourse as it is the accumulation of a literary corpus; as much the product of various functions of power as it is of the tension linking continuous patterns and their inconsistencies. The tradition might be best described as a genealogy, conceived in a Foucauldian sense, in which temporal boundaries can shift as the need arises. The literary texts in question can then be read neither in order to establish patterns of sameness and repetition, and therefore new kinds of grand metanarratives, nor in order to confirm what Francesco Loriggio calls 'readymade norms' (54). Thus, instead of reading diasporic literature in order to verify what we presumably know about ethnicity, we may read it for the discontinuities and discrepancies it might reveal.

My intention to read Grove within the context of ethnicity, then, is not offered as a narrative of progress, a gesture of enlightenment designed to assimilate him into Canada's current multicultural climate. Rather, I want to explore the incommensurability of ethnicity as it is inscribed in Grove's case, and to do so in the context of thinking about both the limits of the Canadian canon and the disruptive effect of ethnic literature as it defies a specific thematic and aesthetic typology. Methodological concerns and the representation of ethnicity, particularly as it has been contrasted to dominant identities and universalist patterns, will form the centre of this chapter, while my reading of *Settlers of the Marsh* will give my discussion its specific focus.

Grove: Universalist = European = Canadian?

Why does Pache counsel his readers against studying Grove as an ethnic writer? Why does ethnicity flirt with danger in Pache's almost aphoristic formulation? Who, or what, does ethnicity endanger? And why has Grove been 'considered to be ethnic' only 'rarely', at least until the early 1980s, as E.D. Blodgett observes (1982, 89)?

Pache's warning against associating Grove with ethnicity comes as the conclusion he reaches after examining him using 'a comparative approach' (12). Taking into account Grove's biography, literature, criticism, and his *'fin de siècle* background' (13), Pache remarks that 'Grove's work defies the categories of literary nationalism: he is modern because he is international' (18). Therefore, Pache argues, Grove lends himself to a 'comparative literature' (12) approach. What distinguishes Pache's approach from, say, Alex Krönagel's reading of Grove as a writer 'primarily concerned with philosophical questions' traced to Nietzsche (472) is his specific intent to posit an image of Grove as 'European' that 'is bound to change our image of Grove, the Canadian' (Pache 14). Neither 'European' nor 'Canadian' is closely examined, though; within the cultural syntax in which they appear, the latter is subordinated to the former while the power structures that bind one to the other remain undisturbed. Pache's argument, as I will attempt to show, points to a misrecognition of some of the central values that have, at least until recently, constituted the Canadian literary tradition. Pache employs two critical gestures to support the European image of Grove against the Canadian one: the first comes from within Grove's work, while the second marks a pivotal moment in his Canadian canonization.

Pache refers to Grove's 'savage attacks on the Canadian literary scene in his early letters, and in entries he later made in his diary "Thoughts and Reflections",'[1] as 'offer[ing] plenty of evidence that his sympathy for existing authors and existing literary movements in Canada was limited indeed, and that he despised most of them for their provincialism and lack of scope' (15). Pache takes Grove's distaste for the Canadian literature of his time to prove, unequivocally, that Grove is not a Canadian writer. Canadian critics, as W.J. Keith rightly observes, 'have learned to be skeptical of Greve/Grove's explanatory assertions' (Grove 1982, vii), but Pache shows no caution in his reading of Grove's remarks. Instead he considers, for example, Grove's diary to offer 'a less literary, and *more documentary* view' of the concerns and themes that preoccupied him (19n.1; my emphasis). In assuming that Grove's references to Canadian literature have a kind of transparency, a truth that coincides with the motives and meaning immediately expressed, Pache accepts Grove at face value; in effect, he is conned. This is not to suggest that Grove thought differently about Canadian literature than Pache argues. Rather, the ideological and epistemological manoeuvring that Grove engages in when he expresses his views on Canadian culture reflects the rhetorical strategies he employs to 'persuade' his reader (Hjartarson 1986, 301), to set the stage for the kind of critical reception he desires.

There certainly are substantial differences between Grove and his Canadian contemporaries. Still, Grove's low opinion of them reveals, I think, the *other* side of his own fear of failure, as well as a certain literary anxiety[2] about his exile from the European tradition to which he sees himself as aligned and the Canadian tradition of the time, into which he presumably does not fit. As his essays, diary notes, and letters clearly suggest, he images himself as the redeemer of culture in

Canada, the philosophical and literary patriarch of a Canadian tradition that is to originate with his writing.

This is the narrative underlying, for example, his truly 'savage' attack on Martha Ostenso's *Wild Geese* in a letter to Austin M. Bothwell, written on 18 November 1925, the year both his *Settlers of the Marsh* and Ostenso's novel had come out.[3] In a rhetoric whose contradictions signify more than Grove intends to disclose, he calls Ostenso's novel 'deplorably, even unusually immature'—a 'natural' thing when 'an immature young girl sits down to write a book', a 'girl' who 'knows nothing of the grim things of life'. He sees Lind Archer, the young teacher in the novel, as a thinly disguised 'Miss Ostenso', a character 'drawn by stencil, pretty, charming, etc., with all the conventional reactions of the NEW WOMAN which exist only in books' (Pacey 1976, 25). Ironically, the objections he expresses reveal more about *Settlers of the Marsh* than about Ostenso's novel: 'The *petty* sexiness of many passages makes a mature person smile. [. . .] Nobody will accuse me of prudishness. What I object to is the incompetence, psychologic and artistic, in dealing with these things . . . .'[4] The unsolicited 'VERDICT' he offers comes as no surprise: 'only trash wins a prize' (Pacey 1976, 26), he says, obviously referring to the $13,500 prize that *Wild Geese* had just received.

This attack may very well be 'savage', and sexist, but it belongs to the writerly tradition of competitiveness and contestation of ideas and styles that is surely characteristic of all times and places. A tradition is founded as much on conflict as it is on consensus. What this assault on a Canadian novel shows is that Grove is not a graceful loser, especially when it means losing to a 'young girl' who writes 'because she has the itch to write' (Pacey 1976, 25). Despite the relative success of *Settlers of the Marsh* at the time, and the fact that it opened a lot of doors for Grove, the literary recognition of Ostenso is damaging to him precisely because its timing and content, not to mention its author's gender, challenge his intent to father a literary tradition in Canada that would 'truly' matter in terms validated by his European background.[5] If Grove, as Pache argues, 'set out to become a writer in Canada rather than a Canadian writer' (15), he would not have been as incensed as he obviously was by Ostenso's success. Notwithstanding the fact that Pache's formulation relies on a homogeneous notion of Canadianness, Grove's criticism of *Wild Geese* could be read as a disguised reading of his own novel, a case of Bloomian anxiety of influence. His vehement attack is a disguised instance of his cultural struggle as an intellectual in the diaspora.

Pache does not explain what constitutes the difference between a 'writer in Canada' and a 'Canadian writer'. Nevertheless, it is apparent that in Pache's binary 'Canadian writer' functions as a sign of negative value, at least to the extent that it refers to Grove's contemporaries. Margaret Turner, who seems to agree with Pache's assessment of Grove (48), suggests that Grove 'works hard to maintain the division of "I" and "not-I" that he repeatedly asserts: the existence of a discrete personality can be proved only by contrast to the natural landscape and by both contrast and relatedness to other human beings' (49). Working against her own insight here, Turner chooses to emphasize only 'contrast' and not the 'relatedness' that she herself notes. Like many critics of Grove, Turner is right to argue that Grove 'constantly compares, either explicitly or implicitly, the Canadian literary community to the circles in which he participated, or wanted to participate, in Europe' (51). But this kind of comparison does not erase Grove's intricate involvement in Canada's literary community. The epistemological position that Grove inhabits cannot be accounted for simply by Turner's binary of 'I' and 'not-I'. The referents of 'I' and 'not-I' in Grove's case are constantly conflated, continually shifting ground, if not value and function. As truth and fiction in his life are not exactly polar opposites but rather share a relationship of complex contiguities, so the question of whether Grove is a Canadian writer depends not only on how we interpret his pronouncements about his peers but also on the process by which he has come to occupy a canonical position. We must therefore examine the Europeanness or Canadianness of Grove within the context of what the concept of Canadian literature entailed in his time.

Ethnicity Under Western Eyes

Although Pache acknowledges that 'Grove's attitude is thoroughly ambiguous' (16), he feels compelled to define Grove's European image by evading the ambiguities to which he refers. In attempting to salvage Grove from 'a new national literature in search of a literary tradition' Pache practises a certain kind of mimicry, employing Grove's own standards. When Pache states that a new national literature like Canada's is founded 'frequently at the expense of simplifying the complexities of a writer whose works are international in more ways than one' (12), he echoes some of Grove's own comments on the same issue.

Here, for example, is the opening of Grove's 'A Neglected Function of a Certain Literary Association':

> It is only natural that a nascent literature, arising in a young country which is on every hand surrounded by older civilizations, should, from a spirit of self-assertion, emphasize those features, conditions, mental and spiritual attitudes which distinguish its life and its nationals from those of other and older countries. (1982, 3)

While Pache's criticism of the appropriating tactics of a new literature is intended to keep Grove apart from it, Grove takes the opposite tack in his essay:

> this young nation forms a mere bud on the larger growth of the great Anglo-Saxon Empire. *Many of us* came to this country saturated with the spiritual achievements of the older parts of that Empire, saturated with the great British tradition; [. . .]

> This great Anglo-Saxon tradition forms one of the directing and living
> influences at work on our literature in the making. (1982, 4-5; my emphasis)

Grove's use of pronouns in this passage is strategic. The inclusion of himself in the 'we' of the new nation and its literary figures is not simply a rhetorical gesture intended to seduce his audience.[6] He means what he says, for he considers himself to be part of the tradition—*as he* defines it. Significantly, here Turner's 'I'/'not-I' paradigm collapses upon itself. Grove's high regard for the British tradition affirms his European values, but in doing so it demonstrates his affinity with what he, like everyone else in his day, sees as comprising the roots of a nascent Canadian literature. On this as on other occasions, Grove promotes at once his vision of literature and himself as its true practitioner, if not its only Canadian father at the time.

Canada's 'cultural wilderness' meant to Grove what the offer of free land meant to the settlers about whom he wrote. Indeed, the 'almost brutal spirit' that he bemoans, 'which tries either to ignore deeper problems or to solve them by the power of force or gold', is exactly the thing on which he tries to capitalize. The Canadian 'spirit of shallow optimism, of a narrow, mistaken, fanatical patriotism' (1982, 6) is the legacy against which he invests the cultural capital he brings to start his life in the 'New World'. His persistent attack on Canadian literature enables him to 'prove up' as a diasporic intellectual.

Pache argues that 'Grove's intention to bring new cultural standards to Canada clashe[s] sharply with Canadian tendencies to establish an indigenous culture' (16). Thus he argues against Malcolm Ross's 1957 'Introduction' to the New Canadian Library edition of *Over Prairie Trails* (1922), the first volume in the series. Ross introduces Grove as 'a *Canadian writer*, wholly absorbed by the Canadian scene and by the pioneer drama of a diverse yet single people' (Grove 1957, v). The emphasis that Ross places on '*Canadian writer*' might be explained, as Krönagel suggests, by 'the literary nationalism that underlies the concept of the New Canadian Library' (471).[7] It should, however, also be attributed to the portrait of Grove that Ross paints, which in turn relies on Grove's own self-fabrications:

> *Over Prairie Trails* was written by a man born in Russia of mixed Swedish, Scottish and English blood. Educated in Paris, Munich and Rome, twenty-one years of age before he came to this country after tours (large if not grand) from the Sahara to Madagascar to the Antipodes to America, Frederick Philip Grove is yet the typical, perhaps even the archetypal, Canadian. (Grove 1957, v)

> *Over Prairie Trails* is the book of a man who is at home, not just 'over here'. (Grove 1957, vi)

It is not difficult to ascertain why Grove qualifies so easily for the 1950s archetype of 'Canadian'. There is certainly a correspondence between the social and cultural credibility towards which Ross's litany of ethnic origins strives and Grove's own invention in the 1910s of his 'mixed . . . blood', which fits the positive figuration of the 'New Canadians' at the time like a glove. In the performative context of Grove's self-fabrications, Scottish and English blood clearly outweighs the accident of his birth in Russia as well as his mother's Swedish origins.

What defines the archetypalism of 'Canadian' in this context is the cosmopolitan image that Grove imports into Canada, which overlaps, ironically, with the kind of internationalism that Pache offers as a corrective to Grove's Canadianness. That Grove allegedly received his education in some of the most prestigious Western centres of knowledge and culture, that he penetrated the mysteries of some of the 'exotic' sites in the East, that he sampled (but ultimately rejected) two 'New Worlds' other than Canada, and that he was familiar with the labours involved in settling and farming—all these result in a fortuitous constellation of invented circumstances that far exceed even the highest, most stringent expectations of immigrants. There is indeed a certain wishful thinking, if not didacticism, in Ross's image of him: it is to the image of such a cultivated and widely travelled man that even 'true' Canadians ought to aspire. No wonder Grove is conceived as an archetypal Canadian.

Ross, at the time, did not have the privilege of knowing about Grove's true origins, which were uncovered by D.O. Spettigue's ingenious research in the early seventies.[8] Contrary to Pache's suggestion that Spettigue's breakthrough has 'modified' Ross's 'emblematic view of Grove' (11), this kind of biographical information has not, it seems to me, cancelled the import of the definition of 'Canadian' that Ross attributes to Grove. In the historical context of Ross's comments, Canadianness is synonymous with the kind of universalism that specifically, and thus paradoxically, advocates the cultural capital of the West. In seeing Grove's fiction as the polar opposite of what he calls an 'indigenous culture' in Canada, Pache misrecognizes what constitutes this indigenousness: its history takes the form of the geographical specificity reflected by the realism of the Canadian West,[9] but it belongs to the temporal continuum of European humanism. The indigenous quality of Canadian literature reflects its particular historical modalities, but it cannot be taken to signify a singular authenticity. The purity of a tradition is a fictive construct revealing more about the *doxa* of a given culture than about the tradition itself. The cumulative differences of Canadian literature from other traditions might point to a certain national character, but they do not necessarily suggest a break from the European master narratives that have shaped it.

Grove's reinvention of his identity obviously corresponds to values and categories he privileges. That he did not choose, for example, Polish, Irish, Ukrainian, Greek, Indian, Jewish, or Italian origins is symptomatic of the way these national identities were constructed at the time. Whatever the intricacies of the family romance dramatized every time Grove embellished his life trajectory, it is no coincidence that the identity values he adopted were the ones judged desirable by the host society he encountered when he arrived in Canada. These shared values in part account for the paradoxes present in his canonized status.

It must be apparent by now why Pache's proposed image of Grove as a 'European' *and* an 'international' writer is at once appropriate and misguided. There is no doubt that, personally and literarily, Grove was rooted in European values, but there is also no doubt that the Canadian tradition depends, rightly or wrongly, on its assimilation of those same values. In this context, Pache's perception of European civilization as a transcultural construct is troubling. When he suggests that a comparative approach—that is, 'taking literary, rather than national or ethnic criteria as points of reference' (18)—would help us to elucidate Grove's fiction, he clearly posits internationalism as a tautology, in effect an affirmation of European values. What is problematic here is Pache's ahistoric presentation of pan-European universalism as a reality; in fact, it is an idealist model that has informed the very discipline under the aegis of which he wishes to see Grove read, namely comparative literature. Pausing for a moment to consider the particularities embedded in this universalism as well as in the foundations of comparative literature will help me move closer to the reasons why Pache's comparativist reading is threatened by consideration of Grove in an ethnic context.

Diaspora and Comparative Literature

While Pache's universalist approach allows nations and ethnicities to be subsumed by Europe, which in turn is absorbed by internationalism, this formulation implies a Eurocentrism of an ethnocentric variety. The humanistic spirit in which Pache reconstructs Grove as a European echoes the tight relationship between the rise of literature (specifically scholarship and philology) as an institution and the rise of nationalism, a movement that assumed 'several different forms during the two centuries between 1745 and 1945' in Europe (Said 1993, 44).[10] '[W]hen most European thinkers celebrated humanity or culture,' Said remarks, 'they were principally celebrating ideas and values they ascribed to their own national culture, or to Europe as distinct from the Orient, Africa, and even the Americas' (1993, 44). Yet the nationalism underlying the kind of literary values and movements that have led to what we now call comparative literature remains, predictably, a covert element in Pache's notion of an international literature that should be read and appreciated without reference to ethnic or national specificities.

Although Canada's 'new national' literature has been shaped by its centrifugal relation with Europe, it does not fit the canonical tenets that Pache endorses. Historically, Canadian literature's colonial relationship with the British tradition has been paralleled by its peripheral sensibility with respect to its location on the other side of the imperial divide. Similarly, its self-consciousness about its fledgling status has been matched by its long-standing adherence, on one hand, to Arnoldian values[11] and, on the other, to its nationalist, but not always necessarily anti-colonial, tendencies. Although the various configurations of these allegiances have often been criticized from our present vantage point, as they ought to be, they follow a historical logic whose elements we cannot easily realign. That the development of Canadian literature *as* Canadian has been integral to the political and cultural discourses constituting Canadian identity has become one of the most common recitations in literary criticism. But it is this kind of negotiation of imperial and colonial signs, of complicity and resistance, of metropolitan aesthetics and cultural differentiation, that refuses Canadian literature the immutability Pache valorizes.

The international literature 'comparatively examined', to which, according to Pache, Grove-the-European belongs, has a different history from Canada's, but both of them have evolved out of nationalism. In Pache's organic argument, though, these historical exigencies remain, subtly, unnamed. Thus we must see the ahistoricity to which Pache's international standards aspire as pointing to its opposite, a figure of history imaged as universal that constitutes a distinctly historical and Eurocentric narrative. The project of 'the pioneers of comparative literature', Said observes, depended on 'the idealist historicism which fueled the comparatist "world literature" scheme and the concretely imperial world map of the same moment' (1993, 48). Pache's call for a comparative-literature approach to Grove is remarkably impervious to the convergence of comparative literature's project and imperial politics.

Emily Apter's view of the history of comparative literature illuminates the ideological trajectory of the discipline, shedding light on the implications of Pache's argument:

> The early history of comparative literature . . . provides a record of the privileging of exile. The émigré founding fathers—Leo Spitzer, Erich Auerbach, René Wellek, Wolfgang Kaiser—arrived at American universities already steeped in a turn-of-the-century culture obsessed with theorizing alienation and subjective estrangement. Marx, Freud, Durkheim, Lukacs, Kracauer, Simmel, Benjamin, and Adorno were among those who had profoundly contributed to the Continental ethos of exile before the fact. After the fact, the early comparatists, concerned to forget the ideology-riven past, developed pedagogies of a panhumanist, theoretical literacy for which, as Denis Hollier reminds us in an article entitled 'On Literature Considered as a Dead Language', 'no visa was necessary'. (87)

Exile, alienation, subjective estrangement—these are indeed the elements that Pache attributes to Grove. Grove's 'escape from life' (Pache 14) in Germany, though, was necessitated by causes decidedly different from those that compelled the founders of comparative literature to immigrate to the United States: Grove was running away from the financial and legal mess he had created for himself, not from historical circumstances that were inimical to his politics and impeded the free pursuit of his intellectual interests.[12]

In reading Grove as a writer who 'sees alienation as an essential part of the writer's existence' (16), an 'expatriate writer . . . able to mediate between self and the world outside' (17), Pache reinstates the appropriating values at the root of comparative literature. He does not simply write from an admittedly unavoidable European perspective; he also writes as the intellectual ancestor of the fathers of comparative literature who saw 'Europe [as] the home of the canonical originals, the proper object of comparative study' and 'so-called remote cultures [such as Canada's as] peripheral to the discipline' (Bernheimer 40). Thus when Pache discusses 'Canadian literature as world literature' (14) he has in mind Grove's 'use . . . [of] Canadian themes as paradigms of universal problems' (15). Universalization is the only way he can address the Canadian content of Grove's fiction.[13]

By denying the cultural specificity of Grove's novelistic material, Pache advocates, among other things, a notion of the novel as a form that transcends the pressures of its content. Pache's understanding of comparative literature is the traditional one that 'expressed universality and the kind of understanding gained by philologists about language families, but also symbolized the crisis-free serenity of an almost ideal realm' (Said 1993, 45). It is precisely Pache's desire for a 'crisis-free serenity' that prompts him to unwrite both Grove's German background and his Canadian reality. But, as I have tried to show, Grove's so-called 'international standards' (Pache 17) do not conceal his origins; quite the contrary, they help the reader confront their historicity directly. Furthermore, if we see Grove's universalist perspective as constructing not 'an abstract, ahistorical setting' (Turner 50) but rather a 'setting' that, in its geographical and intellectual configurations, elaborates the ideology of his artistic project, then we can better examine the domesticating effects of this universalism on his Canadian material, and vice versa.

If Grove is neither German nor Canadian, it is hardly surprising that he cannot be German Canadian either: i.e., ethnic. This worldly condition resembles what Claudio Guillén calls 'counter exile', a tradition where 'exile is the condition but not the visible cause of an imaginative response often characterized by a tendency toward integration, increasingly broad vistas or universalism' (cited in Lagos-Pope 122). We are led to believe that this perpetual exilic condition is desirable if not ideal, that it has emancipatory effects. As to what facilitates this emancipation, Pache admits, 'at the biographical level, the answer is obvious: Grove renounces his German past, de-personalizing it and transforming it into an archetypal *Bildungserlebins*, into the story of initiation into European civilization' (17).

Towards 'A Multicultural Critical Idiom'

As I have tried to show, it is not Grove himself who 'de-personalizes' his German past; instead, this 'de-personalization' is the result of the Eurocentric vision that critics like Pache embrace. Grove's origins were disguised, yes, but they were also inscribed in his writing in more ways than one. He did not 'bur[y] his past, but . . . he slowly reshaped it in terms of his changing understanding of himself'

(Hjartarson 1981, 78). He circumscribes his cultural specificity in the same way that he gives many of his characters specific ethnic origins even though they act in a generalized human fashion. His European image masks his German origins, mimicking the ways in which his Europeanness absorbs the incommensurability of other cultural and nationalist narratives.

The essentialization of Grove's European origins implies a contempt for ethnicity as a condition that threatens the literary topos of the exilic writer. Ethnicity is dangerous because it functions as a sign of specificity contrasted to the generalized subject of European civilization. Against the cumulative, all-absorbing impulse of Eurocentrism, against its ideal of a normative consistency, ethnicity designates difference, the kind of difference that reveals the seams holding Europe together to be insurmountable barriers. The danger of ethnicity lies in its potential to cause havoc, to disrupt the presumed coherence of universalism, to expose the reality of that coherence for what it is, namely a simulacrum of its ideology.

In Grove's case, ethnicity operates as a historical sign that introduces various modalities of representation. The deliberate refashioning of his subjectivity across continents and national borders, his ambiguous self-location on the edge of truth and fiction, his construction of Canada as a sign that is simultaneously desired and repudiated—these and other elements characteristic of his writing spill out of his diasporic condition. In *Settlers of the Marsh*, for example, sexuality, gender, the 'authenticity' of desire, the pathos of innocence, universalism, and the ethos of labour are the corollaries that disclose the inscription of ethnicity in manifest as well as opaque fashions. That Grove has only recently been read as an ethnic author serves to illustrate the extent to which ethnicity has a materiality that is socially and culturally constructed. Besides, the point is not whether Grove, or any other diasporic author for that matter, is labelled ethnic. The crux of the matter lies in the presences and absences, the very ambiguities that inscribe ethnicity, and what ethnicity comes to signify both about itself and about the conditions and contexts that inform its construction.

I would like, then, to appropriate Pache's argument in order to (counter)-propose that Grove's work indeed lends itself to a reading from the perspective of comparative literature, but a comparative literature rethought with a critical difference. If 'comparative' refers to the 'kinds of relations, critical formations, analytical perspectives [that] are relevant' (Chow 1995b, 107) in studying literature, then reading Grove comparatively, within either the Canadian or the European context, involves on the one hand opening up cultural categories and borders and on the other adopting a 'multicultural critical idiom' (Apter 86). Locating Grove's work, and that of writers like him, within such an idiom implies a reading act that takes place across histories and in between the spaces that have kept some of these histories apart or underwritten. A multicultural critical idiom is of necessity comparative, for it attempts to interrogate the diverse forces that comprise the representation of diasporic subjectivities.[14]

A multicultural critical idiom operates as an active transaction between past and future, between (ancestral) origins and host (or birth) countries, between political realities conceived at the same time but in different ways. To ensure that the routes of this transaction are not blocked by abstract determinations of history and identity formation, or paid only lip service by some discourses and institutions that are merely hospitable to ethnic difference while recoiling from political change, a multicultural critical idiom cannot afford to lose sight of the meaning and function of diaspora: dissemination. This involves the constant disjoining and relinking of the chain of events that constitutes diasporic experience, a set of actions that is always marked by political interests.

Reading diasporic writers like Grove from such a perspective would not lead inevitably to the collapse of cultural difference into the assumed 'neutrality' of European civilization or the presumed cohesiveness of Canadian national identity. Nor would it assign to cultural difference a sovereignty that would freeze diasporic writers within a single ethnic idiom.[15] Rather, it means investigating the operations of power and the various acts of nomination that have produced these writers' minority positions. By remaining alert to the socio-cultural frames of a multicultural critical idiom, we would avoid the risk of investing the cultural signature of ethnicity with a determinism similar to the kind that has relegated ethnic difference to the margins. Thus this method of reading should not be confused with the hallowing of ethnicity as an inviolable, everlasting identity. Instead, it requires us to keep in mind that the travel of persons and the traffic of cultures at this point of globalization inflects ethnicity in potentially dangerous ways. Pursuing this critical approach, then, entails taking hold of the Otherness or universalism attributed to ethnic literature in order to examine critically its function as a sign of minoritization and/or idealism. This focus implies, in turn, applying pressure to the cultural and social imaginaries of both dominant and ethnic communities and their respective literary traditions.

The critical effects of the multicultural idiom as I am articulating it here do not conform to, for example, Donna Bennett's notion of Canadian postcoloniality. Hers is patterned around a more or less distinct periodization of literature following the various stages of settlement and immigration of Canadian history. Bennett proposes that the time when Salverson, Ostenso, and Grove published their first books in English was marked by a 'postcolonial longing for a distinct Canadian identity and culture that would blend Continental European and British characteristics' and traces the 'origins' of prairie realism 'in Europe as well as . . . [in] Prairie life' (186). This might be a useful summation of things as they were, or were perceived, but it does not invite a reconsideration of how we are to read writers like Grove today.

According to Bennett, 'The postcolonial model invites us to see—and gives us new ways of seeing—the play of tensions within Canadian culture as well as the tensions between Canada's culture and that of an external centre' (196). Nevertheless, her approach is limited by its focus on a linear development of history, one that does not (against her best intentions) 'give us new ways of seeing'. Instead, it is offered as a 'discourse of the real',[16] a response to a realism structured around a synchronic perspective; it is the critic's viewpoint that lends the period examined its progressivist tenor. Her 'evolutionary model' (195) does not release such authors as Grove or A.M. Klein from the critical and sociopoliti-cal literary periods that she identifies, precisely because her method of presenta-tion adopts the normative attitudes of their times.

The works of Grove, Ostenso, and Salverson, Bennett remarks,

> not only revealed the realities of contemporary settlement life but also recorded new ways of experiencing a frontier. Widely read by British Canadians, these new writers were not perceived as concerned with questions of immigrant or ethnic identity but accepted into the mainstream because they were recording *a settlement experience common to all Canadian immigrants*—an experience that may have been increasingly distant to many English-Canadian readers from southern Ontario and farther east, but one that seemed, nonetheless, to help articulate what it meant to be Canadian. (186; my emphasis)

The paradigmatic reader here is 'British Canadian,' but there is little, if any, differ-ence between that reader's perspective and Bennett's own. Bennett adopts the 'British Canadian' point of view as if she were writing a chronicle. Characterized by 'comprehensiveness', 'organization of materials', and a 'narrative coherency' that 'follows the order of chronology', a chronicle is 'marked by a desire for a kind of order and fullness in an account of reality that remains theoretically unjustified' (White 16-17). All these elements can be found in Bennett's argument.

Though Bennett's chronicle-like approach is steeped in Canadian history, she narrates that history in axiomatic and linear terms. Hence there is no analysis of how Grove, Ostenso, and Salverson, despite their ethnic differences, came to fit so nicely in the mainstream tradition of their time. Bennett's postcolonialism does not examine why the modalities of representation, on the part both of these writers and of their contemporary readers, tend to play down ethnic differences. Thus Bennett contrasts the mainstream tradition to which Grove, Ostenso, and Salverson belong with that of 'identifiably ethnic writing' (187), the beginnings of which she traces to A.M. Klein's work. But the recurrence of such reference terms as 'ethnically identified writers' (186) and 'explicitly ethnic writers' (188), together with her remark that the work of the latter group 'directs our attention to an identity that is external to the postcolonial nation—and at the same time, internal to it' (187), endows her concept of ethnicity with an impermeable authenticity, granting it the function of a privileged signified. Moreover, she renders ethnic identity in binary and spatial terms—'external'/'internal'—in relation to Canada as a 'postcolonial nation', a gesture that not only reproduces colonial tropes but also ignores the politics of a much more complex reality: Canada may be a postcolonial nation with regard to British imperialism, but ethnic minorities are still negotiating their positions within Canada's national imaginary. Above all, to posit Canada's postcoloniality in terms of a linear and progressivist development of history[17] is an affront to First Nations peoples. As Lee Maracle puts it, 'Unless I was sleeping during the revolution, we have not had a change in our condition, at least not the Indigenous people of this land. Postcolonialism presumes we have resolved the colonial condition, at least in the field of literature. Even here we are still a classical colony' (13). That Bennett does not attempt to negotiate the gap between such 'explicit' articulations of difference and the bracketing of ethnicity, in, say, Grove's work shows that her postcolonial perspective operates within a descriptivist framework based on immanent values.

To consider Grove's work within the multicultural idiom I am proposing is not necessarily to imply that Grove's writing uses strategies resisting colonialism or assimilation, a topic he wrote about. Rather, it means reading Grove with and against himself in order to bring to the fore those elements that his writing touches upon but does not directly address. What would happen, for example, if we were to regard the ethnic origins he adopts not as signs of a European or an archetypal Canadian, but instead as elements of hybridity? What would we find if we tested the realism of his writing against the reality that it purportedly imitates? To what extent, for example, is Bennett (and other critics before her) correct in arguing that *Settlers of the Marsh* records 'a settlement experience common to all Canadian immigrants' (186) at the time? Is there anything about the almost instant canonization of this novel that could account, in part, for the fact that other first novels, like Nino Ricci's *Lives of the Saints*, became overnight best-sellers more than half a century later? In other words, what can Grove's case tell us about the reasons why, in the early nineties, ethnic writing became a privileged mode of literary discourse in Canada? What institutions of power mediate ethnicity and the various kinds of value assigned to it? I will address some of these questions later in this book. For now, I would like to examine how, in Grove's first novel in English, universalism barters with ethnicity and vice versa, how ethnicity is at once manifested and superseded. In so doing I hope to shed some light on the way ethnicity is affected by certain power dynamics and how it itself is inscribed in Canadian culture.

Settlers of the Marsh and the Debris of Europe

Perhaps one of the principal reasons why Grove 'is rarely considered to be ethnic' is that the narrative of Niels's life in *Settlers of the Marsh* seems to be at odds with the concerns—resistance to the representation of the ethnic subject as object, emphasis on cultural authenticity and ethnic difference, the Us and Them paradigm, to mention only a few—that recur in many critical studies of ethnic literature. Except on rare occasions in the text, Niels is decidedly unconcerned with his position as ethnic subject. If '[t]o belong to an ethnic minority would seem to guarantee status as an object, as something fraught with difference'

(Blodgett 1982, 86), then Niels's character does not measure up to this definition either. He has to negotiate many differences between himself and those he encounters, but these differences are not ethnic-specific, nor do they relegate him to the position of an object. Along the same lines, if '[e]thnicity presents itself as problem of self-definition,' as Eli Mandel suggests in one of the earlier essays on ethnic literature in Canada (99), then neither ethnicity nor minoritization, nor for that matter belonging to an ethnic community, appears to be of vital importance to Niels's subjectivity. Nor does Niels display, beyond his highly symbolic visions of his mother (more on those later), the kind of nostalgia that is considered to be a stock theme of ethnic literature.

Instead, Niels embodies the psychological and ideological signs of the settler: 'The settler subject is signed . . . in a language of authority and in a language of resistance. The settler subject enunciates the authority that is in colonial discourse on behalf of the imperial enterprise that he—and sometimes she—represents' (Lawson 26). Hence the readiness with which the novel was endorsed by its 'British readers'. Beyond the direct reference to settlers in the novel's title, Niels's position as a settler/colonizer is made apparent in the way he approaches his new environment in Canada: 'In this country, life and success did not, as they had always seemed to do in Sweden, demand some mysterious powers inherent in the individual. It was merely a question of persevering and hewing straight to the line. Life was simplified' (45). Clearly it is not Niels's ethnicity that is at stake here. The 'mysterious powers' that distinguish Sweden from Canada delimit the metaphysical eminence of Niels as a character cast in the commanding role of a settler/colonizer. His subjectivity is thus entrenched in the juxtaposition of European standards of civility, the opacity of the 'mysterious', and the uncivilized status of a yet unformed society, the transparency of the 'new' land.

Even when Niels is represented in an inferior light, his epistemological position remains more or less intact: 'He had emigrated; and the mere fact that he was uprooted and transplanted had given him a second sight, had awakened powers of vision and sympathy in him which were far beyond his education and upbringing' (64). The narrator attributes Niels's spiritual edification not to the cultural specificity of Canada but rather to the very process of being 'transplanted'. Implicitly validated here, too, is Niels's inherent potential as a European subject about to be enlightened, a subject constantly evolving towards a progressivist vision. There is nothing in these images of Niels that would support the minority position so easily attributed to ethnic subjects. Why, then, does Niels perceive himself, at a crucial point in the novel's narrative, as belonging to a class of people he characterizes as the 'wastage' of Europe?

> He looked upon himself as belonging to a special race—a race not comprised in any limited nation, but one that crossed-sectioned all nations: a race doomed to everlasting extinction and yet recruited out of the wastage of all other nations . . . (139)

In this scene, half-way through *Settlers of the Marsh*, Niels occupies a blurred position, for he is the object of a look and at the same time the one producing it. Kristjana Gunnars, in her 'Afterword' to the novel's New Canadian Library edition, is right to see these ruminations of Niels as forming 'perhaps the strangest statement in the whole book. The immigrant as "wastage" from other nations is a low view indeed, and says a great deal about Niels's view of himself and his fellow settlers' (273).

Historically, this 'special race' does not seem to include Scandinavian immigrants, who were among the immigrant groups most favoured by the Canadian government and Canadians in general at the turn of the century. James S. Woodsworth, in his widely read *Strangers within Our Gates* (1909), leaves no doubt as to the general sentiments informing the high opinion of Scandinavians: 'Accustomed to the rigors of a northern climate, clean-blooded, thrifty, ambitious and hard-working, they [Scandinavians] will be certain of success in this pioneer country, where the strong, not the weak, are wanted.' Woodsworth attributes their strength partly to their eagerness 'to become Canadian citizens, and readily adapt themselves to Canadian ways' (77). The Scandinavians are the only 'New Canadians' of whom neither 'the pejorative epithet "foreigner", nor the labels "illiterate" and "unassimilable"' is used (Jorgen Dahlie 102).[18]

Thus when Niels says that he belongs 'to a special race . . . recruited out of the wastage of all other nations', he cannot be thinking of any inferiority attributed to his ethnic group by the presumably homogenized society in Canada. We could not logically assume that he contradicts the social consensus about immigrants at the time; instead, 'wastage' seems to convey a sense of his imaginary projections about himself at this point in the novel. His conceptualization of this 'special race' reflects inferiority, the kind that might be the outcome of hegemonic practices, but its source, at least on the surface, is not in Canada; nor is it given any specific or singular origin. Only by inference can we situate it within Europe. Europe figures as an abstraction, a sign of its self-fashioned universality, but its homogenized image is dissolved by discrepant interests and cultural and class differences. Niels is rather vague, as is usually the case, but it is quite apparent that this 'special race' is the debris produced following the construction of Europe's imagined unity. The distinctiveness of this 'race', what makes it 'special', consists in its precarious condition as at once Europe's 'relation and nonrelation', Serres's definition of a parasite (79).

Niels's statement is perplexing in more ways than one. Within the larger social framework at the turn of the century, his views fall inside the purview of the fears and biases about immigration prevalent in the dominant society's attitudes. Niels's opinion of immigrants as 'wastage' is disturbing, to be sure, but it ceases to be 'strange' if we examine it through the materiality of history.

The Materiality of History and Realism: The Author 'Inside' and 'Outside' the Text, and His Generalized Subject

I wish to make a distinction here between reading historically and reading in a historical materialist way, because understanding the import of Niels's words is not simply a matter of establishing their linear connections to history, their cultural referentiality, or the extent to which they were codified by the immigration policies and popular social views in the early 1900s. To interpret them merely as instances of social realism simulating the dominant or minor ideologies of Grove's time would only expose their evidentiary aspects; it would not address the way historical reality is reconfigured and inflected by elements both extrinsic and intrinsic to the novel.

Reading in a historical materialist way[19] avoids the risk of turning representations of history into literary conceit. Instead, it involves bringing together the social reality external to the novel with that inscribed in it, in order not to match one with the other but to understand how the novel's discourse refracts the master narratives of its time. While a historical materialist reading is responsive to the various strains of cultural discourse embodied in a text, it also remains alert to cultural modulations that elude the text or are suppressed by it. Because this method of reading as I am defining it approaches a text both synchronically and diachronically, it can also reveal the practical and semiotic structures that give shape and direction to our roles both as reading subjects and as social beings. Furthermore, it does not shy away from the psychoanalytic history of the subject; rather, it works together with 'a *situated psychoanalysis*—a culturally contextualized psychoanalysis that is simultaneously a psychoanalytically informed history' (McClintock 1995, 72). Thus such a reading does not aspire to release the subject from its historical entrapments, and it cannot be linear; it must allow for all necessary detours.

In the case of *Settlers of the Marsh*, these detours include testing Grove's notion of the realist novel and deconstructing the realism longed for by his 'British readers', so that we do not rely on history as *doxa* and see Niels as a character typifying the 'experience common to all Canadian immigrants' (Bennett 186). Reading *Settlers of the Marsh* through the materiality of history implies apprehending Niels's identifications and visions as psychic manifestations specific to his character, but also as elements whose meanings slide from historical to literary discourse (with its attendant histories), from Grove's Eurocentrism to his less myopic, but equally troubling, perception of Canada. Considered from this perspective, *Settlers of the Marsh*—despite Grove's universalism, much admired by his contemporaries and some later critics—offers an intriguing representation of the exigencies of diasporic subjectivity. Diaspora, and the cultural difference that it entails, cannot be studied simply in terms of Us and Them, in terms of sovereign positions and minority subjects; it must be examined within the web of complexities that inform ethnic subjectivity and its representations.

Grove's views on realism are well known, but it will be useful to re-examine them here in order to set up my argument. Talking about the purpose of art, Grove states that 'its aim is one; and it consists in the clear and unequivocal expression of the generally human'; he defines 'generally human' as a 'response or reaction [that] is independent of nationality, individuality, station in life, and education' ('The Aim of Art' 1982, 100). Grove's generalized subject depends on the novelist's ability to extract its 'essential' human nature from the elements that tie it down to a subject position conditioned by specificity. But since this subject is produced by 'response or reaction' to the particularities of identities, its universalist nature declares its emancipation from contingencies. Grove's universalist subject seems to have value only insofar as it rises above the factors that give it meaning. But its antithetical relationship to these factors suggests that the distillation process is not complete, that these contingencies of nationality, class, and education are not eliminated: 'What is repressed is always there' (Serres 78). In Grove's case, universalism itself is inscribed as a contingent sign.

This kind of contingency is indeed implicit in Grove's statement that the realist artist 'cannot reproduce except what was potentially in him, he is, in the totality of his creation, present to the spectator or reader. By the very fact that he cannot convincingly represent a character or a happening which finds no echo in himself, he delimits his work by his own personality' ('Realism in Literature' 1982, 61-2). A character structured as a generalized subject is not only haunted by the very specificities she or he is purported to transcend, but is also constructed—automatically, Grove implies—as an example of the author's signature. The character, in other words, functions as a concrete manifestation of the author's authoring and authority, his paternal legacy. What's more, the author does not simply live through his character; he comes alive under the gaze of 'the spectator or reader'. And it is in this guise, at the moment when his past and my present meet under my reading gaze, that Grove figures in these pages.

The author Grove is talking about is the author-as-scriptor who surfaces through the materiality of language, but he is also the author 'outside' the text[20] whose 'personality' resuscitates the particularities wrested from the generalized subject. This 'personality' is not to be readily identified with the sum-total of such biographical details as nationality, gender, and class, although these factors do constitute the 'political force and meaning' that inform 'authorial subjectivity' (Silverman 1992, 162). Thus realist fiction as conceptualized by Grove can never be cut adrift from specific cultural and authorial moorings. As he says elsewhere, seemingly contradicting the above statements, 'a true novel [. . .] will root the crisis and the characters involved in it in the social conditions of the period which it depicts' ('The Novel' 1982, 123). His realism may entail the death of a subject's cultural specificity, but it still holds a tight grip on the specificity of the author as subject; likewise, this realism is movitated by a desire—imbued with moral energy—to 'depict' society. The universalism of Grove's generalized subject, then, is a master fiction in that it attempts to control the intimate connection between the ideological production of subjectivity in a society and its cultural representations.

Grove advocated this kind of realism to his Canadian audience with the fervour of a man convinced he was pronouncing something original. Yet his allusions to the Hellenistic tradition and to such authors as Gide and Zola, together with his essay on Flaubert's art, indicate the derivative quality of his ideas—or, to put it more gently, his indebtedness to the various traditions that his writing amalgamates. In some respects, Grove preached to his Canadian audience with the condescension of a cultural imperialist who thought he knew what they needed to hear. Indeed, he thought his audience 'as stupid as can be imagined' (Pacey 1976, 112); though at least once, when he was in a slightly generous mood, he said he wrote 'for a public which [was] not yet born' (Pacey 1976, 41). It is an ironic coincidence that his was the kind of realism praised by his reviewers.[21]

If we approach *Settlers of the Marsh* through Grove's critical lens as I have just read it, Niels's view of himself 'as belonging to a special race' must be reconsidered as that of the author 'outside' the text who in turn is mediated by the author 'inside' the text. For the sake of clarity I will call the former 'Grove' and the latter 'the narrator'. Thus 'Grove' designates not the man who, for example, while on a nation-wide lecture tour, sent his soiled suits and dirty socks home to his wife for laundering, but rather Grove the subject who is at one and the same time the agent of his multiple acts of self-elision and self-fabrication and the mutated subject that emerges from them. This Grove resides within the cognitive realm of the society that *Settlers of the Marsh* 'depicts', but we can gain access to him only through the novel's narrator.

Niels, his Co-Protagonist, and their Author

We tend to think of Niels as the single protagonist of the novel. Yet because of his inarticulacy, which paradoxically propels much of the action in the text, the leading role he plays as protagonist is shared with the narrator. And I am not referring only to the narrator as the agent that embodies the desire to tell. The sharp contrast between the narrator's discourse and Niels's inability to express his thoughts or take action establishes the narrator as co-protagonist, a character in his own right.[22] For example, the statement that Niels 'was merely a part of that world; not a hero who came, acclaimed by the multitudes, borne high on the shoulders of his followers' (51) is an instance of narratorial intrusion—a pervasive element in the text, signalling that the narrator is not just speaking through or for Niels. Rather, in instances like this, the narrator summons the author who is 'outside' the text.

His letters, essays, and autobiographical narratives reveal the author 'outside' the text to be a man with a highly inflated ego. Indeed, as many of his letters and autobiographical statements attest, self-aggrandizement is at play even when Grove puts himself down. Frequent self-deprecation was among the devices he employed to establish his self-image as a genius awaiting recognition. The failures he experienced—and invented—helped to elaborate his moral tenacity and superiority. That, in his perception, Canada was a cultural wilderness and its intellectuals largely unsophisticated made the country fertile ground for his assignations with his fictional selves. It is through this understanding of Grove's 'character' as the author 'outside' the text that I see Niels as yet another foil for Grove: the more naïve the novelistic character is, the more sagacious and dazzling the author 'inside' the text can appear to be. Seen in this light, Niels occupies a position that often becomes the meeting ground of Grove and the narrator. Niels is, then, a construct emerging from the relation between the authors 'inside' and 'outside' the text. To be more specific, against the immigrant as intellectual and the immigrant as con-man—the double-voiced construct emerging from such narratives as *A Search for America* and *In Search of Myself*[23]—is pitted Niels's figure as paradigmatic settler whose extraordinary naïveté plays a multifarious role.

It is important to note at this point that without the narrator's presence there would be hardly any story for the English-speaking reader to read. From the very opening of the novel, until Niels learns enough English not to feel left out on social occasions such as the gatherings on the Lund homestead, the narrator is inscribed in the narrative at once as storyteller and as translator. '[T]he translator ought, despite or perhaps because of his or her oath of fidelity, to be considered not as a duteous spouse but as a faithful bigamist, with loyalties split between a native language and a foreign tongue' (Johnson 1985, 143). From Benjamin's view of translation as the traffic of differences between cultures, 'language' and 'tongue' can be taken to designate different cultural discourses.[24] Yet 'translation is seldom established on the basis of the equality of the partners' (Chow 1995a, 183), and that is the crucial point here.

Niels's linguistic difficulties in his early days in Canada, together with his psychic problems and inability to express his thoughts even to himself, let alone to others, contrast sharply with the narrator's facility with languages (Swedish, Icelandic, and German are the languages in which various characters supposedly speak); they also contrast with the narrator's propensity to philosophize and analyze, and to do so not always to Niels's benefit.

For example, it is Niels, not the narrator, who fails to understand many of his community's social and sexual codes. 'What was the woman [Clara] in the White Range Line House doing meanwhile?' the narrator asks knowingly, displaying his perspicacity and rhetorical superiority to Niels; Niels himself 'hardly knew' (167). By the same token, I find it interesting, given Grove's sense of realism as a matter of psychological verisimilitude, that it is not Niels who reads *Elements of Political Economy* (177). If it were, we would certainly hear more about it, for both of the books with that title (by Egerton Ryerson and Francis Wayland)[25] have much to say on topics ranging from the material and spiritual aspects of capital to labour and production to agriculture. This is just one example of the way the narrator tells not only Niels's story but also Grove's. Both Ryerson's and Wayland's philosophical arguments about value, capital, and labour within a highly religious and humanistic frame have more appeal, I would like to suggest, for the author 'outside' the text than they do for Niels, who lacks the education and vocabulary, at least at this point in the narrative, to understand the intricacies of such work.

It is within this context that the narrator of *Settlers of the Marsh* functions as co-protagonist, as someone constructing Niels but also constantly engaged in calling upon the author 'outside'. We can see his narrative, then, as the hymen conjoining un/broken land and cultural wilderness, the two elements constituting respectively the frame of Niels's experiences in the novel and the preoccupations of the author 'outside' the text. Thus the hymen—in its connotations as 'neither confusion nor distinction, neither identity nor difference, neither consummation nor virginity, neither the veil nor unveiling' (Derrida 1981a, 43)—designates the narrative as a figural space inhabited by Niels but also frequented by Grove. As co-protagonist, the narrator has an artful role to play: on one hand, he is in charge of exposing Niels's monumental innocence, putting into words Niels's paroxysms of desire and his misbegotten goals; on the other, he translates the effects of that innocence into a discourse that serves the interests of the author 'outside'.

Grove's interests do not always coincide with Niels's. Thus if the concept of a 'special race' doesn't make sense in terms of Niels's ethnicity as inscribed in the novel, it is to the context of the author 'outside' the text that we must trace it. As I have already suggested, there is a paradoxical gap between Niels's construction as a universalist subject—'He was a man!' (74)—and his Swedish background, which is itself contradicted by his deprecatory reference to himself as a minoritized subject. As the title *Elements of Political Economy* points to Grove, so too does the notion of immigrants as 'wastage'.

In fact, this 'wastage' is the single most important sign invoking the critical consciousness of the author 'outside' the text. Within the universalist context of the novel in general and the passage in which it appears in particular, the figure of the immigrant as 'wastage' is a contradictory formation that supplies the novel's counter-discourse of ethnicity. This counter-discourse contests—indeed is interlocked with—the universalism of the novel, which suspends ethnic difference by absorbing it. The spectre of ethnicity that haunts universalism ceases to be submerged when the figure of 'wastage' surfaces. In a discursive fashion, 'wastage' functions as an inscription of various kinds of repression and oppression; it marks, in contradistinction to Niels's universalism, the novel's ethnic signature, albeit as a negative trope.

The interjection of this counter-discourse in the novel is made possible by the narrator's dramatization of the differential relationship between the author 'outside' the text and Niels. As I will attempt to show, the figure of 'wastage' brings into the novel the social paradigms about ethnicity circulating in Grove's time, paradigms that are not always compatible with Niels's character. How this counter-discourse is associated with Grove and what purposes it serves in the novel will, I hope, become apparent in the next two sections.

Between Demand and Supply: The Malady of Ethnicity

Niels represents one of the 'agricultural immigrants' towards whom the immigration policies of Clifford Sifton were geared.[26] Minister of the Interior from 1896 to 1905, Sifton developed a reputation as a 'nation-builder' because of his consistent efforts to encourage—and advertising programs about—immigration and settlement in the Canadian West. 'Our desire,' he wrote, 'is to promote the immigration of farmers and farm labourers. We have not been disposed to exclude foreigners of any nationality who seemed likely to become successful agriculturalists . . .' (cited in D.J. Hall 1985a, 68). Despite his all-embracing gesture toward foreign nationals, Sifton conceptualized and practised his immigration policies in racialized terms that reflected the spirit of his time: 'different "races" had different characteristics which, among other things, inclined some to be farmers and to accept hardship generation after generation, while others either would not succeed on the farm or their children would be likely to leave the farm' (D.J. Hall 1985b, 295). Thus Sifton's image of the ideal immigrant as 'a stalwart peasant in a sheep-skin coat born on the soil, whose forefathers have been farmers for ten generations, with a stout wife and a half-dozen children' (cited in D.J. Hall 1985b, 295)[27] epitomizes his views. The same 'businesslike assessment of ethnic differences' (1985b, 295)[28] is apparent in the diligent fervour with which Sifton pursued his goals: 'In my judgment . . . the immigration work has to be carried on in the same manner as the sale of any commodity; just as soon as you stop advertising and missionary work the movement is going to stop' (cited in Hall 1985b, 288).

In Sifton's project of nation-building, Canada and immigrants are symmetrically balanced as commodities within an exchange system that threatens both equally. Virtually everyone actively engaged in immigration and nationalist projects conceded that 'New Canadians' were badly needed for population, labour, and settlement purposes. Yet that view went hand in hand with a pervasive anxiety over maintaining Canada's Britishness. English-speaking Canadians perceived the influx of non-British immigrants as a threat, against which the assimilationist ideology of Anglo-conformity was their defence, while the immigrants themselves had to contend with the discriminatory practices and views associated with the hegemonic concept of 'Canadian'.[29] The rhetoric of anxiety, reflecting the spirit of the day, is predictably extreme. For example, this is what W.S. Wallace wrote in his article 'The Canadian Immigration Policy' (1908): 'The native-born population, in the struggle to keep up appearances in the face of the increasing competition, fails to propagate itself, commits race suicide, in short; whereas the immigrant population, being inferior, and having no appearances to keep up, propagates itself like the fish of the sea' (cited in Barber, Introduction to Woodsworth xiv).

It is in the context of these debates that we begin to encounter the image of immigrants as 'wastage' in all its possible metaphorical variants. C.A. Magrath talks about 'The European country getting rid of undesirables . . . and Canada receiving and absorbing them into its national life' (116). More feisty and categorical about his racialist and ideological views, W.G. Smith sees immigrants in terms of 'defects . . . [that] may never disappear' (146). 'The game of getting rid of them has always been played enthusiastically by those who are interested in lessening their own troubles,' he states (13); and in a chapter poignantly entitled 'The Refuse of the Tide' he refers to the fear of 'misfits' entering Canada (72). In many of these documents and others of the period, ethnicity figures as a malady, a malignant condition that it is hard for the Canadian state to inoculate itself against. Immigration is synonymous with social failure even before the immigrant tries out a new life in Canada. The immigrant's undesirability is a condition defined by both European and Canadian hegemonic attitudes, characterized by a wilful blindness as much to nativism as to the class and economic factors that necessitated immigration in the first place.

Even *Strangers Within Our Gates*, the book by that 'untypical' Canadian[30] James S. Woodsworth, who was active in such causes as women's rights and penal reform, takes for granted that 'our immigrants are below the average in their own countries' (191). The images of immigrants as 'wastage' that permeate Woodsworth's study exclude Scandinavians but incorporate all other groups, including the English. As he says, 'the trouble has been largely with the *class* of immigrants who have come. . . . England has sent us largely the failures of the cities.' In contrast to the English, whose 'weakness' lies in their 'lack of adaptability' (46),[31] the Scandinavians 'easily assimilate [. . .] and readily intermarry' (76). While Woodsworth welcomes the Scandinavians, who are 'certain of success in this pioneer country' (77), he is 'glad that the Canadian Government is taking steps to prevent the 'dumping' of these unfortunates [the English] into Canada' (51). His celebrated compassion, equivalent to some kinds of liberalism today, is obviously influenced by cultural as well as class biases.

Woodsworth's attitude towards 'the least desirable classes of our immigrants' (138) is no mere instance of essentialism. Indeed, as becomes apparent in his chapter on the 'Levantine Races', subtitled 'Greeks, Turks, Armenians, Syrians, Persians', his view, together with the rhetoric in which it is couched, sums up the layered meanings of human 'wastage'. As he writes, citing Allan McLaughlin at some length,[32] what is undesirable about these immigrants is their 'Oriental subtlety', their 'intrigue, deceit, and servility'. Their 'business acumen' notwithstanding, these 'detrimental and burdensome' immigrants are 'parasites . . . because of their miserable physique and tendency to communicable disease'. They are a 'distinct menace', their 'most consoling feature . . . [being] that they form a comparatively small part of our total immigration' (139). Orientalism clearly falls under the heading of 'wastage', while the fear of these immigrants points to fear of contamination by the Orient. Yet that supposed source of infection has already been infected itself. In fact, 'the Orient' is a misnomer, an instance of colonialist catachresis in which the borders and regions of the Middle East collapse into a phantasmic realm: 'the Orient' is not a real place, but a space right at the edge of Western consciousness where everything undesirable can be 'dumped'. To use a well-known Canadian literary metaphor, it is the 'nuisance grounds' of Margaret Laurence's Christy Logan in *The Diviners*, where the meaning, as well as the value, of refuse changes depending on who does the discarding and who does the divining.

Interestingly, like Niels's 'special race', which resides in Europe (indeed is produced by it) but does not belong there, these immigrants do not become 'parasites' only after they take the route of diaspora. They are perceived to be dispossessed and homeless—already 'parasites'—even before they become geographically displaced. Their parasitic existence has nothing in common with the parasite as elaborated by Serres, which is neither object nor subject but both at the same time, and, above all, the 'astonishing constructer of intersubjectivity' (227). What these immigrants import into Canada is their parasitic relationship with a history viewed as a spatialized and unmediated course of events; hence their undesirability. In this context, the praise Grove has received for his depiction of experiences 'common to all immigrants' is itself an instance of catachresis, for there is virtually nothing in *Settlers of the Marsh*, beyond the loaded reference to 'wastage', that records these commonly held views about most immigrants at the time.

For Woodsworth, the immigrant as parasite is at once refuse and excess. His primary intent is to prevent the arrival of all these 'undesirables', but when it is too late for prevention he hopes to transform—recycle, as it were—this refuse into surplus value with regard to labour and, eventually, assimilation. Thus, contrary to some of his contemporaries, Woodsworth did not entirely despair at the influx of non-British immigrants. He saw 'scatter[ing] the foreign communities among the Canadian' as conducive to 'the process of assimilation' (234); 'labor union[s]' were similarly useful because of their ability to break down 'national differences' (238). Above all, he hoped that 'there are a sufficient number of men who love their country well enough to insist that every boy and girl in Canada have a chance to obtain at least an elementary education' (237). If the representation of immigrants as 'wastage' is strongly inscribed in Woodsworth's book, it is because he endorses it, but also because it serves a strategic purpose in the political platform of his 'social gospel'.[33]

'Riff-raff' and 'Greatness': Grove's 'Jargon of Authenticity'

A similar strategic doubleness informs the motives behind the inscription of immigrants as 'wastage' in *Settlers of the Marsh*. Not only was the history of attitudes I have just recited part of the social climate in which the novel was written, but Grove, who knew Woodsworth,[34] was definitely interested in the immigration debate. His interest, in some respects a reflection of his own diasporic condition, is directly addressed in his essays 'Canadians Old and New' and 'Assimilation'.[35] Furthermore, it reflects both an investment in and an elaboration of his nineteenth-century European legacy, especially the European view of orientalism—a legacy we can trace specifically to, among other things, Grove's intimate knowledge of Flaubert's work and his essay 'Flaubert's Theories of Artistic Existence'.[36] The Grove I am talking about here is the author 'outside' the novel, the author as cultural product and reader of his European and Canadian milieux, but also the author who includes himself 'inside' the text under the heading of 'wastage'.

What is intriguing, however, is that 'wastage' appears only as an aberration in the novel's narrative: the impetus of the story in *Settlers of the Marsh* follows the mode of selective realism. This realism refrains from representing those immigrants whose experiences were predicated on the socioeconomic and symbolic values attached to 'wastage'. Not only are most of the characters Northern Europeans, but even the least financially fortunate among them, Mr. and Mrs. Lund, are depicted as responsible for their hardships; if they suffer, it is not because of any discrimination against them as immigrants. Interestingly, Mrs. Lund is the character assigned the 'task' of making the one explicitly racist comment in the novel—yet another instance of the ambivalent relationship of Grove's realism to the realities of the time. Mrs. Lund, eager to avert critical attention from her husband's uselessness and inability to help sustain their family, attributes her family's lack of success to 'the Jew [who] takes it all', a comment she immediately repeats: 'Whatever we get the Jew puts his hand on' (78-9). Her anti-Semitism is apparently intended to be read either as a mark of her female guile or as an attempt to save face (marks, in turn, of the novel's gender biases); it also brings to the surface of the text, however momentarily, the kinds of reality rendered invalid by Grove's realistic treatment of the generalized subject. Here the figure of the Jew, historically part of Europe's 'wastage', opens up yet another fissure in the text: since there is no specific reference to any Jewish character in the novel, 'the Jew' represents the racist stereotypes attributed at the time to European Jews, and hence functions as an allegory of financial institutions. The figure thus exposes not only the abjection of ethnic subjects, but also the way cultural and historical mutations can be textually inscribed in invisible ink.

In a parallel way, the narrative also eschews representation of the dominant society, for the references to settings and situations that do not immediately relate to the novels' settlers are relatively few and, in the context of the plot, inconsequential. For example, the big city south of the characters' settlement is mentioned only casually, and there are no incidents of conflict between immigrants and Canadians in the town of Minor. While much fiction—from Ralph Connor's *The Foreigner* (1909), whose plot demonstrates normative racist and stereotyping attitudes towards immigrants at the time, and Illia Kiriak's *Sons of the Soil* (1927-28; published 1939-45), which dramatizes ethnic tensions, to more recent fiction like Frank Paci's *Black Madonna* (1982), Wayson Choy's *The Jade Peony* (1995), Austin Clarke's *The Origin of Waves* (1997), and Rabindranath Maharaj's *Homer In Flight* (1997)—situates the immigrant condition and ethnic and racial differences within a social field of contestation arising from the inter-action of 'Old' and 'New' Canadians, Grove's novel decidedly turns away from such confrontations. Still, as I am trying to show here, despite its selective realism, *Settlers of the Marsh* is not devoid of history.

Through the collaboration of the author 'outside' the text and the author 'inside' the text, the novel instils a sense of the permeability of the boundaries separating a community of immigrants from the social structures of the dominant society. The banker in Minor who offers Niels a loan is a good instance of the harmonization of relations between 'Old' and 'New' Canadians in the narrative. This harmonization is intended to 'depict' to Grove's 'British readers' their supposed benevolence towards immigrants, a benevolence that is ironically demonstrated by the notable absence of any character affiliated with the dominant society. Only under the guise of absence does the dominant society materialize in the novel. Like the phantom characters they are, the 'Old' Canadians do not interfere; they leave the immigrants to their own devices, affording them the opportunity to prove themselves worthy of their hosts' trust. Above all, they are not seen projecting onto the immigrants images of 'wastage'. Structurally, their invisibility creates a pointed contrast to the visibility of immigrants; but, in the context of the novel, the visibility of the desirable Scandinavian immigrants functions as a metonym for societal views at large.

So when the narrator puts the sign of 'wastage' under erasure, he produces a story representing the positivism of the dominant society while reflecting the complicity of the author 'outside' the text. The novel's realism, then, attempts to rise above some of the historical specificities of its period. Adopting as he does a selective approach, the narrator tells Niels's story from the point of view of the dominant humanistic ideology. He therefore invokes a spectral history that unwrites the pervasiveness of 'wastage'. From this perspective, the single inscrip-tion of 'wastage' in the narrative can only appear to be a reference to a putative reality. That it is Niels who visualizes himself in terms of debris is, of course, meant to further distance the 'Old' Canadians, and by implication the author 'outside' the text, from the contamination of this sign. Niels's image of himself as expendable is not to be read exclusively as self-referential; in addition, it repre-sents an abnegation of his subjectivity because it serves the author's own purposes. At this point in the narrative, the realism of the novel assumes an archival function.

My suggestion that 'wastage' operates as the textually ironic signature of the author 'outside' the text does not necessarily mean that Grove, following Woodsworth, fully endorses the hegemonic ideology that produces that 'wastage'. Both his self-constructions and the construction of Niels resist the conventional paradigms of diasporic subjectivity, be they the products of diasporic subjects or of the host society, or both. For Grove, though, these paradigms and their hegemonic reformulations are imbricated in the way he fashions his subjectivity and attempts to legitimate the importance of his role as author, as 'spokesman of a race' (1946, 226). In this respect, the representation of Niels as someone who stands above the 'riff-raff'[37] of society parallels Grove's own self-image.

'I felt an exile,' Grove says in *In Search of Myself* (235). This 'exile' has a double signification. On one hand, he refers to the fact that he is physically an exile from Europe; on the other, he says that he 'did *not* feel an exile from any definite country [. . .] I was rapidly becoming extra-European' (236). It is this second sense of existential exile that pains Grove, that subsumes his diasporic displacement. Although he never lets his readers, listeners, or correspondents forget that he was 'transplanted from surroundings of the most advanced European "culture",' that he was destined to do 'things to amaze the world' ('Thoughts and Reflections', Hjartarson, ed. 316 and 319)—an assertion invariably supported by evidence he furnishes from within Europe—European culture dissolves, as I have already intimated, into the kind of global consciousness that a man like him is capable of achieving. What held him back, what constantly nagged at him, was that he 'was being rubbed the wrong way, day in, day out, by those who, for the moment, were my social equals—whom others would have called the scum of the earth; the people who, like myself, were crowded over the edge and into the abyss' (1946, 235-6).

Riff-raff, Europe, exile (intellectual and geographical), European literati, scum, waste, enslavement, abyss: these are the words Grove uses to describe the conditions that produce his subjectivity; they do so by causing him to slide from unlimited potential to self-induced fantasies, from realized aspirations to failure. The undermining of his success, however relative, becomes for Grove the paradigmatic trope through which he reveals himself to be a subject who, like Niels, is never at home. The trajectory of Grove's life-writing follows a kind of syntax that does not tie him down for too long, that does not demand penance, that in fact offers him the abyss as a gift of experience, a syntax replicated by Niels's life. Meanwhile, the 'scum of the earth' that rub him the wrong way are destined to remain just that: faceless and wasted, but endowed with the task of making an aleatory subjectivity like Grove's shift—and shine. This is yet another way in which we can read 'wastage' through the materiality of history.

Thus in his essay 'Canadians Old and New' Grove addresses his mainstream Canadian audience by donning, as he says, the double-faced persona of Janus: 'Like the statues of the ancient Roman deity Janus, this article is going to have two faces, one turned to those who, being born in this country [. . .] invite [. . .] all white nations to come and to make their homes among them; the other, to those who have just arrived in pursuance of that invitation' (Hjartarson, ed. 169). But the Janus mask from behind which he speaks appears to have not just two faces but three, and the third has transmuting or Protean qualities. For when Grove, although an immigrant himself, addresses 'Mr. Canadian Citizen' (170), he speaks not in the voice of immigrants but in the voice of someone who stands above Canadians and immigrants alike.

He identifies with the 'we' of Canadians—'here, in Canada, we cultivate . . . an attitude toward life'; 'In such Crown colonies the foreigner may be tolerated; *we* invite him' (170)—but he also retreats from that identification: 'These people are strange to *you*; but unless *you* overcome that strangeness, it is not likely that anyone else will try' (171). His agency as subject derives in part from the social imaginary of the dominant society. In an Althusserian way, he recognizes himself in this imaginary, but its representation, produced as it is by him, also functions as an instance of misrecognition. What is interesting, though, is that when he stands apart from the Canadian, he does so without taking on the persona of the immigrant. Thus he casts himself in the role of the host only tentatively—'Our guests come from Europe. Europe, as only he can know who has lived there as a poor man, is a bad place to live in' (173); in the meantime he merely flirts with the role of the guest. Yet while he castigates Canadians, he also withdraws from the responsibilities he confers on them as hosts: 'Do you, Mr. Canadian, want to assimilate these people? [. . .] Do not forget that they have brains; for most of them were the underdogs in Europe; and it is precisely the underdog who develops his brains' (174). In this and similar statements uttered by his European persona, he is neither host nor underdog, and thus both inside and outside Canadian society.

But when he 'let[s] the other face of the Janus-head speak' (174), he speaks resolutely from one side of his mouth, and he does so through the sign of the law:

> Mr. Newcomer, we invited you to come among us, and you followed the call. We bid you welcome. We are bound by a promise. [. . .]
>
> You have lived in Europe; so you know that there is no freedom without law. Your freedom depends on your attitude toward that law. You must, for the moment, accept and obey it; or the very machinery that is set in motion for your protection will continue moving to your enslavement. (174)

Although he promises immigrants 'a share in forming that law' (175), and attributes discriminatory behaviour only to those 'belonging to the riff-raff of this country' (175), the law appears as a shadowy figure, shadowy precisely because Grove talks about it without laying it down. If the law is in place to prevent the immigrants' enslavement, it is also there to turn the immigrants into slaves to the very fear that the law inspires. The law, a response to the premise of lingering flaws and faults, is already posited as a judgement of the immigrants' differences. Although in reality one of these newcomers, Grove seems to exempt himself from the emotional enslavement imposed by the Canadian law.

He employs similar rhetorical gestures in his essay 'Assimilation'. He doesn't practise his masquerade trick here; nonetheless, although he often refers to himself as a 'New' Canadian, he does not include himself in the 'ethnic problems' (177) he discusses from inside the collective and dominant 'we' of his address. The advice he offers—'If we want to find settlers fit to do our sort of work, we must go to the poor districts of Europe, to the districts where the hardships of poverty have trained the population for the hardships of pioneerdom' (180)—comes from an intersubjective space. This is a space that supplies him with the power of double knowledge: 'I was tolerably familiar with Europe as it was before the war' (182), he says, and 'I have lived among almost all classes of immigrants; in the open country; and I have lived among them in such a way as to be mistaken for one of their number' (181). To say he has been 'mistaken' for an immigrant means he does not consider himself to be one, and this boastful enunciation of mistaken identity announces the ambivalence and complicity that mark Grove's attitudes. He doesn't quite posit himself as a mediator in whose discourse opposites are united; rather, he places himself within the gap that separates 'Old' and 'New' Canadians, a space he constructs not as a margin but as a third space where the generalized subject assumed by his persona resides. This is not exactly the kind of 'Third Space' that Bhabha talks about. Both are spaces 'of enunciation, which makes the structure of meaning and reference an ambivalent process'; yet while Bhabha's Third Space 'destroys [the] mirror of representation in which cultural knowledge is customarily revealed as an integrated, open, expanding code' (1994, 37), the third space that Grove occupies does not displace 'the narrative of the Western nation' (1994, 37), nor does it point toward 'an *inter*national culture' or the 'articulation of culture's *hybridity*' (1994, 38). Grove's third space may reveal an intolerance of binary identity positions and a reluctance to identify himself exclusively as either a dominant or a minority Canadian, but it sets out to challenge neither. Instead, it divulges his desire to embrace a cosmopolitan identity that rises above the brittle social relations he perceives between immigrants and the dominant society. As he writes elsewhere, 'I, the cosmopolitan, had fitted myself to be the spokesman of a race—not necessarily a race in the ethnographic sense; in fact, not at all in that sense; rather in the sense of a stratum of society which cross-sectioned all races, consisting of those who, in no matter what climate, at no matter what time, feel the impulse of starting anew, from the ground up, to fashion a new world which might serve as the breeding-place of a civilization to come' (1946, 226-7).

Both 'Canadians Old and New' and 'Assimilation', then, disclose his subject position: he is both host and newcomer and at the same time neither. In this respect his discourse seems to embody what, according to Bhabha, exemplifies 'the construction of the Janus-faced discourse of the nation': 'where meanings may be partial because they are *in medias res*; and history may be half-made because it is in the process of being made; and the image of cultural authority may be ambivalent because it is caught, uncertainly, in the act of "composing" its powerful image' (1990a, 3). Yet while Grove's writing displays 'an agency of *ambivalent* narration' (Bhabha 1990a, 3), there seems to be no indecision in the position Grove desires to occupy.

Although he invites his readers to trace such images as 'scum of the earth', 'underdog', 'slaves', 'riff-raff', and 'wastage' to sources outside his discourse, Grove reproduces them not only in order to establish a record of dominant attitudes but also in order to outline the position he desires to hold as subject. He does not explicitly condone these derogatory terms, yet he proceeds to use them repeatedly because he wants to avoid being mistaken for someone embodying the traits associated with those terms. Nor does he show any concern with examining, for example, the causes of poverty in Europe, or the social apparatuses and modes of economic production that generate human 'wastage'. Whether European immigrants are the refuse in Europe or the 'scum of the earth' in Canada is of, at most, secondary importance to him. Their relevance to Grove's argument is that they form the background against which he situates himself. They have a certain fetishistic allure to him; they form the 'jargon of authenticity' that constitutes his subject position.

Grove's identifications and disidentifications with both 'Old' and 'New' Canadians reveal his self-limitations, his hybridization as it were. Even though it might seem that Grove's subjectivity is constituted by a series of reciprocal acts in which the self recognizes itself in the other, the way he executes his shifts from dominant to marginalized subjectivity announces his position to be that of supplement. With regard to Canada and the 'wastage' of Europe alike, Grove is both excess and lack, yet this double figure is not a synonym but an antonym of 'debris'. To use a metaphor that might be a little excessive, he images himself as a kind of transcendental signifier—although I'd prefer to see him as a parody of one. He seeks to transcend his self-inscriptions—a European, a Canadian, an immigrant—by occupying a panoptic position, one that often supersedes even the universalism attached to Europe. He both invests and subverts 'wastage', while rejecting those elements in himself that pull him towards sites of refuse.

Grove's discourse, then, articulates a libidinal economy. In other words, if the process of his self-identification speaks of ambivalence, it is because the displacements and repression undergone by the libidinal energies of his self are sublimated, in part, by the ambivalence that accompanies his diasporic experience. This sublimation enables him to construct an optimum subject position whose desirability and tenacity are as much affected by the symbolic values of the 'riff-raff' and the great literati of Europe with whom he also rubbed shoulders as by his fear of dis/appearing as a diasporic subject. And as his deep concern with immigrant issues reveals, his desire to be a founder of the literary tradition in Canada is similarly filtered through the sieve of his diasporic experience. But at the same time that diaspora helps him to actualize his literary aspirations, it also functions as a source of threat and anxiety, as a signifier of loss and lack. The more he muddles his 'origins' and exposes his ambivalence as to whether he identifies with the 'Old' or 'New' Canadians, the more he reveals his anxiety about who and what he is, the more his fear of symbolic castration becomes evident. Here 'symbolic castration' refers to Grove's fears of psychological and intellectual impotence, his apprehension about lacking, or not having access to, power. His discourse, then, cannot help reflecting his *disposition* to reside simultaneously inside and outside the realms he enters and exits—feigning invisibility and visibility alike. Paradoxically, 'riff-raff' and intellectual 'greatness' become contiguous within the materiality of his writing.

Niels's Dreams: Libidinal Realism and Moral Masochism

It is from the perspective of the contiguity between 'wastage' and 'greatness' informing Grove's libidinal economy that I wish to return to *Settlers of the Marsh*. If, for Grove, 'wastage' is one of the figures allowing him to practise cultural and social cross-dressing, then Niels's self-scornful image belongs to the author 'outside' the text. But this does not imply that there is no connection at all between this sign of ethnicity and Niels as a character.

One of my working principles here has been that the history of a concept like 'wastage' is a kind of *biography* of the Canadian society that is not that different from the textuality of a novel. Thus Grove's libidinal economy 'outside' the text is transferred 'inside' the text in the form of what I call libidinal realism. Thus we can understand libidinal energy as the force that permeates, transforms, and equally intensifies and represses experience. It is what drives Niels away from Sweden and onto the Canadian prairie, and does so in the name of the father—alias Oedipus/alias Grove[38]—veiled by the name of the mother.

The first thing about Niels's reference to 'wastage' that takes the reader by surprise is its context in the novel. It appears in a section hardly two pages long, immediately after Niels has had one of his many 'lightning flashes of pain' (139), recognizing that he must renounce his 'old dream' of a house with Ellen in it. In a manner characteristic of Niels's psychology, this 'negation . . . gave him such an air of superiority over his environment that the few words which he still had to speak were listened to almost with deference' (138). Laurie Ricou's statement that 'Grove's protagonists have little of the king or emperor about them' (38) does not acknowledge Niels's self-satisfaction here. What seems to account for Niels's feeling of superiority is the 'curious' (138) absence of a direct correspondence between his failure with Ellen and the deference that his despondent mood inspires around him. The shift from personal failure to social mastery might be seen as a disengagement from a fantasy that resists fulfilment, a liberation from the shackles of his inner world and a venturing forth into the social realm. But to understand how Niels's failure at this point manages to manifest itself as mastery, I would like to consider first the roots of his 'old dream'.

Those critics who underread its ethnic signature notwithstanding, *Settlers of the Marsh* opens with two immigrants, Nelson and Niels, walking 'blindly' (9) in the middle of a snow storm following a 'trail [that] became less and less visible' (8). It is during this opening scene that we encounter the first of the visions that, later in the novel, the narrator calls Niels's 'old dreams': '[a] vision of some small room, hot with the glow and flicker of an open fire, took possession' of him (9). The site his imagination constructs represents an attempt to egg himself on, but this passage is also the first occasion in the novel when Niels's condition is presented in universalist terms. A hearth in a small room discloses nothing that is culturally specific. Instead, it functions as a generic site existing in homogeneous time—we cannot find a more universal symbol. Yet it is within this symbolic order of the universal that diaspora as the dissemination of various forces appears in the novel.

Neither in this vision nor in its subsequent inscriptions does Niels contemplate going back to Sweden. Grove's writing is certainly not typical of the nostalgia that informs many characters in ethnic Canadian literature. There is, however, a different kind of nostalgia that shapes Niels's character: a nostalgia for the future or, more precisely, a desire for the present. This is why, I believe, Niels's first vision is of a room whose emptiness has 'the topological function of the rim' evoking the 'process of gap' (Lacan 206). The space Niels dreams of shows the margin to be not a space of objectification (the norm in many ethnic studies), but an embryonic space in which the subject is produced through differential relations.

This empty room also holds the seeds of the story, for in both the real and the phantasmic time of Niels's life it will be redesigned and peopled by various characters. Its emptiness evokes his origins, which can never be represented, while foreshadowing his future; it holds his anteriority but, in doing so, it also signals the turns his idiosyncratic idealism will take as he tries to incorporate everything after his arrival in Canada into the house he sets out to build. This empty room, then, is the setting for a primal scene of Freudian and socio-cultural dynamics that helps to establish the course of Niels's life. In accordance with the Freudian scenario of the primal scene, Niels is implicated in it by his position as observer.

The first figure to inhabit this empty room is Niels's dead mother. The narrator presents the mother as the object of Niels's longing, what gives his actions their impetus. It is a longing with a libidinal force—the force that accounts, in part, for his inhibited socialization, for the pathos with which he tries to territorialize himself and, later in the narrative, deterritorialize his wife Clara. Niels's subjectivity is interwoven with his mother; but, all the same, her presence elicits the silence of the father whom the narrative represses.

The first reference to his mother occurs early in the novel during a scene in which Niels attempts to come to grips with the family problems he encounters in the Amundsen household. He is appalled by Amundsen's behaviour towards his wife, who 'reminded [Niels] of his own mother; and like his mother [. . .] aroused in him a feeling of resentment against something that seemed to be wrong with the world' (19). What seems to be wrong in the world, which Niels brings along with him, is the social stigma that accompanies poverty and the low social class to which he belonged in Sweden. While Sweden is represented as a class-structured society, a place where there is 'wastage', Canada is represented as a classless world where '[n]obody looked down upon [Niels] because he was poor' (37).

Grove does not see class in deterministic terms; yet, as we have seen, neither does he analyze it as a social phenomenon. Despite his indictment of American materialism, which we find as much in his fiction as in his autobiographies and letters, he shies away from offering a cohesive critique of labour relations. He is convinced of the power of individuals like himself to fall and rise socially, and he narrativizes this conviction in *In Search of Myself* as well as in *A Search for America*. But while Phil, the protagonist-narrator of the latter, emerges from his tramp and hobo expeditions in triumphant style, Niels seems to begin as one of those unfortunate immigrants that Phil keeps encountering, an immigrant whose faith in himself is shaken by a conspiracy of circumstances (1991, 445).

In Niels's case, though, his bitterness about his past social conditions is lodged in the memories of his mother:

> He longed to be with his mother, to feel her gnarled, calloused fingers rumpling his hair, and to hear her crooning voice droning some old tune . . . And then he seemed to see her before him: a wrinkling, shrunk little face looking anxiously into his own.
>
> He groaned.
>
> The face with the watery, sky-blue eyes did not look for that which tormented him: what tormented him, he suddenly knew, had tormented her also; she had fought it down. Her eyes looked into himself, knowingly, reproachfully. There was pity in the look of the ancient mother: pity with him who was going astray: pity with him, not because of what assailed him from without; but pity with what he was in his heart . . . (59)

Significantly, Niels's longing is not simply for his birth mother. His memory represents her as an 'ancient' figure. The mother's Nordic eyes, instead of casting doubt on her representation as a universal figure, are a reminder that universalism is nothing more than a particular ideology that has achieved normative status. It is in the name of universalism as a hybrid sign that the ancient mother gazes at her son and pities him. Her pity is nothing other than Niels's projection on her of his own anxiety. Anxiety reflects the subject's 'certain non-knowledge, the fact that I cannot know just what I am for the desire of the other' (Weber 161). As 'a constitutive process by which the psyche maintains its coherence and identity' (Weber 154), anxiety also articulates the subject's attempt to come to terms with his 'irreducible heterogeneity' (Weber 161). Niels may be attached to the memory of his mother, but it is the absence of the father that leads him on, the temporary suspension of the Law of the Father[39] that causes his anxiety. Indeed, it is for the paternal/phallic principle embodied in Niels that the ancient mother, in her wisdom, pities him.

The father is mentioned only once, in passing: 'Niels' thoughts [turned] back to Sweden, to his poor home where his father and his mother had died' (36). The ellipses that follow this sentence suggest a 'desire for silence' (Gunnars, Afterword 271), perhaps a reluctance to come to terms with the figure of the father. Both parents are dead: 'They too had worked very hard,' we find out in the following sentence, and that is the last time we hear of the father—a vague but potent figure lodged inside the doubleness of the parental couple. Niels's resentment towards his missing father is revealed through his empathy with his mother. In the inarticulate fashion that is typical of Niels's thinking process, that resentment is reinscribed in the 'fierce and impotent hatreds [that] devastated his heart' (37) while he was growing up as a poor child. These 'impotent hatreds' are caused not only by the rich people for whom his mother worked, who despite their 'good-hearted[ness]' made his family feel like 'being[s] from a lower social, yes, human plane' (37), but also by the father's absence, which contributes to their poverty—both financial and emotional. The father might be invisible because he is dead and because he is not directly memorialized, but he remains in his absence what Bhabha calls the 'bearer of a peculiar, visible invisibility' (1995, 59) entailed by his phallic power, a power that permeates Niels's actions.

Niels's visions of his mother both apostrophize and conceal his father while allegorizing the profound naturalism that informs a male subject's 'amor patriae—the naturalist, phallic identification with the service of the nation' (Bhabha 1995, 59). Love of the fatherland, far from being merely an element of masculinity, epitomizes the presumed imperative that an immigrant feels to revisit the past, to go on embracing tightly the image of the country of origin. In Niels's case, though, amor patriae might be more accurately rendered as amor matris, signalling a substitution of displaced desires, in effect a neurotic naturalism that idealizes the space where Niels locates his origins. Yet at the same time this love also distorts what he takes to be his ethnic authenticity. The coupling of universalism and particularism, of mother and father, of birth and host countries, of man-as-father-to-be and woman-as-mother-to-be—all these elements root Niels's story in the master narrative evoked by the figure of the couple that haunts the novel.

It is Niels's function as a spectator that produces these coupled images. Whether he looks at himself as belonging to a 'special race', or stands outside the rich house where his mother works, or is absorbed by mental visions that rarely include himself, Niels's gaze is what creates his sense of inclusion and exclusion. His gaze reveals the 'appetite of the eye on the part of the person looking' (Lacan 115), an appetite that expresses what he lacks and what motivates him as subject. The figure of the couple, then, is articulated as the locus of Niels's desire. This is a desire that attempts, on one hand, to affirm his cultural authenticity and, on the other, to reproduce a domestic economy: 'By some trick in his ancestry there was implanted in him the longing for the land that would be his: with a house of his own and a wife' (37). The Swedishness of this 'trick' aside, it is property, ownership of land and wife, that promises to heal Niels's fierce and impotent hatreds. The ghostly presence of the father and the vaguely drawn Swedish landowners figure prominently in Niels's libidinal reality.

His desire for 'a house of his own and a wife' motivates him to become an immigrant: 'he had come to Canada, the land of the million farmsteads to be had for the asking' (37). Amor matris is rendered here as amor materiae, a substitution signalling the important role that economy plays in diaspora, economy as the circulation and exchange of the various forces that construct subjectivity. That Niels is unabashedly honest about his materialist motives is hardly surprising, since it is the need to escape dire living conditions that lies, more often than not, at the heart of most migration movements. The formulation of Niels's desire echoes Sifton's rhetoric of barter: it takes the form of a restricted economy with a distinct sense of what is valued, on both sides, in the exchange of Canadian land as commodity—'Here, there were big trees which any one could fell for firewood' (37)—for the labour and displacement of immigrants.

In Niels's case, though, what is interesting is that this restricted economy also speaks of the return of the repressed, here specifically a return to the father whose presence changes the figure of the couple into a triangle of desire. Niels's dream of a house with a wife, which elsewhere in the novel includes 'the pitter-patter of children's feet' (46), reinscribes the father in the narrative. One of the major effects of diaspora, displacement here takes the form of replacement, restoring the absent figure of the father—a replacement that proclaims Niels's nostalgia for the future. Niels attempts to instal himself in Canada as a diasporic subject by acquiring land and fathering children.

Although the narrator presents the desire to acquire land as an element in Niels's cultural background, there is nothing ethnically specific about it. If anything, it is a sign of class aspirations, proof that Niels was part of the 'wastage' of Sweden's economy. Unlike the 'scum of the earth', however, Niels can make earth his own. Yet at the same time land and children are two of the most important signs in the novel that attest to his phallic idealization. That the narrative revolves around a mansion on acres of land but ends with merely a vague promise for children points to the intricate deferrals that Niels's plans undergo. Yet, in its capitalist and psychic functions in the novel, land also becomes Niels's organ par excellence, an instrument of reproduction. Manifestations of Niels's phallic desire, his goals as a settler reflect his desire to satisfy his mother, in reality a desire to (re)instal the Law of the Father.

Ironically, I think this is the main reason why, when Niels sets out to fulfil his aspirations, the narrator configures him in gender-ambivalent terms. The incarnation of Niels's 'ancestral' desire is meant to help him recover the lost power behind his 'impotent' hatred, but his longing for land is 'implanted' in him. He is at once the product of the Law of the Father and its representative. It is the seed of this desire that produces both the gender hybridity of the metaphors at this point in the text and the particular subject position from which Niels operates.

Niels, however, remains oblivious to the cross-gendering of his desire.[40] Already a tool implementing the interests of the author 'outside' the text, he is also embroiled in the various excitations that validate the phallic law of libidinal economy in capitalist terms, an economy that appropriates him, that threatens to castrate him psychically. Still, as the bearer of this 'ancestral' seed, Niels becomes the host of Otherness in Canada. His attempt to build a life in his new country by reproducing the Law of the Father reflects his desire to make himself 'at home'.

The Law of the Father is, of course, already installed in Niels's Canadian milieu, and it also functions as an analogue of Grove's desire to father Canadian culture.

If desire 'constantly couples continuous flows and partial objects that are by nature fragmentary and fragmented' (Deleuze and Guattari 1983, 5), the synergy of Niels's desire for land and for a woman whose 'face [. . .] entirely evaded him' becomes an end in itself. This 'eternal vision that has moved the world and that was to direct his fate' (34) is a paradigmatic instance of the way human commerce is imaged in the novel, the kind of human commerce that is 'confused with an infinite perpetuation of itself' (Deleuze and Guattari 1983, 5). Interestingly, Niels's identity, together with the libidinal economy informing it, is also signalled by another set of gendered metaphors. The narrator tells us that Niels 'felt less a stranger in the bush. Though everything was different, yet it was nature as in Sweden.' But the universality of nature lasts only for the length of that sentence. 'None of the heath country of his native Blekinge here,' we read; 'none of the pretty juniper trees; [. . .] These poplar trees seemed wilder, less spared by an ancient civilization that has learned to appreciate them. They invited the axe, the explorer . . .' (22-3). Niels as an explorer brandishing an axe casts a formidable figure, but the mastery he is supposed to evoke is undercut by the 'still[ness]' of the trees. Niels exercises the ideological imperative of the settler who must clear space in order to make room for his own desires. The sovereignty implied by the 'ancient civilization' functions like an amulet keeping at bay the possibility of castration, easing the anxiety of cultural estrangement.

What I called master fiction earlier is dramatized here by Niels's masculinity, especially as it is expressed by the metaphors through which he identifies with nature in Sweden and in Canada. In Canada his masculinity is affirmed through a gesture of infidelity: 'Already, though he had thought he could never root in this country, the pretty junipers of Sweden had been replaced in his affections by the more virile and fertile growth of the Canadian north' (58). If his detachment from the mother country means he is already oedipalized, his attraction to the Canadian landscape configured in 'virile' terms reflects his desire to prevent himself from being emasculated while at the same time pointing to his ability to plant the 'ancestral' seed he bears to good results. The voicing of this attraction marks the end of Niels's spectator mode—'He had been an onlooker so far'—but it also announces what the narrator takes to be Niels's resolve, namely to live in the present, to 'cling to the landscape as something abiding, something to steady him'. However, the shift the narrator suggests is immediately contradicted by Niels himself, who again 'longed to be with his mother' (59).

The gender ambivalence (with its homoerotic implications) that marks Niels's original vision of the empty room, and its subsequent manifestations, is in keeping with the ambivalence of diaspora. The fact that cultural difference in the novel is represented by a swerving away from specificity is a manifestation of diasporic anxiety, but it is also a sign that the specificity articulated by Grove's text shares the normative patterns of Canadian society at the time. The intricacies of

Niels's visions certainly point to his individual circumstances; their libidinal and domestic economy, though, coincides with that practised and validated by his Canadian environment. It is important, then, to examine what replaces this domestic economy after he seems to come to terms with Ellen's passionate resolve not to marry him, and thus I return to the point where Niels's 'negation' of his 'old dream [. . .] gave him such an air of superiority'.

Niels's feeling of superiority within the settlers' social environment seems to derive from the fear that he believes he inspires. 'Once he heard a man say to Bobby, "I shouldn't care to work for that fellow. I'd be scared of him"' (139). His superiority does not carry the conventional meaning of dominance. Instead, it is a figure of the uncanny, and thus it reflects not the perception of Niels by others, but rather his own wishful image of himself, an image modelled on the author 'outside' the text. In effect, Niels's superiority is inscribed as yet another of his fantasies. This fantasy operates at a number of levels, the conjunction of which is what determines both Niels's notion of a 'special race' and his 'new dream', a dream intent on helping him rise above the 'wastage' of this 'race'.

At one level, it appears that the author 'inside' the text uses the link between the end of one fantasy and the beginning of another (i.e., superiority) to create the tragic image of Niels's character. What is tragic, for Grove, is to 'have greatly tried and to have failed; to have greatly wished and to be denied; to have greatly longed for purity and to be sullied; to have greatly craved for life and to receive death' ('The Happy Ending' 1982, 87). This definition would serve admirably as a summary of *Settlers of the Marsh*, indeed as a recapitulation of Grove's own life-constructions and aspirations; it also discloses the generic role that fantasy plays in his novel.

Behind Grove's privileging of the tragic hero lies a longing for failure, a masochistic relationship with one's own craving for defeat that reveals powerless-ness as 'pleasure in powerlessness' (Paul Smith 78). Thus 'failure' in his lexicon does not bear its conventionally negative connotations; quite the contrary, it mediates the subject's position, and sublimates fantasy. In effect, failure enables Niels to establish his difference with regard both to those around him and to the Name of the Father. Niels's fantasy of superiority validates his suffering, hence the pleasure I think he feels when he becomes an object of fear. His failure to marry Ellen and thus exercise his male performativity in the Name of the Father is provisionally recuperated by the fantasy of superiority that cultivates his image as someone in charge, a substitution that keeps his libidinal economy in circulation.

Were we to dismiss Niels's domineering self-image because it tells us less about him than it does about the narrator's misreading of what transpires at this moment in the narrative, the tragic ethos of the fantasy would remain intact. Immediately after we read the example of how Niels's superiority allows him to keep a certain distance between himself and others, the narrator replaces Niels's superiority with 'the appearance of one insane' (139)—yet another attempt to instil the tragic pathos of the protagonist's circumstances. But what the narrator presents as only a semblance of insanity might be seen as a sign of 'hysterical residues' (Paul Smith 80), an instance of male hysteria that 'can be glimpsed in moments of incoherence or powerlessness in the male body and the male presence' (Paul Smith 92). The external markers of Niels's anguish may not be easily decipherable—at least by his narrator—but the contradictory images they convey disclose the method by which Niels's character is constructed. It is not, then, a matter of deciding what is more veritable at this point—superiority or hysteria—but rather of unravelling Niels's contradictions.

If what drives fantasy is not the desire to dominate someone but rather the subject's desire to position himself within a reality defined now by dominance, now by submission,[41] then it becomes clear why Niels's fantasies constantly shuttle between these two poles of reality. The central paradox of Niels's character lies in the way his fantasies collide and identify with reality while disclosing the masochism behind his attempt at once to evade the Law of the Father and to seek empowerment in traditional patriarchal terms. This leads us back to Grove's definition of tragedy, a notion that in turn defines what he takes to constitute the success of a novel. On one hand, the tragedy of Niels's character seems to derive from his inability to situate himself within a reality that corresponds to his 'old' dream; on the other, it is the elusiveness of this reality, the persistent absence (at this point in the narrative) of reciprocity between reality and dream[42] that guarantees Niels's tragic ethos and thus, by Grove's definition of the tragic, satisfies the demands of his fantasies.

The intricacies of this complex of reality and fantasy are dramatized when we read, in the same section of the novel, of Niels's 'new dream':

> a longing to leave and to go to the very margin of civilisation, there to clear a new place; and when it was cleared and people began to settle about it, to move on once more, again to the very edge of pioneerdom, and to start it all over anew. . . . That way his enormous strength would still have a meaning. Woman would have no place in his life. (139)

Niels moves from the closed space of a house with a woman cloistered there in his 'old dream' to the open, uncharted space evoked by his 'new dream', but the phantasmic structure in both cases remains the same: lack, here imaged in Ellen's retreat from his earlier fantasy, which threatens his masculinity; and land, here reasserted as the instrument that securely lodges him within the symbolic order of power. In this respect, *Settlers of the Marsh* reads like a 'binary machine' (Deleuze and Parnet 20), a construct where '[d]ualisms no longer relate to unities, but to successive choices' (19), 'an important component of apparatuses of power' (21). With woman absent in this 'new dream', Niels is able to posit male subjectivity as 'still' the kind of subjectivity capable of producing 'meaning'. Never mind that he cannot father the children of his old fantasy; as an Adamic pioneer in this 'new dream'—and a Swede at that—he can breed a whole new civilization.

The syntax of his fantasies becomes apparent now: self-degradation spurs self-exaltation. Like an Aeneas of the 'New World', Niels still bends under the weight of the Father. Meanwhile the death of his 'old dream' does not foreclose the regime of failure necessary for what I take to be Niels's moral masochism. Moral masochism, engendered by a sense of guilt that the masochist subject is oblivious to, pursues a victim position, but the suffering yearned for does not involve the body or direct sexual pleasure; neither does it have 'very much to do with virtue'. Instead, the moral masochist 'leaves his social identity completely behind' (Silverman 1992, 190), and strives to fulfil the demands of his super-ego, his conscience. In the context of the maternal and paternal principles that determine his libidinal economy, the moral masochist 'has given up on the desire to be the father' (Silverman 1992, 195).

Niels imagines himself disappearing at the 'very margin of civilization' because of his failure to marry Ellen and thus abide by the Law of the Father. Nevertheless, the miscarriage of his old fantasy is translated into the pleasurable pain of the hard labour and solitude he inflicts on himself in this 'new dream'. Crucially, his fantasy of 'clear[ing] a new place', a place with 'meaning', preserves the Name of the Father and imprints it on the land. Moral masochism 'is at first a way of not having to submit to the law, but, equally important, it turns out to be a way of not breaking (with) the law' (Paul Smith 91). Although the 'new dream' is in keeping with Niels's masochism and thus presents his toil in the guise of defeat, his fantasy embraces both his libidinal economy and the economy of pioneerdom.

The 'new dream' portrays Niels as an arbiter of chaos, a colonial master, a master whose exercise of sovereignty is provisionally deferred in the absence of subjects; thus Niels's moral masochism is satisfied. If the woman of the old fantasy signals impotence, the frontier of the 'new dream' signals virility. This is not a matter of substitution; rather, we may see it as the kind of analogy that has become a stock theme in certain kinds of Canadian literary criticism, namely the casting of wilderness as woman and the reading of woman as wilderness. The feminization of wilderness provides the cure for Niels's own earlier feminization as well as his rejection. Thus while he toils over the land, he continues to romance the Law of the Father. The further he moves into this supposedly uncharted territory, the more persistently he penetrates its otherness. What sustains the scenario of his moral masochism is his self-inflicted isolation, that is, the lack of an observer.

His self-abjection is similarly remedied by his repetitive movements: 'to move on once more, again to the very edge of pioneerdom, and to start it all over again.' In a reversal of the conventional image of the margin as a space marking disidentification and disempowerment, here the margin designates infinite space, a space that does not recede. Instead it expands, becomes a non-site that will achieve definition only through Niels's labour. In a colonialist context, then, there is nothing new about Niels's 'new dream', for it fits the topological imaginary of colonialism: it is 'empty' land. His desire to retreat further into the 'margins of civilization' allows Niels to maintain his authenticity as a subject 'superior' to those settlers who will arrive after he clears the land. He produces a reality that maintains the symbolic structure he needs to preserve: he becomes a founding father of the future to come.

Beyond the Margins: Realities, Realisms, Fantasies

As I hope I have demonstrated so far, the realism in *Settlers of the Marsh* maintains a very precarious relationship to the cultural conditions that inspired it. Grove's realism was lauded by his contemporaries precisely because it was not the kind of 'Critical Realism [that] demanded . . . a critique of others (anti-colonialism) be conducted in the perspective of an even more comprehensive, multifaceted critique of ourselves' (Ahmad 118). Similarly, the value attributed to realism in ethnic literature relies on a supposed unity between literary representation and social reality. What Grove's novel represents, quite faithfully, is Canada's familial ideology—which does not cancel out the notion that, in the rather naïve sense of realism, the novel offers an immediately recognizable image of prairie life at the turn of the century. However, such aberrations in the narrative as the reference to 'wastage' bespeak Grove's ambivalent relationship to social referents; above all, they point to the discursive mode of his novel's realism.

This realism does not merely represent one kind of reality; nor does it conform to a single set of cultural paradigms. The novel's virtually instant canonization indicates that to readers in the 1920s it was a text of pleasure,[43] a text comfortably suited to the critical practices and ideological attitudes of the time. In part, then, its realism reflects the early twentieth-century master narratives of Canada. Because he found himself implicated in them, Grove did not attempt to contradict those narratives. Nevertheless, he slipped in and out of their determinations as he attempted to recuperate the European values he considered threatened by Canadian nationalist sensibilities of his time. This does not mean that we should castigate Grove for not identifying with or representing the kind of reified marginality that some ethnocultural politics foreground with great fervour today; nor does it mean that we should make him fit, or measure his fiction against, current cultural and critical attitudes; the outcome of such efforts would be all too predictable. Instead, if *Settlers of the Marsh*, like all past literature, is to have any relevance today, contemporary Canadians, 'Old' and 'New' alike, ought to read it both inside and outside its time frame, as I have attempted to do here, keeping in mind that a critical representation of Canada's social reality at the time was ideologically beyond Grove's reach. Thus we cannot simply see his novel's realism as conforming to the truth-value that its correspondence to the dominant Canadian social reality would bestow on it. *Settlers of the Marsh* may be marked by its representation of the hegemonic dispositions of its time, but it is equally marked by those from which it dissociates itself.

It is the desire to preserve what Grove valued, what he lacked in Canada, coupled with the demand he felt there was for it, that I take to be the stimulus behind *Settlers of the Marsh*. The desire that writes Grove's fiction, at least to my way of thinking, is interwoven as much with the psychic elements producing identity as with social activity—processes that both overlap and resist each other. If I have focused on the novel's libidinal realism as it is articulated by Niels's fantasies, it is precisely because that realism exposes the limits and guises of the reality overtly depicted in it, and thus brings to the fore some of the realities concealed. The dramatization of this libidinal realism is not reducible to either the dominant or the marginal social plane. The almost extreme idealization that Niels's fantasies express corresponds to the intricate ways in which Grove displaced himself from certain kinds of social reality in order to embrace the reality of the fictions he created. He figured himself by practising an agency whose evident and oblique modalities both camouflaged and disclosed the contestations inherent in diasporic identity. The connections I see between Niels's fantasies and Grove's desire to move towards his culturally validated goals do not limit the textual possibilities of *Settlers of the Marsh*. Instead, they point to the space that exists between fiction and reality. Hence my attempt to pay equal attention to various discourses, the cultural voices at play in the novel, 'not only those heard in aural "close-up", but also those voices distorted or drowned out by the text' (Stam 1991, 256).

If Niels's fantasies have allowed me to get outside the novel and into the socio-cultural context of its time, and thus to test the limits of its realism, I would like to conclude my discussion of the text by reversing this strategy. I would like to see what a reading of a passage that occurs in the novel's 'real', and not phantasmic, time can reveal about the function of its realism.

The Scarlet Colour of Positivist Pedagogy

Every time I read *Settlers of the Marsh* in the past, I remained unconvinced by the representation of Niels as an immigrant who murders his wife in order to appease his cultural and patriarchal demons, his claims on purity and ownership, so that he can be embraced again by Ellen, now a middle-aged maiden—safely neither a 'girl' nor a 'man'—who, cloistered in her prairie bower, waits for the end of his incarceration. I failed to see the inexorable logic in the text that made Clara's death a narrative imperative. Beyond my gender concerns on this matter, I could not reconcile myself to the fact that Niels has to kill the only character in the text who reads a novel, and *Madame Bovary* at that.

Clara dies because the narrator disguises her as an ugly parody of Niels's 'ancient mother', because she offends the morals of the community, and because she cuckolds her husband. But she also dies, I suggest, because she is a reader who identifies with the bourgeoisie, the very object of Flaubert's parody. Clara's murder, perhaps the most important event in the novel, is directly related to the libidinal economy that drives Niels. I would like, then, to conclude this chapter by focusing on some of the conditions that lead to her murder, and by joining, as it were, Niels in jail. Even though his six-and-a-half years of incarceration are afforded only brief treatment in the novel, that period is crucial for two reasons: it prefigures Niels's return to Ellen, and therefore the novel's dénouement; and it serves as an instance of the dominant society's cultural and social competency, a competency measured only insofar as it controls the novel's libidinal realism.

How does Niels fare as an inmate—not in his fantasies but in jail? What happens when, as the convicted murderer of his wife, he finds himself removed from the open space on the 'margin of civilization' and behind the gate of a federal penitentiary, 'a gate, wide and high, but completely closed by steel bars four inches apart' (234)? What does Niels do—he who dreams of 'wastage' but also dreams of running away from the 'riff-raff' of the world—when he has no choice but to move into the midst of '[s]ome two hundred outcasts' (235)? He becomes a friend of the prison warden. He also becomes a 'reformed' man; to put it crudely, he becomes born-again.

Now, before I examine how Niels's relationship with the warden develops, it is important to remember that the prison in question, modelled as it is after the Stony Mountain penitentiary in Manitoba (founded in 1877), is a veritable panoptic structure:

> On top of the walls, at every corner, there stands a small tower from which, also on top of the walls, there stretch two parapeted walks . . . Each of these towers offers, when such is needed, shelter to two men who, armed with rifle, revolver, and sword, walk back and forth, back and forth on their beats. . . .
>
> Yes, when you approach that hill, you cannot get near it without being challenged. [. . .] Should you, by any chance ignore the challenge, your car, disabled, will run into the ditch. In any case, before you reach the walls, every eye is watching for you; every move of yours is being followed. The report of your coming had preceded you, no matter how fast you may have travelled. (234)

This is, interestingly enough, the only section in the novel where the narrator's rhetorical strategies apostrophize the reader, a psychological ploy whose meaning nevertheless is ambiguous: are we supposed to be awed by the penitentiary system and thus impressed by Niels's ability to withstand its rigours? Or is this a warning, a textual device intended to prevent us from lingering too long at this point in the narrative because 'every eye is watching for you; every move of yours is being followed'? Whatever the case, the power architectonics of this penal structure goes hand in hand with the power embodied in and exercised by the warden.

There is, however, a marked difference between the intimidating prison structure and the warden. The narrator introduces the warden as the antithesis of the power dynamics of imprisonment:

And yet, even here a human heart beats, a human sympathy plans the welfare of others: the heart of the warden.

There was a time when the prisoner trembled or scowled at sight of an officer: that time is past.

To-day, when the warden appears, most of the prisoners—those for whom there is hope, hope of a future outside, or of manhood in some form inside—most of them smile.

The warden is a fearless man; he goes unarmed. He is the friend of the unfortunate. He has a way with him which gains their confidence. (235)

I take 'There was a time' and 'To-day' to be in keeping with the realistic depiction of the prison, to reflect the history of the Canadian penal system's development. Yet, however we might compute the novel's chronology in relation to historical changes in Canada's penal system, none of the changes under way in, say, the first three decades of the century advanced the role of wardens in the manner depicted in the novel.

Modelled on the Auburn system employed in the United States, which was supposed to promote a more humane approach and emphasize reform rather than punishment alone, Canadian penitentiaries at the time followed 'stern discipline, no intercourse with the outside world, rigidly enforced internal rules, and the idea that convicts should be *molded, like clay* in the potter's hands' (Skinner et al. 44; my emphasis). Most wardens had military training. Even such an enlightened warden as Samuel Lawrence Bedson, the first warden in Manitoba's penitentiary, who initiated changes in the system that were well ahead of their time,[44] was also known for practices that caused further 'dehumanization' of inmates: he 'introduced a numerical system of convict identification that completely and intentionally replaced the use of proper names during the period of incarceration' (Zubrycki 51).

Niels's warden may not be directly modelled on Bedson, but his humanist ideology bears an uncanny resemblance to the philosophy that inspired the latter's proposed penal reform. As Bedson wrote in his 1885 Report:

A prisoner is a criminal indeed, but in supposing that he is wholly criminal the goodness of the great Creator himself is doubted. . . . He . . . must be educated, he must be trained and disciplined precisely as any other member of society, to induce him, if possible, to give out spontaneously from his own nature that which is right. . . .

You must redeem the prisoner by sympathy and not by extinguishing in him that which is the strongest inspiration of humanity, that which springs eternal in every man's breast except the prisoner's: Hope. Reformation depends entirely upon the amount of this principle you can inspire the prisoner with. (Cited in J.T.L. James 39)

Whatever changes Bedson initiated, the end of his term was followed by 'a rapid deterioration'; in addition, he himself revised many of the humanitarian aspects of his project (J.T.L. James 37). Like Bedson's, the idealism characterizing the warden of the novel has little to do with the reality of the Manitoba penitentiary at the time. Instead, the realism of the warden's representation follows the structure of a fantasy disguised as reality. His remaining nameless is a sign of the universality attributed to him. He is imaged as the embodiment of humanism, an agent at once of repression and of cultural (re)production. His task, then, is formidable: to regulate desire, to construct a generalized subject subliminally instructed not to question his interpellation, not to resist the knowledge imparted by the warden.

Niels enters into a pedagogical relationship with his warden that is intended to teach him, by way of the latter's exemplary generosity and understanding, what it takes to become a 'New' Canadian. 'It was the warden,' we read, 'who made [Niels] think, remember about the past. It was the warden who slowly, slowly made him see that he was not an outcast, a being despised for what he had done. It was the warden who told him that he, too, placed in the same circumstances, might and probably would have acted as Niels had acted' (236). With the jail transformed into a kind of classroom, the warden performs the role of 'the subject who is supposed to know' (Lacan 230). In this 'scene of learning' (Freedman 174), Niels, cast in the role of someone who is blind, who lacks will and agency, is an ideal student. The lesson we observe typifies what I call a positivist pedagogy, a pedagogy that measures its effectiveness by the degree of conformity it instils in students. Its positivism lies in the fact that it fosters knowledge as a finished object, that it teaches its students not to question the value and truth of authority. In other words, it is 'a hierarchical practice, [which] assumes the teacher already understands the truth to be imparted to the student . . . that he or she understands the real meanings . . . and real interests of the different social groups.' In this kind of pedagogy, the teacher is the one 'who draws the line between the good, the bad, and the ugly' (Grossberg 16).

This positivist pedagogy explains why the warden's lesson is not imaged in terms of rehabilitation, as would normally be the case in a penal situation. As far as the warden is concerned, Niels needs no rehabilitation, for he has not committed a heinous act. In fact, part of the warden's lesson involves absolution of Niels's guilt, thus endorsement of his crime: 'he, too, placed in the same circumstances, might and probably would have acted as Niels had acted.' The act of killing a woman is displaced as it is translated into a necessary step toward self-knowledge, a self-knowledge mediated by the colonial ideology that the warden represents. In this context, Clara's murder can be seen as appropriate to the view of colonialism 'as the sublimated sexual outlet of virile and homoerotic energies in the West' (Stoler 1997a, 174). In this last chapter, entitled 'Ellen Again', Clara dies a second death, death by a narratorial discourse that denies her her name. She is simply 'the murdered woman' (233), a vague presence behind the 'thing', the 'it'

(244) that leads Niels to jail. Not even granted the precarious visibility of a ghost haunting Niels's return to his homestead, she is written out of the text. Despite the fact that Niels protests his counsel's attempt to render him insane, that he admits he was 'perfectly responsible for his actions . . . when he shot the woman', that he declares 'he would do so again should the occasion arise' (232), Clara's murder is proclaimed to be merely 'manslaughter' (233). In effect, Niels's pedagogical reformation begins even before, sentenced to 'ten years . . . with hard labor', he arrives 'in the federal prison' (233).

The court decision embodies colonial desire as the wish to regulate desire. The jury, the judge, and the warden all act on behalf of the same regime, the one that holds sexual desire at bay except insofar as it serves dominant society's intention to promulgate its normative ideology. Thus Clara is not 'done in' twice-over merely because she is a woman at a time when female subjectivity and women's rights were still in an embryonic stage, but also because, historically, anything that contravenes the discursive norms of dominant society has been feminized. Indeed, it is tempting to argue that Clara does not exist in the novel as an individual. She seems to be cast in the role of an allegorical character designed to dramatize the risks of degeneracy; she represents the threats of social and cultural anarchy that purportedly appear with any explicit display of sexuality that transgresses the status quo.[45] With her 'coal-black eyes' (26), 'coppery-red' hair, her 'complexion . . . that [is] almost transparent white; her lips, full and red' (100), she is, the narrator tells us, 'intensely feminine, nearly coquettish'. And she is certainly not of Swedish origins. No wonder Niels experiences 'a foreboding of disaster', the coming of a 'terrible destiny' (53). That he feels 'confused' (53) and embarrassed around her when they first meet, and continues to find her 'incomprehensible' (57) even after he marries her, is further evidence that Clara is a dissident with respect to social laws and the familial economy of the time. 'Vogel', her last name, meaning bird, may well be intended to suggest her flightiness. Although there is a direct correspondence between her character and Niels's libidinal economy, the colonial and humanistic forces that make up Niels's trajectory prevent a satisfactory union of what each represents.

The 'gay widow of the settlement' (26), Clara is a promiscuous woman, and as such reinforces the ways in which deviance and unruly behaviour have traditionally been feminized. As, '[i]n the last decades of the nineteenth century, the urban crowd became a recurring fetish for ruling-class fears of social unrest and underclass militancy,' so 'women, particularly prostitutes and alcoholics[,] who were in turn associated with children[,] who were associated with "primitives" in the realm of the empire', were seen as occupying 'a dangerous threshold zone on the border between factory and family, labor and domesticity' (McClintock 1995, 118-19). This cultural context explains why Niels thought she 'looked very lovely', but also that she 'looked like sin' (57). Clara, then, embodies not mere sexual transgression but the very excess element that lurks ominously behind the enlightenment dream of progress, the very dream that Niels as settler aspires to.

It is no coincidence that she is constructed as a scandalous woman.

This layered ideological context also explains why she 'formed a rather strik-ing contrast to all other women present' (25). Far from being a sign that the author 'inside' and 'outside' the text challenges normative views about women at the time, this reiterates how femininity is relegated to the realm of the low, and thus of the expendable. Thus descriptions of Clara abound in such conventional markers of femininity as 'pretty and becoming' clothes, 'with ruffles'. '[B]y contrast to the other women,' there was 'something peculiarly feminine' about her; 'beside her, the others looked neuter' (25). A detailed reading of this passage would take me too far afield. Suffice it to say that the 'neuter' image of the respectable women in the community further indicates that they share in the violence that Clara suffers. Imaged as female eunuchs, they join with this scarlet woman in representing the social repression characteristic of the reality that Grove sets out to fictionalize. The surface inscriptions of sexuality and eroticiza-tion that the community's proper women have learned to repress are precisely what make Clara inspire disgust. But this kind of 'disgust always bears the imprint of desire. These low domains, apparently expelled as "Other", return as objects of nostalgia, longing and fascination. The forest, the fair, the theatre, the slum, the circus, the seaside-resort, the "savage" [and, I would add, the prosti-tute]: all these, placed at the outer limit of civil life, become symbolic contents of bourgeois desire' (Stalybrass and White 191). It is important, then, to understand that this interplay of disgust and longing is identified in Grove's realism only insofar as it emerges from a critical reading that, as I suggested earlier, works both with and against his authorial intentions.

Clara as a figure of nostalgia for repressed desire, together with her murder as a symbol of the desire for order, takes me back to the emancipatory agenda informing the warden's pedagogy. As the representative of the state, the warden delivers a lesson that recapitulates the way colonial discourses of desire produce respectable citizens. His intention is not to reform Niels as the murderer he now is, but rather to cure him of his fantasies of moral masochism. The warden's main objective is to invite Niels to join the humanistic family of generalized subjects. Since the prison, with its two hundred-odd inmates and its rigid social conduct, goes completely against the grain of Niels's 'new dream', it is highly significant that Niels's jail term—no matter how light—is represented as the true gestation period required for his acculturation.

This gestation period is inaugurated when the warden fully condones Niels's criminal act; in so doing he also exposes the phantasmic structure of Niels's character, namely the fact that he represents not the surface reality that most earlier critics of Grove were interested in, but the reality that is repressed. His successful 'intercession with the minister of justice' (236) to have Niels released before he serves his full sentence could hardly be seen as normative behaviour for the Canadian penal system of the time. Far from being portrayed realistically, the warden mimics the desires and ideology of the author 'inside' the text. The latter is a character who approves of the narrative's murderous twist, not for the sake of plot development but for the moral fortitude and vision that Clara's murder suggests—a vision that coincides with that of the author 'outside' the text. In this respect, the warden's discourse resides in homogeneous, empty time. If, as I argued earlier, the Canadian dominant society is inscribed in the novel by its virtual absence, Grove's warden is the construct that translates that absence into presence. If it is gender solidarity that inspires his friendship with Niels, the warden also clearly functions as an allegory of the dominant society's alleged benevolence towards immigrants. In this, the warden reflects Grove's adherence to the system, hence his hyperbolic benevolence; or, conversely, he mirrors Grove's desire for a system modelled on the authorial fantasy discussed earlier. The warden's character, then, dramatizes the emergence of the dominant society with a vengeance: so far repressed in the novel, it now figures as a double sign of penality and edification. As social benevolence incarnate and as the 'voice' of the author 'outside' the text, the warden takes on the role of a temporary father figure in Niels's libidinal economy.

A primary function of the pedagogical lesson that Niels is taught is precisely to reconcile him with the Law of the Father while he is 'prisoner number 187' (236). This demonstrates that, to some degree, his incarceration is not just the result of his murder of Clara; it is also related to his abjection, the stuff of the fantasies that take over after he temporarily renounces his 'old dream'. Thus behind the hard-core realistic evocations of 'prisoner number 187' remains the phantasmic structure of Niels's libidinal economy. Reconciliation with what haunts him involves a recasting of his life in terms that will allow him to emerge as a 'new' man, a man eligible to become a 'New Canadian'. Hence this last chapter opens with a truncated re-enactment of the earlier plot, a re-enactment enunciated, as already noted, by the warden: 'It was the warden who made him . . . remember about the past.' Here the warden functions as the stage manager of Niels's memory of trauma: the trauma is not only a matter of his having murdered Clara, but also of his having yielded to the 'peculiar' femininity and desires that Clara represents.

As the warden tells Niels,

'how you stand with God, I cannot tell. God keeps his own counsel. But let me remind you of the great sinner who had been a bad man all through his life; but on the cross he repented; and Christ forgave him . . . Niels, though you have sinned, I don't think you've been a bad man . . .' [. . .]

And Niels had answered [. . .] 'No; I believe I have tried to do what was right, in most things. I've been self-seeking when I was young . . . I have too often thought of my own life only . . . As for the thing that has sent me here, I don't blame myself . . . Not for that immediate thing . . . But for what preceded it . . . For what led up to it . . . For the very beginning of it . . . Many years before it happened . . . I have long since seen that I had sinned . . .' (244)

Sin preceded Clara's murder. Sin is also, I suggest, what lies behind Niels's singular obsession with his mother, an obsession that allows his empathy with her to emasculate him. This clearly illustrates that '[r]elation with the mother is a dependent object relation' (McClintock 1995, 91), but it also registers ambivalence. Niels idealizes his mother to the point that his aspirations and difficulties as an immigrant are seen as vindicating what his mother went through.

In many respects, we are expected to understand the novel's narrative thrust as Niels's attempt to reinstal his mother in his life by creating a familial scene in which, incarnated in Niels's image of the wife, she moves up the scale of domestic economy. But within the parameters of the culture he is a product of and the society he wishes to enter, this won't do. The reasons are twofold. First, in 'reality', his mother is a servant, more reminiscent of the 'wastage' of Europe than of the European bourgeoisie. In his visions, though, she ascends to the role of a middle-class matron, thus threatening 'one definition of the nineteenth-century middle class in Europe [. . . as being dependent on] its "servant-holding status" . . . [T]hose who served the needs of the *middenstand* . . . were viewed as subversive contagions in those carefully managed' homes (Stoler 1997a, 110). Second, Freudian theory makes it abundantly clear that 'the mother is identified as an object to possess and control rather than a social ideal with whom to identify. . . . [L]oss of the mother is seen not as loss of one of the most profound personal relationships one can have, on which one is dependent for life itself, but as loss of an object. . . . Indeed, identification *with* the mother figure is seen as pathological, perverse, the source of fixation, arrest and hysteria' (McClintock 1995, 91).

These two views do not simply reflect sexual and cultural approaches to motherhood. They preserve a commercial discourse: not only the relations determining the commerce between genders, but also those safeguarding the conditions of economic exchange in Europe and between Europe and its colonies. In this respect, the mother—like Clara, but for different reasons—effects a disjunction in cultural production as her movement from the status of servant to that of 'ancient mother', foremother of civilization, upsets the European standards of acceptability. Since the mother's upward mobility takes place only within Niels's visions, it is the novel's libidinal realism that dares to dispute the social boundaries of the time.

Under the subtly forceful tutelage of the warden, Niels is offered the opportunity to gain the prudence he lacked, to listen to 'reason':

> 'Niels,' the warden had gone on, 'if I'm any judge, God has forgiven you . . . *The killing . . . That, too, was in the atonement* . . . But as for men, you have been judged by your peers, and you have paid the penalty. You have taken life. Yet they have judged you fit to live on. What I'd like you to feel is this. When you go out of here, you can hold your head up. You must hold your head up. As far as human justice goes, you have paid the price . . .' (244; my emphasis)

Not only does the warden make it clear that Clara's murder is not the issue here, but he proceeds to exonerate Niels in both the religious and secular spheres. What mediates Niels's atonement is that he lets himself be 'molded, like clay in the potter's hands', following the rule that, as we've seen, governed the Canadian penal system at the time. Apparently the warden considers Niels an excellent candidate for this kind of subject (re)formation. During this process, Niels becomes in effect infantilized; this is a necessary stage if he is to emerge as a 'new' man. Because he learns to revise his dreams, he enters a libidinal stage that corresponds to the temporal development of his subjectivity. But he also loses his ethnic markers— further evidence that the warden, who never acknowledges Niels's origins, wishes to reconstruct him as a universal subject. If these elements constitute the subliminal nature of this positivist pedagogy, Niels's education is complemented by his attendance at evening classes at the village school, through which he acquires 'a vocabulary which would enable him to read real books' (236).

Above all, Niels learns how to re-establish 'the hegemony of the reality principle over the pleasure principle' (Laplanche and Pontalis 237) and to control his instincts. The warden's positivist pedagogy pays off. As we will see, Niels replaces his attachment to his mother with the phallic economy of the warden's pedagogy. In fact, mothering is now defined in terms that reflect the belief that the subject experiences 'frustrations . . . in earlier infancy because of his mother' (Laplanche and Pontalis 253-4). It is the warden's paternal intervention against the feminization of Niels's subjectivity and his contamination by elements contrary to the dominant society's discursive desire that sets Niels on the 'right' path in his new life.

If one of the reasons Clara has to die, as I intimated earlier, is that she reads novels, then the fact that Niels learns 'to read real books' while he is in jail demands some attention. Not only does Niels discover he has the patience to read, but he also develops into an ironic and critical reader: 'He was often puzzled by the abstruseness of it all. Finally he was amused. He learned to laugh at man's folly in puzzling out such curiosities of the mind . . . What had it all to do with the real problems of life?' (236). The narrator does not explain what constitutes 'real books', but they are certainly not the textbooks through which Niels acquires a rudimentary knowledge 'of French and Latin, of Algebra, Geometry, Science . . .' (236). I think we can safely conclude that 'real books' here represent the kind of books that Grove produced—constructions of identity and narrativized renderings of reality that might offer representational access to truth. Niels's reading of 'real books' is thus a reflexive moment in the novel, an instance also exposing the fallacy, earlier in the text, of his reading *Elements of Political Economy*, a real book indeed. Of great significance here is the fact that the pedagogy that enables Niels to read 'real books' also teaches him to doubt the importance of such texts. Far from suggesting that Niels learns to question received knowledge, his rejection of these books' relevance to 'the real problems of life' rearticulates the complex association between his reality and the representational value of the books he reads—yet another example of Grove's ambivalent relationship to reality and realism.

With his education completed—'He even passed examinations' (236)—Niels's atonement is nowhere more strongly evidenced than in the first vision he has when he is released from prison:

> The vision he saw was that of the homely face of his mother. Yet, her features were strangely blurred; as if, superimposed on them, there appeared those of another; and at last he recognised these as the features of the old man, of Sigurdsen, his neighbor whom he had loved.
>
> Long, long ago, in another such vision, his mother had looked at him reproachfully, seriously, warningly.
>
> And the old man, in the wanderings of his decaying mind, had betrayed to him some corner of his subliminal memories . . .
>
> These two, in vision and memory, seemed to blend, to melt together. Both looked at him, in this new vision, out of one face in which, now his, now her lines gained ascendancy . . .
>
> The wistful face of his mother relaxed in a knowing smile: yes, such was she who had born him . . .
>
> The old man's face took her place: he was moving his lips and muttered, 'Hm . . . tya.' (255)

Lest we think the warden has performed a pedagogical miracle, we are shown Niels wavering. Nevertheless, the result is exactly the one in which the warden has invested all his energy. The mother is 'homely', as befits her low status and life of hard labour, an indication that Niels has learned at least one lesson. The agonistic relationship between the mother and Sigurdsen reinforces the tensions that have characterized Niels's psychic life all along. The mother of the visions relinquishes her hold on him; she is no longer 'the ancient mother', but 'she who had born him', a woman who knows her 'real' place and thus defers to the old man, a surrogate father for her son. Niels reads her 'wistful' expression as proof of her devotion to him: a sign that she assents to being put aside, but also a sign of defeat, a recognition that she is overdeterminedly scripted—as woman, as mother, as social being. When the old man takes her place, the Name of the Father is reinstated, and so Niels is able to move on, to begin planning his future with Ellen.

What we know about Sigurdsen is useful in understanding the alliances meant to be established in Niels's new vision, as well as those intended to be forestalled or, more accurately, erased. Sigurdsen, who, when we first see him, brandishes a shotgun (10), is an Icelandic immigrant who used to be a sailor, abrupt in his behaviour, a loner who gradually softens towards Niels. Little else is revealed about him, but what we find out helps us to construct an image of Sigurdsen that summarizes Niels's fundamental characteristics. In his youth, Sigurdsen was infatuated with a 'girl in Copenhagen' (94), a woman he reminisces about with great relish and in terms that recall the excessive, and therefore dangerous, sensuality attributed to Clara:

'Tya . . . Yo, she laugh . . . and she turn her hips. And her breasts . . . Hi . . . tya. And she bite! Sharp teeth she had, the hussy . . .'

And this decay of the human faculties, the reappearance of the animal in a man whom he loved, aroused in Niels strange enthusiasms [. . .] (95)

That Sigurdsen was a sailor serves as a clue to the woman's lewd character. She may have been a woman he loved, but she may also have been a prostitute—the young Sigurdsen's equivalent to 'the Hefter woman' (137), the double of 'the gay widow' Niels marries. Niels finds the old man's memories inspiring: 'he could have got up and howled and whistled, vying with the wind' (95). At the same time that Sigurdsen's memories announce the psychological affinity between the two men, they also foreshadow Niels's relationship with Clara.

I don't think it's a coincidence that Niels, still a virgin at twenty-nine (103), experiences the surfacing of his own repressed sensuality in the chapter following the one in which his old friend has shared his erotic memories. Nor is it a coincidence that his attempt to come to terms with the instincts 'stirred in him by this woman [Clara], something low, disgraceful' (103), occurs after his self-affirmation that '[o]n his land he was master; he knew just how to act' (102). The conflict between confidence and alarm, between knowledge and intimations of the dark truth lurking behind desire, between strength and vigilance, reproduces the old binary paradigms about body and mind. It also shows that the surfacing of Niels's sensuality cannot be seen simply as a matter of 'nature'—'the animal in a man' wanting to be freed, a prospect that delighted him when he listened to Sigurdsen reminiscing. Rather, it is concomitant with the orthodox hierarchies that constitute gender differences.

In the hotel encounter with Clara that is to mark his destiny, as he so often reminds himself, Niels comes face to face with the values determining sexual difference, values coalescing with the hegemonic principles informing settlers' and other colonies. Clara, who has internalized those values, strokes Niels's ego while also pointing to the gaps in his libidinal economy: 'You are a conqueror, Niels; but you do not know it. With women you are a child. A woman wants to be taken, not adored. But if you are ever to marry, the woman will have to take you . . .' (100). Niels repeats to himself Clara's statement—'Women want to be taken, not adored' (102)—but he fails both to apply this caveat to his awakened instincts and to intuit what it means, let alone to understand the cultural genealogy of such a neat formulation of gender relations. Thus when he and Clara eventually kiss, Niels appears to be a seduced, if not reluctant, participant: he kisses her '[n]ot knowing what he did . . . in a paroxysm of passion, he crushed her against his body, released her, and ran off into the night . . .' (141). Echoing the control and passion of Harlequin romances, this passage reflects the relationship between sexuality and labour, showing the allegiance a man like Niels is made to feel towards the social contract that determines civilization and banishes 'nature'.

The degrading nature of the sexuality Clara represents is made apparent in the figures used by the narrator when he talks about Niels's giving himself up to hard work to forget his troubles: 'a sort of intoxication came over Niels; work developed into an orgy' (73). Agriculture seems to mediate his ignorance of the cultural codes of sexuality and his facility with nature, presumably because, as a successful settler, he finds nature's rules to be manageable. While his orgasmic labour has a therapeutic function, Niels's inability to resist Clara exposes weakness, self-deception, and blindness. These are traits that have the potential, as his case shows, to develop into full-blown pathological conditions, the very conditions the warden's pedagogy is meant to cure.

The most important thing in this context, though, is not that Niels gives in to his 'passion', nor that he does so 'on the evening of the third day' of his hotel encounter with Clara—a suggestion on the part of the author 'inside' the text that Niels is crucified by, falls victim to, femininity's guiles. Instead, what is significant here is the urgency with which he decides to marry the woman whose 'fragrant body . . . envelop[ed] his', whose 'hand closed his mouth' (142). Oblivious to the fact that such female promiscuity is considered a form of barbarism that hegemonic ideology tolerates but does not sanction, Niels straddles social conventions. He finds himself lodged within a *métissage*, not in the sense of intercultural or interracial union, but in the sense that his marriage to Clara 'outlines the fault lines of colonial authority' (Stoler 1997b, 199). It is not only Niels's alignment with Clara's sexuality that crosses over to the other side of the imperial divide. The repeated emphasis on Clara's physiognomy, indulged in by both Niels and the narrator, recalls the way the nineteenth-century 'iconography of *domestic degeneracy* was widely used to mediate the manifold contradictions in imperial hierarchy' (McClintock 1995, 53). If Niels's marriage makes him an outcast in his settler community, it is because he has not yet internalized the fact that *métissage*, 'in linking domestic arrangements to the public order, family to state, sex to subversion, and psychological essence to racial type, . . . might be read as a metonym for the biopolitics of the empire at large' (Stoler 1997b, 199). Thus he offends the morality of his community because his marriage embraces the negative side of the binary structure that determines culture. '[C]ulture is always a dialectical process, inscribing and expelling its own alterity' (Young 1995, 30). Niels yields to what is to be expelled—precisely the transgression that his adopted father does not commit—and is therefore expendable.

This difference between Niels and Sigurdsen is in keeping with the former's resistance to the latter's attempts to promote a marriage with Ellen. Even so, the narrator establishes a bond between the two men, a bond that takes us back to Niels's visions. 'Once a woman had been, his [Sigurdsen's] mother. She had been young, pretty, pulsating, vibrating in every fibre with life: at best she was a heap of brittle bones . . . Did she live on? In him, Niels? . . .' (117). A strange rhetorical question, the answer to which would be ambivalent at best. This pretty mother contrasts sharply with the homely image of Niels's own mother, but echoes the vibrancy of both the Copenhagen 'girl' and Clara. If she lives on in

Niels, she does so as a figure contaminating his character, further disrupting his libidinal economy.

It is when Niels accepts Sigurdsen as a father figure that he begins to recover from his fallacies as well as his fantasies, that he proves the warden's faith in him to be justified. His acknowledgement that he is indeed a patient 'convalesc[ing]' shows that he has learned to control himself when faced with situations that may threaten the nation's health. It is because his libidinal economy is now properly channelled through the dominant discourse aligning the nation's welfare with that of the body that Niels's psychic and social recovery is articulated through a corporeal metaphor: 'It was a painful process: as if the parts of a broken limb were being fitted together, slowly, tentatively, by a skilled but callous physician who did not seem to succeed. It was as if some part were missing' (260). What's missing is the vision that will end the novel: the image of Ellen as Niels's wife, as the mother of his children in his house, will mark the telos of the novel's progressivist ideology. This vision is never described; it is merely intimated, precisely because it forms the overarching cultural and social metanarrative inscribed in the novel. It is supposed, after all, to be imprinted both in Niels and in the 'British readers' of his story.

Instead, the narrative returns to the reality within the novel: 'a middle-aged woman, knitting, with shell-rimmed glasses'; a woman whose 'complexion [is] still that pure, Scandinavian white'; with 'hair, straw-yellow, streaked with grey', 'flat bust; wide, round hips' (257). Purity is (re)installed at more than one level. Ethnicity is not a differential marker, but rather serves to re-establish the lost balance between race and gender, between 'New Canadians' and the Canadian state. Womanhood survives the rigours of Niels's life story, but is imaged only in terms of reproduction; the 'new woman' represented by Clara has been shifted to the background, if not entirely erased. There is a shift in aesthetics here, a move away from the decadence of prettiness and towards a domestic iconography that is intended to be almost anti-aesthetic, as the parallel shift from reading novels to knitting suggests. These dramatic alterations proclaim Grove's views of realism, as I discussed them earlier; they also divulge the 'dangerous liaisons' by which colonialism (both as colonial desire and as colonial anxiety) operates, the overdetermined affinities between subversion and perversion, between femininity and delinquent citizenship, through which hegemonic structures exercise their control.

The narrative's penultimate paragraph leaves no doubt as to what this 'happy ending' entails: Niels and Ellen 'do not kiss. Their lips have not touched. But their arms rest in each other; their fingers are intertwined . . .' (265). There is no room in this developmental telos for sexual desire. Such desire has become subjugated knowledge, disciplined by the power discourses of the nation as they are scripted into the text through the author's 'outside' and 'inside' functions. Sexuality is relegated to the closet.

The pedagogical lesson that Niels learns through his intimate interaction with the warden affirms his 'duty' (236)—the warden's word—to return to his land and to Ellen, to heed Sigurdsen's subtle admonition, earlier in the novel, to marry her. The fact that this curative process is initiated while he is in prison makes it clear that the changes Niels undergoes are not entirely the result of his own agency. The image of prison not as a rehabilitation centre alone but as an educational institution, a school for immigrants, shows how and why Canadian society masks its anxiety of influence. Motivated by the 'fear' that its mode and message of edification 'will not be the only' kind of education available to its new subjects, it believes 'the sole measure of pedagogical success is to be the only teacher the student listens to' (Johnson 1982, 167). It is because of this monologic and homogeneous approach to education that the novel ends by reinforcing domestic economy, by sanctioning ethnicity only insofar as it blends with the values of the Canadian state.

The question Niels asks while a student in jail—what is the connection between the books he reads and his own 'real' problems?—is already answered by the amusement he feels at 'man's folly' in attempting to deal with reality through books. I take this to be yet another instance in which Niels is speaking on behalf of the author 'outside' the text. This question-and-answer reflects Grove's abiding interest in books, but it also has a paradigmatic function addressed to 'New Canadians' as readers. 'New Canadians' must develop themselves as model citizens by relying not on 'real books' like *Settlers of the Marsh* or *Madame Bovary*, which reveal a libidinal economy that might lead us astray, but on 'the real problems of life'. How not to be seduced by the disciplinary and homogenizing control of the dominant society seems to be 'the real problem' here. I believe that, in his own way, Grove understood this. Perhaps this is why his novel apostrophized its 'British readers' more than it did the immigrants of its protagonist's time. We can appreciate the ambivalent meaning of this double apostrophe only if we read the novel as a *real* book about diaspora.

Chapter 2

Sedative Politics:
Media, Law, Philosophy

The word and the history are only paper. But the experience, especially the experience of suffering. Open your eyes and ears, open your door, open the leaves of your table, open your heart, open your homes, your arms. Open what philosophers most often seek to close. Everything but the mouth. Give what they hold back. So? So: the noise for your ears, stereotyped behavior for your eyes, the crowd who eat the last scraps from your table. The noise of their chewing produces a noise in the organized cloud of those whom I can only call parasites.

Michel Serres (9)

I
Media Discourse and Representational Economies

Multicultural Fatigue:
The Politics of Scandal and Disavowal

Between the 1920s, when Grove wrote his first novel in English, and the second half of the 1990s, when I am writing this, a lot has changed about the perception and status of ethnicity in Canada. Notably, the literature written by the descendants of the 'New Canadians' of Grove's time and by later immigrants has gained a measure of both popular and academic legitimacy and of cultural and political weight. Yet the recent rise of multicultural rhetoric and postcolonial critical discourses, curricular developments in secondary and postsecondary institutions reflecting Canada's multicultural make-up, and the success of such authors as Rohinton Mistry, Evelyn Lau, M.J. Vassanji, and Nino Ricci do not necessarily imply either that ethnicity has become an integral part of the literary canon or that Canadians have finally come to terms with the diversities inherent in Canada.

If Grove, like many of his contemporaries, felt compelled by circumstances to lecture on his national tours about the pros and cons of assimilation, it is the entanglement with diversity, together with the pressures entailed by the concept and practice of tolerance, that has dominated the many debates about ethnicity since the early 1970s.

When the Canadian government introduced multiculturalism as an official policy in 1971, entrenched it in the Charter of Rights in 1982, and tabled the Canadian Multiculturalism Act in 1988, it made substantial proclamations of responsibility concerning ethnic diversity. The Multiculturalism Act (also known as Bill C-93) recognizes the cultural diversity that constitutes Canada, but it does so by practising a sedative politics, a politics that attempts to recognize ethnic differences, but only in a contained fashion, in order to manage them. It pays tribute to diversity and suggests ways of celebrating it, thus responding to the clarion call of ethnic communities for recognition. Yet it does so without disturbing the conventional articulation of the Canadian dominant society. The Act sets out to perform the impossible act of balancing differences, in the process allowing the state to become self-congratulatory, if not complacent, about its handling of ethnicity.

More often than not, multiculturalism is perceived as, in Robert Stam's words, an 'abrupt jettisoning of European classics and of "western civilization"', as 'systematically, reflexively anti-European', a concept that is a 'misunderstanding'. While multiculturalism has always been marked by ambivalence and viewed as a concept fraught with contradictions, 'a slippery signifier onto which diverse groups project their hopes and fears' (Stam 1997, 190),[1] the hegemonic views that have shaped the dominant literary tradition continue to operate. 'Is multiculturalism a threat to the status quo?', Michael Valpy's article published in *The Globe and Mail*, is one example of media discourse that attempts to define, and to show the erosion suffered by, the dominant tradition following the advent of multiculturalism.[2] In a paradoxical fashion not uncommon in the media's coverage of similar issues, Valpy endorses and celebrates multiculturalism only insofar as it guarantees assimilation. Its merits 'are obvious to those of us with children attending multicultural urban schools, who witness the near-magical transformation of our offspring's classmates within a brief few months—from little strangers into ordinary Canadian kids' (D5). The tension between 'little strangers' and 'ordinary Canadian kids' announces the writer's staunch support for dominant values. Multiculturalism's potential to cause havoc is juxtaposed to the stability of the mainstream—yet another commonplace in conventional interpretations of multicultural policy. Valpy's view preserves the binary thinking that is integral to the 'status quo'—indeed, crucial to its survival. Moreover, it demonstrates that one of the principal and, sadly, most effective strategies employed in journalistic reportage and analyses of immigration and ethnicity is the deliberate bracketing of any serious critique of the mainstream. Media discourse posits itself as a source of information for the public while in fact it fashions the public's views and fears, as is obvious in the prevalent mode of address: presumably a collective 'we', but a 'we' that invites identification only with those Canadians who see themselves as products of the dominant culture.

If such representations of multiculturalism by the mainstream media[3] are at all indicative of the public's view of racial and ethnic diversity, then complacency and, conversely, a tendency to demonize diversity are the norms today. In fact, it wouldn't be too cynical to argue that to the constitutional fatigue that afflicted Canadians in the early 1990s we can now add multicultural fatigue. This fatigue directly reflects the dominant society's comfortable assumption that multiculturalism, through implementation of the official policy and the proliferation of discussions and forums about it, has already fulfilled, if not exceeded, its mandate.

The view of multiculturalism as a *fait accompli*, and displays of saturation or impatience with anything related to racialization and ethnicity, are symptoms of this multicultural fatigue. This phenomenon reflects the mass media's tendencies to dismiss calls for radical change in the current social and cultural landscape, to look for quick answers to systemic problems, and to identify multiculturalism as too complex or idealistic to be workable; thus the media absolve themselves of the responsibility to deal with it in earnest. The result is twofold: universalizing the political and cultural import of specific events; and circumventing a more sustained and historical approach to the issues at hand. That media discourse about diversity has reached this stage of complacency and exasperation is evident in the two predominant signs through which it represents multiculturalism, which I call the signs of disavowal and scandal.

If we consider further the discourse on multiculturalism that has appeared in *The Globe and Mail* in the last few years,[4] we notice that, with few exceptions, Canada's 'National Newspaper' is indeed reluctant to embrace a rhetoric of pathology or of biological determinism. Nevertheless, as we read *The Globe's* coverage of multiculturalism we witness the emergence of a new political rhetoric, a rhetoric intent on disavowing ethnicity, a disavowal that goes hand in hand with the intent to present multiculturalism as scandalous. This phenomenon is not unique to *The Globe and Mail*. As Stuart Hall argues, the media 'are, by definition, part of the dominant means of *ideological* production. What they "produce" is, precisely, representations of the social world, images, descriptions, explanations and frames for understanding how the world is and why it works as it is said and shown to work.' Thus if they undermine support for an openly multicultural society, and if they do so by depicting certain multicultural events as scandalous, it is because of their belief that they reflect their mainstream readers' ideology. But beyond functioning as more or less accurate registers of common opinion, the media 'are also one place where ideas are articulated' (1981, 35). This is the reason why a selective review of journalistic discourse on multiculturalism is an appropriate preamble to what I wish to discuss in this chapter: how ethnic diversity is given legitimacy, and what this legitimacy entails.

Multicultural Gothic: A Narrative of Cultural Unease

Gina Mallet's 1997 article 'Multiculturalism: Has diversity gone too far?'[5] typifies the function of the double trope of disavowal and scandal. She sets out to impress on her readers that multiculturalism has not just accomplished its objective, namely 'to promote tolerance', but 'has, in fact, gone too far' (D2). Her litany of examples disavows any efficacy that the multiculturalism policy may have had: in 'the view of many . . . right across the ethnic spectrum, the drive to recognize diversity has not served Canadians well at all' (D1). Although her article includes comments on how immigrants have found 'the demands to conform incompatible with their dignity' (D2), her gaze is fixed on the present moment; thus she disregards the formidable historical legacy of racialization and discrimination.

It seems that, for Mallet, Canadian history began in 1971. Multiculturalism is a misbegotten ideal, its failure measured 'by hundreds of millions of dollars—no one knows how much—in multicultural grants' (D1). The anxiety she attempts to instil regarding the amount of funds subsidizing multicultural projects is the leitmotif of her article. It is also a frequent element in most media discourses about diversity, discourses that dehistoricize multiculturalism by seeing it only as a manifestation of the contemporary moment, and this only insofar as it belongs to the machine of commodification.[6]

We have moved, then, from the assimilationist debates of the first two decades of the century to the consumerist impetus that drives us toward the millennium. The cultural and economic determinations have changed between then and now. Still, the position of minority Canadians has shifted without any radical alteration in their construction as ideological objects. Formerly objects of at worst contempt and overt discrimination, at best tolerance and assimilation, they are now often seen as threatening subjects. This shift in attitude reflects, on one hand, the social and cultural achievements of minority people and, on the other, changes in federal policies and social attitudes, but such accomplishments are viewed as threats to the dominant society's self-image. As Ian Angus argues, 'Violence against the other is one major response to the perceived threat of the loss of identity' (135). Violence here is not to be understood so much in a physical sense as in the sense of virulent politics, a politics that more often than not is characterized by a 'rhetoric of opposition' (Angus 145). Thus, although the terms used in discussing ethnicity have changed, it would be safe to argue that minoritarian Canadians still remain Other to the national imaginary. In the realm of media discourse, they continue to be defined in terms of a counternarrative that now changes, now erodes, what Canadian identity is presumed to mean.

Mallet concedes that 'differences must be respected,' but it is 'the many things we have in common' (D2) that she wishes to see consolidating the Canadian state. Whether she questions Canada's need for a multiculturalism policy or the effect of the federal policy itself is unclear. What is certain, though, is her disavowal of a politics of difference, a disavowal made possible by her assumption that there are no epistemologically privileged subjects in Canada. Yet she belies her own perspective by identifying diversity as the frontline of the battle she envisions between Us and Them. Ironically, it is precisely her strategy of verbal terrorism that reveals the imperative need for a multiculturalism policy, although not necessarily the existing one.

'Everyone these days has a multicultural horror story,' says Mallet, and she proceeds to rewrite identity politics by adopting a style reminiscent of the gothic genre that Margaret Atwood used in developing her thesis about Canadian identity. Mallet's gothic is a narrative of cultural unease: 'to criticize any aspect of multiculturalism is to risk being called a racist, a word as incendiary as "witch" was in 17th-century Salem. The r-word is the only epithet that is still heard in public discourse. The others (Taffy was a Welshman, Taffy was a thief) have gone *underground* where, if anything, they gain intensity, surfacing only among friends, over dinner, or a jar at a bar. In public, euphemisms and code words have taken over real language' (D2; my emphasis). Putting herself on the line as she does by spelling out the 'r-word', Mallet rewrites her involvement in diversity politics as a coming-out story—one that, we are led to believe, it takes courage to tell: 'Those who talk do so at their peril' (D2). What emerges from this media discourse is an image of the dominant citizen[7] as cultural guerrilla, as the promoter of a particular set of cultural values.

A self-appointed target of her witch-hunt plot, Mallet sees herself as occupying a heroically vulnerable position—exposed and unarmed—in the multicultural wars. 'Often,' she declares, 'multicultural policy seems like a pistol pointed at the heads of people of British descent' (D2). She is the central character, then, in her gothic tale, coming out of the closet determined no longer to operate 'underground'. 'Eurocentric has become a dirty word. Freedom of speech is called racism' (D2); yet Mallet feels safe enough to publicize her views in the Saturday *Globe*. This fact alone undermines the vehemence of her argument. It also shows that the culpability of multiculturalism for her condition as a threatened 'Eurocentric' subject is largely a matter of her reductive and ideologically loaded strategies. It is the displacement of neat borderlines between centre and margins that seems to put her belief in sovereign subjectivity under siege.

Apparently under duress, but also out of conviction, she brandishes a weapon that suits her emancipatory discourse perfectly: 'the only antidote . . . is the Western European belief in reason—which is no longer taught' (D2). This is of course the ultimate 'horror' in her gothic scenario, for she has already proclaimed 'Western liberal culture [to be] under attack' (D2). With her only weapon presumably disabled, she resorts to psychological warfare. 'Horror' itself becomes her definitive strategy, one not aimed directly at minorities but geared towards rallying support, shaking Canadians—descendants of the two 'heritage nations' or those assimilated into those dominant groups—from their complacency. '[P]eople,' she states, 'are identifying themselves in the census as simply "Canadian". But they are losing ground. There is still a crèche [sic] at the

University of Toronto's Hart House but the Gospel of St. Luke's recounting of the nativity is no longer read at Christmas—in case someone is offended. David Moll, chairman of the Toronto Board of Education, says "British history has been expunged from the schools here"' (D2).

Lamenting the alleged demise of Western values, which she takes to be stable, Mallet proclaims a moment of emergency. Even though she considers minority subjects to be Canadian, her notion of 'Canadianness' implies transcendence of ethnic difference, a homogeneous identity. One would think Mallet has never heard of colonialism or decolonization—or that, if she has, she dismisses that history entirely. To borrow Said's words, 'The thing to be noticed about this kind of contemporary discourse, which assumes the primacy and even the complete centrality of the West, is how totalizing is its form, how all-enveloping its attitudes and gestures, how much it shuts out even as it includes, compresses, and consolidates. We suddenly find ourselves transported backward in time to the late nineteenth century' (1993, 22). Indeed, although Mallet adopts the narrative perspective of Marlow in her 'horror' narrative, and puts herself in the besieged position of the colonized subject, her dramatization of the Us and Them conflict is both ahistorical and anachronistic.

The 'horror' she speaks of is not that different from Kurtz's. If anything, the darkness she fears is potentially more terrifying, for it lacks a particular geography and reverts to a mythology that reproduces the double bind of the Enlightenment, fighting prejudice while validating reason itself as prejudice. Because she does not consider the materialist and historical conditions at the heart of the issues she examines, she attributes ultimate authority to Western reason, seeing it as completely free from history. Mallet's is the darkness that comes after the demise of Western logic: the cultural and political anarchy of multiculturalism; diversity imaged as sheer instability, bedlam resisting control, defying order.

Multicultural Fairy Tale: A Success Story

If the impetus for Mallet's article is her determination to see multiculturalism eliminated, other instances of media discourse employ the rhetoric of disavowal not to attack diversity as such, but to advocate, in subtle and not so subtle ways, a new brand of multiculturalism: residual diversity. 'Laying to rest "this whole immigrant thing"', the title of Val Ross's article on the publication of *Where She Has Gone* (1997), the third volume of Nino Ricci's trilogy, is an example of the kind of disavowal that permeates many recent treatments of popular Canadian authors in the media. Ross adopts the fairy-tale form to tell Ricci's life story:

Once upon a time on a farm west of Toronto there lived a boy named Nino who dreamed of becoming a Catholic priest. Nino's parents, who had immigrated from Italy before he was born, grew vegetables under a sea of glass houses. On Sunday mornings in the spring, Nino worked in the fields sowing seeds, his mind and hands numbed by the repetition. If there were no crops to plant, he and his father and his brothers attended mass. In church, the flickering candles on the stained glass and icons mesmerized him.

. . .

Of course, Nino Ricci never did become a priest. Instead, at 38, he has become one of this country's most accomplished and acclaimed writers. . . .

The fairy tale inscribed in these opening lines is not offered as a form of idealism, but as a realistic representation of immigrant experience in Canada. If traditional readings of fairy tales privilege their presumed universality, a similar archetypal quality defines the Ricci family's narrative of ascent. The son's movement from agriculture to the most promising pastures of Canadian culture is offered not only as a sign of individual talent and success, but as unshakeable proof that Canada is hospitable to immigrants; this social mobility, like the universal settings of myths and fairy tales, fulfils its promise that the immigrants' toil will yield a happy ending.

Ross presents immigrant experience as an obstacle to be overcome. She writes: 'Ricci's early life was difficult. Most devotees of Canadian literature already know the broad details—the anti-Italian sentiment he encountered in Leamington, Ont., where he was born; the resultant self-loathing and feelings of displacement and alienation; the strain of living with too many people in too small a house.' Without problematizing her shifts from Ricci's real life to the reality represented in his fiction, Ross depicts these difficulties as part of a transition period that makes the multiculturalism policy redundant. Yet Ricci's life would not be a fairy tale without his immigrant background. What is significant in Ross's approach is the readiness with which she dodges the 'self-loathing' and 'displacement' Ricci experienced as a child. She attributes these feelings to the Canadian mainstream environment, positing Canada as a nasty stepmother, a necessary ingredient in her narrative mode. She opts to focus on negative memories of family life that corroborate some of the stereotypes about immigrants. 'We're always fighting. I thought it was an immigrant thing,' Ricci tells her. Ross does not examine the conditions and systemic attitudes that made young Ricci feel alienated, or why he believed that conflict in his family 'was an immigrant thing'. Instead she reinforces what is clearly an instance of the way he has internalized negative stereotypes with a dramatic embellishment: 'Ricci's brow still creases at the recol-lection' of strife in his family. Ross's journalistic method allows her to ascribe the memory of trauma to the immigrant family alone, thus releasing Canada from its legacy of immigrant relations. Like Mallet, she avoids the question of history.

There are two things that matter in her narrative: Ricci's Christian vision of 'the redemptive power of good works' and the fact that his first novel, *Lives of the Saints* (1990), 'sold close to 80,000 copies'. Although Ricci 'relinquished his Catholicism early in high school', he says his religious vision helped him to '"see things [he] hadn't seen before—and it was all tying into a good/evil dichotomy and this whole immigrant thing".' Ricci's binary thinking holds the key to the disavowal of multiculturalism announced by the article's title. There is no doubt as to whether 'this whole immigrant thing' is the positive or the negative part of the dichotomy here. Diversity is the ore to be mined for literary works that soothe the dominant public's anxieties about multiculturalism. In this context, the figure of 80,000 copies functions as the benchmark of the cultural value of ethnicity. It reflects the selective memory that makes acceptance of ethnicity possible. Moreover, the greater the assimilation and commodification, the greater the mainstream's endorsement. When ethnicity becomes yet another signifier of the culture of marketability, when diversity becomes synonymous with liberalism, then the success of ethnic literary discourse is, more often than not, measured by the success with which ethnicity can be translated into a commodity product. The dissemination of ethnicity in this way turns diversity into the familiar sign of use value. When diversity becomes equivalent to consumption, then the immigrant condition survives only as the residue of its historical materiality. Once a sign that marked a subject indelibly, now ethnicity acquires relevance because it serves to prove the imperative for the ethnic subject to transcend it.

It is the scandalous absence of history that lends Mallet's thesis of 'horror' its shape, and it is the absorption of history into a happy ending—'they [Ricci and his wife] will live a full and happy life'—that gives Ross's fairy tale of immigrant experience its putative reality.[8] This is also one of the reasons why books like Dionne Brand's *Bread Out of Stone* (1994) or Himani Bannerji's edited collection *Returning the Gaze: Essays on Racism, Feminism and Politics* (1993) did not receive similar coverage by *The Globe*.

Multicultural Bodies: The Scandal of Numbers

My use of the word 'scandal' here is meant to suggest the dramatization of multi-cultural conflicts in ways that enact and mobilize the historically and psycholog-ically rooted anxieties of dominant society. Also scandalous in this treatment of diasporic writing is the bracketing of a big chapter in Canadian history, that on ethnic relations, not to mention the treatment of First Nations peoples. Consider the coverage given to the PEN international conference sponsored by PEN Canada in Toronto and Montreal (1989),[9] the Royal Ontario Museum's 'Into the Heart of Africa' exhibit (Toronto, November 1989-August 1990),[10] and the anti-racist guidelines developed by the Women's Press.[11] Most of *The Globe's* treatment of these events locates multiculturalism exclusively within a site of controversy, a strategy embedded in the media's overall approach to constructing narratives. 'Certain events and topics are what *count* as news,' says Fred Inglis; 'If other things happen which don't fit the news-processor's categories, they are either transcribed until they do fit it [*sic*], or they are ignored.' The media 'cannot report process, sequence, the uneven development of history which is life-in-earnest' (149). Thus reporting on such volatile issues as ethnic diversity and racism by manipulating the complex politics involved has the invariable result of 'focus[ing] on the drama of an incident . . . ; the medium simply intensifies the problem by accenting the conflict' (Snow 23).

I am not suggesting that *The Globe* is in the habit of inventing conflict where there is none, or that its coverage of ethnicity is always the same, but rather that its editorial policies and manner of reportage define multicultural conflict in ways that solidify the Us and Them categories while often reversing the referents. Through such media narratives, multiculturalism is presented to the Canadian imaginary as an explosive issue. This is not surprising, since the federal policy, as I discuss it in the next section, promises at once to recast and to maintain the social and cultural master narratives that have formed Canadian history. But the projection of multiculturalism chiefly through images manufactured by the media that take on an iconoclastic function does little to promote a complex under-standing of what a multicultural Canada entails. Such media narratives are reduc-tive because they do not ipso facto lead to changes or to a subtler understanding of how these conflicts are engendered by society at large; they are also perilous because they do not necessarily challenge the inherited assumptions that locate ethnic subjects in sites of trouble. If anything, the representation of multicultur-alism through the sign of scandal obscures the need to examine the historical co-ordinates of minority subjectivities. It creates an image of diversity that at best is manageable by the system and that at worst feeds the very anxieties and misun-derstandings it seeks to address. Because it tends to employ stereotypes without necessarily considering the history that produced them, multiculturalism as a media-manufactured scandal circumvents the systemic structures of which it is both symptom and effect.

A recurring element in this kind of media representation is the effort to force the national imaginary to confront multiculturalism through body images, images already racialized and ethnicized. When, for example, the media approach the representation of difference through stories that focus on numbers (for example, how many dollars are granted to multicultural projects, or how many people of colour serve on Canada Council juries), they offer a crude way of exposing the power dynamics inherent in such issues. However we may analyze or resolve the politics of these events, the body is instrumentalized as the locus of multicultural-ism. It figures as a zone of representational economies in which difference is 'removed from the language of biologism' while it is 'reworked' and 'displace[d . . .] within a hegemonic project of national unity' (Giroux 33). The deployment of these representational economies by contemporary public discourse, and sometimes also by members of ethnic communities, translates the representation of minority subjectivities into a representation of body numbers—precisely what I take to be scandalous. '[R]epresentations are . . . real, but we still need to keep a clear grip on the distinction between representations and the reality they represent' (Appiah 1993, 88). The scandal, then, lies in confounding the 'multicultural "fact"' with the 'multicultural "project"' (Stam 1997, 188). In other words, public discourse tends to confuse the representation of minorities with a pragmatism that reflects, indeed fuels, national economies, which flourish while minorities remain othered.

A notable example of the deployment of the body as representational economy is evident in the media coverage of Writing Thru Race: A Conference for First Nations Writers and Writers of Colour (Vancouver, 30 June–3 July 1994), organized chiefly by Roy Miki. When it became known that the conference, expected at the time to be subsidized in part by federal funds, would restrict enrolment of participants to First Nations writers and writers of colour, there was what might safely be described as a hysterical response, which began in the Writers' Union and the House of Commons and culminated in the mass media. It is no coincidence that the writers and journalists who published articles support-ing the conference in *The Globe* felt compelled to adopt a tone of apologia. As the titles assigned by *The Globe* to Myrna Kostash's 'You don't check your colour at the door', Bronwyn Drainie's 'Controversial writers' meeting is both meet and right', and Roy Miki's 'Why we're holding the Vancouver conference' suggest,[12] the authors had already been put on the defensive, primarily by the ways in which *The Globe* had already been reporting on the conference. Its coverage included, among other pieces, an editorial, 'Writhing thru race', a tongue-in-cheek treat-ment of the conference as a natural extension of the government's 'mandated discrimination', and an article by Robert Fulford, 'George Orwell, Call Your Office', that accused the Writers' Union of 'reinventing apartheid'.[13]

'We have apparently moved,' Fulford wrote, 'from the era of pluralism to the era of multiculturalism. The old liberal pluralism holds that each of us has rights as an individual. . . . The new multiculturalism, on the other hand, focuses on the rights of groups, and sees each of us as the member of a racially designated cluster.' In Fulford's binary thinking—not unusual, as we have seen, in debates on multiculturalism—the kind of liberal pluralism that neutralizes differences is synonymous with some old kind of multiculturalism: hence a policy on diversity is redundant. Fulford's view of Writing Thru Race as a threat to the 'era of plural-ism' was an ironic reminder of what had occasioned the conference in the first place.[14] His attitude summed up both the rhetoric and the ideological vestiges of universalism characteristic of most of the conference's media coverage. As Miki wrote in response, '"Multiculturalism" . . . was intended to acknowledge the cultural and ethnic pluralism of Canadian society. The kind of pluralism Mr. Fulford yearns for is really the resurrected form of an earlier assimilationist ideol-ogy that was used historically to promote Anglo-European values and traditions as the Canadian norm' (1994).

The public debate about the conference, whose scheduled readings and recep-tions were attended by many white writers, continued unabated even after the event itself had ended. The fact that debate was sparked by the exclusion of white writers from the conference sections reveals how the policy of multiculturalism, together with the public understanding of it, begins and ends with the racializa-tion and ethnicization of bodies, bodies that are not white. Whiteness is already excluded from the mandate of the multiculturalism policy. If included at all, it is as the normative—and therefore invisible—category it still is, one whose 'epistemological stickiness and ontological wiggling' (Hill 3) came to the surface in that summer of 1994. Indeed, one of the major accomplishments of Writing Thru Race was that it showed white Canadians, including those of ethnic origins, that they are as racialized as black or aboriginal Canadians are. Those who found the conference's exclusion of whites to be scandalous did so precisely because it forced them to confront the fact that whiteness is not paradigmatic. This is the kind of scandal that reveals the alleged invisibility of white bodies to be a myth.

Many of those who objected to the exclusion of white writers tied their position to the conference's public funding.[15] The conjuction of bodies and funds brings to the fore the double economy that informs the way public discourse treats the politics of cultural production: the value of multiculturalism policy measured in terms of public funds expended; tolerance to diversity conceived as an exchange process (I'll tolerate you if you'll tolerate me). These two elements, with their implied reciprocity, can effect only a precarious balance of differences. If anything, they inflate the gap between mainstream and minority. The controversy about Writing Thru Race, then, seemed to offer an answer to the question posed in another *Globe* column, 'Will Ayatollah's curse turn multicultural dream into nightmare?' the last column that Mavor Moore wrote for the paper.[16] 'Are we ready for . . . radical remedies?' he asked, 'Ready to pay for them?' The rhetorical question betrayed Moore's fear that the answer was, as it continues to be, a resounding 'no'.

'If multiculturalism works in Canada,' Moore wrote, 'we shall have given the world a useful model. But its chances rest unequivocally on vigilant tolerance of each other's traditions.' There is a price to pay, he argued, for dealing with the cultural 'traumas' and self-defence mechanisms that come into play when the relationships between society and culture are reformulated with the intention of addressing long-standing inequities and the redistribution of power. The most significant price by far is that 'the mainstream . . . is having to assimilate.' '[C]anons are being deconstructed' today, but 'the question is whether the mainstream can survive at all without catering to the new many-headed audience— . . . building a whole new repertoire to accommodate visible minorities and reflect a mixed society.' A fuzziness in the structure and logic of Moore's argument is evident in, among other things, his proposition that the mainstream cultural industries must both survive and be 'deconstructed'. What is clear, though, is that the economic terms in which he articulates the 'rewriting' of the canon—demand and supply—do not suggest any systematic analysis of differences. The market economy that informs his argument depends on his recognition that the audience is diversified. For Moore, though, this diversification, an invalid analogue of diversity, portends dangerous consequences not only for national culture, but also for the state. He thus posits multiculturalism as leading the state to the brink of a possible national disaster: 'What price multiculture if culture fails?' he asks, fearing the erosion of Western culture and its values. The vertical relationship of multiculturalism to culture at large consigns to the former the instability and undecidability that are presumed to trouble the cohesiveness of the latter. Were 'culture' not to 'fail', multiculturalism would have to rearrange itself as identical to mainstream culture.

Beyond the Fantasy of Homogeneity

Like similar arguments about diversity, Moore's is determined by an alignment of the cultural and the economic. There is a 'complicity', Gayatri Spivak says, 'between cultural and economic value-systems [that] is acted out in almost every decision we make' (1985, 83). But as she and others argue, this complicity is coupled with a tendency towards 'reducing "noneconomic" values to economic values' (Guillory 326). That this is a risky matter becomes apparent every time we encounter in public discourse the juxtaposition of diversity to hegemonic culture. Multiculturalism is accepted only insofar as it promises to enhance the cultural capital of the mainstream. This is one of the reasons why a large portion of the public reaction to Writing Thru Race conveniently forgot that the conference was about writing.[17] Moore's statement that 'multiculturalism must work or modern Canada will not work' only feigns to remedy this problem. Since, as he claims, 'the common denominator among multicultural audiences in Canada . . . [is] a taste for the dominant culture of the continent: the American,' he seems to be advocating a functional multiculturalism, one that can be used to enhance the cultural capital of the dominant society. Meanwhile, his caveat that multicultural audiences are complicit in the erosion of the mainstream targets them as a force to be restrained. That the Americanization of Canadian culture was an issue even before the advent of official multiculturalism does not affect the fashion in which Moore constructs minorities.

My sampling of media discourses on multiculturalism illustrates the major shifts that have occurred in the way Canadian dominant culture positions itself. Whether the subject is residual or functional multiculturalism or multiculturalism as 'mandated discrimination', media discourses betray an underlying belief that Canada's survival and future success depend on its being a homogeneous community whose coherence is to be achieved through mastery of the Other. Both residual and functional multiculturalism strive towards harmonization of differences. But in effect they still advocate uniformity, for such harmonization depends on the domination of the Other by national will, a process that reifies minorities as that which the cohesive nation is not. These discourses of the media, then, reflect the tense relation between what Charles Taylor calls 'difference-blindness', 'a politics of universalism, emphasizing the equal dignity of all citizens' (1992, 40 and 37), and what he calls 'a politics of difference', a politics wherein 'Everyone should be recognized for his or her unique identity' (1992, 38). Each condition often finds itself under siege by the other. No matter how we configure this state of affairs, the present climate of Canadian cultural politics seems to have reached a checkpoint—that point in time and space fraught with the ambiguities that surface when difference disrupts the dialectic of centre and margin.

Evidently, the challenge of identity politics to Canada's presumed homogeneity has led to the emergence of counternarratives. Thus one way of understanding multiculturalism would be not as an umbrella term that includes all Canadian Others, but as a counternarrative intended to undo the inherited binary conception of Canadian society, a counternarrative that should be read alongside the master narrative of the nation. But the absence of a single, cohesive counternarrative that would realign hegemonic conceptions of Canada makes it difficult to appreciate that even if one did exist, it could not possibly open a new chapter in Canada's future history wherein all differences would be, depending on one's politics, eradicated or legally endorsed. The common assumption in media discourse that the absence of a cohesive approach to multiculturalism among minorities themselves[18] is itself a sign that diversity has gone too far only demonstrates the real 'danger to democracy': namely, 'the foreclosure of the field of contestation' (Butler 1993a, 5).

Nevertheless, some view the lack of a coherent counternarrative as the most serious weakness, the Achilles heel, of multiculturalism. Others translate that absence into a pluralism that alternates between threatening to erode the Canadian nation and celebrating a state that doggedly attempts to edit, not necessarily rewrite, cultural mythologies such as that of the two 'founding nations'. Others still, and I count myself among them, believe that the absence of a cohesive new paradigm is inevitable, for comprehending, and dealing with, diversity is a continuous process of mediating and negotiating contingencies.

Recent debates about the metanarratives of the federal state and cultural discourses—the Constitution, the Charter of Rights, the Official Languages Act, the literary canon—have shown that we can no longer remain trapped within a national self-image of cohesiveness. Yet the signs that some might read as symptoms of cultural and political malaise might also be seen as indicating a healthier state of affairs. Whatever the stakes might be in recent cultural and political debates, there is one recurring point of great importance: people are becoming increasingly aware that the political and the cultural are inextricably interrelated, in fact that they inhabit the same discursive site. Thus the convergence of previously exclusionary discourses and sites reflects, among other things, the 'new' designation allotted to minority issues. The racial and pedagogical conflicts that occasionally afflict Canadian universities,[19] whether they come under the rubric of 'academic freedom' or proposed 'codes of ethics', are determined by the same disjunctions, occurring as the result of the perceived need to recast and articulate the meanings and positions of racial, ethnic, and gender differences. But to overcome the stalemate in the debates about cultural politics today—the polarization, between, say, 'difference-blindness' and 'the politics of difference'—the articulation of difference ought to take place within a critical dialogue that will seek to produce a community not of consensus but of hybridity.

II
'Hey, you there!'
Law and the Discovery of Ethnicity

The Legitimation of Ethnicity

A diasporic author does not automatically occupy a position of marginality in Canada. But the prominence of ethnic discourse today is certainly not an unequivocal sign that multiculturalism has succeeded. Rather, it is symptomatic of a culture in which 'the contradictions that arise within . . . society are resolved in ways that assure the continuation of a ruling group's hegemony' (Ryan 11). No matter how we interpret the federal government's legitimation of ethnicity, it is indisputable that the state's multiculturalism policy, together with some of the ways it has been implemented, has facilitated the development of ethnic literary discourse. But the same policy has also given rise to vehement arguments about the representation of ethnicity both inside and outside ethnic sites. Multiculturalism may 'not [be] by definition good or bad' (Gutmann 172), but the introduction of legislation about it marks a turning point in the national imaginary.[20]

Because 'law . . . is fundamentally an interpretive process,' an interpretive act that involves a 'critique, and indeed rejection, of past arguments and past principles' (Cornell 1136 and 1170), law recognizes and acts on the materiality of history. It is a constituent part of the social technology that produces, and includes, the discourses that construct and contain us. Multiculturalism legislation, then, accounts for the ways in which our knowledge about ourselves and our communities circulates, the ways in which ethnicity becomes a discursive sign of differentiating practices. Since ethnicity is an ambivalent concept, a cultural synonym both of Otherness and of incommensurability, it does not suffice to examine the discourse produced by ethnic writers alone. Unrepresentable in its totality, ethnicity must be examined as a product of a knitting together of social and cultural factors, including legal realities. When the ethnic subject speaks of and through herself, she does so by interpreting how she has already been constructed, thus speaking back to, or together with, what defines and delimits her as ethnic. Even when she seems to be entirely motivated by a discourse of resistance to the surrounding hegemonic discourses, she cannot distance herself completely from them. Ethnic subjectivity is never utterly free and of itself. This does not mean, though, that ethnic subjectivity is entirely alloyed, or that it lacks agency. Purity is not an element intrinsic to ethnicity. Since '[i]dentity is always . . . a structured representation' (Stuart Hall 1997, 174), the technology of ethnicity, what produces and is produced by it, is part and parcel of the larger systems within which it operates.

To what extent, then, is ethnicity produced by the letter of the law? What are the contending forces that characterize their relations? What is the difference between multiculturalism as legislated by the state and multiculturalism as it

operates within the state? What histories are inscribed in official multiculturalism? Can the federal policy help us to reconcile the simultaneous rise of marginal
discourses and multicultural fatigue? My purpose here is to examine closely the
very text that sanctions the structural conditions enabling ethnicity to circulate
with legal authority.

The Canadian Multiculturalism Act / Loi sur le multiculturalisme canadien: Translation and the National Imaginary

As is the convention with federal government documents, The Canadian
Multiculturalism Act / Loi sur le multiculturalisme canadien[21] is printed in two
parallel columns of English and French. In this sense, it is already more than one
act even before we begin to read it. It is posited at once as law and as translation,
only it is not exactly clear which of the two texts is the translation of the other. In
fact, the conventional notion of translation—in which a source text operates as the
origin and semantic double of a text written in a different language—is suspended
by the Act/Loi, which declares that 'the Constitution of Canada and the *Official
Languages Act* provide that English and French are the official languages of Canada
and neither abrogates or derogates from any rights or privileges acquired or
enjoyed with respect to any other language.' Translation is also put under erasure
not only because I have obviously cited the Act in English alone, but also because
the two texts are not, strictly speaking, translations of one another.

The premise that in translation 'the forms must be altered if one is to preserve
the content' because 'all languages differ in form' (Nida and Taber 5) is not the
only issue here. The French version of the section cited above differs from its
English equivalent by going beyond alterations made for the sake of faithfully
translating meaning. We read, for instance, that the Constitution of Canada
'proclame . . . le statut du français et de l'anglais comme langues officielles du
Canada'. The order in which 'French/français' and 'English/anglais' appear in the
document's two versions asserts, respectively, each language's claim to official
status. This doubleness reflects both textual and political asymmetry and the
'bigamist' mode of translation (Johnson 1985, 143). The law of language—in
reference both to official bilingualism and to the law of translation as being
'always . . . the translation of *meaning*' (Johnson 1985, 145)—introduces a
cultural syntax of agonistic relations that deconstructs the intention of the legal
text. Although the Act/Loi seeks to enshrine national stability by legislating on
ethnicity, it discloses that contestation is not only what produces ethnic
Otherness, but also what binds together the two 'heritage' groups as a single
nation while keeping them apart.

The relationship between the English and the French texts of the document,
then, is both dialectical and diacritical: at the same time that the document in its
entirety affirms the official status equally shared by both English and French, thus

constituting a balancing act, the French and the English texts establish a differential relationship to each other that deconstructs, linguistically, the mastery claimed by both of them. As each language becomes an analogue of the other, it articulates, strategically, the assumption that the legitimacy of law is linked to mastery of language; but the bilingualism of the document gives the lie to either language's mastery.

Thus English and French in the Act/Loi are not simply translations of one another. In fact, since both languages are official, neither of them needs to be translated into the other; I may be reading them as translations of one another, but they are both originals. This simultaneity exemplifies what Benjamin argues is a fundamental element in translation, namely the original's 'great longing for linguistic complementation' (1969, 79). Beyond suggesting that the original is always incomplete, and therefore 'translatable' (Benjamin 1969, 81), the idea of the original's longing for complementation also implies that, as Chow argues with great insight, 'translation is primarily a process of *putting* together. This process demonstrates that the "original", too, is something that has been put together' (1995a, 185). In complementing each other as simultaneous originals and translations, the French and English texts of the Act/Loi point to a third original and 'literal' text (1995a, 186), namely Canadian society. If 'the original' refers, as Chow argues in her study of Benjamin, not only to the language translated, but also to the translator's own language, then 'translation is a process in which the "native" should let the *foreign* affect, or infect, itself, and vice versa' (1995a, 189). From this perspective, the Act/Loi shows Canada to be a community whose 'nativeness' includes, indeed is determined by, elements 'foreign' to it: namely the ethnic communities and, above all, First Nations peoples. In fact, the indigenousness, as well as the national and linguistic diversity, of the latter serves to bring home that Canada is not only an officially bilingual state formed by two 'heritage' groups, but also, and more significantly, a state that is already 'foreign' to Natives, a state that becomes 'native' to itself only insofar as it acknowledges its own 'foreignness'.

Interestingly, this 'foreignness' is inscribed in the Act/Loi through exclusion. The definition of 'federal institution' in its 'Interpretation' section, which lists those institutions in charge of implementing the multiculturalism policy, specifically 'does not include'

> any institution of the Council or Government of the Northwest Territories or the Yukon Territory, or . . . any Indian band, band council or other body established to perform a governmental function in relation to an Indian band or other group of aboriginal people.

Whether these institutions and councils are excluded because the First Nations peoples are considered to fall outside the mandate of the Act/Loi or because they deserve 'distinct' treatment, given their aboriginal claims and rights, is unclear.[22]

As a hermeneutic act, then, the Act/Loi is itself a translation of what it interprets, that is, 'the cultural and racial diversity of Canadian society'. But it performs its hermeneutic task 'ironically, transplant[ing] the original into a more definitive linguistic realm' (Benjamin 1969, 75). For de Man, this 'gesture' allows translation to make 'its own version more [canonical] than the original' (82). This canonization reflects the authority of law, an authority that speaks of the legal text's intention to function as a master narrative, a narrative that attempts to discipline ethnicity.

The textuality of law operates in much the same way as that of any literary enterprise.[23] Yet, whether law as interpretation is limited by 'textual determinism' or is a case of '[b]ounded objectivity' (Fiss 743 and 745),[24] the performance of its disciplinary gesture operates as an instance of cultural appropriation. This is a feature of the Act/Loi's ironic intention: in setting out to legitimize ethnic and racial diversity, it recognizes the suffering of minorities, but this recognition is modified by its bilingual framework and by its framers' desire to manage contingency. This desire is made clear in its stated aim to 'advance multiculturalism throughout Canada in harmony with the national commitment to the official languages of Canada'. Bilingualism, in this instance, is a matter not just of two languages, but of two discourses whose conjunction is intended to prevent the production of a third one, what in 1964 Senator Paul Yuzyk called the 'Third Force—a coalition of all non-English and non-French ethnic collectivities' (cited in Kallen 57).[25]

Thus the epithet attached to both English and French, 'official/officielle', functions both as a matter of law and as a signifier pointing inadvertently to those languages in Canada that are not declared to be official. It would seem that the Official Languages Act avoids the singularity of monolinguism and ethnocentrism; as it is embedded in the Multiculturalism Act, however, it asserts its own epistemological laws about cultural and linguistic diversity. Law, which cannot exist outside language, adjudicates on the very medium that makes it operable. My examination of the tropes through which the Act/Loi legislates on ethnicity is meant to elucidate how the minority subject, when imaged by legal discourse, himself produces a discourse with the potential to alienate him from himself (an issue I discuss in the next chapter), a sign of the 'foreignness' that contaminates subjectivity.

Two Official Languages = No Official Culture = Multicultural 'Ideal'

The paradox inherent in the doubleness of official discourse and its verbal stratagems structures the immediate legal framework within which diversity is located. The Act/Loi is further complicated by yet another official discourse: the statement delivered by Prime Minister Pierre E. Trudeau in the House of Commons, namely the 1971 White Paper on multiculturalism. This document functions as both a supplement to the Official Languages Act and a subtext to the Multiculturalism Act.[26] Trudeau's comments at once legislate and explicate, attempting to prevent any misunderstanding of the policy, or at least of the government's intentions. As the White Paper states, 'although there are two official languages, there is no official culture, nor does any ethnic group take precedence over any other.' Behind the self-contradictory, if not impossible, intention of keeping language and culture apart, there is the implication that the government is reluctant, in fact unwilling, to acknowledge an official culture.

'Official', in this case, has a double sense, meaning at once legally endorsed and dominant. Thus Trudeau's statement functions as the blind spot in this legal discourse, for in refusing to acknowledge the interrelatedness of language and culture, it pretends there are no dominant cultures in Canada.[27] I say 'pretends' because it is common knowledge that the impetus behind this White Paper was the desire to capture what is still called the 'ethnic vote'. Linda Hutcheon sees Trudeau as '[o]ne of those who "glimpsed" the possibilities of a different Canada', and the White Paper as his 'acknowledge[ment]' of the contribution of ethnic groups (Hutcheon and Richmond, eds 1990, 12 and 13). However, Trudeau's vision of Canada as 'a truly pluralistic and polyethnic society' had specific boundaries, for it was to be realized only through regional 'autonomy' (Trudeau 177 and 178). As for his federal vision, there was no doubt: 'The die is cast in Canada: there are two main ethnic and linguistic groups; each is too strong and too deeply rooted in the past, too firmly bound to a mother-culture, to be able to engulf the other. But if the two will collaborate at the hub of a truly pluralistic state, Canada could become the envied seat of a form of federalism that belongs to tomorrow's world' (Trudeau 178-9). As Manoly Lupul puts it, multiculturalism was 'not central to Trudeau's thinking' (96). The bureaucratic (dis)coordination of multicultural affairs within the federal government is just one indication that Ottawa's multiculturalism policy was not proactive, but a reactive gesture in response to external pressures.

When the Canadian Multiculturalism Act was passed in 1988, the prime minister at the time, Brian Mulroney, had his own political motives, but one political reality remained the same: Canada as an 'original' was to remain unaffected by its translation into a multicultural state. When tabled, the Act/Loi was expected to pay homage to minorities, bowing to the pressure to acknowledge them, while maintaining the 'original' state made up of two 'heritage groups' intact. This is a good illustration of Benjamin's argument that 'translations . . . [are] untranslatable' (1969, 81), that the 'original' cannot be retrieved as 'original' via its translation. If one test of multiculturalism is that it 'permits a multiplicity of social voices and a wide variety of their links and interrelationships' (Bakhtin 263) to coexist, the Multiculturalism Act fails. At first glance, it would seem that the Act/Loi attempts to 'put together' these contradictory discourses; that, as Hutcheon argues, 'Even if some people remain unconvinced that this act is not just paying lip-service to an undeniable social fact, or concealing assimilationist impulses behind a mask of tolerance, few would deny that its ideal is a worthy one' (1990, 13).

Yet, however 'worthy' the policy may be, if we keep in mind even some of the political subtexts behind it, it is quite apparent that the Act/Loi represents not an 'ideal' but a political effort to maintain the status quo. Hutcheon would call this interpretation a 'cynical response [that] is just too easy, and may not be fair' (1990, 15), but the question raised for me here is, fair to whom? And on what terms? Accepting the policy as an 'ideal' that is 'worthy' does not encourage us to probe into the concrete circumstances that have given rise to multiculturalism. Such acceptance is 'idealism as the act of idealizing—of envisioning and asserting goodness and perfection in the thing or person perceived' (Chow 1993b, 10). Idealizing the Act/Loi means looking at it only from the perspective of those who put it in place, adopting, as it were, their gaze. But since this is a gaze that has displayed a remarkable consistency in objectifying and containing Canadian Others, identification with it would not be an instance of mere complicity—a condition that, as Hutcheon's work on postmodernism has shown us, we cannot avoid—but rather an instance of what ˘   calls 'symbolic identification'. Symbolic identification marks 'the point from which we are observed', the point that 'dominates and determines the image' that we idealize and identify with (108). Because this image does not manifest itself in its entirety, what we identify with is 'inimitable, . . . eludes resemblance' (˘   109). We idealize it precisely because it seduces us by denying its history, by revealing only a positive image.

alerts us to the fact that 'names which *prima facie* signify positive descriptive features already function as "rigid designators"' (109). For this reason, 'every political demand is always caught in a dialectics in which it aims at something other than its literal meaning' (112). And in the same way the Act/Loi pretends to offer us a model of diversity that exceeds its limits while denying the liminality of dominant as well as minority subjectivities.

It is against the backdrop of these differential relations that the main text of the Multiculturalism Act is introduced. The Act/Loi is framed by eight 'preambles' that subordinate it to such legal covenants as the Constitution and the Canadian Human Rights Act. This framing, I suggest, is crucial for two reasons: it shows the Act/Loi to participate in a process of repetition and interpretation; and it discloses, albeit obliquely, the historical materiality of Otherness in Canada. Yet the fact that the legislation itself is preceded by these preambles affirms the anteriority of the national imaginary to ethnicity. Because the Act/Loi does not introduce a disjunctive present in its representations of national will and ethnicity, its function is both descriptive and prescriptive. 'Prescriptive texts are as amenable to interpretation as descriptive ones' (Fiss 751), but the prescriptiveness of legal texts suggests that '[l]egal interpretation seeks to resolve ambiguity' (Brest 770).[28] Irrespective of the ambiguities inherent in its language, law by definition commands obedience. What the policy's declared purpose—to 'recognize and promote the understanding that multiculturalism reflects the cultural and racial diversity of Canadian society'—demands is that we comply with its construction of ethnicity. Compliance in this instance would amount to acquiescent complicity, the kind that gives in to a totalized view of history. The Act/Loi enunciates what constitutes the nation, thus repeating its history, while it totalizes ethnicity by practising a 'syntax of forgetting': 'To be obliged to forget—in the construction of the national present—is not a question of historical memory; it is the construction of a discourse on society that *performs* the problem of totalizing the people and unifying the national will' (Bhabha 1994, 160-1). It is in this context that I would like to explore how the two main premises behind the Act/Loi—the ethnic subject's resistance to acculturation within a state that forgets it is still attempting to define itself, and the perceived potential of ethnicity to infiltrate dominant culture—work to legitimize ethnicity.

Legal Positivism and Pan-Canadianism

To legislate on ethnicity is to signal both a recognition of existing diversities and a desire to govern, to regulate, the phenomenon of disparity. The Multiculturalism Act, then, operates as what Bhabha calls 'the nation as a form of narrative—textual strategies, metaphoric displacements, sub-texts and figurative strategems' (1990a, 2). Such a nation-narrative, however, does not operate rhetorically alone, as the figures of Bhabha's statement may suggest at first glance. Its rhetoric of articulation serves the politics of the prescriptive act it performs. Thus the intent to legislate on ethnicity begs a double question of apostrophe. To whom does the Act address itself? As for the referents of ethnicity, is multiculturalism postulated as the supplement to a dominant culture that is persistently concealed by the Act's discourse? Or is it unwittingly posited as the Canadian culture par excellence, since we have been told that there is no official culture?

The Multiculturalism Act apostrophizes 'all Canadians, whether by birth or by choice'. But if 'all Canadians' are indeed the subject of apostrophe here, and if the Act makes multiculturalism the subject of its discourse in that it 'reflects the cultural and racial diversity of Canadian society', ethnicity strikes a bizarre figure. It appears to be a sign of the equality of 'all Canadians' under the letter of the law—a sign of its totalization—but also a strategic gesture.

Treated as a sign of equality, ethnicity loses its differential role. Instead, it becomes a condition of commonality: what 'all Canadians' have in common is ethnic difference. As an all-embracing concept, ethnicity ceases to function as the counternarrative that it has been. No longer a thorn discomfiting Canada's nation-narrative, it affirms that 'multiculturalism is a fundamental characteristic of the Canadian heritage and identity.' It would appear, then, that ethnicity is what sustains Canada's national imaginary. But since the Act endorses, and appropriates, *ethnos* by teasing out a presumably neutral meaning, its inscription of ethnicity within homogeneous time raises more questions than it resolves. Canada is conceptualized as a nation-narrative whose mark of difference consists not in hybridity but in yet another kind of commonality: 'all Canadians' are members of the same *ethnos*, Canada. This statement, however, is historically both true and false. It is true in that 'all Canadians' are, at least technically, members of equal standing within the state of Canada. But the statement is also false in that it dehistoricizes the social and political conditions that have discriminated against many Canadians, the same conditions that, through colonial history, contributed to the formation of the Canadian state. Moreover, it is belied by the fact that many Canadians reside within the space of the hyphen; whether it is immediately perceptible or not, fully embraced or brimming with ambivalence, the hyphen is the sign of diaspora. A figure at once of double allegiances and 'reciprocal displacement' (Radhakrishnan 1996, xiii), it does not necessarily suggest an identity crisis. Instead, it dramatizes the disjunctiveness of history, and the composite genealogies of the self. Ironically, the Act's double-dealing with history is consistent with Canada's mis/appropriation of ethnicity, a good example of the way legal discourse embodies the materiality of cultural difference. What happens when the sign of ethnicity is posited as an agent that circulates freely within a nation that, with regard to ethnicity, constructs itself as a general-economy state, a state whose cultural and political practices cannot be reduced to rigid formulations?

The first apparent result of this construction process is that ethnicity becomes manifest as something residual to the make-up of Canada, hence not a sign of contestation. Seen in this way, the Act would appear to be a paean to the Canadian *ethnos*. Not intended to appear as a remedial act, although in fact we know it to be one, it recognizes and advocates a sort of pan-Canadianism through a universalizing rhetoric evidenced by the recurrence of such phrases as 'all members of Canadian society'. By releasing 'all Canadians' from the specificity of their histories, this legal document seeks to overcome difference rather than to confront incommensurability. Belying its intent to address systemic inequities, it executes an emancipatory gesture in the name of homogeneity and unity.

This process is the result of the Act's reliance on legal positivism. Although, as Chief Justice Antonio Lamer of the Supreme Court of Canada remarked, the kind of '[l]egal positivism [that] says that what is right is what the law says is right' was ended in Canada in 1982 by the Charter of Rights and Freedoms, it would seem that the Act still operates within this mode. By pretending to construct an image of Canada without interpreting it—by relying, as it were, on the premise that its discourse has a 'plain meaning' (Cornell 1137)—the Act can legislate on ethnicity while bracketing the history of ethnicity by *naturalizing* 'all Canadians'. In legal positivism there is 'an implicit belief that there is usually a plain and obvious meaning to the words that make up the precedents, the statuses, and the regulations'. Thus 'law rests on the acceptance of the "master rule of recognition"' according to which the meaning of the law is self-evident. (Cornell 1137). It would be too easy, then, to argue that the Act simply reproduces what it attempts to remedy; instead, it overdetermines ethnicity. Thus it mimics not so much the desire of diasporic Canadians to be treated with equality and dignity as it does the dominant society's tendency to regulate difference.

From this perspective, the Multiculturalism Act postulates cultural relativism as defined by Gutmann, as a process that 'relies upon the standard of dominant understandings, . . . identif[ies] justice with the social understandings of dominant groups, . . . [and] implicitly denies that justice can serve as a critical standard to assess dominant understandings' (176). Precisely because there is no cohesive social understanding, cultural relativism 'does not fulfill its promise of dissolving multicultural conflicts' (Gutmann 178). Thus the all-inclusiveness of the Act's apostrophe, far from redistributing cultural power within the Canadian state, asserts the state's own power as law.

The Act's address to 'all Canadians' can also be interpreted as signalling the intent of this legal discourse to make ethnicity palatable to the dominant society; or, to put it more subtly, to operate pedagogically by showing ethnicity to have a normative function. This is clear in the Act's recognition of 'the diversity of Canadians as regards race, national or ethnic origin, colour and religion'. Despite this acknowledgement, the Act addresses no specific group of Canadians as ethnic. Only in the clause about 'the existence of communities whose members share a common origin and their historic contribution to Canadian society', and in the two instances when the words 'minorities' and 'minority' are used, can we infer a non-integral relation between these 'communities' and 'Canadian society', a relation in which ethnicity is inscribed as a differential sign.

It is no coincidence that nowhere in the Act is there a reference to immigrants. As Harney remarks, 'Leaders have generally preferred to think of those they represent as ethnic groups rather than immigrant groups since *immigrant* conjures up the thresholds of acculturation while *ethnic* implies a permanent quality of otherness' (68). The assumption here is that immigrants are outsiders whose differences are defined by their origins, while the differences of ethnic subjects are defined by the surrounding culture. This (un)naming gesture reinforces the legal discourse that absorbs ethnicity into a formal and situational policy—one of the ways in which the Act sets in place the technology that produces a disciplinary image of ethnicity. The ethnic subject becomes undifferentiated, and therefore essentialized. When law and culture meet, the (un)naming of the ethnic subject speaks of the ongoing crisis that marks both legislation on multiculturalism and ethnicity itself.

The strategic fashion in which the policy addresses 'all Canadians' irrespective of their diasporic origins places the ethnic subject in a fictional position. The marginality of the groups that the Multiculturalism Act seeks to protect is nullified by its rhetoric of normalization. The 'norm', François Ewald argues, 'is related to power, but it is characterized less by the use of force or violence than by an implicit logic that allows power to reflect upon its own strategies and clearly define its objects' (139). Defining ethnic subjects by normalizing them stresses those elements of their subjecthood that conform to 'Canadianness' rather than those about which they beg to differ.

This strategy is in keeping with the Act's intention to construct ethnicity through a collective subjecthood and thus to institutionalize the 'minority' status of diasporic Canadians. Although many clauses in the policy refer to 'individuals and communities', much emphasis is placed on 'communities', 'organizations', and 'institutions' that represent the 'diverse cultures of Canadian society'. The 'Implementation' section of the Act declares that the minister responsible for multicultural affairs is expected to 'encourage and assist individuals, organizations and institutions to project the multicultural reality of Canada in their activities in Canada and abroad'. Yet if we hear echoes of the White Paper in this clause, it becomes obvious that the individuality of a person is measured and acknowledged primarily through that person's ties to a specific community. 'The royal commission,' the White Paper says, 'was guided by the belief that adherence to one's ethnic group is influenced not so much by one's origin or mother tongue as by one's sense of belonging to the group, and by what the commission calls the group's "collective will to exist". The government shares this belief' (8545). Clearly, this declaration reflects the state's desire to forge a collective image of ethnicity, an image intended to construct a state that is at once centralized and decentred in that it is situated within the spaces linking the communities of the various ethnic groups. While in the official bilingualism and biculturalism policies 'origin', French or English, is treated as a natural law, official multiculturalism suspends the importance of mother tongue and ethnic origin.

What, then, is to promote the cohesiveness the Act assumes to be necessary for the definition of a community? Moreover, what constitutes the Canadianness of subjects who share a language and origin other than English or French? The Act remains silent on these matters, except in the slippages that appear when we look at how the policy is to be implemented. The minister responsible 'may', among other things, 'assist ethno-cultural minority communities to conduct activities with a view to overcoming any discriminatory barrier and, in particular, discrimination based on race or national or ethnic origin'. In asserting the fight against racism to be one of the principal imperatives of multiculturalism, this statement confirms what various legislators and politicians have taken pains over the years to deny, namely that there is a dominant culture, a culture whose dominance is implicit in the 'discriminatory barrier[s]' it erects when confronted with the Other Canadians. This is a moment in the Act when its construction of Canada as a general-economy state vis-à-vis ethnicity is disrupted. The empirical element introduced by the words 'discriminatory barrier' produces a difference where previously there was none. The Act yields to history (albeit in too mild a fashion), but this isn't to say that its pledge to facilitate the 'overcoming' of discrimination necessarily corresponds to anti-racist work, or that the state openly acknowledges its complicity with systemic discrimination. The counter-archive that emerges at this point is produced only by the Act's nod at the historical legacy of racial and ethnic relations in Canada, a gesture that shows the Act to be a double inscription of history: the history of discrimination that belongs to 'minority' Canadians insofar as they have been on the receiving end of its effects, and the discriminatory, and therefore disciplinary, history of Canada's dominant culture.

Hailed by the Law: 'Sorry, you've got the wrong person.'

What is important in this double inscription of history is the way the policy proposes to manage its supposed generalized notion of ethnicity by practising a restricted-economy approach. That is, it sets out to apply to ethnicity a proceduralism that is informed by the privileged values of conservation and restraint. It is hardly coincidental that the two central sections of the Multiculturalism Act, 'Multiculturalism Policy of Canada' and 'Implementation of the Multiculturalism Policy of Canada', are marked by repeated reference to 'preservation', 'enhancement', and 'sharing'. More than anything else about the policy, these concepts have been embraced as offering a (facile) interpretation of multiculturalism and at the same time they have elicited vigorous criticism. Every time they appear in the Act—and more often than not they appear as a threesome—they constitute a discursive site where 'ethnicity' designates at once a subject position and Canadian marginality. It is a site where multiculturalism is held together as a manifestation of legal positivism but also where it falls apart, and hence is fraught with ambivalence.

Louis Althusser's concrete example, the 'police (or other) hailing: "Hey, you there!"' (131), which he uses to illustrate that one is not a subject, not fully constituted as such, unless one is hailed by the law, discloses how the Act is able both to discover and to misrecognize ethnicity. As I've tried to show, the Act discovers ethnicity as a belated historical necessity. The result of its strategy of sedative politics, this discovery wields the power to 'recruit' (Althusser 130) the ethnic subject from his history of un(re)presentability, but in doing so it shows the law to be 'intolerant of its own history' (Derrida 1992, 194). Ethnic subjectivity as a delayed and summoned condition opposes the policy's pan-Canadianism. But, as Althusser argues, the law as an act of interpellation always 'contribute[s] to the same result: the reproduction of the relations of production' (117). Thus mobilized by the law itself, ethnic subjectivity emerges as a condition inhabiting the same discursive site in which it was previously silenced and discriminated against. Because representation is always the product of codes and values that are historically determined, it is inevitable that the enunciation of the ethnic subject can take place only within the same codes that have produced the law itself.

The policy may suspend subjectivity with one hand while granting it with the other, but this doesn't mean that we must see ethnic subjectivity as permanently reiterating the conditions of its historical marginality. Because the epistemic violence manifest here affects both the law and the ethnic subject, it becomes clear that the ethnic subject's agency is constructed 'in part through being implicated in the very relations of power that it seeks to oppose' (Butler 1997a, 382). Still, to recognize that the subject hailed by the law is us does not necessarily mean that we fully endorse the law's act of interpellation and the way it designates us as subjects. 'What if,' Terry Eagleton asks, 'we return the reply: "Sorry, you've got the wrong person"?' (Eagleton 145). Or we may reply, 'That's me, but you've got my name wrong'; or vice versa, 'You've got my name right, but I'm not what you think I am'. Eagleton is right to draw our attention to this blind spot in Althusser's theory of interpellated subjectivity, for 'there is no reason why we should always accept society's identification of us as this *particular* sort of subject' (Eagleton 145).

Thus in the case of the Multiculturalism Act, identifying with the subject as defined by the law does not necessarily mean conceding to the ways the law constructs us. This identification entails a double recognition: recognition of the way ethnic subjectivity has been historically inscribed, and recognition of the fact that those historical designations involve misrecognition. This is why the ethnic subject must continue to reside within the same regime of history that has caused his marginality: not in order to keep insisting on his position of victimage, which would amount to reifying his interpellation, but in order to 'disarticulate . . . [his] position in the discourse of "multiculturalism"' (Stuart Hall 1992, 257). The disavowal of what grants the ethnic subject a conditional agency involves an epistemic shift, a reversal, from his interpellation as ethnic and a move towards articulating his misrecognition. This involves disobeying the law,[29] deciphering its blind spots, and writing into them ethnic subjectivity not as a disciplinary condition but as one that develops through and against the law, in effect by disciplining law itself.

The triad of 'preservation', 'enhancement', and 'sharing' occurs at the conjunction of this recognition and misrecognition, the place where at once the law attempts to discipline ethnicity and the ethnic subject must inscribe her resistance. 'Preservation' endows the ethnic subject with a stability that belies the incommensurability of identity. Consistent with the other contradictions embedded in the Act, the insistence on 'preservation' affirms the history of ethnic subjectivity as a differential sign, but it does so by appropriating that difference. While no subject can exist outside the history that has produced her, history is imaged here as a finished product—for how else could it be 'preserved'? Also implicit in this image of history is the notion of ethnicity as a permanent condition; this suggestion of permanence disguises the law's hailing act while ignoring the impact and discontinuities effected by diaspora. Since these particularities are put under erasure, the difference of the ethnic subject's history is obviously determined in relation to the history of the dominant society. Thus the policy inserts a break in historical continuity by locating ethnicity at the limits of dominant history, but it also posits history as a totalization 'dependent on a notion of chronology which assumes a synchronic homogeneous notion of time' (Robert Young 1990, 46). Both gestures point to what Spivak calls '"[r]eified" history', 'our monumentalized national-cultural history of origin' (1997, 471). 'Preservation' of ethnicity, then, can operate only through 'a syntax of forgetting', a syntax that pays no heed to historical discontinuities, that forgets that all the events in a series do not necessarily belong to the same temporality. Keeping in mind the Act's pan-Canadianism, multiculturalism then advocates the coexistence of different, unrelated, and totalized histories within a homogeneous time—hardly a plausible proposition.

That the Act's appeal for the 'preservation' of ethnicity has been embraced by some ethnic communities and attacked by others with equal vehemence shows that not all subjects respond in the same way to the legitimation of their differences. The 'preservation' of ethnicity lodges the ethnic subject within a museum case because of a 'heritage'—another touchstone in the Act—that is presumed to be stable and unambiguous, and therefore easily reproducible. Such a notion of heritage implies that what differentiates minority communities in Canada from the mainstream is that they hold on to unitary lineages of tradition, that they live through homogeneous and neatly shaped histories. In reality, though, this notion of heritage is a far cry from the unproblematic recycling of 'authentic' features in an ethnic community's self-identification. Rather, it is a contaminated heritage, as its cultural expressions are inevitably decontextualized, and are the result of an overdetermined promotion of ethnicities that says as much about the Canadian state as it does about the origins of ethnic communities themselves.

The Politics of Heritage:
Greek Canadian Folk Dancing as a Case Study

Caterina Pizanias' study of Greek folk dances in Canada is a good example of the way heritage is pruned and tended before it is performed for the audience of the host country. When the performative manifestations of heritage are viewed not only in the present tense of their performance but also diachronically and across cultures, then we may encounter what Pizanias calls 'the arbitrariness' of that heritage: 'when we go public, so to speak, as Greeks in multicultural Canada, we are expected to perform a heritage that in many ways is as awkward, foreign, and exotic to us as it is to our audiences' (17). Ironically, such performances, while considered to project a unified image of a given ethnic community, disidentify many of its members; this irony is not one we can attribute exclusively to the erosion that heritage undergoes when it travels or when it is manipulated by the host country. Rather, it points to the way the inescapable cultural markers of diasporic imaginaries are often invested with deterministic agendas. These agendas are responsive to official multiculturalism's call for impermeable ethnic identities, but they also convey a unified front with respect to what is deemed exportable from the country of origin. Pizanias' study focuses precisely on the very historical discontinuities that the Multiculturalism Act wilfully suspends. This is the reason why she examines the politics of 'cultural brokers' in Canada in general, and in the Greek Canadian community in particular.

While Pizanias was invited to work with a Greek Canadian community in the areas of contemporary Greek poetry and theatre, she very quickly learned that government *funding was plentiful if the group was involved in folkloric activities*—such as dance—*but there was almost no funding for contemporary poetry* and/or Greek theater. The problem was that I neither knew much about nor cared to learn folk dancing, something I had never done in Greece outside the mandatory lessons during basic schooling. But the opportunities to obtain grants for costumes, travel, and teaching were tempting, so 'folklore' sustained our main interests. Because of our *expected participation in heritage celebrations*, I began inviting dance instructors from eastern Canada, the United States, and even Greece to teach us how to dance. (12; my emphasis)

Support for folklore promotes the exotic image of Others—a view that has become commonplace. The availability of funds and the media's readiness to report on such heritage performances create a web of complicitous relations and dubious obligations that guarantees the 'preservation' and 'enhancement' only of the kind of culture that fits the fictionality of the diasporic subject as imaged by the state. At the same time, though, it is important to consider some of the implications of this sanctioned exoticism. One thing implied here is that the promotion of folkloric cultural expressions prevents ethnic subjects from maintaining or discovering contemporary expressions of their original culture. The intention may be to foster a tighter bond with the adopted country, but the result is the construction of folklore as the ethnic subjects' only 'contact zone'[30] with both their country of origin and their new country.

Folklore, then, is employed both to obscure and to reveal. Endorsed and promoted as the most transparent form of cultural authenticity, it can also lead to cultural insiderism,[31] an absolute belief in essential differences. It encourages and feeds the sort of nostalgia that results in cultural mutation, locking ethnic subjects between 'here' and 'there' while feigning to resolve their fragmentation. Thus even as it affords them the opportunity to celebrate and share their heritage, it detemporalizes them, creating the semblance of historical continuity, in effect a form of hegemonic modernity. If this is the function of heritage festivals in an official multicultural state, what does folklore signify for the diasporic communities themselves?

From the perspective of ethnic communities, I suggest, folklore plays an equally ambivalent role. As a one-time member of the Greek Canadian community in Edmonton and a former artistic director of its dance group for young adults, Pizanias realizes that the '"correctness" and "authenticity"' of folk dancing 'boiled down to nominal variations stemming not from historical research but from the technical abilities of the teacher/dancer/keeper of tradition for any given dance' (13). Moreover, whereas Pizanias wished to include in the performance group 'anyone who wanted to dance', community members reminded her that

back in the village participation . . . depended on generational, kinship, and gender matters, not on some outsider's decision. . . . For them the performances were an opportunity for their daughters to dress in the old ways, an opportunity to show off their children rather than to live up to some aesthetic ideas of an 'outsider'. . . . They were looking for a connection with their past village life, and all they were getting were polished stage productions. (14)

It may seem that the community's perception of folklore reveals some aspects of the social and gender structure of Greek culture, but the point here is that those structures are usually determined by regional and class factors—as is the case with most folkloric traditions. As Pizanias' experience testifies, they should not be taken to represent a singular Greek identity.

What is performed on Canadian stages as Greek folk dance was (and still is in some rural locations) an integral part of life in Greece, one whose meanings and aesthetic shapes are now, by definition, unlivable and resistant to narrativization. If the Canadian state's emphasis on folklore as authentic heritage involves a pedagogy whose objective is to teach diasporic subjects how to practise and perform their ethnicity, this is the kind of pedagogy that promotes totalized knowledge while showing the state remaining wilfully ignorant of the diversities inherent in ethnic communities.[32] Folklore, in this context, produces a normative cultural narrative; it becomes a portmanteau, a carry-all from the old country in which cultural values and images are preserved in supposedly pure condition. But as Pizanias demonstrates, this carry-all is in fact a Pandora's box.

Pizanias' research shows that what constitutes contemporary Greek folk dancing in the Greek diaspora is largely the elaborate construction of a single woman, Dora Stratou, in collaboration with the ideological values of official politics in Greece at the time. '[A] ballet dancer in the mould of Martha Graham and Isadora Duncan', Stratou was 'Greece's John Murray Gibbon' (26).[33] She 'put together a spectacular stage show' of 'hundreds of dances and collected dozens of costumes' from various regions of Greece, 'regardless of the effects the decontextualizing and dispersement might have [had] on the originating village tradition, or . . . on the audience' (26). The show proved popular among Greeks and tourists alike. What is crucial here is, first, the fervour with which the Greek diaspora responded to Stratou's travelling troupe—here was a flamboyant way in which to 'enhance' and 'share' their ethnic image—and, second, the fact that Stratou's project involved tracing the origins of Greek folk dance to antiquity. Her objective was to authenticate the continuity of Greek history,[34] an enterprise that many studies of Greek folklore by both Greek and non-Greek specialists have shown to be fraudulent.[35] Integral to Pizanias' argument is that Stratou's project was supported by, and was also the ideological product of, the political agenda of the 1967–74 fascist military regime. But while many of the spectators in Greece were in a position to separate the aesthetic pleasure provided by Stratou from her facile nationalism, audiences in the diaspora do not have ready access to the political referents of such events. Not only is it difficult to know and evaluate the historical and cultural aspects of a performance, but the history behind a performance may, consciously or unconsciously, be concealed—just as the heritage that the Multiculturalism Act expects ethnic Canadians to celebrate is sanitized, deprived of its historical contingencies. Pizanias' cross-cultural reading not only reveals the commodification of ethnic differences but points out how the performance of Greek heritage can be understood, ironically, as an element in the Greek state's own constructions of nationalism at that time.

I am not suggesting that every performance of ethnic heritage is traceable to similar instances of carefully manufactured national imaginaries turned ethnic in the diaspora. Nonetheless, Pizanias' study does illustrate how the 'preservation', 'enhancement', and 'sharing' of ethnic heritage constitute a performance that may very well repeat narratives of dubious genealogy. These narratives often develop into master narratives (if they are not so already) because of their iterative function and their representation of collectivities. The point here is not that these heritage festivals ought to be abandoned because there is something inherently suspect in folklore. Rather, I wish to stress the need to view folkloric culture, especially the kind that travels through diaspora, not as an unadulterated manifestation of a community's purity—which would amount to a reductive response to the rich complexity of folklore—but as a palimpsest where various histories and intentions may be inscribed.

Such heritage festivals should be distinguished from events like Desh Pradesh, an annual festival and conference in Canada focusing on South Asian cultural practices in the West,[36] or arts projects like 'Self Not Whole: Cultural Identity and Chinese-Canadian Artists' and 'Racy Sexy: Race, Culture & Sexuality', both sponsored by the Chinese Cultural Centre in Vancouver.[37] Cultural events of this kind explore the imbrications of race, ethnicity, gender, and sexuality through contemporary art and politics. Their significance is three-fold: they create a critical dialogue among various diasporic artists, their respective communities, and the mainstream; they showcase art that might otherwise be ignored; and they engage with difference by exposing the historicity of history and of the present moment. The result is that such artists renegotiate their relations both with their own ethnic communities and with the dominant culture. Cultural exhibits of this kind intervene in the well-controlled and total-ized image of the representation of ethnicity. At the same time that they question exhibition as a medium of cultural representation, they give us access to the multiple gazes through which culture is produced.

Heritage and Diasporic Mimicry

The danger I see in heritage performances lies as much in the patronage they receive under the Multiculturalism Act as in their immediate and subliminal effects on ethnic communities and the mainstream audience. Patronage in this instance is to be understood as perhaps the most important strategy of official multiculturalism's sedative politics. It furnishes proof of the circulation of ethnicity while securing for minority Canadians a space where they remain visible as Others. The emphasis is placed on reproducible and therefore reductive heritage images, precisely because they are seen as reflecting a past irrelevant to Canada's and therefore of little, if any, political pertinence to Canadian culture. Such displays of difference promote a fetishization of ethnic imaginaries: they cast minority Canadians as objects of national voyeurism by keeping them, as it were, under surveillance. Not only do these displays appear to be easy targets for the rhetoric of disavowal and scandal I discussed earlier, but they also fail to register how some ethnic subjects resist their definition by the law. Instead, they function as discourses of mimicry, but mimicry not exactly as defined by Bhabha. In fact, they reverse the structural relation at the core of Bhabha's 'mimic man', imaged as an Indian civil servant educated in English who projects a familiar yet distorted image of his colonizers.

For Bhabha, 'mimicry emerges as the representation of a difference that is itself a process of disavowal. Mimicry is thus the sign of a double articulation; a complex strategy of reform, regulation and discipline, which "appropriates" the Other as it visualizes power' (1994, 86). The 'profound and disturbing' effect of Bhabha's mimicry, and therefore its value, depends on its visualizing the cultural markers of those in power in a fashion that unsettles power dynamics. By contrast, the mimicry in heritage displays has no such efficacy: subject and object here are one and the same, for the ethnic subject reproduces herself through a self-defined form of ethnicity. Because of this identification, the ambivalence that marks Bhabha's mimicry is not necessarily present in what I call diasporic mimicry. The 'ambivalence of mimicry', for Bhabha, resides in the 'area between mimicry and mockery, where the reforming, civilizing mission is threatened by the displacing gaze of its disciplinary double' (86). Keeping in mind the Greek Canadian example discussed above, I would point out that mockery is not a trope employed in diasporic mimicry; instead, the operative trope there is a discourse of authenticity, a discourse intended to project ethnicity as what defines a sovereign identity. But because this sovereignty often takes on an image of voided history, diasporic mimicry functions ironically, at the expense of the ethnic subject herself. While the value of Bhabha's mimicry lies in its potential to disturb 'certain forms of stereotyping', enabling power and producing loss of agency (Robert Young 1990, 147), diasporic mimicry tends to reinforce ethnic stereotypes. The agency lost here belongs to the domain of the ethnic subject, not that of mainstream culture. The mimicry performed by the 'preservation', 'enhancement', and 'sharing' of ethnic traditions is of the kind that, more often than not, maintains the dominant society's disciplinary gaze intact.

If colonial mimicry is a 'menace', it is because it speaks of the 'desire to emerge as "authentic"' while operating only as 'partial representation'. Its 'double vision . . . disclos[es] the ambivalence of colonial discourse [but] also disrupts its authority' (Bhabha 1994, 88). In diasporic mimicry, however, this disruption occurs primarily within the discursive site of ethnic communities, usually under the auspices of the Canadian state. For Lacan, who is the source of Bhabha's theory of mimicry and double vision, mimicry is a 'function of adaptation', but is not 'bound up with the needs of survival' (98 and 99). Lacan in turn follows Roger Caillois, who argues that mimicry is a 'drama' where 'the living creature . . . is no longer the origin of the coordinates . . . it is dispossessed of its privilege and liter-ally *no longer knows where to place itself*' (29). Thus the subject of mimicry experi-ences loss of identity as he 'feels himself becoming space . . . . He is similar, not similar to something, but just *similar*', a process Caillois calls '*depersonalization by assimilation to space*' (30). The ethnic subject as a simulacrum, then, lacks any agency whatsoever. From this perspective, heritage shows make visible the point where the ethnic subject's misrecognition by the law coincides, ironically, with his (mis)recognition of himself, an example of the misprision that occurs when self-identification functions as a response to the subject's legitimation.

The 'preservation' strategies of official multiculturalism do not guarantee that the survival of diasporic traditions will substantially alter the way ethnicity figures in the dominant society. Still, neither this lack of guarantee nor the bracketing of the ethnic subject's agency means that heritage shows as instances of diasporic mimicry necessarily lack the potential to introduce a differential, and therefore ambivalent, element as performances of diasporic self-representation. Along with simulating an ethnic community's own image, diasporic mimicry has the poten-tial, I suggest, to resist both how ethnic subjectivity has been stereotyped by dominant society and how diasporic identity is engineered by the nationalist agendas of the countries of origin. To accomplish this, it ought to undo its struc-ture as an apparently seamless history of identity, to resist submitting itself to the determinations of national imaginaries. Diasporic mimicry, then, should stress diaspora and the ideological mediations that inform it rather than the reproduc-tion of myths of undivided identities. To do this, it must remove the ethnic subject from the field of visibility where he operates as a pawn in the political gerrymandering of hegemonic intentions.

If I am stressing less the positive potential of diasporic mimicry than its negative function, it is because I think there is always something disfiguring that survives the performance of diasporic mimicry. This surviving element is what Lacan would call 'the stain' (74), what the mimicking subject imitates, namely himself. The subject 'becomes a stain, it becomes a picture, it is inscribed in the picture. This, strictly speaking, is the origin of mimicry' (99). Significantly, the stain is not something that can be seen. Thus in mimicry the subject's position is 'that of someone who does not see. The subject does not see where it is leading, he follows' (75). The stain leaves a 'track', 'a trace' we can follow, a 'thread' (74) we can unravel, but it never fully manifests itself. If it lacks the kind of visibility we can identify with, this is precisely because it belongs to the field of visuality, because it is what has already formed our image of ourselves, an image already *stained* by misrecognition. As Lacan says, 'the function of the stain and of the gaze is both that which *governs* the gaze most *secretly* and that which always *escapes* from the grasp of that form of vision that is *satisfied* with *itself* in imagining itself as consciousness' (74; my emphasis). The stain that marks diasporic mimicry survives in the metonymic way in which cultural displays relate to a community's ethnic self-image. It also survives in the space where the law and the ethnic subject encounter each other in their common desire to adjust reality, a desire whose performative function often reveals that desire and reality to be at odds with each other.

Mimicry, Lacan casually points out, depends on mutation (73). In diasporic mimicry, mutation 'enhances' the split of the ethnic subject from the dominant society, but it also reveals a split within ethnic communities. The latter is effected by official multiculturalism's strategy of constructing ethnicity in collective terms. Thus it recognizes a subject's ethnic difference only insofar as that subject identifies herself with a given, coherently structured, community. In this regard, the policy affirms diversity as a plurality of ethnic communities, but refrains from acknowledging that the ethnic communities are themselves plural. As heritage displays promote what Joan Scott calls 'false clarity' (19), so this homogenized image of ethnicity reflects a false community identity.

If community, as Iris Marion Young argues, 'is an understandable dream, expressing a desire for selves that are transparent to one another, relationships of mutual identification, social closeness and comfort' (300), the reality of that dream is that it 'always depends on excluding some elements, separating the pure from the impure' (303). This is the paradox in the Multiculturalism Act's pan-Canadianism. In this legitimation politics, the performance of ethnic identities in putatively authentic terms serves to keep diasporic communities totalized, and therefore manageable, but it also enables the state to argue for the authenticity of mainstream society. Authenticity bears the stain of much that is pernicious in identity politics, be it practised by the state or by ethnic communities themselves. By legitimizing cultural diversity, the Canadian Multiculturalism Act strives to lay the ground for an 'ideal' community. In this 'ideal' community, differences are granted nominal positions. Diversity is respected and supported only insofar as it is presumed to articulate subjects rehearsing collective identifications that are determined categorically and not relationally—precisely the point of the federal policy's sedative politics.

III
Charles Taylor's 'Multiculturalism'—and Herder

Western philosophy coincides with the disclosure of the other where the other, in manifesting itself as a being, loses its alterity. From its infancy philosophy has been struck with a horror of the other that remains other—with an insurmountable allergy.

Emmanuel Levinas (346-7)

Studying the Other

Having already examined what the legitimation of ethnic diversity entails in media and legal discourse, I would like now to consider how multiculturalism has been viewed at the other end of the cultural spectrum, that is, in philosophy. I will focus on Charles Taylor's 'The Politics of Recognition',[38] an essay that has elicited a lot of critical attention. 'The Politics of Recognition' presents a powerful, if troubling, argument about the need to support through legislation the survival of cultural minorities. If the media approach multiculturalism through disavowal and scandal, and the Multiculturalism Act does so through politically sedative strategies, Taylor enters the arena of multicultural debate by advocating a politics of critical judgement that will allow us to address 'marginalization without compromising our basic political principles' (63).

Taylor calls upon us to embark on 'the study of the other'.[39] 'There are other cultures,' he says, 'and we have to live together more and more, both on a world scale and commingled in each individual society' (72). This statement defines, at some level, his understanding of multiculturalism. As Himani Bannerji puts it, Taylor's recognition 'that many (perhaps too many) "others" have been allowed in, stretching the skin of tolerance' is an instance of 'plain realism' (1996, 112). In Kalpana Seshadri-Crooks's words, Taylor 'deplores as hypocritical at worst and condescending at best the form of multiculturalism that demands not just respect and recognition but equal worth before study' (50). What he's looking for is a median point 'between the inauthentic and homogenizing demand for recognition of equal worth . . . and the self-immurement within ethnocentric standards.' The answer seems to be what he calls 'the presumption of equal worth' (72). Taylor is being rhetorical when he claims he is 'not sure about the validity of demanding this presumption as a right' (68), for his essay makes it abundantly clear that this presumption is 'logically' wrong. Hence he argues in favour of a study of the other. The purpose of studying the other is to determine whether a minority culture deserves recognition of equal worth. As I understand the logic of the 'multicultural' pedagogy he is proposing, a minority culture is deemed worthy until proven unworthy; the other, then, is placed in the position of defendant. The question raised here is whether the minority subject as an object of study would place the dominant society in the role of judge, prosecution, or jury.

Taylor's attention to the other comes from his recognition that 'Western liberal societies are thought to be supremely guilty . . . partly because of their colonial past, and partly because of their marginalization of segments of their populations that stem from other cultures' (63). Significantly, he is unwilling to address the imperative to examine the way history, as told by the dominant society, has muted minority subjects and mutated their sense of culture. His argument is a response to 'what is today called the politics of "multiculturalism"' (25), to the '*awkwardness* [that] arises from the fact that there are substantial *numbers of people* who are *citizens* and also belong to the culture that calls into question *our* philosophical boundaries' (63; my emphasis). Taylor rejects the kind of 'liberalism' that advocates 'cultural neutrality' as an answer to this 'awkwardness'; instead, he 'espouse[s]' his 'hospitable variant' (62) of 'nonprocedural liberalism' (63)— 'hospitable' because of its willingness to make '[s]ubstantive distinctions' (62) based on study of the other.

There is an irony in Taylor's calling his nonprocedural liberalism 'hospitable', which is reinforced by the implicit distinction he draws between 'our philosophical boundaries' and 'how we do things here' (63). Implied in this formulation is the paradigm of Us and Them, 'Them' referring to persons 'whose center is elsewhere', 'people' he calls 'citizens', thus juxtaposing their legal status to the homologous relationship between 'Us' and the state. Suffice it to say that this distinction does not alter the status of those 'citizens' (irrespective of the fact that 'substantial numbers' of them may very well have been born within 'our' state) as other to the dominant position occupied by Taylor's 'we'. The hospitality he extends to them renders him a host to their parasitic existence.

Notwithstanding his 'hospitable' gesture, host and parasite here are not imaged in Serres's terms, where the two are inextricably interrelated. For Serres, the parasite is always 'at home' (156), while 'the host is both the local man and the stranger' (221). This paradoxical reciprocity, Serres tells us, speaks of 'the theory of relations' (185) where what is conventionally seen as disorder is the order of things (167). Because the parasite is always defined by its proximity to the host— 'para- means "near", "next to", measures a distance. The *sitos* is the food' (144)— it is an integral part of the 'circulation' (161) and exchange that define their relations. Determined by an organic interrelationship, the parasite's proximity to the host allows it to function as 'the active operator and the logical operation of evolution, of the irreversible time of life' (188).

For Taylor, though, this proximity is 'disturbing' (63), makes 'awkward' waves. His recognition that 'all societies are becoming increasingly multicultural, while at the same time becoming more porous' (63) is underlain by anxiety. In view of the fact that the 'commingling' of disparate cultures may already have resulted in what we could call a community of those who have nothing in common,[40] Taylor is anxious to reconcile the local with the global traffic that disturbs the former's cohesiveness, and to do so without resorting to compromises that may further disturb what produces that cohesiveness in the first place.

The fact that he locates the departure point of his study of the other in global traffic discloses some of Taylor's presumptions, notably his belief that a culture— his example is that of Quebec—reserves the right to design policies for its 'cultural survival'. These policies include 'actively seek[ing] to *create* members of the community' (58-9) who will guarantee the continuance of that culture. Despite, or because of, his nonprocedural liberalism, Taylor's project with regard to minority rights, like the project of the Multiculturalism Act, is reactive rather than proactive. Serres's teasing challenge, 'Harmony gathers what noises kept apart. . . . You shall love the odor of others' (145), would be diametrically opposed to the route Taylor proposes to take towards recognition of the equal worth of others.

Taylor's attempt to defend the 'preservation' (58) of a culture such as Quebec's demands a delicate, if not perilous, balancing act. He believes that a culture has a moral duty to shield itself from forces that may undermine its 'integrity' (61) and render it 'porous'. But he also wishes to legitimate this goal 'without this being seen as a depreciation of those who do not personally share . . . [that culture's] definition' (59). This double objective, together with Taylor's rejection of 'a liberalism of rights . . . inhospitable to difference' (60), may explain the nature of the pedagogical strategy that he proposes. Recognition of diversity, he suggests, ought to entail 'a willingness to be open to comparative cultural study of the kind that must displace our horizons in the resulting fusions' (73). The conclusion of his essay, this would appear to be a welcome alternative to the federal policy's approach to ethnic heritage. The problem is that, notwithstanding Taylor's call for a multicultural pedagogy, there is little if anything in his essay about how this study ought to proceed. Indeed, his attempt to reconcile the 'resulting fusions' of such a study with his double emphasis on the authentic self and minority groups' demand for equal recognition shows his 'multicultural' pedagogy to be unworkable.

The 'Authenticity' of the Modern Self

The difficulties in Taylor's essay arise as much from the lacunae in his philosophical argument as from his methodology. Taylor's argument is elaborate and condensed, but it is not only the compressed way in which he sails through 'multiculturalism' (which he frames in scare quotes) that raises questions. The impetus behind his thinking here, as in his earlier work, is his desire to establish a linear trajectory of the modern self's development, a history securely rooted within one strain of the Western tradition. More specifically, the philosophical anchors of his argument are Montesquieu, Rousseau, Hegel, and Herder, along with Trilling's concept of authenticity in *Sincerity and Authenticity* and Bakhtin's dialogism. Thus the philosophical background of 'The Politics of Recognition' is not particularly original in the Taylor canon. Indeed, *Sources of the Self: The Making of the Modern Identity* (1989), *The Ethics of Authenticity* (1992), *The Malaise of Modernity* (1991), and *Reconciling the Solitudes: Essays on Canadian Federalism and Nationalism* (1993) outline in greater depth and detail the philosophical traditions from which Taylor's notions of selfhood and authenticity are derived.[41]

Taylor has explored the history of the modern self with remarkable consistency and force. Yet his insistence on seeing the modern self in terms of epistemic shifts that are answerable only to the same epistemes undermines his argument. Taylor traces 'the modern preoccupation with identity and recognition' to 'the collapse of social hierarchies, which used to be the basis for honor. . . . For some to have honor . . . it is essential that not everyone have it' (26-7). In the modern era, however, 'Democracy has ushered in a politics of equal recognition [and] dignity. The underlying premise here is that everyone shares in it' (27). Few would disagree with Taylor's insistence on the importance of understanding what constitutes identity before attempting to recognize the dignity and respect that the identities of others demand.

Nevertheless, tensions arise when his argument begins to swerve toward what becomes its centre, 'the ideal of "authenticity"' (28):

> There is a certain way of being human that is *my* way. I am called upon to live my life in this way, and not in imitation of anyone else's life. (30)

> Being true to myself means being true to my own originality, which is something only I can articulate and discover. In articulating it, I am also defining myself. I am realizing a potentiality that is properly my own. This is the background understanding to the modern ideal of authenticity, and to the goals of self-fulfillment and self-realization in which the ideal is usually couched. (31)

Here the self is imaged as a whole; 'originality' attests to the self's unitary essence; and 'authenticity', 'properly' articulated, is a guarantee that the self's wholeness remains undisturbed. This definition clearly dispels any notion that the self is marked by alterity. It may be Taylor's concept of the modern self, but behind this modernity lies the phantasm of humanism, the legacy of which has a lot to do with multicultural politics today.

Taylor sees Fanon as one of 'the key authors' who have inaugurated the 'transition' (65) to our age, an age in which 'the demand for recognition is now explicit' (64). This reference would seem to suggest an acknowledgement of humanism's responsibility for the construction of marginalities, but Taylor offers only a cursory and reductive treatment of *The Wretched of the Earth*. Indeed, his representation of Fanon's discourse on violence comes close to being a wilful misreading. Fanon, Taylor tells us,

> argued that the major weapon of the colonizers was the imposition of their image of the colonized on the subjugated people. These latter, in order to be free, must first of all purge themselves of these depreciating self-images. Fanon recommended violence as the way to this freedom, matching the original violence of the alien imposition. (65)

It is ironic that Fanon, the only writer mentioned in 'The Politics of Recognition' who stands on the other side of the cultural divide from Taylor, is depicted here in a manner that recalls the same Manichean logic he himself so rigorously exposed.[42] At the same time that Taylor concedes that '[n]ot all those who have drawn from Fanon have followed him' in his call for violence, he creates a reductive image of Fanon that does not take into account either the historical contingencies of his argument or the question of agency. Taylor views Fanon's 'struggle for a changed self-image' as the 'main locus' in the debate over multicultural education (65). Beyond that, he doesn't pause to consider that when Fanon talks about violence he is not referring simply to the 'avalanche of murders' (Fanon 1967, 252) committed in the name of European colonization; nor is he referring only to the necessity for certain groups to engage in armed battle, or to the 'native intellectual tak[ing] part, in a sort of *auto-da-fé*, in the destruction of all his idols' (1967, 36). What determines the signification of violence in Fanon's work is, above all, the 'violence which is just under the skin' (1967, 55), the violence that 'hammered into the native's mind the idea of a society of individuals where each person shuts himself up in his own subjectivity, and whose only wealth is individual thought' (1967, 36). Many Fanon readers have paused to problematize his notion of violence; yet, even among his detractors, Taylor stands out for his tight grasp on a literal and therefore restrained meaning of violence.[43]

Fanon characterizes as 'narcissistic dialogue' (1967, 36) the humanistic ideologies that legitimated colonization and similar projects spurred on by the belief that the European concept of the essential self had universal value. It is strange, then, that Taylor pays no heed to that aspect of Fanon's argument nor to Sartre's preface to Fanon's book, which problematizes humanism. As Sartre wrote, throughout Fanon's argument 'the settler which is in every one of us is . . . savagely rooted out. . . . [W]e must face that unexpected revelation, the striptease of our humanism' (Fanon 1967, 21).[44] Despite Taylor's promise that he will approach these issues 'gently and gingerly' (44), the 'originality' and 'authenticity' that mark his notion of the modern self partake of the same humanistic tradition that Taylor's nonprocedural liberalism supports. This explains, in part, the vehemence with which he rejects what he calls the 'subjectivist, half-baked neo-Nietzschean theories . . . [d]eriving frequently from Foucault and Derrida' (70). In fact, rejection of the 'neo-Nietzschean standpoint' (66) has become a kind of tic in Taylor's work, an ironic *noblesse oblige* nod at precisely those shifts in philosophical and historical discourses that might point to a different understanding of why, as he puts it, the modern self is concerned 'not [with] the need of recognition but [with] the conditions in which the attempt to be recognized can fail' (35). This failure is, presumably, one possible outcome of the study of the other, if the other proves to fall short of the values of a dominant community imagined in totalized terms.

Taylor alludes to poststructuralist views of history and subject formation as 'radical' and lacking 'coherence' (66); they 'claim that all judgments of worth are based on standards that are ultimately imposed by and further entrench structures of power' (70). But they do so only when seen in Taylor's summary fashion. There are, as Thomas L. Dumm remarks, 'thoughtless' and '[t]houghtful "deconstructionists" . . . just like there are [thoughtful and] thoughtless liberals and communitarians' (170). In a facile way, Taylor reduces poststructuralism to a 'power and counterpower' (70) thesis. The easy alignment he makes between this notion and multiculturalism as a 'politics of difference' which 'asks that we give acknowledgment and status to something that is not universally shared' (39) discloses the problem of his reasoning to lie in a 'morality' that he takes to be indeed 'universally acknowledged', the universe of ideas here being a specific construct of Western thought, that is, rationalism.

That 'morality' is the issue in what Taylor considers to be the 'organic' flaw in 'neo-Nietzschean' theories is more clearly evident in *The Malaise of Modernity* (his Massey Lectures) than it is in 'The Politics of Recognition'. A long quotation is in order here:

> Morality as normally understood obviously involves crushing much that is elemental and instinctive in us, many of our deepest and most powerful desires. So there develops a branch of the search for authenticity that pits it against the moral. Nietzsche, who seeks a kind of self-making in the register of the aesthetic, sees this as quite incompatible with the traditional Christian-inspired ethic of benevolence. And he has been followed and exceeded by various attempts to champion the instinctual depths, even violence, against the 'bourgeois' ethic of order. Influential examples in our century are, in their very different ways: Marinetti and the Futurists, Antoine [sic] Artaud and his Theatre of Cruelty, and Georges Bataille. The cult of violence was also one of the roots of Fascism.
>
> So authenticity can develop in many branches. Are they all equally legitimate? I don't think so. I am not trying to say that these apostles of evil are simply wrong. They may be on to something, some strain within the very idea of authenticity, that may pull us in more than one direction. But I think that the popular 'postmodern' variants of our day, which have attempted to delegitimate horizons of significance, as we see with Derrida, Foucault, and their followers, are indeed proposing deviant forms. The deviancy takes the form of forgetting about one whole set of demands on authenticity while focussing exclusively on another. (1991, 65-6)

Of the philosophers and writers he mentions in this context, Foucault and Nietzsche are two that Taylor has given considerable attention to in his earlier work,[45] but, as is the case with Fanon, no elaboration is offered in 'The Politics of Recognition' relevant to the charges he lays against them. Taylor may be one of the most rigorous critics of the Enlightenment tradition today, but his caustic rhetoric and the trenchant manner in which he dismisses so-called neo-Nietzschean thought undermine his attempt to pose a 'coherent' history of the modern self. If anything, his method shows his insistence on 'coherence' to be suspect.

Taylor's notion of the modern self derives precisely from his overdetermined view of the history of philosophical and historical discourses that, when faced with contradictions, proceed to ignore or absorb them following the conventions of their own logic. While Taylor acknowledges that one of the 'sources' of the modernity of the self may be the need to recognize diversity, he considers this need to be fraught with perils. Thus he configures diversity as a 'source' of danger, because it threatens to realign the direction of the modern self's authenticity. 'The notion of authenticity,' he says, 'develops out of a displacement of the moral accent in this idea. . . . What I'm calling the displacement of the moral accent comes about when being in touch with our feelings takes on independent and crucial moral significance. It comes to be something we have to attain if we are to be true and full human beings' (28).

His juxtaposition of what he privileges about the modern self, namely its 'form of inwardness' (29), with the implied outwardness of diversity, shows in full relief that Taylor's objective in this essay is not multicultural politics as such but a general project of management. How to reconcile the individual self with a society whose purity has been disturbed by global traffic and that has therefore become too porous for its own 'good' (59); how to curtail, if possible, the very conditions that result in multicultural states; and how, in the case of horizons already fused, to develop 'new vocabularies of comparison, by means of which we can articulate' what we find 'strange and unfamiliar to us' about the others amongst us (67)—all these, as I understand Taylor's argument, constitute his mandate in the study of the other. In order to appreciate the implications of what these 'new vocabularies' would say, I would like to examine first how Taylor's modern self relates to its own community, and then how it responds to differences within its community.

Whither the 'Multicultural'?

A long-standing pursuit in Western thought, the attempt to reconcile what Taylor calls 'the intimate sphere' and 'the public sphere' (37) exposes one of the blind spots in his argument. Far from questioning a totalized notion of the self in relation to the construction of history, Taylor would seem to imagine a self resistant to the historical exigencies that effect change or require that it question what it holds dear. If 'the source we have to connect with is deep within us,' as Taylor argues (29), then, following this logic, it becomes obvious why diversity, whose 'source' is in the social, threatens to erode the modern self's responsibility to its authenticity. The problem with diversity today, as Taylor sees it, is that it applies pressure on the self to reconsider, and radically, its 'displacement of the moral accent'. This is the main reason why he casts diversity not only as a force with the potential to erode the modern self's accountability to its own originality, but also as a force that is partially responsible for what ails the modern self.

It becomes apparent at this point why Taylor eclipses both the problem-laden history of humanism and poststructuralism's differentiated notions of history and the formation of the subject. In fact, he practises the same kind of 'forgetting' of which he accuses neo-Nietzscheans. Perhaps this explains why 'multiculturalism' in this essay, far from referring to the broad spectrum of issues and perspectives that characterize the construction of ethnicity today, is largely synonymous with political correctness in both Canada and the United States. In fact, there is precious little in 'The Politics of Recognition' that displays intimate or scholarly knowledge of multicultural debates.[46] As Dumm points out, none of the other essays in the volume where Taylor's essay appears acknowledges 'any of the works of contemporary scholars associated with multiculturalism in the academy' (172).[47] One wonders, then, why a volume inclined to identify multiculturalism almost exclusively with practices that have come to be known as political correctness, and that is completely disinclined to address, even in passing, any of the recent scholarship on cultural diversity, was initially called *Multiculturalism and 'The Politics of Recognition'* and subsequently retitled simply *Multiculturalism*.

Along the same lines, Taylor's habit of addressing the demand for recognition by lumping together minority subjects and their groups (i.e., women and aboriginal people) is in keeping with a reductive view of history. As other critics of his work have noted, these groups may be minorities, but the differences among them cannot be neutralized by considering them all under the same rubric.[48] Taylor's methodology exacerbates his problematic use of the term 'multiculturalism': he is more concerned with the legislative implications of one cultural group's aspirations to become a sovereign nation (Quebec) than with the individual and collective rights of diasporic groups within a nation. That Fanon provides the only example (and a distorted one) of anti-colonialist discourse; that the only concrete example of multicultural conflict is an extreme one (whether 'one . . . forbids murder or allows it', the subject being 'the Rushdie controversy' [63]); and that Quebec's separatist movement virtually monopolizes the discussion, preventing any close attention to the historical realities of minorities in Canada, or elsewhere for that matter—all these factors disclose Taylor's dubious relationship to the historical realities he claims to address, as well as his indebtedness to a particular history of philosophy. These presences and absences function, in effect, as strategies of exclusion that sanction his version of the modern self.

In Dialogue with 'Others'

Related to these omissions and misreadings is an essential contradiction about Taylor's modern self. This contradiction is evident in his belief in an authentic and original self and his equally adamant position that the 'crucial feature of human life is its fundamentally *dialogical* character' (32). For Taylor, the modern self is characterized by its 'capacity to listen to [its] inner voice', by its penchant to 'find the model by which to live [. . .] within' itself, thus following 'the principle of originality' (30). Yet he also argues that 'We define our identity always in dialogue with, sometimes in struggle against, the things our significant others want to see in us' (32-3). This dialogue appears to be the first promising point in relation to the study of the other. It seems to evoke the process through which 'our standards' must be transformed before we set out to study 'a culture sufficiently different from our own' (67). For a moment, this dialogue may even appear to imply what we could call 'mutual interpellation'—not the Althusserian one-way apostrophe ('Hey, you there')—but a 'reciprocal address' that speaks of community (Fynsk in Nancy xxv).

I say 'appears' and 'seems' because Taylor's understanding of dialogue in this context does not suggest the kind of community that may result from 'mutual interpellation', community as 'nothing other than what undoes, in its very principle, . . . the autarchy of absolute immanence' (Nancy 4). Because Taylor's theory is unwilling to relinquish the self's originality, the immanence implied by the 'moral accent' on its authenticity forestalls the possibility of alterity. For Taylor, the self already has an inner knowledge of itself before it joins in dialogue with its significant others. In fact, it is the contradiction between the self's original/authentic core and its dialogic structure that points to what I find problematic in his 'multiculturalism'.

Taylor may rightly acknowledge that the 'genesis of the human mind is . . . not monological' (32) in that 'I negotiate [my own identity] through dialogue, partly overt, partly internal, with others' (34), but he falls short of arguing that the self is coextensive, co-originary, with the social. Hence his dialogism remains at odds with the self's originality. If the community of significant others were the originary point (the 'genesis') of the self, the self would not be able to claim that in 'articulating [my originality], I am also defining myself' (31). Beyond his general emphasis on the self's moral responsibility to remain authentic to itself, Taylor does not address what the self's own articulation entails, how the self performs its selfhood within society, and how its performative acts affect its significant others. His statement that '[w]e need relationships to fulfill, but not to define, ourselves' (33) suggests to me that the self stands apart from the sources of its fulfilment, wherever or however they may be found—that it doesn't 'fuse' with them.

Although Taylor repeatedly stresses his rejection of 'the monological ideal' (33), the authenticity of the self is left undisturbed by his notion of dialogism. In this scheme of things, the self's external and internal dialogue takes place within firmly established parameters, within a self-contained community. In the case of external dialogue, Taylor concedes that 'real judgments of [the other's] worth suppose a fused horizon of standards . . . ; they suppose that we have been transformed by the study of the other' (70). Still, he doesn't discuss how an authentic self can proceed to change its values while maintaining its authenticity immune to that change. What is more, when he writes about the 'demand . . . that we all *recognize* the equal value of different cultures' (64), culture is inscribed as monologic and pure, and difference as extraneous to it. Taylor's is not a community that has been formed through the intermingling of various peoples, or that acknowledges its members' identification with such differing social structures as class. This explains why the only extensive evidence of 'multiculturalism' he furnishes concerns Canada as a '[m]ultinational' (64) state and Quebec's sovereignty movement, not the demands for recognition of Canada's First Nations and minority groups. As for the internal dialogue, we are led to believe that the self may be troubled by or considerate of differences, but that it remains sovereign in the authenticity and originality that designate it as distinct. Thus the Taylorean self can absorb only those differences that derive exclusively from the community that is homologous to it. It is, then, caught in a double bind that echoes the Enlightenment formulation of human values and ideals.

Herder's Trojan Horse

Taylor's 'dialogicality' flows from Herder, to whom he attributes 'the ideal of authenticity' (30), and not from Bakhtin, as he would like us to believe.[49] Herder, one of the fathers of German Romanticism and nationalism, also inspires Taylor's crucial shift from the self to its significant others.[50] 'Herder,' Taylor tells us, 'applied his conception of originality at two levels, not only to the individual person among other persons, but also to the culture-bearing people among other peoples. Just like individuals, a *Volk* should be true to itself, that is, its own culture' (31). From the perspective of Herder's *Outlines of a Philosophy of the History of Man* (1784-91), 'every man is ultimately a world, in external appearance indeed similar to others, but internally an individual being, with whom no other coincides' (163). But because 'he is actually formed in and for society, without which he could neither have received his being, nor have become a man' (209), he is a microcosm of his culture, his originality reflecting what is authentic in his society. This is why his '[s]elf-preservation[,] . . . the first object of every existing being' (208), coincides with—in fact necessitates—the emphasis that Taylor, following Herder, places on a culture's survival, specifically Quebec's. But Taylor's endorsement of cultural survival is not to be confused with support for multiculturalism.

Although 'dialogicality' appears to be crucial to Taylor's argument, he does not expand on the self's relationship to its significant others. When he says, in a rather casual fashion, that we cannot '*prevent* our identity's being formed by the people we love' (33), he muffles what he is actually saying about cultural survival. Herder provides the missing link in this and other related points that are unarticulated but nevertheless operative in Taylor's position. Herder's answer to the question 'whether there be innate ideas' is 'in the negative', but he proceeds to establish the self's relationship to its community in unequivocal terms: there is a 'hereditary' (180) relationship between the self and its culture that propels Herder's, as well as Taylor's, theory.

As Herder says:

> Race refers to a difference of origin. . . . For every nation is one people, having its own national form, as well as its own language: the climate, it is true, stamps on each its mark, or spreads over it a slight veil, but not sufficient to destroy the original national character. This originality of character extends even to

families, and its transitions are as variable as imperceptible. In short, there are neither four or five races, nor exclusive varieties, on this Earth. Complexions run into each other: forms follow the genetic character: and upon the whole, all are at last but shades of the same great picture, extending through all ages, and over all parts of the Earth. They belong not, therefore, so properly to systematic natural history, as to the physico-geographical history of man. (166)

Herder puts forward an absolutist definition of culture, one that relates organically (178) both to its members and to its geographical location. His vision of culture as 'a complicated knot' (180) may be eloquently expressed, but it does not help Taylor to understand the reality of multiculturalism: 'See the negro in Europe,' Herder tells us; 'he remains as he was. Let him marry a white woman, and a single generation will effect a change. . . . So it is with the figures of all nations: . . . by intermixture with foreigners, in a few generations every mungal, chinese, or american feature vanishes' (180-1). Herder does not tell us what lies beyond this vanishing point, what results from interracial and intercultural minglings. What is certain, though, is that for him miscegenation is synonymous with human 'degeneration' (179). His geopolitical and genetic understanding of culture[51] demands that cultures not circulate, that no substantial exchange take place among different societies.

In Herder's view, then, study of the other would inform one culture about another, would provide ample evidence of the universality of human nature, but would also disclose that this universality is tempered by naturally inviolable laws affirming the impossibility of cultural transmutation. Indeed, deep understanding of what characterizes the particularity of a culture is not possible. As he says, 'The european has no idea of the boiling passions and imaginations, that glow in the negro's breast; and the hindoo has no conception of the restless desires, that chafe the european. . . . In short, the human feelings have received every form, that could find a place in the various climates, states, and organizations of our Globe' (221-2). Thus for Herder it was a wonderful thing that nature 'separated nations, not only by woods and mountains, seas and deserts, rivers and climates, but more particularly by languages, inclinations, and characters; that the work of subjugating despotism might be rendered more difficult, that all the four quarters of the Globe might not be crammed into the belly of a wooden horse' (224). Herder delights in the plurality of cultures, 'a labyrinth of human fancies' (201), but he laments their commingling.[52] He considers the 'enlargement of states, the wild mixture of various races and nations under one sceptre' to be 'unnatural' (249) in terms of both the function of such culturally mixed states and the degeneration of their 'national character' (250): 'glued together indeed they [different cultures] may be into a fragile machine, termed a machine of state, but destitute of internal vivification and sympathy of parts' (249). This 'gluing together' may be, perversely, an apt metaphor for what we today would term a multicultural state, but the image of it that Herder suggests leaves no doubt as to the spectre that haunts Taylor's argument.

Herder employs a powerful, if disturbing, metaphor that summarizes his vision. Such mixed states, he says, 'appear in history like that type of monarchies in the vision of the prophet, where the lion's head, the dragon's tail, the eagle's wings, and the paws of a bear, combined in one unpatriotic figure of a state' (249-50). Here Herder may be speaking like the Lutheran pastor he was, but there is no doubt about the message his figure of a mixed state is meant to convey. Imaged as a freak, a grotesque aberration violating the organic laws of nature, a mixed state is 'unnatural' and therefore stands no chance of success. Its disintegration is just a matter of time:

> Such machines are pieced together like the trojan horse; guaranteeing one another's immortality, though destitute of national character, there is no life in them, and nothing but the curse of Fate can condemn to immortality the forced union: for the very politics that framed them are those, that play with men and nations as with inanimate substances. But history sufficiently shows, that these instruments of human pride are formed of clay, and, like all other clay, will dissolve, or crumble to pieces. (249-50)

The inevitability of the disintegration he anticipates has the force of natural law: 'where she [nature] could not gratify with giving, she has fought at least to satisfy in refusing' (221). Thus Herder's 'notion of incommensurability' (Pagden 145) respects the singularity of individual nations, but posits the encounter with cultural differences as fatal to a culture's distinctiveness, damaging to 'the internal genius' (179) of the self.

It was his genetic approach to culture that led Herder to consider travel to other nations—read European imperialism—a dangerous thing, not only because it sought to change the 'nature' of the peoples encountered, but also because it had a negative influence on the colonialists themselves. As he wrote, '*Too sudden, too precipitate transitions to an opposite hemisphere and climate are seldom salutary to a nation*; for Nature has not established her boundaries between remote lands in vain' (185). Herder's indictment of colonialism spoke against the universalist inclinations of his contemporaries. At the same time, though, as mentioned above, it reflected his belief that a culture was a self-contained entity, an organic whole; such a culture could survive only if it remained uncontaminated. Even in reference to the nations of Europe, he insisted that the distinctiveness of a given nation was peculiar to itself, and that nothing about that distinctiveness was shared by other European states. Here fear of contamination is synonymous with cultural insularity, with a tightly integrated society whose members are related to each other and to the whole in a homologous fashion. Thus a nation's homogeneity attests to its people's authenticity—and vice versa.

It is in this context that Taylor's understanding of decolonization—'European colonialism ought to be rolled back to give the peoples of what we now call the Third World their chance to be themselves unimpeded' (31)—overlaps with Herder's dual concept of nationalism and authenticity. As Seshadri-Crooks puts it, this 'is a way of returning them to their authentic selves' (50). What Taylor leaves unanswered at this point is the degree of authenticity that the departed colonialists or a settler society can claim after contact with other peoples, the extent to which colonialism or diaspora can be seen to function 'dialogically'. For, while Herder wrote passionately of the pathology of colonial traffic, of the extent to which it contaminated bodies and minds,[53] Taylor only alludes to the singularity of individual identity and the homogeneity of a people. His positivist mode conceals the negativism of Herder's belief in the incommensurability of cultural identity, a belief that stigmatizes 'multiculturalism' as unnatural. This is why, for example, Taylor, supports 'the schooling provisions of Quebec's Law 101 [that] forbid (roughly speaking) francophones and immigrants to send their children to English-language schools, but allow Canadian anglophones to do so' (55).

When Taylor says that people's cultural identity is 'determined by their place in society, and whatever roles or activities [are] attached to this position' (31), he endorses Herder's essentialist construction of the *Volk*. '*Volk*' functions as a rendering of Rousseau's 'people', replacing 'citizen dignity' (35) with a fervent belief in nationhood. Taylor acknowledges that '[w]e can recognize here the seminal idea of modern nationalism, in both benign and malignant forms' (31), but he refrains from elaborating on the negative manifestations of nationalism, or the degree to which he has appropriated Herder's philosophy. Along the same lines, he also strains the differences between nation and culture, as evidenced by his exclusive use of Quebec as an example in his 'multicultural' argument. His conflation of culture and nation explains, in part, why the 'hospitability' of his nonprocedural liberalism is so closely aligned to legal discourse. The view of Quebeckers as a *Volk*, and their province—the geopolitical place that defines them as a 'distinct society' (53)—as contained and affected by 'English Canada' (54), reflects at once Herder's caveat concerning the commingling of cultures and Taylor's position on Quebec.

Quebec and 'The Position of the Immigrant': Between 'Natural' and State Law

While lamenting the fact that Canada is 'under threat of breakup' (1993, 188) and wanting to see Quebec stay within Canada, Taylor makes a passionate plea for the recognition of Quebec's status as a 'distinct society'. But because—the possibility of separation aside—the prospect of restoring Quebec to its 'natural' state is virtually nonexistent, he resorts to the force of the law. Thus he sees, for example, Quebec's use of the 'notwithstanding' clause in the Canadian Charter of Rights to be in keeping with its 'collective goal of survival' (53). Similarly, he views the failure of the Meech Lake Accord—intended to accommodate Quebec's 'distinct society' within the federal Constitution—as reflecting 'in part . . . a spreading procedural outlook in English Canada' (60), an outlook that he earlier dismisses as an 'inhospitable' variety of liberalism. Law is the remedy that Taylor suggests when the 'natural' laws that determine the cohesiveness of a culture have been upset. Only within the technology of law can Quebec remain 'true to the culture of our ancestors', can 'Quebec governments' practise what they consider 'axiomatic', namely 'that the survival and flourishing of French culture in Quebec is a good' (58).

The Quebec question, whether it presents itself in the form of a 'distinct society' clause or of separatism, is certainly relevant to Canadian multicultural-ism. After all, legally and politically, multiculturalism has a cause-and-effect relationship with bilingualism and biculturalism. Nevertheless, Taylor does not address the complexity of this relationship. Instead he appropriates the concept of minority from multicultural politics and applies it to Quebec while bracketing the question of minorities within Quebec. Even in *Reconciling the Solitudes*, which focuses on the Quebec question, he takes the same reductive approach. One difference, however, between 'The Politics of Recognition' and *Reconciling the Solitudes* is that Herder's influence on Taylor's thinking is more clear in the latter than in the former.

For Taylor, what is 'axiomatic' in Quebec politics is that Quebeckers 'intend to survive, and therefore the position of the immigrant is fundamentally intolerable for them—not only in Canada, which is supposed to be their country, but partic-ularly in the province of Quebec, where they are in a majority' (1993, 11). Here the 'position of the immigrant' reflects Quebeckers' view of their position within Canada—precisely the thing they cannot condone. Beyond the familiar reasons why this position is indeed 'intolerable' to Quebeckers, it is important to note that the image of the immigrant as deployed by Taylor in this instance is not to be confused with the construction of immigrants and other, ethnically diverse, Canadians in the Multiculturalism Act. As a philosopher and a Quebecker, Taylor views the immigrant as someone who 'axiomatically' is expected to lose his or her language, in effect to become assimilated. According to Taylor's (and Herder's) logic, immigrants, because they are already detached from their place and culture of birth, are destined by 'natural' law to suffer cultural 'degeneration'. Quebeckers, however, residing as they do in a province where a 'higher propor-tion' of the population 'is *pure laine*' (1993, 161), have the right to protect by law the survival of their culture. There are two kinds of law at work here: 'natural' law derived from a biological theory of culture, which can be punitive for some people but sustaining for others; and state law, a law designed to uphold heredi-tary rights, which comes into play when 'natural' law is under threat. There is a contingency between these two orders of law, the kind that at once unleashes and binds the condition of otherness.

Taylor's recognition of Quebec's 'axiomatic' claims does not acknowledge the heritage status granted to Quebec in the Multiculturalism Act. At the same time, though, he bestows on Quebec a special kind of heritage in which the notions of original and originary are collapsed into one another. Clearly a strategic move, this allows Taylor to configure Quebeckers at once as others in Canada and as a group with 'natural' rights. It might seem that Taylor is proposing a notion of contingent identity, but this identity is contingent only in relation to the 'natural' laws that give birth to it; he thus argues for a *sui generis* identity, one whose originality becomes its origin. This kind of identity does not simply ask that it be recognized as equal in worth to other identities; it demands its 'survival through indefinite future generations' (41n.16). Hence the need for laws that would '*create* members of the community*' (58-9) willing or conditioned to contribute to the survival of a '*pure laine*' identity. His emphasis on *creation* invites a double reading: 'natural' law, procreation of the same; and creation as the forging of citizens (Quebeckers with a federalist vision, and minorities) in the image of the same, in effect as the manufacturing of a specific kind of citizenry sanctioned by 'natural' law and authorized by the legal system. Yet there is hardly anything 'natural' about Taylor's 'creative' project.

This is the point where the key concepts in his argument—the self's authenticity, dialogism, and the cultural survival of homogeneous groups—begin to blur. Herder argues that 'the history of man is ultimately a theatre of transformations' (164) that include 'degeneration', or, more subtly, the transmutation that individuals undergo when they are transplanted into different cultural and linguistic milieux. Even the genius of language, the centre of Herder's philosophy, is capable of being improved, as he argues in *New German Literature* (1767) with respect to the German language. For this purpose Herder, a translator himself, does not hesitate to use foreign languages as a means of ameliorating German, thus 'changing the other into an object of assimilation' (Kristeva 1991, 213, n.15). Taylor, though, perhaps because he has learned Herder's lesson too well, is silent regarding the kind of transformation a culture may undergo. Interestingly enough, he is also silent when it comes to the origins of Quebec. His historical omissions and totalized vision of Quebec would suggest that Quebeckers were not settlers, that they had nothing to do with colonization, that they were the indigenous population in what is now the province of Quebec. By gliding over history in this fashion, Taylor makes a strategic departure from Herder's philosophy. '*Pure laine*', in this context, functions as a fiction, the fiction that Quebeckers originated in Canada; hence Taylor's frequent association of them with the First Nations peoples.[54]

Critical of 'difference-blind' liberalism, and thus of the Charter of Rights, Taylor attempts to locate himself between a politics that does not override individual autonomy and authenticity and one capable of accommodating the recognition demands of 'minorities [like Quebeckers] who define themselves as historic societies' (1993, 194)—a difficult, if not impossible, position to uphold. Meanwhile, the slippages in 'The Politics of Recognition' from the self's authenticity to a community genetically defined, and from 'natural' to state law, contribute virtually nothing to our understanding of ethnic differences in a multicultural state. Indeed, it would seem that ethnicity is the name of the malaise afflicting immigrants. Taylor's statement that 'the demand for equal recognition is unacceptable' (71) serves to dismiss the Multiculturalism Act—obviously not for the same reasons I have critiqued it—although he never refers to the Act directly. Along the same lines, when he says that the 'porousness' of multicultural states 'means that they are more open to multinational migration; more of their members live the life of diaspora, *whose center is elsewhere*' (63; my emphasis), he displays a limited, if not distorted, view of diaspora. In fact, this is all he has to say about diaspora. The view of diaspora that forms the subliminal text of 'The Politics of Recognition' is articulated quite clearly in *Reconciling the Solitudes*: 'homogeneity is an advantage' (1993, 189).

While the Act offers a particular interpretation of the Canadian Charter of Rights, Taylor is concerned only with the latter both in 'The Politics of Recognition' and in *Reconciling the Solitudes*. If this concern contradicts his belief in the self's authenticity, it also shows his interest in multiculturalism to be grounded in his deep concern with the Quebec question. Thus despite the fact that he employs Canada and Quebec as his chief examples in the former text, the closest he ever comes to addressing Canadian multiculturalism is in the latter.

Discussing the 'terms' by which '[t]he language and culture by themselves mark us [Quebeckers] off from Americans, and also from other Canadians', Taylor views 'multiculturalism' as 'more problematic' than the Charter of Rights; still, he never addresses multiculturalism directly. Here are two specific references he makes to it:

As a federal policy, multiculturalism is sometimes seen as a device to deny French-speaking minorities their full recognition, or even to reduce the importance of the French fact in Canada to that of an outsized ethnic minority. Meanwhile, within Quebec itself, the growing diversity of francophone society is causing much heartburn and anxiety. (1993, 162)

A wide coalition, including those who pressed for a policy of multiculturalism, some women's groups, and others, saw the answer to their aspirations in a Canadian Charter of Rights, conceived as guaranteeing equality between individuals. . . . ; but for minorities who define themselves as historic societies and want this acknowledged, it cannot serve. . . . We are at an impasse. In a similar way, the sense of regional alienation has been translated into a concept of justice that entails equality between provinces. This is then taken as incompatible with a recognition of a distinct society.

. . . Quebec has not been innocent of this in the past. The famous formula of the 'two nations' fitted very well Quebec's own sense of itself as a nation, but involved projecting the same kind of unity onto 'English' Canada, where it never really applied and has become steadily less apposite over the decades. (1993, 194)

In this context, 'the position of immigrant' marks the source of alterity, precisely what Taylor's theory fails to accommodate. Taylor recognizes differences within a 'religious' frame, Herder's vision, wherein 'variety of culture' is intended to contribute to the 'greater harmony' of the universe (72). The dissemination of differences threatens to realign the structural manifestations of the divine; 'on the human level' (72), Taylor does not so much adopt Herder's cultural relativism as relegate diasporic subjects to a theatre of observation where they are cast as the ones providing the spectacle.

His study of the other involves the other only as an object, not as an inter-locutor. He feels morally bound to reject 'the politics of difference' because it 'can end up making everyone the same' (71). From the perspective of Taylor-cum-Herder, 'everyone' bears the stamp of universalism, of the 'natural' laws that at once value difference and relegate it to a self-contained place. 'Everyone' refers not only to the assimilation of the other, but also to the contamination of the culture advocating the politics of difference. Taylor attempts to act out Herder's definition of cultural heroes, those who 'succeed in removing wants from the creation, falsehoods from our memory, and disgraces from our nature, [who] are to the realms of truth, what the heroes of mythology were to the primitive world; they lessen the number of monsters on the Earth' (Herder 165). Similarly, Taylor feels morally compelled to keep the other at bay, for in his view the 'position of the immigrant' is already bastardized.

His theory of authenticity, his belief in the 'pure' originality of cultural identity, does not permit the modern self to question its values radically before conducting a study of the other. There is, then, no room in Taylor's theory for constructive dialogue, dialogue that would allow the other to cross the boundary that circumscribes it. His study of the other, far from offering a multicultural pedagogy, serves to reinforce what validates a 'distinct' society in its own terms. In this, the possibilities of real dialogue are severely limited. 'The Politics of Recognition', then, contradicts Taylor's own philosophy from two different perspectives. From the perspective of minority subjects, because otherness may be proven worthy yet continue to function under the influence of the 'distinct' society's representational economies, this study does not promise to return to them any of their appropriated subjectivity and agency. From the perspective of the modern self, we cannot afford to engage in serious study of the other, for this would mean submitting the modern self's image of originality to scrutiny, if not radical revision—even to conceding that what it takes to be its authentic core may be nothing more than the other installed in the self. Dialogue that would suspend oppositions, that would eliminate the centre-margin dialectic, would prevent assimilation, yet Taylor dismisses such dialogue as the 'free play' of the neo-Nietzscheans.

Towards a Mastery of Discomfort

My critique of the process by which ethnicity is legitimated in Canada does not mean that the Other, as inscribed in this country, is not in need of legitimation—in effect, that its desire for recognition has already been met. What I have tried to show is that ethnicity, when defined by master discourses—positive or negative, procedural or nonprocedural—is addressed in terms that speak of communities designed in a positivist fashion. Instead, I think we should strive 'to form a community in which the recognition . . . of the Other is always also the failure to know that Other' (Butler 1993a, 5).

Failure to know the Other means failure to accommodate existing stereotypes and failure to produce new ones. It means failure to assimilate the Other into cultural and political discourses that appropriate its differences. It also means failure to accept universal principles in good faith, and failure to see the Other as a fully knowable entity. Failure, in this context, is a kind of negative capability that both reveals the alterity of the Other and exposes the fallacy that dominant culture is transparent, dominant in and of itself, a community of pure hegemonic will or one that fully knows itself. Lest I seem to advocate a politics of failure in which the Other becomes reified once again, my use of the word 'failure' is intended to eliminate, if possible, the yoke of the capital 'O', the object/ified position; to release ethnic subjects from their condition of marginalized Otherness. It is because I think we still have a long way to go that I do not speak in emancipatory or messianic terms.

Whatever the ideological allegiances of the various contesting groups, there ought to be a will to carry on with the negotiation of diversities, not with the aspiration of reaching consensus, but with the resolve to address diversity without (re)fashioning it according to familiar paradigms. Only by deconstructing both sides of the Us and Them paradigm can we begin to address, and move beyond, the historical categories that have given rise to the existing paradigm in the first place. The goal, as I understand it so far, is not to construct a reality of comfort, but rather to view comfortable positions with suspicion; not to 'dramatize victimage' as Spivak warns us (1993, 63), but to expose how we still remain lodged within systemic structures, and to go beyond the simple act of naming them; not to capitalize on the currency of diversity, which would amount to fetishizing minoritarian identity, but to resist designing boundaries that would discipline diversity and to reconsider the overdetermined value assigned to it. The goal, then, is mastery of discomfort, a mastery that would involve shuttling between centre and margin while displacing both.

Chapter 3

Ethnic Anthologies:
From Designated Margins to
Postmodern Multiculturalism

I
The Anxiety of Ethnic Differences

An absence, . . . as much as a presence, is a good point for a beginning.
And when any situation is replete with both—where a pervasive absence
signifies an absent presence, and a fleeting presence itself signals to a
hidden imperative of invisibility, then that is precisely where work of
inquiry and description must begin. We begin with what we have—our
invisibility.

Himani Bannerji (1993, xii)

When we talk about ethnicity today, as Bannerji's epigraph reminds us, we engage
in a dialogue that has barely begun. It may take place in fits and starts, it may
stutter as it looks for the critical idioms to express the cultural and political
pressures of a given moment, or it may exude confidence because it has already
carved out a niche for itself, but any discourse about ethnicity inevitably
confronts the tension between absence and presence, visibility and invisibility.
This doubleness does not necessarily mean that we remain lodged within the
inherited binary structures that have given rise to the construction of Otherness.
Rather, it points to the fact that such discourse moves away from the very boundaries these paradigmatic structures have installed; in this case, boundaries do not
separate, but mark the point from which something begins.

The many ethnic anthologies that appeared between the mid-1970s and mid-
1980s marks the first such concentrated unfolding of ethnic writing in Canada.
As it emerges from the Other side of Canadian literature's cultural syntax, this
writing brings into play what was previously disregarded. It makes present what

rendered it absent; it brings into relief the boundaries that separated it from the mainstream tradition. And so it stands on the threshold of what Canadian literature has become since those 'strangers within our gates' took it upon themselves to cross the boundary separating those who are silenced, who are written about, from those who give voice to themselves. These writers often journey towards an originary home, but they also recognize that they are destined never to return to it, that they have been permanently cast out of a house of familiar knowledge. Their voices sometimes converge, sometimes remain dissonant. Whatever the case may be, these writers set out to legitimate ethnic voices in their own terms, but also in terms that reflect the given cultural and political climate.

How diasporic literature circulates within the Canadian literary tradition as a symptom of difference, as a designated margin, and as a sign of cultural excess will be my focus in this chapter. I will explore ethnic writing in relation both to itself and to the advent of multiculturalism. For this purpose, I will undertake a comparative reading of the first wave of ethnic anthologies, especially as they are framed by their editors' statements and strategies, but I will also pause to examine a few individual contributors at some length. What marks ethnicity when it is defined by diasporic subjects themselves? What inscriptions characterize the immigrant experience? What kinds of negotiations and resistances speak of ethnic subjects' relations to their communities? These are some of the issues I will address in the first section. In the second, I will deal with a major shift that has occurred in the field of ethnic anthologies, namely the compilation of writing in comprehensive volumes intended not to represent distinct ethnic groups, but to bridge their differences. *Other Solitudes: Canadian Multicultural Fictions* (1990), edited by Linda Hutcheon and Marion Richmond, the first such anthology to have a major impact, will be my focus.

Diaspora Anthologized / Anthologies as Archives

I grew totally perplexed when people demanded that I should look like myself.

Walter Benjamin (circa 1900)[1]

It ain't where you're from,
it's where you're at

Paul Gilroy (1993, 120)

One Out of Many, ed. Liz Cromwell; *Harvest: Anthology of Mennonite Writing in Canada 1874–1974*, ed. William De Fehr et al.; *Roman Candles*, ed. Pier Giorgio Di Cicco; *Other Voices: Writings by Blacks in Canada*, ed. Lorris Elliott; *A Shapely Fire: Changing the Literary Landscape*, ed. Cyril Dabydeen; *Arab-Canadian Writing: Stories, Memoirs, and Reminiscences*, ed. Kamal A. Rostom; *Transplanted Lives: Dutch-Canadian Stories and Poems*, ed. Hendrika Ruger; *Italian-Canadian Voices*, ed. Caroline Morgan DiGiovanni; *Chilean Literature in Canada*, ed. Naín Nómez; *Yarmarok: Ukrainian Writing in Canada since the Second World War*, ed. Jars Balan and Yuri Klynovy; *Voices: Canadian Writers of African Descent*, ed. Ayanna Black.

I am offering this long catalogue as a double act of naming: belatedly making present, if only by name, anthologies that appeared around the time multiculturalism was introduced as an official policy in Canada; and calling to attention the fact that these texts remained virtually ignored, that they made no dent in the canon either at that time or later.

I focus on these texts because anthologies are usually designed around principles shared by their contributors. As efforts to make a collective statement, or to convey what is current, anthologies, perhaps more than individual titles, reflect the values shaping a given tradition or, conversely, a perceived need to revise that tradition. Together, the ethnic anthologies I have listed offer the first consistent compilation of ethnic literature in Canada. They function as an archive illustrating the manifold ways in which ethnicity is represented not only within ethnic communities, but also within the context of official multiculturalism. The significance of anthologies lies in, among other things, the access they provide to a variety of works that are often difficult to locate. This is one of the reasons why I have chosen to examine these early ethnic anthologies here. A second is that by making available new as well as traditionally ignored and marginalized authors, these texts also make visible, in direct or indirect ways, the cultural and political histories that inform the production of this writing.[2] Given their wide scope, I could not possibly address—let alone resolve—all the issues they raise. My intention is of necessity limited: to sketch out, on one hand, the varied, and often contrary, constructions of ethnicity that emerge from these collections, and, on the other, the editorial policies that frame them.

The contents of these anthologies are disparate in many ways, but ethnicity emerges as an overriding concern, endowing the writing featured in them with a dynamism that has ideological and cultural implications. To borrow Nancy Hartsock's words, they 'develop an account of the world which treats [their] perspectives not as subjugated or disruptive knowledges, but as primary and constitutive of a different world' (171). Read separately, they appear as distinct expressions of individual ethnic groups; read collectively, they come to embody Canada's cultural heterogeneity. What they share is the intention of translating their writers' image as Others into a self-defined specificity. They are presented as texts invoked by historical necessity, reaching the reader from a point of view that is at once marginalized and affirmative. Yet they do not function as what Alan C. Golding calls 'revisionist' collections 'intended to shift an academic canon defined mostly by teaching anthologies' (283). Their editors are 'revisionist' only insofar as they expose the ideologies informing the mainstream canon. They do not set out expressly to question such canon-making texts as Margaret Atwood's *Oxford Book of Canadian Verse*, Gary Geddes's *15 Canadian Poets x 2*, Robert Lecker and Jack David's *New Canadian Anthology*, and Russell Brown and Donna Bennett's *Anthology of Canadian Literature in English.*[3] Instead, their goal is to preserve and disseminate what the tradition represented by mainstream anthologies skips over. These specifically ethnic anthologies thus serve a paradoxical function: on one hand, they ratify by default the very tradition that has disregarded ethnic literature; on the other, they move beyond that tradition and draw our attention to its margins.

To put it differently, their editors do not simply seize the opportunities granted by funding agencies, universities, and publishers when these institutions find themselves under duress to acknowledge ethnicity. By redefining ethnicity as a centre of cultural production, they redraw the blueprint of power relations. Moreover, as I will try to show, these anthologies do not present a uniform view of ethnicity. In them ethnicity is celebrated and condemned, sought after and rejected, defined over and over again. It is virtually impossible to extrapolate from them a single working definition of ethnicity. If there is any consistent message, it is that diasporic discourse cannot be abstracted from the forces and conflicts that delimit it, that ethnicity is always a matter of 'fluctuating identities' (Christian 243). Thus the agency of the ethnic subject is always located within a dense web of relations. Even though it is difficult to negotiate all these relations in a single discussion, it is imperative at least that we keep them closely in mind, that we study ethnicity within the set of cultural and political specificities that produce it.

The heterogeneity of these ethnic anthologies is one of the reasons why their potential to revise the canon has remained largely unrealized. Although intended to reach a group of readers that has stubbornly ignored ethnic writing, they were published by small if not obscure presses, and hardly reviewed at all; thus their readership was actually very small. What these anthologies failed to do at the time of their publication—no fault of their own, it should be stressed—has been accomplished more recently by the publication of works by individual authors, authors who have been published by major presses or firmly established small ones, and who have attained public recognition of various degrees or become the subjects of critical discussion. Recognition of this kind has eluded these anthologies primarily because of the time when they were published, namely before multiculturalism gained literary and cultural currency. In this chapter I am interested in exploring how the representations of ethnicity in them at once support and contradict the group-identity mentality and the essentialist view of origins evident in the public response to diversity as well as in the official multiculturalism policy.

Diaspora: Between Faction and Fiction

If the anthologies in question differ in the ethnic and racial origins of their contributors, they also differ in their interpretations and implementation of multiculturalism. Their editors acknowledge indebtedness to the official policy because of the financial support they received through multicultural programs, but also, and most important, for the policy's sanctioning of ethnicity. In this sense one may conclude that the Canadian Multiculturalism Act has succeeded in fulfilling one of its principal mandates, namely the 'enhancement' of diasporic experience. Conversely, the self-contradictory images of ethnicity that emerge from these anthologies defy the ideological assumptions of the Canadian Multiculturalism Act: that ethnic subjectivity, understood and contained in collective terms, is always determined by reference to a distant, and often dehistoricized, past. Thus these anthologies demonstrate the need for the ethnic subject to articulate ethnicity at a specific historical moment,[4] yet, despite the common ground they share, they offer no cohesive 'grammar' of ethnicity (Kroetsch 1989). Instead, they function as alternative sites of cultural production. Ethnicity emerges from them as both faction and fiction.

Here 'faction' refers to the way much of this writing, because it is a fictional rendering of the author's own immigrant experience, presents that experience as the essential determinant of subjectivity. The empiricism of this literature, even though it signals difference, is given an ironic privileged status as it reifies both the essentialism of ethnic identity and its marginalized position. 'Fiction', in turn, refers to what is deemed irrelevant to diasporic experience; yet the elements that are excised from these narratives, presumably because their presence would signal fabrication, constitute a paradoxical figure speaking truths that are usually unacknowledged. The truth is that displacement is not necessarily the single most important factor defining diasporic identity; the truth is, too, that the disunity the self experiences is not necessarily the direct result of that displacement alone; finally, the truth is that the longing for one's ancestral country is no guarantee that returning there will restore unity, for that place functions as an allegory of values that are often commemorated while the historical and social contingencies informing them are ignored.

This interplay of faction and fiction—sometimes operating unconsciously, at other times employed with heavy irony or, conversely, with blind faith in the transparency of empirical truth—informs most of the writing in these anthologies. It also raises the question of representation, an issue that emerges at the point where the difference that constitutes ethnicity is strategically renamed as Otherness. This recasting of the diasporic subject is the inevitable effect of fusion and intervention. As DiGiovanni says in her introduction to *Italian-Canadian Voices*, 'Today, multicultural manifestations are not only accepted but actively promoted as the kind of national identity Canada wants to present to the world' (17). To give credence to her statement she refers to Pier Giorgio Di Cicco's earlier anthology of Italian Canadian poetry, *Roman Candles*. 'Assisted by funding from the Canada Council,' she observes, 'DiCicco's [sic] work as an editor contributed to multiculturalism as a national policy. He brought out a book which gave all Canadians access to the creative self-expression of one ethnic group'; the writers in Di Cicco's anthology, she adds, 'celebrate their culture without apology' (19).

The question of how many Canadians took advantage of the availability of *Roman Candles* aside, her summation is accurate, but also interestingly misleading.

Whereas DiGiovanni emphasizes the singularity of cultural expression, Di Cicco tells us that the 'impetus behind' (10) the writers included in his anthology is their 'bicultural[ism]' (9). In a deliberately ironic move, Di Cicco presents a definition of biculturalism that differs from that of the Official Languages Act. He attempts to 'map out' 'a journey towards a new citizenship, one that has little to do with anti-Americanism or the convenience of a melting pot' (10).[5] Although his choice of the word 'citizenship', with its connotation of legal rights, would seem to imply that ethnicity is always grounded in the legislating mechanisms of states, Di Cicco does not pursue this notion. What emerges from his preface is an anxiety of ethnic difference—'I'd been a man without a country for most of my life' (9). The paradoxical duality of his condition, wherein two countries equal a zero home/state, reflects not a cosmopolitan identity,[6] but anxiety about the location of selfhood, a concern that is also inscribed as a longing for stability and certainty. The fact that anxiety and longing are also pervasive in Canadian literature that is not, strictly speaking, diasporic, but rather bears residual signs of colonialism, does not diminish the import of what Di Cicco is saying. It is the historical specificity of diasporic experience that constitutes the ethnic signature of the anxiety and longing in question here.

To illustrate this Di Cicco concludes his preface with John Robert Colombo's poem 'My Genealogy'. I will quote a few stanzas because it typifies the way, in these anthologies, anxiety of ethnic difference is engendered when heterogeneity displaces singularity, when ethnic purity disappears in the symbolic exchange of values and states.

1.
My great-great-grandfather
played in the streets
of Milano, I am told.
I take it on faith.

2.
His son, the artisan,
immigrated to Baden, Ontario,
as a decorator or builder.
I believe this, but never met him.

3.
My grandfather was born
in Baden, and he married
a German girl there.
I remember him well—

he spoke English
with a German accent.
. . .

7.
I remember quite distinctly
my mother's parents, my grandparents. My grandfather spoke
with a thick Greek accent,
and my larger grandmother,
a nasal Quebec French. Yes,
they made a colourful couple.
. . .

11.
I seldom feel close
to the Rocky Mountains,
the Prairies,
the Great Lakes,
or the cold St. Lawrence.
What am I doing in Toronto?

12.
If this means being Canadian,
I am a Canadian. (10-12)

'My Genealogy' deconstructs the configuration of ethnicity as the unified entity
for which DiGiovanni, inspired by official multiculturalism, argues. Colombo
points to the falsity of the dualism implicit in the Multiculturalism Act's bifurca-
tion of residents of Canada into Canadians proper and persons belonging to
minority groups, as well as the assumption that persons are defined by their affiliation with a single ethnic community.

Colombo reformulates these conventional views, suggesting that multiculturalism can construct only a conditional identity. The irony of the poem's title, then,
offers us an index to the complicated ways in which ethnicity signifies. There is a
polar tension between being a legal resident of a country and feeling other to its
culture, but this cannot be viewed as a matter of binary opposition alone. In
Canada, which images itself as a state founded by settlers, the construction of
ethnicity cannot be accommodated by a simple binary model. Colombo eschews
this model; instead, he constantly defers the identification of a stable origin. In so
doing, he demonstrates that ethnic difference is not always synonymous with the
marginalization that might result from a state's political and social manoeuvring.
Difference, in this instance, is coincident with one's own ambivalent subject
position, a position sustained by resisting both internal and external fixities. The
tension between what he remembers and what he takes on faith dramatizes the

ambivalence of ethnic subjectivity. Thus he claims to be Canadian only after showing 'Canadian' to signify a hybrid genealogy, a genealogy that speaks of filiation and affiliation, of belonging and detachment, of mimicry and contamination all at once.

Before and After Diaspora: The Epistemology of Ethnicity

From the point of view suggested in Colombo's poem, the lack of a solid, unamalgamated origin suggests that ethnic difference is predicated not as a minority position but as a differential sign. Hence what arises as a pressing issue is the epistemological process by which ethnicity is understood as a condition of identity constructed in marginal ways. How does a subject respond to the experience of having what was a normative position in the country of origin become Other under the scrutiny of 'foreign' eyes? To put it differently, how does the ethnic subject know herself to be ethnic—that is, both inside and outside a dominant society? What are the discourses she employs to manifest her desire to make herself present?

Such questions are treated variously in these anthologies, but certain elements recur in all of them. One of the most important is the near absence of questioning, overt or covert, as to what constitutes subjectivity prior to diasporic movement. The cultural and national realities left behind do not seem to cause any ambivalence as to who the subject was prior to immigration. Just as Canadian society does not usually problematize its whiteness, because that whiteness is normative, the signature of the country of origin appears to be taken for granted. The ethnicity of the subject becomes an issue only after relocation has occurred. For example, the voices of European origin speaking in some anthologies do so from the position of a formerly unified subject who has undergone a collapse of his subjectivity because of his diasporic experience[7] and the discrimination that frequently accompanies it. In contrast, when the ethnic subject originates in a former colony or is defined as racially Other to the normative whiteness of Canadian society, he approaches his diasporic experience with a sharp sense of displacement and discrimination already in place—a knowledge, however, that is explored principally through references to the Canadian context.

Whatever the racial group represented in an anthology—white, black, or other—two factors are essential in determining the construction of ethnicity: the subject's perception that she is now defined as Other by the mainstream society, a definition that in effect forces her to function as parasite on the host environment; and the painful awareness of the loss of a familiar (no matter how troubled) world, the distancing from an indigenous past. The consciousness of no longer belonging to a cultural continuum induces a feeling of lack. Lack is imaged in terms both of a distant originary place and of the subject's lack of sameness vis-à-vis the dominant society. The writing in these anthologies articulates this lack. Although it cannot always compensate the ethnic subject for the experience of loss, language both mediates and records these acts of knowing. More important, these anthologies demonstrate that as soon as the ethnic subject enters the site of her own discourse she becomes empowered. Ethnic discourse tends to entwine the experience of loss and of being othered in a web of old and new cultural registers, showing the ethnic subject to inhabit an in-between position.

Yet there appears to be a reluctance to acknowledge the ambivalence of that position. Irrespective of the particular experiences represented, the starting point of the epistemological process inscribed in these anthologies invariably occurs when the difference that ethnicity signifies is translated into a sign of minoritization. The crisis that results from this process of translation—in effect a process of objectification—marks the moment the subject is 'born' as ethnic within the host society. I do not intend to suggest through this biological metaphor that these subjects have no prior histories or identities—quite the contrary. A recurring figure in these anthologies, the birth metaphor signals how those histories and identities are appropriated by the dominant society in its efforts to stabilize and, by implication, to frame and reduce their meanings and their impact on itself. Hence the consternation often expressed in the anthologized poems or stories when the speakers fail to recognize their own image in the Otherness mirrored in the dominant society's gaze. The moment they encounter that spectral image of themselves that is not themselves is the moment when they are 'born'—that is, reconstructed—as Others. Thus the writing in these anthologies often centres on the ethnic subject's experience of being constructed as Other by the dominant society, but it also records how the subject initiates the process of self-definition, his attempt to articulate *and* dissemble his recognition of his othered self.

The hiatus between *being*—who the ethnic subject was, who he thinks he still is—and *becoming*—what becomes of him in Canada, how others perceive him—is what structures 'the spectacle of otherness' (Bhabha 1982, 151) that these anthologies invite us to interrogate. I am not implying here that the ethnic subject has a fully formed, teleological identity before joining the diaspora, although this is often the case with the ethnic subjects, regardless of their origins, who appear in these anthologies. My distinction between *being* and *becoming* is intended to express the disjunction that occurs when the ethnic subject enters a process in which she recognizes her Otherness to be a symptom of difference not defined by herself. Thus the ethnic subject's diasporic experience constitutes an instance of self-identification by negation, a negation that affirms the subject's belonging to Canada. If such belonging suggests any stability, this is manifested through the pervasive sense of ambivalence that marks the otherness of subjectivity and subjectivity as Otherness.

Here is a statement by Aruna Srivastava that speaks to this issue:

What . . . am I to make of those who . . . accuse me of being a 'professional ethnic'? Who, benignly, assume my automatic knowledge of and identification with a particular community? Which one, I want to ask? South Asia? Do any of us/them identify with that geographical fiction? India? Pakistan? Trinidad? Sri Lanka? The Philippines? What really unites us/them, makes us cohere? Not any fictional nation. For we are all here now, for now, *Canadian South Asian* women, deterritorialized, unhoused in a country that has severe doubts about its own territory, its homeness—the myths of multiculturalism, even of biculturalism and bilingualism, unraveling as I speak. Our otherness, inessential, ephemeral, defined by—what???—perceived gradations of colour, by accent, by name, is defined against our Canadianness, so that we 'not-not quite Canadians', to use Bharati Mukherjee's apt phrase, are always, already continuously, dispossessed, and displaced. (111-12)

Ethnicity as we experience it in Canada, as it is inscribed in much of the writing in these anthologies, does not originate in what Srivastava rightly calls a 'geographical fiction'. Instead, it is 'born' the moment a subject is exposed to discursive modalities that contest or threaten what it has known itself to be, what it is becoming. Ethnicity, then, is the result of being 'deterritorialized' not from an original birthplace, but while 'here now', in Canada. Srivastava's deconstruction of the conventional mode of nostalgia shows the imperative to address ethnicity not in relation to some remote place, however attached we might still be to it, but in the context of our present place and time. This temporality of ethnicity, the need to examine the historicity of its history, together with all that it entails, is not always operative in these anthologies. Many of the writers perceive identity as a totality of a pre-given horizon or have internalized the ways in which the dominant society has designated ethnicity as an essential margin. Yet even when ethnicity is not viewed as a condition produced by particular power relations, examining the experience of being 'unhoused' in terms of a 'fictional nation' discloses the need to release ethnicity from a metaphysics of origins.

The 'Birth' of Othered Bodies: Desire and Racialization

Consider an example of how ethnicity is 'born' in Youssef El-Malh's story 'Jumping in Air', included in Kamal A. Rostom's anthology of Arab Canadian writing:

> Licking her upper lip with the tip of her tongue, she said indifferently:
> 'You have a strange accent. Where do you come from?'
> Without giving me the chance to answer, she resumed, looking fixedly into my eyes:
> 'India?'
> 'I am an Arab.' [. . .]
> 'Here is one of you.'
> 'What do you mean one of us?'
> 'Indian!'

I followed the movement of her eyes and saw a dark girl walking shyly on the beach. There was a brief period of silence, while my eyes wandered between the two bodies, the dark and the white. Then I started in an awkward manner to explain the difference in origin between Indians and Arabs, but she seemed absentminded and distracted, as if she had lost interest. My whole being was overwhelmed by the disturbing feeling that I was nothing . . . nothing at all, that I lacked so many things to become a human being like her. Those people moving on the beach represented the civilized race. As for me, I was a different creature, uncivilized and inferior; my skin is dark, you know. (22-3)

Up to this point in his two-page story, El-Malh has disclosed the race only of the woman his narrator was picked up by in a bar, and he has done so in a casual fashion that raises more questions about gender and sexuality than about racial difference. We read of her seductiveness and the 'passionate intensity of her love-making', but also of her 'blond hair' and 'her white body stretched voluptuously on the bed' (22). These qualifiers reverse the normative paradigm that renders white skin invisible because it is taken to be symptomatic of the status quo. It is not accidental, then, that the narrativization of Otherness here is initiated by the male narrator himself. At the beginning of the story, this narrativization coincides with his resistance to being the object of the woman's desire in the bar when she singles him out. Gradually, however, the narrative shows signs of real discomfort, culminating in the beach scene cited above, where what launched the characters' liaison is acted out again, this time at the verbal level and on a social plane larger than that of the bedroom.

The symmetry of the 'couple' they were for one night having already been broken by the presence 'of all these white bodies' on the beach, the man realizes that he is visibly a minority; this realization leaves him 'without desire or sensa-tion' (22). What is played out here is the structural politics between the private and the public. The characters' racial difference is specified only when they find themselves in a public milieu. Hence the symbolic transience of their mutual passion. Their desire for each other dies away once they have to function as members of a society that privileges one but ostracizes the other. The contrast between the private and the public spheres, between 'the dark and the white', between 'human being' and 'creature', between the sexual boldness of the white woman and the shyness of the (presumably) Indian girl, between the reductive racism and ignorance of the white woman and the abjection of the Arab man, is emblematic of two kinds of difference: denotative, in which difference is a matter of description; and connotative, in which difference is a matter of value judge-ment. Before these casual lovers go to the beach, their differences operate at the denotative level; as soon as they find themselves in the public sphere, those same differences acquire a connotative significance.

Otherness as difference is not always articulated in such a neat manner, nor am I suggesting that the distinction between denotative and connotative difference marks discrete stages in our relations with others. It is at the level of structure, of the way a story is plotted, that we find this distinction operating. An example in El-Malh's story is the narrator's apostrophe to the reader: 'my skin is dark, you know,' he tells us, although we have known this for some time. It is this unnecessary explanation, at once an affirmation of the way his self-definition reflects his skin colour and a negation of the way he is perceived, that marks the moment the narrator is 'born' as ethnic.

The historically loaded and problematic metaphor of being 'born' as ethnic at this point is intended to stress a particular aspect of ethnic ambivalence, the kind that shows how corporeality functions in the realm of ethnicity. Corporeality encompasses the various conditions of the body and the forces that affect it, ranging from its physicality and sex, its pathology, and its socialization, to the body's registration as a site where specific power relations are both acted on and produced by it as a set of limits that can be perceived as boundaries but also as instances of the body's capacity for change.[8] In El-Malh's story, and in other writings in these anthologies, the ethnic subject's body, both ethnically and sexually, is reproduced as the manifestation of power relations that the narrator can identify and articulate but not overcome—at least not in the context of the story.

The Arab man's recognition of his racialization, then, is not determined by biology, is not simply an epidermic phenomenon. Instead, it demonstrates that he feels he is 'nothing' only after the white woman categorizes him in a 'meta-biological' (Berel Lang) manner that assumes there are essential traits that define groups of people. Crucial in this scene of the 'birth' of the other as Other is the fact that the white woman is oblivious to the offence she gives the Arab man. Still, her attitude, the seemingly innocuous but no less disturbing question with which she begins their dialogue—'You have a strange accent. Where do you come from?'—dramatizes the systemic and internalized nature of racism. Thus the Arab man is 'born' as Other the instant the white woman's internalized racism is translated into his abjection. Far from suggesting that the man has not previously experienced discrimination, this instant has a paradigmatic function in such literature. The racialization operating here is different from what Appiah calls 'racialism', the neutral evaluation of a group in terms of shared attributes that, he argues, precedes racism (1992, 13 and 14). Although this is a useful distinction, the chronological order that Appiah proposes is, as Berel Lang shows, problematic historically: 'the search for categories of racial difference has typically been motivated by racism—the attachment of invidious weight to racial characteristics—rather than the other way round. That is, racism has been primary and racialism secondary' (18).

Equally crucial in this story is that racialization as racism coincides with the Arab man's loss of desire for the white woman. This doesn't mean that the body is a metaphor, a screen on which racial objectification is acted out; rather, his loss of desire shows the extent to which 'race and sex . . . are inextricably bound up in each other as signifiers that seep through the constraining boundaries of rationality' (Miles 138).[9] It becomes apparent at this point that racialization is already present in this one-night stand, well before the Arab man names it. Her picking him up may have initially appeared as a reinforcement of his masculinity but, in this racial/sexual scenario, it is a performative act that reproduces the way gender, sexual, and racial stereotypes function. While they are still in the bar, both the Arab man's initial awkwardness and the white woman's attraction to him reflect the 'cognitive construction' of stereotypes (Rapport 271). As she is turned on by his racial difference, he is at once excited and taken aback by her proposition. Thus while a gender stereotype (men are the predators, women the prey) is reversed, a racist stereotype (dark lovers are highly sexualized and desirable objects) is affirmed. This reading is easily inferred from the opening paragraphs of the story, although the protagonist does not enunciate this scenario until he is verbally insulted. Language—whether in the form of a 'strange accent' or of the cultural codes that inform this liaison—is the realm where ethnicity is produced. Loss of desire, the effect of this production of ethnicity, is not to be understood only in terms of the Arab man's sexual desire for the white woman; it is metonymically related to his loss of subjectivity, to his *becoming* 'nothing at all'.

Totalizing Origins / The Body Cultural

The racial, ethnic, and gender dynamics that El-Malh dramatizes reappear in many contributions to these anthologies. Furthermore, his narrator's unnecessary explanation ('my skin is dark') exemplifies the ethnic writer's sense of obligation to combat the opacity of language. The relentless recording, through language, of the concrete signatures of accent and race is a recurring element in these anthologies, demarcating the shifts in the characters' knowledge of themselves as subjects and objects. The means used to record those signatures vary, but the need to inscribe and critique them remains constant. How this need affects the desire informing ethnic subjectivity and its epistemological grounding is certainly a crucial question, but it cannot easily be answered here. Suffice it to say we cannot know the ethnic subject on his own terms unless we have access to the manifestations of his desire to make himself known—otherwise we have access only to images of ethnicity as it appears to the dominant society. That desire, always discursively produced, expresses itself with a forked tongue. On the individual level, it speaks of the need to address the difference between being ethnicized within a hegemonic structure and affirming one's own ethnic difference by choice. For example, my being defined by others as ethnic, or seen as a tourist in some cases (both in Canada and Greece), because of my accent, suggests a meaning of ethnicity that is different from the ethnicity implied when I myself choose to foreground my Greek origins. In the first instance my ethnic difference is appropriated; in the second my own agency is at work. On a more general level, the desire to name oneself as ethnic speaks of the mutable nature of subjectivity, a condition that is not exclusively determined by the various specificities underlying ethnicity. In both cases, ethnicity surfaces as a historical reality that, although not equivalent to gender, sexuality, and class, cannot be understood without reference to them.

Nevertheless, some of the writing in these anthologies represents ethnicity as a totalized form of identity that defines a person solely in terms of country of origin. In this case, unity and disparity, affirmation and negation, abjection and resistance are offered as faithful portrayals of a social body that is not always recognized as one determined by hegemonic self-interest. At the same time that we must heed the message much of this writing seems to convey—'This is what it is like to be ethnic'—we must also remain alert to the risks involved when ethnicity is postulated in mimetic terms, terms that tend to give it a value based on an authenticity that the epistemology of the ethnic subject often takes for granted, the conditions of diasporic mimicry discussed in the previous chapter. Interestingly enough, sometimes this overdetermination of ethnicity is not to be found in the contributions themselves but in the editors' prefaces. The editorial approach of Hendrika Ruger, the editor of a 'series of Dutch Canadian antholo-gies' (1989, 7), is a case in point.

Like DiGiovanni, Ruger presents her contributors' ethnicity in an unprob-lematized, if not essentialized, manner. In *Distant Kin*, for instance, she tells us that 'The "Dutch elements" in these literary works are found in details of obser-vation, in descriptions of typical Dutch-Canadian immigrant experiences, in a certain "Dutch outlook" of the authors, and in their perception of the world around them' (8). In her desire to highlight 'Dutchness', Ruger neglects to offer any kind of functional definition and misrepresents a number of her authors.

Cornelia Hoogland's 'How Our Feet Go On', for example, a long poem in the voice of a Dutch female immigrant, traces its narrator's longing for an 'assured Dutch self' (Ruger 1989, 40). Although it is punctuated with Dutch phrases, and expresses the acute sense of disappointment and loss caused by the difficulties the narrator faces as an immigrant woman, I would be hard-pressed to say what constitutes the ethnic specificity of her 'Dutch self' or 'Dutch outlook'. Nor does the absence of any specific indicators of 'Dutchness' suggest that Hoogland is part of what Sneja Gunew calls the 'unprecedented assault on the concept of the fixed subject by all those women, minorities, non-Westerners who realized they were excluded from its purview' (10). Unlike authors such as Claire Harris, Kristjana Gunnars, Ven Begamudré, and Yasmin Ladha, Hoogland is one of the many writers in these anthologies who endorse a unitary ethnic identity. Thus even though the narrator explicitly blames her husband for her disappointment and loss—'I should have known this was a trap. / Emigrate with me, he said. / So why am I shut in the women's quarters / with the stench of diapers and worse' (27)—Hoogland's emphasis on her search for an 'assured Dutch self' implies that its rediscovery will restore a wholeness shattered by immigration. Here ethnicity follows the model of a sovereign identity: sovereign first in the sense that it remains determined by birth origins, unyielding to processes of change, and second in the sense that it promises control and fulfilment.

In contrast to this approach to ethnicity, which both proves and disproves Ruger's claims above, the narratives 'Whoopers' and 'Who Speaks for Running Waters?' by the third-generation Canadian Kevin Van Tighem (Ruger 1989) do not thematize ethnicity, at least not directly. Instead, these poignant and evocative stories reflect their narrators' attachment to the Canadian landscape, an attachment that in turn reflects not assimilation, but the subject's process of acculturation. The characters' Dutch names, besides justifying the stories' inclusion in the anthology, draw attention to the differentiation the ethnic subject undergoes, a process that should not always be understood in minority terms. Ruger overlooks the fact that Van Tighem disproves the reductive assumption that his writing will be about things Dutch.

Moreover, Ruger does not explain why her anthologies are not called Dutch *and* Belgian, since she gathers in them writers with roots in Belgium as well as the Netherlands. She does not take into account the historical ties and differences between the two countries, which were united for a brief period; nor does she consider any distinctive national feelings the Dutch-speaking writers of Belgium might have, let alone the relations between languages and nationalities in the Netherlands and Belgium, and what happens when they are 'transplanted' to Canada. Ruger's inclusion criteria smack of a positivism that subsumes any contesting elements in her contributors' construction of ethnic subjectivity or the apparent lack of interest among some of them in ethnic matters. Her view of ethnicity borders on 'ethnic absolutism' (Gilroy 1992). She tends to ignore the relationship between ethnicity and nationalism, to leave little if any room for cross-cultural influences, and to overlook the different ways in which a given writer might deal with assimilation, or express a vision of integration or resistance to Canada. The result is an apparently seamless ethnicity, from which the diversities or conflicts that might be part of an ethnic community's history are excluded. In a state with an official multiculturalism policy, ethnicity runs the risk of becoming both an inescapable label and a master narrative that subordinates the subject in the present to her roots in the past.

Ruger's strategy of drawing from more than one origin but privileging only one ethnic identity raises questions when she tries to account for John Weier's inclusion in *Dutch Voices*. Weier, born in Winnipeg and raised as a Mennonite, is included because the Mennonites' religious roots go back to the sixteenth-century Dutch preacher Menno Simons. As Ruger puts it, 'For the Mennonites . . . the journey has been long and the times hard. Their family names still remind us of the fact that their roots were in The Netherlands' (1989, 7). Yet many Mennonites are of German descent. Ruger's generalization brings ethnicity to the fore in terms that echo the state discourse on multiculturalism. The same essentialist approach is evident in her long biographical notes on the contributors, which list in detail their ancestors' migrations.[10] The construction of ethnicity here is the result of an overdetermined act of nomination. Ruger appears to believe that one ought to maintain an ethnic, and by implication marginal, identity even if one's family has been in Canada for three or four generations. The problem with this position lies not in the 'natural' fact that many authors acknowledge their roots, but in the underlying assumption that those origins are the exclusive determinants of subjectivity. By conflating, if not confiscating, national histories, by equating religion with ethnicity, and by ignoring aesthetic issues, Ruger demonstrates the elasticity of ethnicity, but also the dangers implicit in its overdetermination. Treating ethnicity in such a way manifests an epistemology in which the object position is already installed in the subject.

Naturalizing the Body Cultural

Ine Schepers' story 'Discovery in Delft' serves to illustrate Ruger's ideology. After the opening paragraph's description of the market square in Delft, the narrator wonders:

> What am I doing here? For the first time since our emigration to Canada, twenty-seven years ago, I'm back in Holland alone, without husband or children. I am out of touch with my country. Restless between large, fun-filled family reunions, I'm gripped by an indefinite yearning like those cravings during pregnancy when I don't even know what I'm craving for. (Ruger 1988, 11)

Despite her feelings of estrangement and anxiety—inscribed in the story by a series of questions such as 'Did it happen the way I remember it?' (14)—the narrator concludes: 'This is my country. Mine forever' (15). The biological nature of her 'cravings' suggests that the narrator is 'forever' destined to look backwards, seeking to recover the missing bond with the mother country. This desire for a reunion with the symbolic order of the maternal body is presented as a romance that, we are led to believe, remains unadulterated by any feelings of attachment to Canada that the story's immigrant narrator might develop. Indeed, the only sign that the authenticity of these yearnings might be compromised, the fact that she finds herself singing in English the words of an old Dutch hymn, is quickly put aside.

> A Mighty Fortress is our God—*Een vaste burcht is onze God*. The Dutch words of the hymn flow easily now. I say them silently, sentence after sentence, while floodlights suddenly illuminate the contours of the New Church, accentuating the darkness of the sky. I leave the market square and walk back to the car. . . . The silent presence of history vibrates in the cool night air. A sense of permanence and stability invades me. Flashes of memory flood my mind . . . (14)

The metaphysical overtones of the narrator's reunion with the mother country, although narrated in the present tense, privilege the past. The religious context of this scene sanctions the immigrant's desire to embrace the maternal body, to authenticate her origins. Thus the hymn's translation from English into Dutch parallels the symbolic conversion from the status of immigrant to that of 'natural' denizen.

Yet the narrator's epiphany at this point is made possible only by a breakdown of temporality and logic. There is a contradiction between the narrator's claiming the Netherlands as hers 'forever' and her putting this feeling into practice by 'visiting all those places' (15). The violence and transgression implicit in the metaphor of 'invasion', instead of affirming the narrator's transcendence of the diasporic condition, expose the inauthenticity of her proprietorial claim ('Mine forever'). The epistemological position she assumes (that she knows who she is, where she belongs, and what is rightfully hers) appears to be as transient as her desire to prove herself to be, in Chow's words, 'non-duped' (1993a, 52). 'Because the image, in which the other is often cast, is always distrusted as illusion, deception, and falsehood, attempts to salvage the other often turn into attempts to uphold the other as the non-duped—the site of authenticity and true knowledge.' But as Chow proceeds to show, 'those who think they are undeceived are the fools' (1993a, 52). It is from this double perspective of deception and presumed authenticity that the story, I suggest, oscillates between faction and fiction. The elation with which the narrator asserts her knowledge is tenable only insofar as she suspends her immigrant condition and what makes her different in Canada. Ironically, it is Canada as the originary point of the journey to the Netherlands that enables her to claim this experience of certainty. Her 'host' country, Canada, now appears as the parasite to the narrator's 'discovery of Delft'. The metaphor of pregnancy, besides signifying that she carries her immigrant condition within her, indicates that she herself gives birth to the maternal body; this image is typical of the biological tendencies of certain kinds of multicultural discourse, but it also indicates the extent to which the power of origins lies in how they are constructed, not in any 'natural' essence.

Even more interesting than these tensions are the religious and cultural sites within which the immigrant narrator positions herself in the story. The polarity between the darkness of the sky and the illuminated contours of the church (implying an entry into cosmic time), between forgetting and remembering the mother tongue, between recalling Delft's distant history and knowing nothing of its present, relegates the immigrant to the position of a damned figure awaiting redemption. Written in English, and published in Canada for Canadian readers by a Canadian company called the Netherlandic Press, 'Discovery in Delft' deconstructs its own ending. It addresses the immigrant's relationship to Canada and at the same time shows that relationship to derive from the immigrant's immanent experience in the country of origin. If this story's reading of diasporic experience has the authenticity presumably recovered in a moment of near ecstasy, what is the immigrant to do when temporality is restored, when the excitement of her transcendent rediscovery of 'home' subsides, when she returns to the host country only to discover that she has had a home there for 'twenty-seven years'?

Characters who speak of the return to a homeland—a recurring motif in these anthologies—tend not to concern themselves with such questions. Instead, they are inclined to reify what their longing produces, reconstructing their subjectivity by privileging a past cut off from social and political realities. Such narrators assume a paradigmatic role as they exemplify official multiculturalism's views of the ethnic subject as remaining the same 'forever'. Ethnicity is thus configured as a 'natural' condition, the outcome of displacement, that cannot (must not?) be absconded from or adulterated. Identity defined in ethnic terms, it is suggested, can be understood only as permanent and stable. This reluctance to seriously examine what ethnicity signifies, and how, suggests that ethnicity, together with the origins that are often taken to be its principal referents, is a construct produced by the anxiety and loss that accompany displacement; often, it is also the result of the subject's mistaking her legitimation by the law as an Other for a benign acknowledgement of her presence.

Beyond the Determinism of Origins

Not all texts in these anthologies, however, articulate ethnic difference in essentialist terms. Some of them deconstruct the assumed determinism binding diasporic subjects to their birth or ancestral countries and certain inherited premises about ethnicization. Take, for example, Nigel Darbasie's poem 'Conceiving the Stranger', from *Voices: Canadian Writers of African Descent*, edited by Ayanna Black:

> First define the tribal self
> in skin colour, language
> religion, culture.
> Add to that
> boundaries
> of nation, city
> village or street.
> And there you are:
> out of place
> a foreigner
> the strange other
> a moving violation
> of tribal differences. (Black 1992, 58)

The proliferation of names designating the immigrant points to the diversity of the border lines that separate indigenous from non-indigenous subjectivities; it also points to the impossibility of attributing marginalization to a single source or agent of power. The speaker perceives ethnicity as a construct situated between the overlapping and conflicting meanings of difference and Otherness. Being ethnically different does not necessarily mean being a 'strange other'. Otherness is conferred on the subject, and it says more about those who use it as a discriminatory gesture than about those marginalized by it.

Consider Cyril Dabydeen's poem 'I am not', from the same anthology, which powerfully resists ethnic nostalgia:

> I am not West Indian
> I am not—
> let me tell you again and again
> let Lamming and Selvon talk of places
>   too distant from me;
> let me also recover and seethe
> & shout with a false tongue
> if I must—
> that i am here
> nowhere else . . . (Black 1992, 31)

The immigrant speaker's affirmation of his ties to Canada reverses the tradition of ethnic writing that privileges nostalgia for the past; in effect it denounces what Kristeva calls 'the cult of origins' (1993, 2). The shift from 'I' to 'i' undermines the sovereignty of identity and reflects the mutability of the subject. Far from being oblivious to the presence of boundaries—'we fashion new boundaries / and still i do not know' (32)—the speaker acknowledges the constructedness of the dividing lines that usually delimit ethnicity. Not unlike Jorge Etcheverry's poem 'Ethnical Blues' in *Chilean Literature in Canada*, edited by Naín Nómez, Dabydeen's 'Multiculturalism', also in *Voices*, offers a definition of multiculturalism contrary to the one propounded by official ideology that insists on separating one ethnic group from another. Its speaking 'I' bemoans 'The ethnics at our door / Malingering with heritage' (Black 1992, 29), but dons, among others, Chinese, Japanese, black, aboriginal, and Québécois identities. Far from presenting a utopian vision in which specificities have been eliminated, this floating 'I' is lodged in the political realities of 'employment equity', the 'police shootings in Toronto', 'vandalism at a Jewish cemetery' (30).

These poets' visions, then, span political as well as emotional and geographical distances. As Manuel Aránguiz, another poet represented in *Chilean Literature*, says:

> We are not separated by a different song
> nor by the colour of our skin
> nor by our stature.
> It is the coming and going of commodities
> the legal plundering
> the inhuman coveting
> of things. (Nómez 4)

Here the racial and cultural differences that many ethnic writers and ethnic studies tend to valorize in their treatment of ethnicity are shown to be subject to political and legal commodification. The ideology implied here reflects the impossibility of understanding ethnicity in essentialist terms—terms that disregard the complex roles played by political, economic, and legal systems in its determination.

The Literariness and Thematics of Diasporic Discourse

The complicity between official multiculturalism and some ethnic anthologies often becomes apparent in the writing itself, some of which seems to have been selected specifically to represent the putative collective ethos of an ethnic community. This strategy often tends to reproduce—unwittingly, one presumes—clichéd images about immigrants, and to fulfil stereotypical expectations. For example, Marieke Jalink-Wijbrans' 'Immigrant', in *Transplanted Lives* (Ruger 1988), more a document of personal anguish than a poem, reflects a need to make the immigrant's plight public and (like many other selections in these anthologies) suggests that the act of writing has the therapeutic or documentary function of exposing the tension between faction and fiction:

> Because I'm different
> I will never
> really belong.
> I left my country
> where I now
> don't belong either.
> I live in a vacuum:
> I belong neither
> here nor there. (52)

Beyond its nod towards poetic notation, 'Immigrant' is artless. Its inclusion in the anthology is symptomatic of the tendency to make the immigrant experience the primary, defining element of ethnic writing.

This raises a number of questions, among them what Carole Boyce Davies calls 'the loaded question of literariness'. The fact is that some of the selections in these anthologies were 'never intended to be introduced to the public as "works of literature"' (6). Although Jars Balan and Yuri Klynovy remark that the Ukrainian émigrés and Canadian-born writers of Ukrainian descent included in *Yarmarok* 'were asked to contribute pieces that drew on their ethnic background or experience', they argue that 'in neither case was content invoked as a criterion of acceptance.' Yet they admit that 'Some of the writing encompassed in this volume is primarily of historical or sociological value, and only secondarily of aesthetic interest. It has been included for the benefit of Ukrainian Canadianists and others working in the field of ethnic studies' (xii). Like some other editors of ethnic anthologies, Balan and Klynovy make it clear that their selection criteria are informed by the intention to document their ethnic group's experience and 'express a contemporary Ukrainian' identity (xi).

This editorial approach is to some extent in keeping with the criteria used by the government officials who fund ethnic writing projects and heritage festivals. It becomes quite obvious that such criteria are not meant merely to ensure representation of what presumably already exists in ethnic communities; they also reflect the overdetermined definitions of ethnicity outside ethnic communities and are complicit with the various policies that attempt to situate ethnicity inside certain parameters. When editors, overtly or tacitly, concede that writing of dubious literary merit may be included in their anthologies, they give credence (ironically) to the excuse traditionally given by mainstream publishers for excluding minority writers from publication. This, of course, raises the question not only of which, but also of whose aesthetic values determine the publication of ethnic writing.

Lorris Elliott, Cyril Dabydeen, and Naín Nómez problematize this issue in a context that reveals the dynamics of cultural production and the marketing practices of publishers. Elliott, the editor of the black writing anthology *Other Voices*, acknowledges in his preface the financial support and the instigation of the Secretary of State in the production of a survey of literary writings by blacks in Canada, but he also challenges the expectations that multiculturalism raises in readers concerning the thematics of ethnic writing.[11] In an essay that documents his experiences as an editor and bibliographer of black writing in Canada, Elliott observes that, 'despite the expressed desire of the Canadian government that minority ethnic groups remain visible and not be melted into one faceless Canadian mass, one finds that the creative output of Blacks in Canada is yet to be fully recognised, made available and properly assessed' (1990, 170). Elliott elaborates on the systemic discrimination he refers to here by asking whether 'work written by Blacks in Canada' is 'of an inferior quality to [that] written by others' (1990, 170). Since the obvious answer is no, he addresses the problem by talking about the lack of 'commercial viability' that publishers at the time attributed to ethnic writing (1988, 5; 1990, 170), which led to facile rejection of it. Significantly, these practices had a negative impact not only on the dissemination of black writing but also on black writers' own attitudes towards publishing. As Elliott says, 'One of the most surprising obstacles in my way—one that is most ironical—was the reluctance of Blacks themselves to provide samples of their work for possible publication. I eventually discovered that this attitude was a result of the fact that they had been frequently duped by people who came full of promises, but delivered nothing' (1990, 171). Despite the difficulties he encountered in compiling his anthology of black writers 'of various regional and ethnic origins' (1990, 170), Elliott saw no reason to compromise his literary standards.

A similar concern with ethnic difference and aesthetics underlies Nómez's bilingual anthology *Chilean Literature in Canada /Literatura Chilena en Canada*. Its title introduces us to a national literature represented by established and new writers who immigrated to Canada primarily for political reasons. The editor's discussion of the writers' contributions is informed less by a need to prove their ethnic difference than by a desire to address the politics of cultural production in Canada. Nómez argues in his foreword against 'a synthetic, totalizing culture that denies expression to the majority of the people', and goes on to define culture as 'a plural phenomenon, a constantly renewed place of encounter and dialogue between the various cultural groups co-existing in the country' (vi). In fact, the specific ethnic focus of the anthologies under discussion here does little to advance the dialogue among various ethnic groups, but almost exclusively reflects each group's interaction with the mainstream society. Nevertheless, Nómez makes it very clear that his main concern is not to appease any anxiety about ethnic difference but to locate his contributors within the various traditions of Chilean literature. '[W]e cannot expect these writers,' he says, 'to fully identify with their present historical situation, nor with Canadian literary production. They must be seen,' he insists, 'within a literary tradition that has fought in this century to free itself of its European (and especially French) influences, and to find its own mode of expression, whose most salient traits are the telluric American world, interpersonal relationships, struggles for social liberation and the reconquest of a non-colonized language' (viii). Language and exile, as Claudio Durán says, go hand in hand:

> Exile and grammar—each possessed
> of its inexorable rules,
> like the polar flight of migratory birds that fall
> in Lake Ontario
> never to stop resting. (Nómez 16)

Having lost their 'natural audience', these writers have to decide whether to write in Spanish or in one of Canada's official languages. But Nómez does not address this dilemma; instead, he is concerned with these writers' 'task', which is 'twofold: they must maintain their links with their native language and culture, and assimilate their experience in Canada and its culture' (x). By locating these writers in what Abdul JanMohamed would call their 'generative ambience' (1983, 2), Nómez investigates the principal theme of their work, namely one's relation to the country of origin, but he does so without endorsing the nostalgia that informs much of the tradition of ethnic literature, at least in its early days. The main reason for this, perhaps, is the 'traumatic experience' of political 'repression' (x) in Chile—in many cases the experience that occasioned the writers' exile. When political exile is the reason for emigration, nostalgia for the place left behind does not lead to a mythologizing of origins. Instead, as much of the writing in this anthology demonstrates, it leads to the task of remembering why these writers were 'lost to the history of their nation' (x). Such remembering has nothing to do with cherishing tender images of the mother country. Quite the contrary. Gonzalo Millán writes in 'The Break':

> They peel fruit and smoke
> and joke among themselves and with me
> while I hang upside down by my feet. (Nómez 62)

Not all of the writing in this anthology is about torture and political persecution, nor does Nómez attempt to suppress the individual differences among his contributors for the sake of presenting a collective ethos of exile.[12] His main editorial intent is to locate the poetry and fiction he has selected in a specific cultural, social, and political context. He does not perpetuate the construction of cultural icons suggesting an unalterable national or ethnic identity. Instead, he is concerned with the way this writing records the inevitable changes that occur after exile.

If the importance of Nómez's anthology lies in his, and his writers', resistance to a unified thematics of ethnicity, DiGiovanni's *Italian-Canadian Voices* attempts to consolidate the assumption that ethnic writing is always about the same themes: it 'speak[s]', as Pivato argues in his preface to her anthology, 'to the modern Canadian experience of the immigrant, the ethnic and the exile' (DiGiovanni 13). This assumption, still prevalent today, ascribes to ethnic writing an essentialist thematics that, on one hand, reflects the goal of official multiculturalism to 'preserve' and 'enhance' ethnicity as a stable entity and, on the other, posits ethnicity as the principal determinant of subjectivity. A certain ethnic essentialism may be necessary, as Spivak argued, although, as I have already suggested, ethnicity is surely one element among many regulating subjectivity. Yet there is an ironic twist in Pivato's essentialist approach, for he does not situate exclusively in the mother country the past that such writing tends to embrace.

For example, to demonstrate that ethnic discourse is conditioned by history and creates history, he begins with a short litany of names: 'Caboto, Da Verrazano, Tonti, Marini and Bressani.' They are not, as one might expect, the names of writers featured in the anthology; 'these are the Italian names,' he tells us, 'that appear in the early history of Canada. These explorers and military heroes remind us that Italians have had a long association with Canada.' And he goes on: 'In this century thousands of immigrants from the boot-shaped peninsula have come to this country and have made their labour felt in our social and economic life. More recently a few of these immigrants and some of their sons and daughters have begun to make a contribution to the literary life of Canada' (DiGiovanni 13). Exploration, military bravado, social history, genealogies: these are not just rhetorical gestures acquainting us with new literary voices. In endowing the Italian Canadian writers he is about to introduce with a Canadian past as long as the one Canada itself can claim, Pivato remaps Canadian history. While pointing out that most of the writing in the anthology deals with what he calls 'the trauma of dislocation', and drawing attention to the 'authenticity' of its 'verbal expression' (DiGiovanni 13), his opening remarks, subtly yet purposefully, bid the reader to review the ideologies that have shaped the Canadian cultural canon.

Pivato's way of stating his claim on Canadian history changes the image of the ethnic subject as a foreign Other, and thus works against the ideology of official multiculturalism that defines the ethnic subject by strategically privileging her origins outside Canada. He proposes an ethnic subjectivity that is domesticated not because it has been appropriated by state policies, but rather because of its continuous historic presence.[13] Here, as in some anthologies of black writing, ethnicity is defined as a 'naturalized' presence. To do this, Pivato employs the double gaze that structures the conventional expression of ethnic experience. This gaze is characterized by temporality—the *now* and the *then* of Canadian history that he claims as ethnically his. He attempts to strengthen the position of Italian Canadians by presenting the diachronic view of ethnicity that is lacking in the Multiculturalism Act. The writers in *Italian-Canadian Voices* are exactly that, Italian Canadian. Pivato's hyphen functions to assert difference, but that difference is not total. The hyphen thus performs an interesting balancing act; Pivato, I believe, wishes us to hear not the articulation of a gap in the space of the hyphen, but a self-identity doubly stressed. As a link, functioning like the conjunction 'and', the hyphen does not cancel out either the Italian or the Canadian identity. Identity becomes synonymous with the kind of difference that separates one group from another. Pivato's rhetoric may be much obliged to official multiculturalism, but it does not condone that policy's ideology of passive domestication.

Between 'Here' and 'There': The Politics of Collective Ethos

The complex politics of representing a collective ethnic ethos takes a different configuration in the anthologies of writers of colour. For example, *A Shapely Fire: Changing the Literary Landscape*, edited by Cyril Dabydeen, presents what its editor calls an 'evolving literature' of Caribbean authors framed by 'the *there*, the place where one came from', and 'the *here*, temperate Canada, where the Caribbean spirit asserts itself in the desire to forge a wholesome and meaningful existence' (10). The spatial metaphor of Dabydeen's double gaze may emphasize the Caribbean, but it also illustrates the diversity of race, ethnicity, and language that may characterize a single region. In this respect, his anthology is a mirror of the multicultural and multiracial realities in Canada.

He tells us that Claire Harris's work 'is expressed in the form of a spiritual odyssey to Africa as the speaker [in her poems] fuses those experiences with the present'; in Marlene Nourbese Philip's work, he continues, we see 'virtually the same fusion but with a distinctive cadence'; in Neil Bissoondath's story he finds 'attempts at bridging to the *here*'; while in 'Anthony Phelps, both *here* and *there* are finally welded into a mythopoeic paean distinctively African and Caribbean and extending to the universal through the energy of sheer texture' (11). Fusing, bridging, welding—these metaphors suggest a coming together, a union both expressive of the desire to coexist in a space of diversities and antagonistic to the distinctiveness that his contributors advocate. Far from wanting to eliminate this paradox, the result of racial and ethnic hybridity, Dabydeen highlights it through the writing he selects. For example, Horace Goddard's 'Mamaetu' foregrounds the very difference that marginalizes its speaker while at the same time relegating the reader to the margins of understanding:

Oh iponri
Oh iponri
Damballa Hwedo
Ogun Batala
Ogun Balanjo
Damballa Hwedo

Mother, we are here (Dabydeen 112)

The poem's concluding line might strike an affirmative note, but any universalism or utopianism the reader might wish to attach to it is curbed by its irony. 'Here' echoes Dabydeen's spatial metaphor, but it does so in a reverse fashion, for Goddard's 'here' signifies Dabydeen's 'there'. As a floating signifier, this 'here' speaks of the anxiety of belonging.

One Out of Many: A Collection of Writings by 21 Black Women in Ontario (1975), to my knowledge the first anthology of black writing in Canada, and of women exclusively at that, similarly announces a collective ethos, only this time it is informed by race and gender. With 'a great deal of pride and trepidation', the editor, Liz Cromwell, introduces her contributors by addressing not only Canadian readers in general but other black women specifically: 'If the work inspires other Black women to write,' she says, 'then it has succeeded' (5). This statement comes after what DiGiovanni would call her apologia:

> While some people are obsessed with involved language that [attests] to their great learning, I believe seldom does this contribute to clarity. I regard the poems in this book as successful. Because they are not trivial in concept or inconsequential in message, and speak of experiences common to people in the group labelled 'visible minority'. And while I recognise the work has many weaknesses, I am still convinced that the words of the women must be heard and read, because the message is undeniably clear. (5)

In its stated intentions, Cromwell's anthology is multicultural in a literal sense, yet it also goes beyond the official multicultural imperative to preserve and enhance a collectively defined ethnic identity. Her preface lacks any of the self-conscious strategies that would allow her to plead ethnic—she speaks as a writer about other writers. Indeed, instead of looking backwards in an attempt to consolidate the ethnic presence of her contributors, she looks forward in her desire to encourage more writing by black Canadian women.

The history of race and gender represented here questions the solidified notion of ethnicity that marks other first-wave ethnic anthologies. As Cromwell says, some of the contributors 'migrated from the United States, Jamaica, Trinidad, Guyana, Africa, South America and elsewhere', and some are 'native born Canadians whose parents or grandparents came from somewhere else' (5). The experiences of immigration, ethnicity, and nationality are secondary to the experience of being a black woman. In privileging race and gender, Cromwell invites us to reconsider the dogmatism that might lurk in the claims made in other ethnic anthologies. In its hybridity, *One Out of Many* offers—more than any other volume examined here—the kind of 'inter*national* dimension' that Bhabha talks about; it stresses not homogeneity but 'the margins of the nation-space and . . . the boundaries *in-between* nations and peoples' (1990, 4).

This 'inter*national*' component presents an alternative to the tendency of official multiculturalism to treat ethnic difference as an instrument that reinforces dualism. Ironically, however, this complex of factors determining subjectivity is compressed in Cromwell's attempt to make her anthology fit within the 'emerging' canon of ethnic voices. '[A]ll other ethnic women have been heard before,' she says, 'except Black women' (5).[14] This statement would lead us to assume that 'black' and 'ethnic' belong to the same semantic category. This collapse of differential meanings demonstrates both the competition among ethnic groups that official multiculturalism and its programs encourage, and the problems that arise when ethnicity is defined in exclusively racial terms. Further, this anthology suggests that the politics of ethnicity and/or race does not subsume the politics of gender or class. Radhakrishnan's suggestion that 'the politics of the "one" typically overwhelm[s] the politics of the "other"' (1992, 78) is answered here unequivocally. These women authors never lose sight of any of the forces that mediate their subjectivity; they keep them in clear view, with great panache and irony.

For example, the title of Andrea de Shields' poem 'Return' parodies the 'craving' to return to one's origins. The 'return' here signals that 'Black is back' after 'hiding in a nigger's head / Sleeping in a negroe's bed' (Cromwell 41). Similarly, Vera Cudjoe's poem 'Enough' articulates a politics of resistance that defies the representation of ethnicity through mimicry:

Rass man! Rass!
Enuff o'dis
Blasted romantic stuff
Enuff is enough.
Rass man! Rass!
Enuff o'dis
Blasted white man tic stuff

Enuff is enough.
Is all I can take
O' dis sugar cake stuff
And 'your skin is like silk'
And 'mine is like milk
Next to you'n.'
Shit! Enuff is enough.
Take yur tongue from my ear
I had it to here man
don't tell me to say
What you want to hear.
Cause how much I like it
and how much I want it
And how well we fit
Is all fantasy shit
A nail is a nail
A screw is a screw
Or didn't you know
I'm having an experiment with you.
And enuff is enough
O.K.   (Cromwell 37)

The double spelling of enough/enuff signals the poem's double talking, for its 'blasted' language demythologizes both the gendered and racialized codes of romance and inherited definitions of ethnicity. The clash between written/ hegemonic and aural/oral discourse, the scrambling of standard English by the speaker's black dialect (with its deliberate defamiliarizing impact on the white reader), the deafening repetition—all help to explode the stability that is often attributed to the ethnic subject in these anthologies. The speaker's 'experiment' is already working: not only does she display her agency in showing that her racial and gender otherness must not be understood as the only characteristics by which she is defined, but she is acutely aware of the politics of seduction and resistance. In her poem, to borrow Said's words, 'culture . . . is a source of identity, and a rather combative one at that.' This return is 'accompan[ied by] rigorous codes of intellectual and moral behavior that are opposed to the permissiveness associated with such relatively liberal philosophies as multiculturalism and hybridity' (1993, xiii). Indeed, the speaker shows this kind of liberalism to be 'fantasy shit'.

Derailing Essentialist Definitions and Canonical Questions

I have tried to read one ethnic anthology through another and each through its preface, in search of an understanding of the diasporic subject's process of self-reflection and self-representation. The conclusions that can be drawn about this corpus of writing are neither final nor straightforward. The heterogeneity of this ethnic discourse demands that we study the cultural context that (re)defines the diasporic subject as object, that we examine her 'marked subjectivit[y]' (McCallum 432), and that we articulate the relations of complicity and power that inform her work. This is why the ethnic anthology functions contrapuntally—it is always responsive to the forces that would relegate it to the margins. Reflecting, structurally and ideologically, forces that construct ethnicity, each editorial preface functions as a metanarrative of the cultural and psychological anxieties experienced by the diasporic subject.

In these anthologies, ethnic subjectivity, be it securely accepted or radically questioned, involves an epistemological process intended to recuperate the agency lost through displacement. The subject's discourse textualizes the discursive relations binding individual identity to collective ethos, and the cumulative impact of the construction of the past and the ethnicization of the present. This writing is the product of the thematization of ethnic experience, and it is marked by a direct and unambiguous foregrounding of the authors' origins. In these texts, the 'death of the author' announced by poststructuralism is annulled. The ethnic specificity of the author's name comes to signify authority and authenticity. The displaced author finds a 'home' in writing. Or, to put it differently, characters and personae reflect their authors' politics of self-location.

If the anthologies examined so far suggest that ethnic discourse produced in the 1970s and early 1980s remained on the margins of mainstream culture, and paid only scant attention to the ideologies informing ethnic 'authenticity', the 1990s mark the beginning of a new trend in the anthologizing of ethnic writing, as testified by the many collections published by both small and large presses.[15] Interestingly, though, while the publication of such texts coincides with what we have come to call the 'canon debate', ethnic discourse is rarely mentioned in arguments about canonicity. Thus the questions that, for example, *Telling It: Women and Language Across Cultures* raises are not thematized either by the critical dialogue between Robert Lecker and Frank Davey,[16] or by Lecker's edited collection *Canadian Canons: Essays in Literary Value*.

Edited by The Telling It Book Collective, comprising Sky Lee, Lee Maracle, Daphne Marlatt, and Betsy Warland, *Telling It* is described as 'the transformation of a conference' of the same name that took place in Vancouver in 1988. It affords us a historical look at the politics involved in the lives and writing of these lesbians and women of colour. As Daphne Marlatt says in her introduction, the conference from which the book emerged was 'an attempt to form a meeting ground on the very fractured margins we [the contributors] inhabit' (15). At once a meeting ground and a field of 'cultural difference', the collection has a polyvalence that contests not only the Canadian literary canon, but also those social, cultural, and political institutions that have attempted to render the contributors to the collection[17] invisible or inconsequential.

Telling It thematizes difference without eliding either its complexity or the difficulties it raises. It does so by contesting difference from within the 'margins' to which difference is relegated. '[T]here was a certain idealism,' Marlatt observes, 'that fueled this conference. But the trouble with idealism . . . is that it can overlook the pain of real differences in oppression for the sake of some fantasized solidarity. Differences did surface, sometimes in suppressed, even suppressive ways . . . but differences also surfaced in lucid and edifying ways' (13). Contestation figures as the political and cultural value accompanying these writers' political and literary output. Far from being simply a matter of attitude, contestation 'augurs', in Marlatt's words, 'a contextual shift so basic it shakes the edifice of values we live inside of' (18). What makes this kind of shift possible is the increased, if not unavoidable, recognition of the material reality of difference and its contingent relation to the materiality of language. The ideological margins separating the literary and the political, as they have so far been perceived, are not merely touched upon in this collection; they are named and problematized as the discursive site where contestation occurs and where alternative courses of action ought to be pursued.

In contrast, even though Lecker introduces *Canadian Canons* as belonging to the tradition of 'interrogations [that] are inevitably contentious' (1991, 3), his collection illustrates what happens when literary values are questioned while the edifice containing them remains intact. Lecker presents this volume as ground-breaking and timely—'the first collection of essays to focus on Canadian literary canons' (3)—but the ground it works is hardly new. Most of the contributors plainly ignore not only the ethnic literature published up to that point, but also the multicultural debate in Canada. Given that the theoretical and critical sources (for example, John Guillory's work) acknowledged in Lecker's introduction have their departure point in identity politics, it is ironic that cultural difference remains largely invisible in this collection.

Instead of signalling contestation, the reference to the plural 'canons' in Lecker's introduction is merely a conciliatory gesture; in fact, he fails to acknowledge that the materiality of language manifested in literature occurs at the interface of political and cultural production. Indeed, Lecker shows a reluctance to shift the debate away from canon formation and towards those excluded sites that help to circumscribe the Canadian literary tradition. As he says:

> this book cannot avoid becoming a field of contestation both within and outside its covers, for canonical enquiry is deliberately aimed at destabilizing authority through its analysis of the intermingling structures that uphold the political, economic, social, and cultural institutions that house the prevailing versions of literary history, tradition, form, and taste. Any analysis of canons must consider the status of these institutions. Who rejects them? Who sees them crumbling? Who feels locked out? Who feels locked in and can't leave? Who loves their shape and size? Who is determined to remodel? Who holds their keys? (1991, 3-4).

The questions Lecker raises are both relevant and timely, but they remain rhetorical, for he does not venture to answer them; nor do the majority of his contributors.

Although all the essays in the collection offer intriguing and important rereadings of canon-formation in Canada, most of their authors are similarly unwilling to raise radical questions about the making of the Canadian literary tradition. In their essays ethnicity remains, to repeat Bannerji's words, 'a pervasive absence [that] signifies an absent presence'. Most of the contributors do not acknowledge their complicity in taking as givens the very 'values' they intend to examine. Dermot McCarthy, for example, rightly states that 'Any critique of the contemporary Canadian literary canon which does not address these issues [how the canon is structured both 'theoretically' and 'concretely'] risks envelopment in the very structure it seeks to challenge or dismantle' (30). Yet, even though most of the critics here deal with historical developments, and in fact historicize their arguments, the histories they discuss are marked by a 'monomania' similar to the one McCarthy attributes to the making of Canadian literary history (45). Thus while they are concerned with the formation of a national canon, no consistent argument is offered to the effect that the nation under question is unthinkable without the history of immigration. Granted, a number of the authors, like Carole Gerson, focus on periods when hardly any ethnic writing was published. But, except for Sherry Simon, no contributor thematizes the absence of such writing. This glaring omission is not just an instance of the inevitable blind spots that, as Lecker says, characterize the critical practice (6-7). Rather, it is symptomatic of the fact that, as Lorraine Weir puts it in the same collection, 'What has been canonized is, . . . always, what can be absorbed with least resistance or noise in the institution' (194).

Simon's reference to 'minority writing' in Quebec (175) is the collection's only reminder of the other literatures in Canada, aboriginal and ethnic. Although she focuses on Québécois literature, the central premise of her argument applies to English Canadian literature as well. As she writes, 'In some ways, the terms of the discussion relating aesthetic judgments to socio-political pressures have remained stable in the Quebec literary tradition. . . . Revisionist assault on the canon . . . comes less in the form of an alternate list of works than in a shift in the site at which this essential link is discerned' (167). This lack of an 'alternate list' of works through which to re-examine social and aesthetic values also characterizes the so-called canon debate about English Canadian literature. Thus behind Lecker's editorial intention to put together a collection of essays that are 'understandable, accessible, and therefore, safe' (7) lies the fact that *Canadian Canons* tends to reproduce the very values it analyzes. When contestation emerges in the collection, it is the result of the coming together of the presumed interiority of the canonized value systems and the rhetorical tropes that facilitate their discussion. This kind of contestation, though, is too gentle to effect any change in the way canon formation in Canada operates in relation to ethnic writing. By contrast, *Telling It* posits contestation as a discursive site within which cultural production is to be examined.

It is hardly surprising, then, that contestation arises mostly from within groups that have been socially and politically marginalized. Perhaps they are not concerned with 'safety' precisely because they have nothing to lose, because they're used to taking risks. In this context, while Lecker's editorial project fails to change the ideological and cultural systems that have put in place the tradition of English Canadian literature, *Telling It* succeeds as an intervention into the canon and multiculturalism because it does not shy away from its internal contradictions, because its contributors do not hide, or hide behind, their ideologies. *Telling It*, then, is an instance of what Bhabha calls 'affective writing', writing that 'overcome[s] the pedagogical predictability of the sententious professor and the politician', and 'attempt[s] to construct modes of political and cultural agency that are commensurate with historical conjunctures where populations are culturally diverse, racially and ethnically divided' (1992, 57).

Towards Relational Knowledge

The anthologizing of ethnic writing since 1990 reflects a determination to foreground ethnicity not only as compensatory knowledge emerging from within the binary paradigm of Us and Them but also, and more significantly, as relational knowledge. In this context, 'the word "multiculturalism" has no essence; it points to a debate' (Shohat and Stam 47). This debate takes the form of a dialogue among various cultural communities. Ethnic voices are no longer segregated within the space of individual ethnic groups; they converge as they speak with each other, but—the most important element here—they do so without being reduced to sameness, as they often speak across each other as well. Thus they do 'not preach a pseudo-equality of viewpoints' (Shohat and Stam 48). Instead, they generate a dialogue that invites us to contest inherited assumptions within both ethnic communities and the mainstream. This kind of dialogue, however cacophonous and discordant it may be at times, demands that both interlocutors change (Shohat and Stam 49). Thus authenticity may still be privileged, but this privilege is counterbalanced by a growing disbelief in the transparency of self-evident truths about both ethnic communities and the dominant society. Ethnicity no longer functions merely as a symptom of difference, as a designated margin that has to be managed. Instead, it points to the gaps in identity, among ethnic and non-ethnic Canadians alike. That not all those inhabiting the conventional centre position are aware of this dialogue, and, similarly, that some diasporic voices insist on reifying their inherited minority positions, does not alter the import of the shifts that have occurred.

The shifts I am talking about here do not suggest that minority identities, racist constructions, and other such discriminatory practices have been eliminated. As many recent studies illustrate, the changing economic climate and recent immigration policies 'make it more difficult for immigrants to obtain work and to utilize support services. The upshot of these trends is the establishment of a permanent underclass of visible minorities concentrated in the major cities of Canada. This situation is conducive to racial strife and to the crystallization of barriers to the integration of visible minorities. Thus we can confidently predict an escalation of racial problems in Canada in the 1990s' (Stafford 90). Beyond their representation in ethnic literature, these realities have an impact on the literary realm in terms of what kinds of writing get published and given prominence. The shifts I am talking about point to the need to reconceptualize the power relations that have determined both ethnicity and hegemony. And it is important to stress here that, more often than not, these developments occur on the cultural margins—a reminder that dominant society still feels more comfortable operating within its syntax of forgetting. These shifts speak of the gradual reinscription of Canada's social imaginary in ways that address the need to view minority Canadians 'not as "interest groups" to be "added on" to a preexisting nucleus but rather as active, generative participants at the very core of a shared, conflictual history' (Shohat and Stam 48). It is because of such conceptual turns that ethnic writing since 1990 has received critical attention and been incorporated into the curricula of secondary and postsecondary institutions.

II
Ethnicity as Cultural Excess

> But the other is also *other*. To recognize the other as other is to sense the imperative weighing on his or her thought. It is to sense its imperative force—a force that binds me also.
>
> Alfonso Lingis (25)

The 'Other' of the Canon

Other Solitudes: Canadian Multicultural Fiction (1990) was the first anthology of ethnic writing to have a broad critical and pedagogical impact. This anthology inaugurated a decisive shift in the articulation of ethnic difference in Canada, for—unlike the ethnically and/or racially singular first-wave ethnic anthologies— it brings together writers from various ethnic, racial, and national backgrounds. It is a multicultural anthology in the literal sense of the word. Nevertheless, its editorial strategies and the sensibilities they reflect demand careful scrutiny, for they perform a double legitimating act: they endorse the sedative politics of the Canadian state's appropriation of ethnicity, and they construct ethnicity as a normative identity. As Marion Richmond says in her preface, quoting Atwood, 'we are all immigrants to this place even if we were born here' (np). Similarly, Hutcheon elsewhere explains that *Other Solitudes*,

in placing well-known Canadian writers like Michael Ondaatje, Joseph
Skvorecky, Joy Kogawa, and Mordecai Richler in the (for some, surprising)
context of multiculturalism, sought to undo the kind of thinking that separates
the 'central' from the implicitly 'marginal' by showing how many of Canada's
canonical texts are indeed written from the so-called margins of ethnicity. There
is an argument to be made that the canon in Canada has been, from the first, a
creation of women and 'minorities'. (1996, 12-13)

If *Other Solitudes*, as its editors argue, disputes the 'canon' of ethnic marginality, it
does so only because Hutcheon and Richmond operate according to an understanding of ethnicity that shares some of the premises of the Canadian
Multiculturalism Act while concealing the history of cultural politics behind the
prominence that contributors like Rohinton Mistry and Dionne Brand have
recently gained. This is, in fact, the only anthology among those I have examined
that rejects the recurring argument made by editors that it is time to do away with
the limits of the Canadian literary tradition, give serious consideration to ethnic
literature, and address the systemic problems that have led to its marginalization.
On the contrary, *Other Solitudes* seems to argue that ethnic writing has always
been part of the canon.

The view that the Canadian canon has been, 'from the first', a product of
'minorities' (in quotation marks)—because, for example, Mordecai Richler has
long been a major figure—cannot be supported without redefining canonicity or
examining Richler's position in the Canadian national imaginary. That Jewish
writers like A.M. Klein, Leonard Cohen, Irving Layton, and Eli Mandel have
always held prominent positions in the Canadian literary tradition does not
negate the fact that ethnicity is more than an identity marker different from those
of the two 'founding' nations. Ethnicity is not simply a matter of origins. It is
indeed a matter of cultural and social contingencies, but Hutcheon's view of the
Canadian canon as a product of minorities tends to obscure the history of exclusionary and appropriating tactics. Perhaps Hutcheon puts 'minorities' in quotation marks in order to dispel the historical inferiority of ethnic subjects, but the
result is a revisionist history that reproduces a reality constructed through institutional forgetting. This kind of revisionism does not help us to understand what,
for example, Bannerji, a contributor to this anthology, means when she says that
the official policy is 'a way to contain and marginalize us' (Hutcheon and
Richmond 146).[18]

Other Solitudes, I suggest, has become a prominent text of its kind not because
ethnicity has always been a part of the canon, but because it affiliates itself with
two dominant national narratives: that of the mainstream literary canon and that
of the official multiculturalism policy. Along the same lines, its publication by a
major publishing house guarantees it wide distribution and, by extension, critical
attention; its exclusive focus on fiction, the most accessible and commodified of
literary forms, is also a factor contributing to its marketability. Similarly, the fact

that its title is clearly intended to remind readers of Hugh MacLennan's canonical text *Two Solitudes*, an icon of Canadian cultural politics, aligns the anthology with the very canon it wishes to be an extension of, while inviting us to believe that the politics of ethnicity today is not different, at least structurally, from the politics of the two 'founding' nations. Its second-last section, 'The First and Founding Nations Respond', which includes interviews with (but not writings by) Tomson Highway, Jacques Godbout, and Robertson Davies, addresses the title's allusion and is meant to demonstrate the plurality of Canadian culture.

It would seem, then, that *Other Solitudes* is designed to erase the marginalization of ethnic writing. Whereas its selections take a critical look at many aspects of multiculturalism and ethnic experience, its editorial strategies counterbalance what minority as a political and cultural sign entails. The overall editorial intent is to present a single model of Canadian history, a model affirming the magnanimity of the majority culture whose celebration of diversity becomes yet another way of containing it. Thus ethnicity is inscribed in the editorial statements as a domesticated identity. The editors leave no room for representation of ethnicity as what Abdul JanMohamed and David Lloyd call a 'product of damage—damage more or less systematically inflicted on cultures produced as minorities by the dominant culture' (4). This editorial approach is in contrast to the writings and comments of contributors like Austin Clarke, Dionne Brand, Janice Kulyk Keefer, and Yeshim Ternar, who, for different reasons, if they embrace official multiculturalism at all, do so without the ease that the editors do.

Despite these contradictions, or because of them, the writing and interviews included in the anthology, when read in a contrapuntal fashion, point to the risk involved when marginality is reified to such an extent that it becomes impossible for the minority subject to shift her position. Most of the writing included in *Other Solitudes* avoids this risk, but the tendency to see the ethnic subject in reified and essentialist terms often surfaces in individual interviews. For example, Karen Mulhallen's interview with Katherine Vlassie focuses mostly on Vlassie's Greek background and has very little to do with her writing: Mulhallen remains oblivious to Vlassie's complaint that 'anyone who has questioned me about the book [her novel *Children of Byzantium*] seems to stress the fact that [its protagonist] Eleni is Greek and asks about my particular background' (118). Mulhallen's interviewing strategies reflect the extent to which 'the discourse of the marginal,' as Jonathan Crewe remarks, 'include[s] the risks of a revived positivism, of re-essentializing oppositions from the "side" of the marginal' (123).

By contrast, Hutcheon herself is eager to recuperate minority identity from the margins. As she puts it, 'the Kogawas, Ondaatjes, Bissoondaths, Mistrys, and Riccis in their very diversity have been—and are becoming—as *defining* of what is Canadian as the Atwoods or the Findleys have ever been' (1996, 13).[19] There are two difficulties with this statement: first, the tension between its present perfect and present continuous tenses, and, second, the choice of names. Hutcheon does not tell us how many 'Ondaatjes' or 'Bissoondaths' there are; nor does she consider what the relationship is between the representational modalities in the writing produced by the 'Mistrys' and 'Riccis' and the way such authors are treated as icons in her view of Canadian culture. There appears to be a desire to establish diasporic subjects as *having* already *been* a part of 'what is Canadian'. In this generalized view of Canadian culture, ethnicity is at once transparent and opaque, in circulation and condensed to the point of invisibility, particular and a part of the Canadian totality. What are the ideological implications of this contradictory view?

Reception: Towards and Away from the 'Personal'

Considering the history and contexts of the reception of ethnic writing, it is hardly astonishing that *Other Solitudes* has elicited a 'debate', a 'furor' of responses as Hutcheon sees it (1996, 10). What is remarkable, rather, is that 'the vehemence and range of responses surprised' the two editors (Hutcheon 1996, 10)—even though Hutcheon herself acknowledges that multiculturalism is rigorously debated, a sign of the health of the state of multicultural affairs in Canada (1996). This 'heated debate', which prompted Hutcheon 'to examine the problematics of *reading* multiculturalism' (1996, 10), demonstrates that Canadian ethnic writing remains a 'touchy (if timely) topic' these days (1996, 11).

The anthology was criticized for, among other things, being too close to the mainstream canon and, conversely, for valorizing difference at the expense of universal assumptions; and for being too intellectual.[20] The last level of attack, although significant, is the least relevant to my argument here. The 'strong anti-intellectualism directed against both the introduction and the interviews' (Hutcheon 1996, 15) is in keeping with the Canadian intellectual tradition, especially as it is represented by public discourse. Hutcheon's and Richmond's anthology is one of many texts that have been dismissed by reviewers because they take an 'intellectual' (read informed or academic) approach to issues. Hutcheon's impassioned plea that we continue to 'talk' because 'talk is what both the writing and the reading share; talk is what creates what we call identity' (1996, 17) is a much needed reminder of the work required to combat the reductiveness that comes with anti-intellectualism. This kind of criticism aside, though, the negative response the anthology has received and the success it has enjoyed are as much a measure of the kind of writing included in it as they are symptomatic of the ways its editors situate *Other Solitudes* within the Canadian national imaginary and its literary tradition.

Hutcheon's introduction presents *Other Solitudes* as a representative instance of the Canadian state's narrative of multiculturalism. This intention is reinforced by an appendix that reprints the text of the official multicultural policy 'without comment—in order for readers to compare the stated policy with the rest of the volume's testimony of its lived reality and its literary inscription' (1996, 12). This statement is puzzling, for it is belied by Hutcheon's introduction, especially its section 'Multicultural Policy and its Discontents' (12-16). Not only does she, like many other editors of ethnic anthologies, endorse the policy for the 'positive changes' it has brought about (14), but, as she wrote in her first critical treatment of Canadian ethnic writing, she 'find[s her]self reacting against the seemingly cynical view[s]' (1991, 47) of critics of multiculturalism. The recurring terms in which she refers to criticisms of the policy —'sadly' (13), 'sad' (1996, 12), 'cynical' (15)—together with her penchant for seeing the policy as representing an 'ideal' (12), make her position on it clear. Indeed, her fusing of literary and legal discourses points to one of my arguments: that there is a correlation between the construction of ethnicity and official attitudes. But what ideological affinities inform this relationship?

No matter how one interprets the Multiculturalism Act, it would be difficult to deny that it has been instrumental in engendering dialogue and counter-dialogue on race and ethnicity, and that it has facilitated the publication and dissemination of ethnic writing. Why then does Hutcheon, whose 'idealism' validates, and is validated by, the Act, dissociate her critical discourse from its context? Why is she unwilling to engage seriously with the questions that critics of the Act have raised? 'Whether one reads this document as a sad irony or as a still valuable ideal is probably a matter of personal politics, as well as personal experience' (1996, 12), Hutcheon says, putting the issue to rest.

Given the theoretical frame of both her introduction and her response to the anthology's reception, her use of the word 'personal' strikes a dissonant chord. On one hand, 'personal' is positively inscribed as what the writing in the anthology articulates: it 'explores both the *lived* experience and the *literary* expression of multiculturalism in Canada' (1); 'this book is an exploration of the meeting-ground of experience and literary expression in individual writers' (4). Yet on the other hand, when it comes to a critical response to the Act, 'personal' views are dismissed as irrelevant to serious criticism (positive, negative, or ambivalent) whether of the anthology or of multiculturalism in general. There is a contradiction, then, between the way the 'personal', in all its ambivalent configurations, is manifested in the fiction and interviews included in *Other Solitudes*, and the way it is bracketed by Hutcheon in her critical response in favour of what appears to be a disinterested approach. The answer to this fundamental paradox in her argument lies in her position on history and the canon, a position informed by her notion of the postmodern.

The Other as the Postmodern 'Ex-centric'

Postmodernism is not mentioned in her editorial introduction, but Hutcheon's configuration of multiculturalism as 'a way of thinking and talking about ethnicity and race', as 'an innovative model for civic tolerance and the acceptance of diversity that is appropriate for our democratic pluralist society' (14 and 15), is informed by her notion of the postmodern. This becomes apparent in her response to the criticism of *Other Solitudes* when she refers to Mark Cheetham's *Remembering Postmodernism: Trends in Recent Canadian Art* and to her own *A Poetics of Postmodernism: History, Theory, Fiction*. '[H]istory or memory,' she says, 'is the defining feature of Canadian postmodernism . . . as also exemplified in postmodern architecture's effort to recall history after the modernist ahistorical infatuation with the new. . . . This concern with history and memory is combined with a valuing of difference rather than of the universal that is the legacy of the still dominant liberal humanist ideology' (1996, 13). This is the case with most general definitions of postmodernism; but what does postmodern historicization, as defined by Hutcheon, mean for ethnicity? What does it do to 'the universal'? How does an opening up of history, in Hutcheon's terms, help us to address the 'lived' experience of minorities both in the present and in sites of memory?

Hutcheon's postmodernist injunction in her response to the reception of *Other Solitudes* demonstrates that, in postmodern terms, ethnic difference is endowed with political value precisely because it is named, because naming allows identities previously ignored and subjugated to become present. But this presencing, as I will attempt to show, makes ethnicity a sign of cultural excess: ethnic identity is one of the many 'ex-centric' identities that Hutcheon's postmodernism embraces and, in some ways, commodifies. In the postmodern world of today, Hutcheon writes in *A Poetics of Postmodernism*, 'The centre no longer completely holds. And, from the decentred perspective, the "marginal" and what I will be calling . . . the "ex-centric" (be it in class, race, gender, sexual orientation, or ethnicity) take on new significance in the light of the implied recognition that our culture is not really the homogeneous monolith (that is middle-class, male, heterosexual, white, western) we might have assumed' (1988, 12). One of Hutcheon's operative modes, the 'ex-centric' depends on a (*the*?) centre that, although not 'completely' intact, although reconceptualized as 'fiction', retains its hegemonic function; it is still understood as 'necessary, desired' (1988, 58).

Celebrating the visibility of one side of the Us and Them dialectic while asserting the necessity of the other does not promise a 'militantly anti-humanistic' (1988, 176) way of critiquing the legacy of binary thinking. Within this postmodern view of the world, the term 'ex-centric' functions not so much to designate a condition, or a site where the ethnic subject resides, as it does to recast marginality as a palatable, and thus consumable, cultural product. In this heterogeneous yet logocentric postmodernism, ethnicity never moves beyond the 'ex-centric' alliance of '(. . . black, ethnic, gay, and feminist)' issues (1988, 35). This is not an alliance that suggests solidarity or promises to dissolve limits; rather, it is presented as a chain of interchangeable signifiers, what facilitates postmodernism's 'intertextual play and . . . intellectual contingency' (1988, 54), a spectacle that speaks of a postmodern narcissism of differences. Hutcheon's parentheses[21] hold in (their) place this alliance of Others; they also dramatize her master trope of postmodern poetics and politics, irony. She names ethnicity, but that naming act itself serves to re-repress the already repressed.

However nuanced Hutcheon's irony is,[22] it does not propose to radicalize the centre. Instead, the 'ex-centric' serves to recast marginality in terms that affirm the 'worldliness' (Arac 281) of her postmodernism. From architecture to photography, from music to museums, from literature to advertising—virtually all cultural expressions that are referential and self-reflexive, and thus infused with an ironic view of history, are eligible for Hutcheon's 'postmodern' label. This capacious postmodernism may announce 'how difference operates, as opposed to only considering what difference is' (Lubiano 208), but it does not set out to challenge what the 'centre' in 'ex-centric' stands for. Hutcheon's postmodernism functions as a master narrative, one in close alliance with the master narratives it purportedly sets out to dismantle. It is a postmodernism that resembles the 'rationalist narratives of the knowing subject', narratives 'full of a certain sort of benevolence towards others, wanting to welcome those others into [its] own' (Spivak 1990, 19).

The benevolent intent behind Hutcheon's postmodernism is nowhere more strongly asserted than in the following statement:

> What has been *added* most recently to [postmodernism's] list of 'enabling' differences is that of ethnicity. The ethnic *revival* of the 1960s in the United States has been well documented. . . . Studies . . . [of ethnicity] *are made possible* by postmodern rethinking of difference in the face of modern urban, industrial society that was expected to efface ethnicity. Instead, ethnic identity has changed from being a 'heathenish liability' to being a 'sacred asset'. . . through a very postmodern, contradictory divided allegiance . . . (1988, 71; my emphasis)

Hutcheon grants ethnicity the standing of an additive. Once a subjugated identity, now ethnic identity is posited as a subordinate condition. Behind the suggestion that the problems facing ethnicity have been resolved is the implication that there was a time when ethnic difference was already accepted and respected—what else could 'revival' mean in this context? This is not just an instance of utopian discourse, a hopeful imagining of the future; utopia is already installed in the present moment, usurping history, arresting politics, foreclosing the possibility of any interruption of the mechanisms of social formations. Most important, Hutcheon denies ethnic subjects any significant role in the development her rendering of history points to, in effect denying them agency. Instead, it is the 'postmodern rethinking of difference' that is credited with having liberated ethnicity from the margins. This redemptive function of postmodernism is a clear case of what William Spanos would call 'the amnesiac strategy of *accommodation*', a strategy in which ethnicity as a positive name 'appear[s]' (69) as a mere symptom of postmodernism, accommodated and curtailed at the same time. If Hutcheon's postmodernism views history in such syncopated terms, what does this tell us about her approach to multiculturalism?

Pluralized Difference / Neutralized History

Hutcheon delineates her perception of Canadian multiculturalism in postmodern terms in contradistinction to Fredric Jameson's reading of American multiculturalism in *Postmodernism: Or, The Cultural Logic of Late Capitalism*. I will quote her at some length:

> [Jameson] calls this postmodern emphasis on difference a 'booby-trapped' . . . concept and suggests that the 'spirited defense of difference' may be simply 'liberal tolerance, a position whose offensive complacencies are well known but which has at least the merit of raising the embarrassed historical question of whether the tolerance of difference, as a social fact, is not the result of social homogenization and standardization and the obliteration of genuine social difference in the first place' (341). While this may well describe the situation in the United States in which Jameson writes, it might be a little different north of the border. For Jameson, ethnicity 'in the postmodern, in other words—*neoethnicity*—is something of a yuppie phenomenon, and thereby without too many mediations a matter of fashion and the market' (341). In multicultural Toronto or Montreal or Vancouver, no one would want to argue that ethnicity is totally divorced from the market or fashion, but in that country [Canada] it is also a matter of formal government policy and open public identity debate in a way that has seemed foreign to the American context. . . . The very terms of that debate—a postmodern one in that very different Canadian sense of the word— are articulated in all their diversity and tension in the critical reception of *Other Solitudes*. (1996, 13-14)

There are differences, as Hutcheon rightly points out, between the American and Canadian versions of multiculturalism. But while she questions Jameson's totalizing impulses, she adopts his notion of commodified ethnicity without regard for the context of his argument. Her notion of ethnicity as a fashionable and marketable commodity implies that the relationship of ethnicity to history is determined by a visible, one-dimensional present, existing only 'in the "new" time of advertising and the media' (Shohat and Stam 131). The Chicago Cultural Studies Group are among the critics who call this phenomenon of ethnic visibility the 'Benetton effect' (532). What constitutes the postmodernity of ethnicity here is that it signifies elimination of critical distance, not displacement of stereotypes or racism. Hutcheon's image of ethnicity as fashion indicates the way her postmodernism collapses differences into neutral modalities, at once closing the space between Us and Them and suggesting a closure of history. This is the kind of postmodernism that Appiah defines 'as a retheorization of the proliferation of distinctions that reflects the underlying dynamic of cultural modernity, the need to clear oneself a space' (1991, 346). But clearing oneself a space, treading (however gingerly) on the catwalk of ethnicity-as-fashion, and doing so under the auspices of a government policy, does nothing to help us look history straight in the face as a system of power relations that we wish to change. By recontextualizing history in postmodern terms Hutcheon may ironize hegemonic structures, but she refrains from transforming the past, in Benjamin's fashion, into a future that will be.

Jameson's postmodernism, some critics have argued, is flawed by its singular emphasis on class and capitalistic relations, especially when he examines these in the context of subjugated identities. Still, I think his view that many discussions of difference today merely reflect liberal tolerance is accurate—and applicable to Hutcheon's approach. Jameson is certainly too quick to move beyond the connection he establishes, what we may call his 'omni-subsumptive vision' (Appiah 1997, 425), and he is only too eager to see postmodern discursive practices 'as a symptom of the simulacral logic of late capitalism' and not 'as an instrument committed to [its] critique' (Spanos 71). But, within the context of my argument, his approach helps to clarify the nature of the postmodernism that Hutcheon celebrates, which he calls 'a cultural dominant' (Jameson 6): a culture whose 'internal and superstructural expression' is marked by 'economic domination throughout the world'. The 'underside' of this culture, he reminds us, 'is blood, torture, death, and terror' (5). These are precisely the conditions put aside by Hutcheon's formulation of the postmodern; the culture she envisions is one that 'deoppositionali[zes]' (Appiah 1997, 425) the very binary oppositions that determine its centrality. Thus while Jameson may disregard the specific problems and politics of his simultaneous local and global formulation, Hutcheon herself elides the way her terms of reference pluralize difference. She states that the 'past as referent is not bracketed or effaced, as Jameson would like to believe: it is incorporated and modified, given new and different life and meaning. This is the lesson taught by postmodern art today' (1988, 24). Nevertheless, her overall argument collapses the distinction between postmodernity and postmodernism.[23] Although she offers intriguing readings of postmodern cultural manifestations, she does not always examine the premises and politics behind the theories informing them.

Apparently Hutcheon's dismissal of Jameson is intended to support her view of Canadian multiculturalism as an 'ideal'. Her assertion that multicultural debates don't take place south of the Canadian border is simply not true. Similarly, her dismissal of Canadian criticism of the federal multiculturalism policy as 'cynical' shows her reluctance to abandon some of the foundational assumptions behind her postmodernism. As I argued in the previous chapter, the Canadian Multiculturalism Act privileges precisely the kind of cultural production that results in the 'postmodernist mode of ironic pleasure' (Ahmad 94). This is the kind of pleasure that comes from seeing the counter-history of minorities diversify the social imaginary without actually changing it. Quite the contrary: ethnic differences are appropriated in order to enhance the dominant society's cultural capital. As yet another narrative configuration of the postmodern, this kind of multiculturalism represents nothing more than Western societies' concession to no longer being the only normative cultural centre. This is Hutcheon's notion of history, and it is precisely what allows her to subsume multiculturalism into a generalized notion of the postmodern.

'In our postmodern world,' she says in the concluding paragraph of 'Multicultural Furor', 'the positive valuing of difference has been translated into something that not all of us want to dismiss quite so easily: making room for other voices to be heard, voices that may not always have had access to publication and thus to a general reading public as well as an academic one' (1996, 16). But, as I have already suggested, making room for such voices does nothing to change their minority positions. Hutcheon's concern about the anxieties this process of translation generates is justified, but 'the positive valuing of difference' suggests the kind of pluralism that, as JanMohamed and Lloyd remark, 'disguises the perpetuation of exclusion insofar as it is enjoyed only by those who have already assimilated the values of the dominant culture. For this pluralism, ethnic or cultural difference is merely an exoticism, an indulgence that can be relished without significantly modifying the individual who is securely embedded in the protective body of dominant ideology' (8).

Postmodern Multiculturalism / Canada as a Virtual Nation

How, then, is this pluralism to be reconciled with Hutcheon's references to Canada's racist history in her introduction? What exactly does she mean when she states that, '[u]nlike the United States, Canada is trying today simultaneously to articulate a *totalizing national discourse of consensus* and to make space for negotiated difference, so to speak, within that consensus' (1996, 11-12; my emphasis)? A telling rhetorical gesture, 'so to speak' identifies Hutcheon's position and at the same time shows her ambivalence to be steadfast.

To understand how Hutcheon proposes to embrace Canada as simultaneously negotiating differences and constructing 'a totalizing national discourse of consensus', consider what she says about this totalizing impulse in *The Politics of Postmodernism*:

> The function of the term totalizing, as I understand it, is to point to the *process* . . . by which writers of history, fiction, or even theory render their materials coherent, continuous, unified—but always with an eye to the control and mastery of those materials, even at the risk of doing violence to them. It is this link to power, as well as process, that the adjective 'totalizing' is meant to suggest, and it is as such that the term has been used to characterize everything from liberal humanist ideals to the aims of historiography. (1989, 62)

Hutcheon does not criticize the desire to master history. Instead, in an elegant move that has become predictable in her work, she attempts to contain and thereby manage it, her instrument here being postmodernism's complicity.

Postmodernism 'both inscribes and challenges' (1989, 64) this totalizing impulse. Hence the ambivalent potential of the pluralism she advocates: 'we now get the histories (in the plural) of the losers as well as the winners, of the regional (and colonial) as well as the centrist, of the unsung many as well as the much unsung few, and I might add, of women as well as men' (1989, 66). The paratactic structure of this sentence articulates an image of culture determined by horizontal, as opposed to vertical, relations, an instance of what I would call, borrowing from Robert Young, the 'white mythologies' (1990) of Western history. In her earnest wish to liberate ethnicity from the margins of history, Hutcheon homogenizes heterogeneity and transposes the ethnic subject within a temporality that is 'post-' revolutionary. I say 'post-' because the ethnic subject must already have broken free of hegemonic history if Hutcheon is to conceptualize ethnicity as she does.

As she writes:

> Certainly, if the term 'ethnic' were limited, as it usually is, to non-Anglo or non-French, then the associations have indeed traditionally been of 'less' and 'marginal' within what was once called the 'vertical' mosaic of Canadian social hierarchies. Yet, just as even the English and French were once immigrants to Canada, so too are they 'ethnic', at least insofar as they possess distinctive cultural customs and languages. If you don't consider the British as 'ethnic', think about cricket and Yorkshire pudding. (1991, 47)

Hutcheon's reference to John Porter's classic *Vertical Mosaic* is followed by the comment that 'the change has been slow and is in no way complete' (1991, 66). But this qualification does not alter the import of the ways in which she theorizes ethnicity. Her proposition that difference is a universal condition is not historically accurate. Difference here becomes a banality, frustrating any attempt not only at revisiting history but also at recognizing the exigencies of the present. Hutcheon's method, as I understand it, involves a double and simultaneous gesture: she redefines the Canadian nation as a multiethnic state, and disengages ethnicity from marginality. The result is an image of Canada as a virtual nation that accounts for neither the way the national subject has tempered its hegemonic role nor the processes through which the ethnic subject has reached a 'post-' ethnic subjectivity.

Hutcheon's postmodern vision of multiculturalism 'does not in any way deny the existence of the past real, but it focuses attention on the act of imposing order on that past, of encoding strategies of meaning-making through representation' (1989, 66-7). But endowing with political efficacy the postmodern 'self-consciousness' about the way the past is narrativized (1989, 71) is not that different in its totalizing impact from Jameson's positing of postmodernism as a symptom of the state of global relations and late capitalism. Hutcheon concedes that postmodernism 'exploits and yet simultaneously calls into question notions of closure, totalization, and universality', but she chooses not to view this ideological complicity 'as a sign of decadence or as a cause for despair'; instead, she argues, 'it might be possible to postulate a less negative interpretation that would allow for at least the *potential* for radical critical possibilities' (1989, 70). In the context of her kind of postmodernism, however, these 'radical critical possibilities' lie in the strategies of parody, irony, and double-coding, strategies that allow postmodern discourse to de-conceal the past, to '"de-doxif[y]" received notions' (1989, 78). But these tropes do not necessarily lead to dismantling of what her postmodernism 're-presents'. The problem here lies in the emphasis she places on postmodernism's iterative function. The postmodern 're-presentation' of the past does not remove the subject from a troubled history; rather, it promises to 'impose order' on that past, to contain hegemonic trespasses. Situating 'the past in the present' (1989, 70) makes history visible in a way that, in the paradoxical fashion of Hutcheon's postmodernism, has no substantial impact on the subterranean links between the construction of identity and structures of domination.

Within this economy of visibility, rendering past inequities manifest does little to remedy the sense of injustice on the part of the 'losers', let alone to restore what they have lost or make them 'winners'. History emerges as a single narrative—with a difference: it now includes its own nervous double, those trajectories it previously submerged or justified in the name of exploration and progress. Thus the 'losers' and the 'unsung' are brought forward into the light; yet now, strangely enough, the 'losers' and the 'unsung' find themselves inscribed in this kind of history exactly as such: 'losers' and 'unsung'—namely 'ex-centric'. This is the kind of history that completes the emancipation project of Enlightenment progress. The 'simultaneous' existence of differences becomes the measure of that project's success. Hutcheon's postmodernism, then, recognizes historical realities, but its 're-presentation' of the past works in tandem with the Western desire to master history. The 'order' that this postmodernism seeks to 'impose' on the past may be the result of artistic construction, but it also reflects the desire not to displace that past, and hence to leave undisturbed the construction of minorities. Postmodern multiculturalism emerges as a benign master narrative in which the agency of the ethnic subject is still determined by the dynamics of the very system that mediates it.

Hutcheon's work on postmodernism makes it clear that she cannot be oblivious to the questions I am raising here. Still, she chooses to render multicultural reality in terms that don't disturb 'civic tolerance'. Her writing on ethnic subjectivity exemplifies her definition of the postmodern subject: a subject that 'lives . . . in full knowledge both of the power of and desire for those humanist master narratives and also of their impossibility, except as they are acknowledged to be necessary (if illusory) consolations' (1988, 191). This is why she celebrates a heterogeneity in which differences become homologous to each other—a totalizing and totalized heterogeneity. As she says:

> When the center starts to give way to the margins, when totalizing universal-
> ization begins to self-deconstruct, the complexity of the contradictions within
> conventions—such as those of genre, for instance—begin to be apparent. . . .
> Cultural homogenization too reveals its fissures, but the heterogeneity that is
> asserted in the face of that totalizing (yet pluralizing) culture does not take the
> form of many fixed individual subjects . . . , but instead is conceived of as a flux
> of contextualized identities: contextualized by gender, class, race, ethnicity,
> sexual preference, education, social role, and so on. . . . [T]his assertion of
> identity through difference and specificity is a constant in postmodern thought.
> (1988, 59)

A situation in which heterogeneity was a constant would be desirable, had we
already entered what Radhakrishnan calls the 'post-Ethnic' temporality (1990,
71)—that time in the future when the diasporic self will have dealt with its
'entrapment in multiple temporalities and histories', 'empower[ed] itself as
"identity" and, at the same time, realize[d] its potential to be a site, the *topos* of a
revolution that is also its own meta-revolution,' namely its having moved beyond
'the hegemonic grid of 'identity" (Radhakrishnan 1990, 67). I want to believe that
this is the time and place we're moving towards. But we aren't going to get there
by embracing a multicultural ethos modelled on a postmodernism that 'questions
centralized, totalized, hierarchized closed systems: questions, but does not
destroy' (Hutcheon 1988, 41).

What Hutcheon's view of multiculturalism postulates is—in typical postmodern fashion—a paradox: a Canada that 'articulate[s] a totalizing national
discourse of consensus and make[s] space for negotiated difference'. Hutcheon
does not explain how this consensus is to be achieved when differences are still
under negotiation, when the negotiations (as I understand her formulation) are to
be conducted by a society whose self-image as dominant remains intact. Perhaps
the resolution of this paradox lies in her defence of official multiculturalism as an
'ideal'. In this context, a 'totalizing' national discourse can bring about Hutcheon's
proposed unity only if it suspends differences as counter-discourses. It is in this
way—the same way in which official multiculturalism 'gives us subjects without
history' (Robert Young 1990, 68)—that Hutcheon's Canadian national imaginary
can encompass ethnicity. The consensus by which this national discourse can
remain 'totalizing' and at the same time embody ethnicity has a disciplinary
function: however ethnicity is defined, it must yield to the 'totalizing' impulse of
such a nation. A consensual community of this kind, a community presumably
without ethnic margins, would include 'negotiated difference', but for this negotiation to succeed, minorities' experience of difference would have to be subsumed.
Instead, such a multicultural nation will continue to assert its allegiance to the
modernist discourses of nationalism. It will be an imagined community, the kind
that occupies homogeneous, empty time, a community whose historical materiality will consist in its misremembering of its past.

Chapter 4

The Body in Joy Kogawa's *Obasan*: Race, Gender, Sexuality

Silence and speech are the two determining elements of Joy Kogawa's *Obasan*: they correspond to oppression, the flagrant violation of human rights, and to revisionism, political activism that sets history straight. At least this is what many critics, irrespective of their methodological differences, seem to agree on. As Roy Miki puts it, 'all [academics] tend to incorporate a resolutionary (not revolutionary) aesthetics in their overall critical framing of the novel. The agreement seems to be that Naomi resolves her silenced past, so establishes peace with the human rights violations that caused such havoc and grief to her, to her family, and to her community' (1995, 143). Miki's distinction between 'resolutionary' and 'revolutionary' aesthetics is crucial. It articulates the problematic desire to embrace the all-consuming myth of progress, to see the novel as a developmental narrative and its narrator as the agent of progress. Thus Naomi is credited with resolving the political and moral crisis at the heart of the novel's historical narrative. Far from suggesting revolutionary potential, this interpretation of *Obasan* proposes a forced conversion: Naomi's move from a history marked by humiliation and turmoil to a present—'where I am' (247)—in which she embraces her 'Grief' through 'the familiar lost eyes of Love' (246) and makes peace with the tortured and torturing images of the past.[1]

This resolutionary movement reflects modernity's impossible impulse toward order, but it ignores the existence of disparity, the other of order, as well as the unassailable fact that '[t]he discovery that order [is] *not natural* [is] discovery of *order as such*' (Bauman 6). Grounded in this myth of order, most interpretations of the novel tend to read into it an inner logic that affirms universal morality and law, a logic whose triumph is allegedly evidenced by Naomi's conversion from a silent woman into an eloquent narrator. But the novel, as Miki reminds us, does not close with reparation; it doesn't end on a note of 'Love'. Instead, it ends with 'a matter-of-fact document asking the government not to deport Japanese Canadians, signed by three white men. . . . At the novel's closure, then, following

Naomi's own private resolution, the silence still haunts in the absence of a Japanese Canadian name on this political document' (1995, 144).

How, then, are we to reconcile the materiality of the document ending the novel with the universalist faith in order allegorized by Naomi's vision of 'Grief' and 'Love'? Is its inclusion nothing more than a gesture proclaiming 'the "eternal" image of the past'? Or is it a performative gesture, the 'constructive principle' of Benjamin's materialist historiography (1969, 262), intended to make a difference? If the latter is the case, as I am suggesting, how is the reader to reconcile the intent to rip apart the sameness of history with Naomi's 'Love', which echoes the novel's biblical epigraph[2] promising the reward of 'hidden manna' to 'him that overcometh'?

Neither in *Obasan* nor in its sequel, *Itsuka*, does Naomi seem to overcome the histories she embodies. This is not to say that the novel fails to confront history, that at its end we find ourselves at an impasse, caught between the past and the present. If, however, there is any 'revolutionary' potential in this novel, it does not lie in the reconciliation of its apparent paradoxes and contradictions, in seeing Naomi as the 'synthesis' of Obasan's silence and Aunt Emily's activism, as Marilyn Russell Rose suggests (1988, 220);[3] nor does it lie in the disclosure of familial and collective histories. Rather, this potential is suggested by the way the novel reconstructs history and, above all, by the way Naomi's character operates as a montage—not a 'synthesis'—of different historical discourses. The reconciliation of contesting forces implied by synthesis is, of course, tempting, for it promises the containment, if not erasure, of disparities. Such a synthesis may be perceived in the poetic discourse towards the end of the novel's penultimate chapter, in the utopian, if not stereotypical, image of a rainbow—'a place where the colours all meet' (246). Portraying history's unfolding as a natural process of synthesis, this image hints at forgiveness, but it is hardly a political answer to the ravages of the past, or to the view of present as 'this new hour filled with emptiness' (245). Far from representing reconciled differences, Naomi's character at the end of the novel 'counteracts [the] illusion' (Buck-Morss 67) of harmony suggested by this Benetton-like 'United Colors' solution. Hence my choice to see Naomi as a character embodying history as a montage, in which 'elements remain unreconciled, rather than fusing into one "harmonious perspective"', a montage that 'interrupts the context into which it is inserted' (Buck-Morss 67).[4] Although I am aware that my proposed reading may be to some extent contrary to the author's intention, it is not 'Love' that seduces me as reader at the end of the novel. It is the 'stain[s]' on Naomi's fingers that hold my attention, the fingers with which she reads 'the forest braille' (246), an intricate image that exposes the artifice history can be when it mimics the linear, evolutionary progress of natural history. I am interested, then, in her rejection of the body as a house 'fit for human habitation', in her desire to create her body anew: 'Let there be flesh' (246).

Grove, as I showed in Chapter One, responded to his material reality by producing a generalized subject in *Settlers of the Marsh* whose in-betweenness as ethnic and universal was up to the reader to recognize. Kogawa, writing at a time when ethnicity had already achieved a certain visibility, created in Naomi a protagonist who makes it impossible for the reader to overlook the historical and psychological dynamics of her character.

'A moving novel of a time and a suffering we have tried to forget'—this is how *Obasan* is described on the front cover of its paperback edition. Indeed, the novel unfolds as a narrative of repression. Repression, psychological and political, is at the heart of the story this novel tells, both at the collective level of the Japanese Canadian community and at the specific level of Naomi's family. Especially when understood as a concept whose meaning and structure are always political, repression explains why *Obasan* narrativizes what has been repressed and represses what threatens to unleash forces that do not promise immediate or comfortable resolution. Keeping in mind Freud's comment that repression 'pleads a failure of memory' (14.16),[5] in this chapter I will argue that Naomi's body functions as a memory site where the constructions of race, gender, sexuality, and nationalism are implicated in each other while remaining distinct dimensions in her formation as subject.

'Yoku nakatta ne.'

'Nomi is fine. She's so silent though. I've never seen such a serious child before,' writes Emily in her diary addressed to her sister, Naomi's mother (105). Naomi disputes this definition of herself while admitting that she recoils from speech. 'It isn't true, of course,' she says in the opening of Chapter Eleven, 'that I never speak as a child. Inside the house in Vancouver there is confidence and laughter, music and meal times, games and storytelling. But outside, even in the backyard, there is an infinitely unpredictable, unknown, and often dangerous world. Speech hides within me, watchful and afraid' (58). The dialectics of inside and outside, laughter and fear, speech and silence, form the correlates of Naomi's subjecthood. It is important to note that she does not align herself with either of the two sides in these binary constructions, but locates herself in the spaces between them. As 'Canada and Japan do not afford the reader symmetrical discourses' in the novel (Brydon 98), so is there no satisfying balance between the silent Naomi and the Naomi who is a loquacious narrator. Absence, displacement, humiliation, deferral, desire, and the disfiguration of the maternal body—literal or figurative—are at the centre of her story. These conditions determine her silence, but they also show that silence to be ambivalent, to both sustain and traumatize her. Naomi's childhood memories help us to understand how this asymmetrical relationship of silence to speech is brought about, and how it relates to the history of her community in Canada.

The last incident Naomi remembers before her 'mother disappears' (66) involves Naomi putting a 'dozen cotton-batten-soft yellow chicks' (58) in the wire cage of a hen that strikes at them with her beak and claws until most of them are dead; the rest are saved by Naomi's mother. "'It was not good, was it," Mother says. "Yoku nakatta ne." Three words. Good, negation of good in the past tense, agreement with statement. It is not a language that promotes hysteria. There is no blame or pity. I am not responsible. The hen is not responsible. My mother does not look at me when she says this' (60). As Naomi gratefully admits, what keeps hysteria at bay is the presence of her mother, who is able to manage an unpleasant episode without making Naomi feel any worse than she already does. The mother accomplishes this by stating what has happened in a negative sentence structure that allows her to substitute good for bad. 'It was not good' forestalls hysteria because it lays no charges of guilt or responsibility. Those potential charges are averted because, although the mother does not deny what has happened, she addresses not Naomi but the event itself, relieving her daughter of agency in the incident. 'It was not good' is a constative act, describing what happened, but it is heard by Naomi as a performative utterance[6] that accomplishes the opposite of the action it describes: it is good for Naomi not to be driven to hysterics for causing the death of the chicks.

The mother, by unwriting Naomi from her sentence as the agent of the action that was not good, and thus by allaying Naomi's fears, prefigures the elaborate process of negotiation with the constructions of ethnicity, race, sexuality, and gender that the novel engages in. Unwriting of the past and rewriting of the future are also signalled by the mother's use of the past tense, which frees Naomi from any ill feelings at the present moment, and points to negotiation as opposed to rejection or attribution of blame.

But does the mother's efficacy in this incident prevail over the rage and paralysis that Naomi feels when, for example, some time later, she witnesses the killing of a hen (155)? Does Naomi's mother succeed in warding off hysteria for good, so to speak? The answer is no. In fact, as I will attempt to show, the entire narrative represents a series of attempts to reveal what Naomi has repressed personally, familially, and historically.

Bodies Speaking

'Yoku nakatta ne', perhaps the mother's most important utterance in the novel, has implications that go beyond the episode of the chicks: it brings to the fore the condensed history of Naomi's character. The statement is effective precisely because it does not address Naomi. Yet its effectiveness depends on Naomi's knowing exactly what the statement does not name: her body. This becomes evident in the silence that precedes her mother's utterance:

> 'Mama————'
> Without a word and without alarm, she follows me quickly to the backyard. The arena is punctuated by short piercing trills as the hen keeps pecking and the chicks squeal and flutter, squeal and fall.

With swift deft fingers, Mother removes the live chicks first, placing them in her apron. All the while that she acts, there is calm efficiency in her face and she does not speak. Her eyes are steady and matter of fact—the eyes of Japanese motherhood. They do not invade and betray. They are eyes that protect, shielding what is hidden most deeply in the heart of the child. She makes safe the small stirrings underfoot and in the shadows. *Physically, the sensation is not in the region of the heart, but in the belly*. This that is in the belly is honoured when it is allowed to be, without fanfare, without reproach, without words. What is there is there. (59; my emphasis)

Here silence signifies love and protection; it is to be understood not as lack of words, but as a discourse of the body. The body's language—steady eyes, calm face, deft fingers—is translated into silence in the realm of linguistic articulation. Naomi may employ language as a metaphor in describing how the chicks' squeals of pain 'punctuate' the air, but it is through a metonymy of physicality that communication is achieved between the mother's and daughter's bodies. The point is not that language is redundant, but rather that a language of a different order, that of corporeality, the visceral stirring 'in the belly', is characteristic of 'Japanese motherhood'.

Indeed, at the end of the previous chapter, Naomi sums up her experience of early childhood by foregrounding body talk:

To travel with confidence down this route the most reliable map I am given is the example of my mother's and Grandma's alert and accurate knowing. When I am hungry, and before I can ask, there is food. If I am weary, every place is a bed. No food that is distasteful must be eaten and there is neither praise nor blame for the body's natural functions. A need to urinate is to be heeded whether in public or visiting friends. A sweater covers me before there is any chill and if there is pain there is care simultaneously. If Grandma shifts uncomfortably, I bring her a cushion.

'Yoku ki ga tsuku ne,' Grandma responds. It is a statement in appreciation of sensitivity and appropriate gestures.

I cannot remember that I was ever reprimanded or punished for anything, although that seems strange and unlikely now. The concept that a child could do wrong did not seem to exist. There was no need for crying. (56)

These bodily acts are speaking acts that do away with the Cartesian dialectic of body and mind. The body is not an instrument that mediates consciousness, that channels the inside outside; nor is it a purely biological entity, organic but passive, with no interiority of its own. The relationships of these female bodies suggest that the 'body is not only anterior to language' (Butler 1997b, 6),[7] but has the ability to register its own 'knowing'. These three women's bodies engender their own discourse, one that affirms the body's agency.

These bodies differ substantially from what Butler, drawing on Shoshana Felman, defines as the 'speaking body', 'the body from which speech is uttered', and which 'becomes a sign of unknowingness precisely because its actions are never fully consciously directed or volitional' (1997b, 10). Felman insists on 'the relation between language and body: a relation consisting at once of incongruity and of inseparability', one that, because it belongs simultaneously to 'the realm of the performative' and 'the domain of psychoanalysis', is 'scandalous'. The scandal consists in the fact that a speech act 'cannot *know what it is doing*' (Felman 1983, 96). Even though both Felman and Butler argue, and persuasively, that this scandal has the productive effect of problematizing the mind/body dichotomy, in their theory the body is not seen as producing its own language: as Butler puts it, 'the body is the blindspot of speech' (1997b, 11). While not ignored and not quite metaphorized, the body in these formulations is conceived as relational to the speech act.

In Naomi's childhood experience, however, the scandal lies not in the body's unknowingness, but in its very knowing. Most important, implicit in this knowing is Naomi's image of her childhood in terms of a dialogic corporeality, that 'most reliable map' graphed by the contiguous bodies within whose realm she could do no wrong. The reciprocity of the three bodies—mother's, grandmother's, and Naomi's—shows their discourse to be at once constative and performative in that they do what they say, and they say what they do. Here 'saying' denotes a discourse of physicality that expresses the libidinal energies connecting these bodies to each other. The corporeal map that links them is produced by the constant flow of these women's desires, a circuit of exchange established by their bodies' knowing. Those bodies function as 'the agents of knowledge, [. . .] an intensely energetic locus for all cultural production' (Grosz 147).

The cultural implications of this dialogic corporeality become apparent when Naomi refers to two things that her mother's and grandmother's bodies teach her: that there is nothing profane or shameful about her body, and that a child can do no wrong. '[N]udity at home' is not only 'completely thinkable' (48) but an example of the way a certain corporeal attitude signifies cultural difference. Naomi's memory of bathing with her grandmother[8] illustrates the organic relationship between the materiality of the body and ethnicity. 'I will suffer endless indignities of the flesh,' such as scalding hot water, Naomi says, 'for the pleasure of my grandmother's pleasure.' And so Naomi's 'body is extended beside' her grandmother's in the bathtub: 'Once the body is fully immersed, there is a torpid peace.' They 'lie in this state forever', while her grandmother's loving fingers rub every nook and cranny of the child's body (48); no part of her anatomy is marked as not-to-be-touched. Thus the socialization Naomi undergoes in her familial environment involves her body as 'signifying and signified' (Grosz 18). Meanwhile she experiences the intimacies that link her to her mother and grandmother as integral to herself, as evidence of the permeability of the body—'I am supremely safe,' she says (49). Within the Nakane household,

Naomi's subjecthood is interpellated through her lived body, 'the body as experienced by the person it is, [. . .] the home of the distinction between self and body' (Schatzki and Natter 5).

Naomi sees this dialogic corporeality, marked by tenderness and silence, as an embodiment of 'Japanese motherhood'. Teruyo Ueki confirms this: 'calmness, quietness, thoughtfulness, efficiency, and being matter-of-fact in the face of agitation, confusion, and suffering—[these attitudes] are counted as key components' not only 'of Japanese motherhood . . . but also [of] the Japanese-Canadian community as a whole' (12). Similarly, King-Kok Cheung argues that 'Whereas in English "silence" is often the opposite of "speech", the most common Chinese and Japanese ideogram for "silence", is synonymous with "serenity" and antonymous with "sound", "noise", "motion", and "commotion"' (127). She calls this silence 'attentive', attentive 'to a maternal tradition in Japanese culture' (148).[9] At this childhood stage of Naomi's life, then, her silence, like that of other Japanese Canadians in the novel, is not 'an inadvertent bow to the occidental hegemony which legitimizes their abuse', as Rose argues (1987, 293). On the contrary, it is a sign that Naomi's ethnicity is determined in part by her gender difference. Although brought up with similar love and care, Stephen is not silent, nor does he figure in the dialogic corporeality in which his sister's childhood is enmeshed.[10] 'I am more brave, more praiseworthy than Stephen,' Naomi remarks; 'He will not bathe with Grandma' (48). His reluctance to participate in this dialogue of bodies speaking may be a sign of his age difference (he is older than Naomi), but it also reflects the way ethnic inscriptions vary with gender.

The Physics of the Body Cultural

> A culture never repeats itself perfectly away from home.
>
> Robert Young (1995, 174)

The difference between Naomi and Stephen echoes that between their mother and her sister Emily, and, like other elements in the novel, it illustrates the fact that although Japanese Canadian culture may be cohesive, it is not homogeneous. I am referring not only to the generational differences between the Issei, the Nisei, and the Sansei[11] that *Obasan* is in part concerned with, but also to variations in ethnic articulation that reflect gender, sexuality, and other aspects of socialization as they affect a subject's formation.[12]

When, early in the novel, Naomi looks at family photographs (a conventional narrative device that gives the reader access to her genealogy), she remembers that 'the Nakanes and Katos were intimate to the point of stickiness, like mochi' (20); her Aunt Emily confirms this memory:

> My parents, like two needles, knit the families together carefully into one blanket. Every event was a warm-water wash, drawing us all closer till the fibre

of our lives became an impenetrable mesh. Every tiny problem was discussed endlessly. We were the original 'togetherness' people. [. . .]

After that—there was the worrying letter from Grandma Kato's mother in Japan—and there were all the things that happened around that time. All the things. . . .

If we were knit into a blanket once, it's become badly moth-eaten with time. We are now no more than a few tangled skeins—the remains of what might once have been a fisherman's net. The memories that are left seem barely real. Grey shapes in the water. Fish swimming through the gaps in the net. Passing shadows. (20-1)

While the metaphoric substitution of 'mesh' for 'mochi' reflects the cultural hybridity of Naomi's background, the shift from a densely woven blanket to a ragged net obviously alludes to the ravages both sides of her family suffer because of the rampant racism of the Canadian state at the time. Also important here, though, is the textural rhetoric that Naomi employs, which reflects the tactile physicality of her Japanese Canadian upbringing—the physics of her family, as it were. This texture attests to the density of her childhood experience and the materiality that informs the structural relations of her family.

This is the reason, I believe, why her memory of the family as an 'impenetrable mesh' is later modified: 'Who is it who teaches me that in the language of eyes a stare is an invasion and a reproach? Grandma Kato? Obasan? Uncle? Mother? Each one, raised in Japan, speaks the same language; but Aunt Emily and Father, born and raised in Canada, are *visually* bilingual. I too learn the second language' (47; my emphasis).[13] Here the 'fibres' that hold the family together are realigned; although all family members share a common body language, the family is already hybridized. Naomi's question may be a gesture toward self-understanding, but it also signals that a certain disparity has always been lodged within the family's texture. The interrogative mode of her memory, together with its almost accusatory tone, suggests that this reference to the family carries no trace of the *jouissance* associated with the image of the family as 'one blanket'. Instead, this memory is interwoven with the anxiety that accompanies Naomi, the epistemic problem she has to deal with when she finds herself outside the safe haven of her family.

Although Naomi is exposed to hybridity within her household, she has to learn to become a hybrid outside it, and to do so on her own terms. Most important, she has to negotiate the various kinds of hybridity she encounters—for example, those embodied by Emily and Stephen. Thus while, for her, being 'fed on milk and Momotaro' is an instance of '[c]ulture clash', for Emily it is a matter of being Canadian: 'Everything a Canadian does is Canadian' (57). Hybridity is not homogeneous; moreover, it demands that the subject straddle the various parts that constitute her identity both in reference to individuality and in relation to diaspora as the latter is produced by the travel of national imaginaries. Naomi's attempt to articulate the coexistence of milk and Momotaro in terms that 'clash' reflects the asymmetry that baffles her as a child and that she tries to understand as an adult. In asking her question, then, she seeks to authenticate her hybrid identity. Yet this authentication has nothing to do with the discovery of an essential model of selfhood; rather, it is a gradual process that coincides with Naomi's narration of her life. The 'second language' she has learned to speak seems to register not a split from a bona fide Japanese self-core but a liminal space, a third space. Thus she sets out to problematize the locus she inhabits as a Japanese Canadian child both inside and outside the family economy.

Pedagogy of the Gaze

'Race'—that four letter word, making headway on visibility: the zone of the body scanned . . .

Or 'Colour', with a 'you'. How 'we' has to figure it out. How some of us can't make a move without thinking it. How some of you never think it, don't have to, don't even bother because it is no bother to you. . . . Invisible. Except for a name, a history, a dream, a resonance, a trace taste that becomes a hunger, a deep need, to spit it out. (Miki and Wah 5)

Crucial to Naomi's process of self-understanding is the pedagogical intention behind the question 'Who is it who teaches me that in the language of eyes a stare is an invasion and a reproach?' Naomi positions herself as student, but her professional identity as teacher also informs what she sets out to unravel. For this reason, I believe we should hear the question not merely as one asking 'who' instructs her on this definition of a stare—on a certain level, the answer is Naomi's mother and what she allegorizes in the novel—but also as a metapedagogical question concerning familial pedagogy. 'Who is it who teaches me . . .?' also asks *how* and *why* this lesson is taught, as well as *what* it means. Therefore it is significant that, although Naomi wants to dispel the 'danger' of the 'outside' world, to demystify her 'mortifi[cation]' and 'discomfort' when she is stared at (47), her need to understand exactly what it is about a stare that incites in her feelings of alienation draws attention at once to those staring at her and to the cultural and social implications of the stare's 'invasion' and 'reproach'.

Given her upbringing as we have seen it so far, it is no coincidence that she attempts to understand her socialization with regard to her family and the world at large by reading the body. As a speech act, her question derives directly from the body's instrumentality, more specifically from the technology of the gaze; this is signalled in the text by the fact that she remembers her first staring experience while looking at a photograph:

In the picture I am clinging to my mother's leg on a street corner in Vancouver. A small boy is standing hugging a lamp post and is staring at us. His thumb is in his mouth. I am mortified by the attention. I turn my face away from everyone. My mother places her cool hand on my cheek, its scent light and flowery. She whispers that the boy will laugh at me if I hide. Laugh? There is no worse horror. Laughter is a cold spray that chills the back of my neck, that makes the tears rush to my eyes. My mother's whisper flushes me out of my hiding-place behind the softness of her silk dress. Only the sidewalk is safe to look at. It does not have eyes. (47)

Here is her second experience of an unsettling stare:

My mother and I are on a streetcar. She boosts me up on the seat and I reach for the cord. We will be getting off soon. As I scramble down to the floor, I see a man sitting hunched forward, his elbows on his knees. He is looking around quizzically, one dark eyebrow higher than the other. When our eyes meet, he grins and winks. I turn away instantly, startled into discomfort again by eyes. My mother's eyes look obliquely to the floor, declaring that on the streets, at all times, in all public places, even a glance can be indiscreet. But a stare? Such lack of decorum, it is clear, is as unthinkable as nudity on the street. (47-8)

There are striking structural similarities between these two remembered incidents. To begin with, both of them occur in public spaces that contrast sharply with the self-sustained economy of the Nakane family. The mother's presence in both episodes seems to suggest a continuum between the Japanese Canadian household and the public sphere. Yet once Naomi finds herself in the discursive space of the latter, she seems to lose the self-confidence that permeates her lived body at home. The transparency of desires that defines home as a comfort zone does not translate into confidence, not even an approximation of it, in the public space. Instead, the knowledge she acquires in public space conflicts with what she 'knows' as the daughter of the household. Moreover, while part of the value she ascribes to her recollection of family life involves a tacit accommodation, if not complete acceptance, of her needs and desires, her relation to social space is mediated by a disciplinary discourse, however gentle. Her mother's warning that the boy will laugh at Naomi if she hides is an admonition she pays heed to, but it is ineffective in allaying the 'horror' that makes her cling to her mother's leg. The 'hiding-place behind the softness' (47) of her mother's dress is metonymically related to the textural image of the family. Here, though, home as a safe haven is reinscribed as refuge, a sanctuary that signifies both the security it affords and the threat it tries to ward off.

Thus the street and the streetcar where staring is perceived as a threat are social locations that stand in sharp contrast to home. Public space ruptures the familial cohesiveness that Naomi knows; it dispels the naturalness that infuses her identity as a child. If at home she is interpellated through bodies speaking *with* her body, in this outside space she is interpellated by bodies speaking *to* her, and doing so in a manner that she is at a loss to decode.

Racialization and the Optics of Power

Viewed from a diasporic perspective, this contrast is hardly surprising. While the present-tense narrative of *Obasan* focuses on historicizing and negotiating the differential elements that characterize Japanese Canadian subjectivity in relation to Canada, the episodes from the past suggest how the difference of the diasporic subject is 'born' and determined. But the past here should not be understood exclusively in terms of the historical events thematized in the novel, the Japanese attack on Pearl Harbor and its consequences for Japanese Canadians—the events on which most historiographic readings of *Obasan* focus.[14] Attentiveness to specific military, political, or legislative events of the early 1940s is necessary. But reading the novel only 'along the legal axis of definitions of citizenship' (Lowe 11) does not necessarily permit us to see how the racialization process operates outside the context of the law, that is, how it functions when its procedures are not visible and are therefore easily missed.

The taxonomic tendencies of the eighteenth century and the expansionism of the nineteenth, scientific theories of racial hygiene and the pathology of the body, the multiplicity of philosophical discourses on purity and nationalism—all these have shaped racialization. Lest I appear to be suggesting that there is a universal-ist logic, external to a given society and its history, that points to a foundational origin of racialization, or to be arguing the case for a contingency so rigid as to constitute a new kind of determinism, I should say that it is the permeability of the body and cultural identity I am trying to stress here. Racialization is a matter of permeability; racism is part of a continuum even when the materiality of this continuum is obscured by the tendency of the real to render normative what regulates and produces it.

In other words, recognition of racism is, more often than not, consistent with the fact that racist behaviour makes visible precisely what it seeks to eliminate. Similarly, the fight against it is often, sometimes inevitably, caught within the visuality of racism. As Chow says, 'the production of the West's "others" depends on a logic of visuality that bifurcates "subjects" and "objects" into the incompatible positions of intellectuality and spectacularity' (1993a, 60). Thus, while part of what impels us to act when confronted with racism is its visual element, we often fail to realize that what makes racism insidious is the fact that bodies are already racialized. Because the racialized body is constructed not only spatially and temporally, but also diachronically and synchronically, it reproduces what consti-tutes it. This double act of construction and repetition means that even when the racialized body repudiates its racialization, it cannot relinquish what it has already absorbed: in other words, it is permeable.

Precisely because racism tends to operate in a highly forceful and visible fashion, some readers find themselves compelled to focus on its concrete manifes-tations in the novel as events bound to a transparent view of history. But a discourse on or against racism that does not thematize racialization as a discursive field tends to construct a racist event as a self-contained episode rather than a symptom of ideologies and practices that foster purity and the normalization of society. To understand, then, why a Japanese Canadian child feels threatened when a boy stares at her, or how a country that was declared a 'democracy', that was 'not', in Emily's words, an 'officially racist regime' (81), came to sanction and practise racist policies, we must look into the genealogy of the novel's historical events. This involves consideration of discourses on race as a metanarrative that gives rise to social and cultural formations on small and large scales. More specifically, we must confront the discursive nature of the 'Oriental Problem'.[15] Although this history is ostensibly glossed over by Naomi's idealized family memories, it is referred to, albeit briefly, by Emily in her first diary entry: 'We're used to the prejudice by now after all these long years' (80). Here the reader is invited to consider a history that had already begun before Japan bombed Pearl Harbor, to read the text through events that are not directly addressed in *Obasan*. This history includes the cultural fantasy of the 'yellow peril',[16] the social and political ramifications of which have played a role in the treatment of Japanese Canadians on the west coast of North America since their arrival.

'The "Yellow Peril",' Ken Adachi writes in his history of Japanese Canadians, 'according to the fevered imagination of the daily press, stood poised, ready to engulf into its maw, if it was not already devouring, the livelihood and security of the white population.' What had been seen as the virtue of Chinese and Japanese immigrants, the hard labour that initially made them welcome in North America, was almost instantly construed as their vice. Not unexpectedly, that change in perception was supported by the 'evolutionary process that has been in progress for centuries': 'The propagandists were simplifying and distorting Darwin's biological thesis to conform with their particular interests, because they saw the Japanese becoming potent competitors in the labour market' (65-6). The spread of these racist stereotypes, clearly fuelled by economic anxiety and the rise of capitalism, reflects the way natural law is constructed and appropriated as an allegory of social regulation intended to discipline and manage the movement of certain diasporic subjects. Far from providing evidence of essential biological differences, the pervasiveness of stereotypes makes it clear that racialization is part of the ideology behind the '"bio-regulation by the state" of its internal dangers' (Stoler, citing Foucault, 1997a, 82). Ronald Takaki's example of a 'memorandum acknowledging receipt of an order for'

bonemeal
canvas
Japanese laborers
macaroni
Chinamen (24-5)

shows that Japanese were already racialized in the capitalist labour systems of nineteenth-century North America. The hegemonic logic behind this commodification of Asian immigrants points to the continuous and disjunctive manifestations of the materiality of history. The implied equivalence of these immigrant workers and, say, canvas exposes the normative and dehumanizing nature both of racialization and of the epistemologies that posit the movement of people as distribution of labour products.

But taking these kinds of epistemologies out of the closet is not an easy thing to do when examining how racialization is inscribed in a novel like *Obasan*, precisely because its plot foregrounds the material, visual nature of racism in a particular period. Racialization can be hard to discern, let alone articulate. 'You have to remember,' Aunt Emily tells Naomi; 'You are your history. If you cut any of it off you're an amputee' (49-50). But Naomi has no choice; no matter what she does, she is already an amputee. Even before she and her community become 'enemy aliens', in public space she experiences self-alienation in terms reminiscent of Fanon. Shocked out of his self-identification by the gaze of a white Swiss child on a train who cries out, 'Mama, see the Negro! I'm frightened!,' Fanon writes:

> I could no longer laugh, because I already knew that there were legends, stories, history, and above all *historicity* [. . .] Then, assailed at various points, the corporeal schema crumbled, its place taken by a racial epidermal schema. [. . .]
> I was responsible at the same time for my body, my race, for my ancestors.
> . . . What else could it be for me but an amputation, an excision, a hemorrhage that spattered my whole body with black blood? (1963, 112)

Fanon recognizes that his racial interpellation involves not only that child's stare, the surgical instrument of the amputation, but also his body as that which was taken away from him through the 'historicity' of racialization. The fact that the body becomes part of a network of forces that dismember and warp it, that it dissolves under the weight of history, is exactly what I mean by saying that the body is permeable. Naomi's body, because it is permeable, already bears the stain of the socio-political history that determines *her own* history's script.

The Family as Nation (or Vice Versa) and the Grotesque

Naomi's racialization may be part of her history, but it does not account for the pain she experiences when she remembers how much 'more splendid' the family's Vancouver house was 'than any house [she has] lived in since' (49). We feel compelled to contrast this splendid house with the maggot-infested 'Pool' where the Japanese Canadians of Vancouver were first gathered, with the stinking outhouse in Slocan where Naomi's family was sent, or with the dispersion of the Nakane and Kato families. Predictably, at least today, we recognize that racism is evil, but our response, at least initially, is triggered by history and the visuality of the experience. But this recognition alone does not immediately divulge how racialization as a body of knowledges so pervasive that they operate as ideology permeates Naomi's daily life. It is not easy to understand why Naomi, as a child still enjoying the comforts of that beautiful Vancouver house, feels invaded by the stares of two strangers. Nor is it easy to understand how a woman as politically astute and passionate as Emily, who is capable of recognizing that '[i]n one breath we are damned for being "inassimilable" and the next there's fear that we'll assimilate' (87), can regard 'Canadian' as the quintessential liberal national identity. Emily dedicates her life to restoring dignity to her community, but she draws her energy and political will from her unproblematized notion of Canada as a democracy. Because Emily never concedes that racialization is embedded in the foundations of the Canadian state, she unwittingly reproduces the liberal ideology that justifies racism within a democratic framework.

Emily's liberalism becomes clearer when we read the letters and essays of Muriel Kitagawa, who served as one of the documentary anchors for *Obasan* in general and Emily's character in particular. Kitagawa, a formidable woman, was both vociferous and eloquent in responding to what happened to her community.[17] Yet, like Emily, she never lost faith in what it means to be Canadian. 'We're Canadians and can expect decent treatment from decent people,' Kitagawa wrote in December 1941 (74). But a huge part of what being Canadian meant for her also involved, as she said in a 1948 speech, fighting 'racial discrimination of any kind in Canada, whether it be against the Japanese, the Negro, the Jew, the Chinese, Indian or anyone else', because it 'affects not only the victims but the aggressors as well' (272).

Nevertheless, for Kitagawa being Canadian also meant a certain degree of assimilation for Japanese Canadians:

> Slowly but surely, the Nisei women are emerging from the custom-bound past and catching up with their Caucasian sisters. A sociologist once said that the women of today were twenty years behind the times, and that the Japanese women were twenty years behind that again. The change hasn't come about without many tears and recriminations. (266)

The progress desired in terms of gender is envisaged through the West/Orient dialectic that is essential to racialization. While national, ethnic, and cultural differences disappear for the privileged totality of Caucasian women, Japanese women stand out in their racial and ethnic specificity as representatives of a tradition that is considered backward.[18] The difference between Caucasian and Japanese women is not only legitimized by a sociological study whose racialist assumptions are left unexamined; it is already confirmed by a racial hierarchy to which Kitagawa— predictably, given the historical times she was a product of—remains oblivious even though she is a victim of it. Kitagawa understands assimilation as progress both for Canadian society at large and for Japanese Canadians, but she does not take into account the difference between assimilation and integration.

Kitagawa's discourse illustrates that the formation of a nation itself is a gendered process. If the connection between gender identity and ethnic and racial differences goes unnoticed in this example, it is precisely because this connection is part and parcel of the ideology of racialization and the modelling of the nation after the familial economy. As McClintock writes, 'Because the subordination of woman to man and child to adult was deemed a natural fact, hierarchies within the nation could be depicted in familial terms to guarantee social difference as a category of nature.' Kitagawa's text dramatizes what McClintock calls the 'metaphoric depiction of social hierarchy as natural and familial' (1997, 91). Further, it shows the permeability of the family as a social body, and suggests that the domestic sphere, a gendered space itself, is where national identity is fostered.[19] If the nation is modelled after the family, then the family is the school where national subjects are made.

An excerpt from one of the letters Kitagawa wrote to her brother Wes exemplifies the organic relationship between family and nation:

> Ugh! I hate wars, and I've had one already, though I wasn't old enough to know anything then. Now I'm going through a worse one. War, active war, is easier to bear with courage than this surging up of mass hatred against us simply because we are of Japanese origin. I hope fervently that it will not affect the lives of Shirley and Meiko . . . After all, my kids, as only proper being my kids, are so thoroughly Canadian they would never understand being persecuted by people they regard as one of themselves. Already Meiko came crying home once because some kid on the block whose father is anti, said something. Yet I try to rationalize things for them, so that they won't be inundated by self-consciousness. Children are so innocent, but they are savages too, and reflect faithfully their parents' attitudes. . . .
>
> Remember when Shirley was little she was more shy of Japanese strangers than she was of the hakujin?[20] *She used to stare goggle-eyed at them.* Because they, even now, rarely see Japanese people out here, and the ones they see they are so used to that they don't even see the difference in colour. One day they asked me whether they were Japanese or Chinese or English or Scotch or what in the world? It made me laugh. I told them they were Canadians, and that is what they sincerely believe. (74; my emphasis)

I take this passage to be the historical parallel to Naomi's experience of the invasive stares. Shirley's and Meiko's education at home, although as rigorous as Naomi's, involves a different lesson. The normative environment in which two sisters are brought up is totally Canadian, one that Canadian liberalism would fully condone.

Precisely because of the visual dynamics of the racialization that already permeates this Japanese Canadian household, the national identity fostered in it is marked by a grotesque paradox. The Canadianness that Kitagawa's daughters learn embraces them unconditionally, yet it disfigures their cultural specificity to the point of erasing it. If Shirley stares goggle-eyed at Japanese Canadians, it is because she has learned to image herself as white, whiteness being the implied mark of Canadians. But the slippage between what Canadianness means in the Kitagawa home and the way it operates in the public sphere belies the value of the liberalism at work in this familial and national pedagogy. The problem here is not that Kitagawa is not 'so thoroughly Canadian'. On the contrary. The problem lies in her understanding of Canadianness as embodying unity when in fact that unity is overshadowed by differences that the historical constitution of the nation cannot accommodate. Kitagawa's faith in this supposed unity is so deep that she 'laughs' when her daughters ask her 'what' they are. Ideally, her answer that they are Canadian should have sufficed; but Canada's 'national "family"' at the time did not include a 'family of nations' (McClintock 1997, 91).

The irony in Kitagawa's familial pedagogy becomes evident in the grotesque reversal mentioned in her letter: what proves that Shirley is a Canadian through and through, the goggle-eyed stare that she directs at Japanese Canadians, mimics the stares of hatred directed toward Japanese Canadians, including herself. This grotesque reversal reveals what happens when the desire for a unified identity operates at the expense of hybridity. Putting together elements that are incongruous both structurally and formally, the grotesque signals heterogeneity; it is also a byproduct of the attitude that takes homogeneity to be the natural order. In its inclusiveness, Kitagawa's definition of Canadianness is certainly a radical revision of this order, but the familial pedagogy at work fails to take into account the discontinuities in the national imaginary. Thus while Shirley and Meiko, in voicing the uncertainty of their identity, draw attention to the racialization that remains unspoken in the family, their mother recomposes their identity by reaffirming their Canadianness. The anxiety the children experience is not merely the result of physical perceptions. It also reflects the fact that Canadianness, in practice, is far from the seamless identity that Kitagawa perceives.[21] Kitagawa thus embodies the liberal quandary articulated by Geoff Dench: 'By all means declare a belief in future justice and equality. This is part of the role. But do not expect it to materialize' (259). What prevents it from materializing, at least most of the time, is the seductiveness of the logic of visuality.

Though Emily displays an understanding of Canadianness akin to Kitagawa's, *Obasan* attempts to deconstruct this liberal ideology in subtle but still powerful ways. 'None of us, [Emily] said, escaped the naming. We were defined and identified by the way we were seen' (118). She ascribes to the dominant society the visual logic of racialization, thus pointing to the genealogy of racism. Although the novel does not appear to address this, it is still possible to imagine what the impact is on the object of the stare when racism is not immediately perceptible. 'The body will not tell' (196), Naomi says; but, given the ambivalence of bodily construction, the body always does.

'Discovering' the 'Secret of Race'

That the pedagogy Naomi herself practices as a teacher employs the stare as the paradigmatic instance of the 'birth' of diasporic subjectivity is in keeping with the way immigrant and ethnic subjects are defined in public as Others to the dominant society: through a 'look'.[22] This look, be it an inquisitive stare or an averted glance, operates on the pretense of acknowledging heterogeneity. Nevertheless, more often than not it expresses a monologic ideology that resists whatever would diversify a presumably homogeneous community. Reflected here is Herder's belief that homogeneity is the desired, if not natural, state of affairs, whereas heterogeneity—which he associates with mongrelization—is a recipe for social and cultural disaster. It is in this context that I want to examine two consistent elements in *Obasan's* two episodes of staring: invasion and racialization. These two elements reinforce not only the disjunctions that occur between familial and outside spaces, but also the way the look operates, both psychologically and racially.[23]

The boy and the man in these two episodes are white, although Naomi does not say that either of them is. But it is the absence of racial specification that holds the key to racialization; this is why Naomi experiences the stare of a boy, young enough to still suck his thumb, or the approving wink of a man[24] as invasive. It is because whiteness is the default mode that it goes unmentioned here. Its invisibility, its 'unmarked or "blank"' category, makes it 'aparadigmatic' (Chambers 189), but no less tyrannical as a norm.

The unmarked racial specificity of the boy and the man changes the nature of the dialogic corporeality that produces Naomi's perception of the familial space. The body maintains its instrumentality in the public sphere, but the terms in which it speaks here are drastically different. The stare visualizes Naomi's body, foregrounding her physical appearance: the body still shapes her identity, but it is the dynamics of a look that determines her sense of difference and alienation. It is through this logic of visuality that Naomi enters the realm of the body politic.

But Naomi's understanding of what these moments mean subsumes the issue of racialization into questions of cultural differentiation and of difference within a given culture. While Naomi interprets the two staring incidents only as indicating 'a lack of decorum', there is clearly more at stake here than cultural etiquette. It would not be too far-fetched to argue that Naomi ascribes the blame for her feelings of alienation partly to the ethno-cultural fidelity with which she has been brought up. But if she unravels these memories in her attempt to understand why as a Canadian-born child she, unlike Shirley and Meiko, has been offered only the Japanese definition of a gaze, a third staring episode reflects, in contrast, Naomi's need to defend what she has been taught about the Japanese semiotics of staring.

I am referring to the aftermath of the scene where the white hen pecks to death the yellow chicks, an incident observed by Mrs. Sugimoto. Imaged by Naomi as a 'white hen, always fussing over her boys', Mrs. Sugimoto demonstrates that 'even a glance, if it is not matter of fact, is a betrayal' (59): '[Mrs. Sugimoto's] face is not matter of fact like Mother's. Her eyes search my face. Her glance is too long. She notes my fear, invades my knowing' (60). If Mrs. Sugimoto 'invades' Naomi's 'knowing', it is not only because she makes Naomi feel naked, her body and innermost thoughts transparent to the scrutinizing eyes of this 'fussy' mother, but also because she 'betrays' Naomi's understanding of Japanese culture as homogeneous. From young Naomi's perspective, Mrs. Sugimoto exemplifies neither idealized motherhood nor Japanese decorum. Thus Naomi's characterization of her as a 'white hen' is an indictment of Mrs. Sugimoto's departure from the Japanese ethos that Naomi has internalized. Naomi experiences a comparable sense of invasion when she looks at the photograph in which the interfering presence of the boy disrupts the contained image of the family. Similarly, the fact that the man's conspiratorial wink is not observed by Naomi's mother alienates Naomi from her. What connects—and keeps apart—Mrs. Sugimoto and the boy and man is 'the secret' that racialization is supposed to be. The invasion of this 'secret' forces Naomi into a liminal space where the physical intimacies of home are translated into ethno-racial interjacence.

We begin to see, then, that in *Obasan* the invasion of the stare reifies difference as a negative sign, but that it also goes beyond the cultural boundaries of difference. It foregrounds the discomfort Naomi experiences when she is confronted with a 'knowing' of the body that contradicts the corporeal knowledge embedded in her familial environment. This somatic knowledge mediates the privileged body politic. It shows her body to belong to a culture intent on triumphing at the expense of the racialized difference she is made to represent. And this is precisely what is unsavoury and painful about the invasion of the stare: the recognition that one enters the real through the body, but at the same time the growing awareness that, once invaded by the stare, the body turns on itself, its physicality becoming a pathological condition—in short, racialized subjectivity.

As Marylynne Diggs says:

> The construction of difference as biologically, and therefore essentially, pathological, and of difference and pathology as essentially degenerative, worked as a technology of control and regulation, constituting difference as a shameful secret and thus ensuring self-surveillance. Both racial and sexual identity were thus something you could discover about yourself and something you must keep secret from others. (8)

Diggs' argument[25] helps us to understand that Naomi's reticence about the whiteness of the boy and the man is not simply a matter of the silence that characterizes her as child; it is auxiliary to the double 'secret' of race and sex that marks her subjectivity. Keeping their race unmarked seems to convince Naomi that she can 'pass' unmarked herself. The racialization performed by the staring eyes that behold her is translated into self-surveillance. This self-surveillance, though, reproduces itself with a critical difference in Naomi's reflexive pedagogy, in effect functioning as the kind of subjugated knowledge that challenges hegemonic discourse. Thus we must understand 'invasion' here as referring not just to her racialization, but also to the invasion of her body by Old Man Gower, and to the dominant society's perception of her community as enemy aliens threatening it with invasion. This understanding of invasion shows in full relief that Naomi as subject is constructed in several ways at the same time.

Before I return to the effects of the pedagogical question that unleashes Naomi's memories of being stared at, I want to examine two of these ways: first, Naomi's representation of the racism directed against her and her community during their internment; and second, her silence about her sexual molestation.

'That death day . . .':
Wherein a Lesson in Colours Reveals the Rules of the 'Game'

Slocan, 1942. After almost drowning in a lake accident, Naomi is in the hospital. A nurse combs her 'tangled hair, pulling so that the roots clinging to the scalp strain the surface of the skin' (150). 'Why is this spectacle being made of me?' Naomi wonders. 'If I cry now while I sit on this bed, all the people will turn and look' (151). Naomi does not cry; she maintains the same determined composure with which she has experienced the stare. But her hospital stay, which opens Chapter Twenty-Two, sets the tone for the delirium-like narrative that unfolds. As she reads the fairy tales from the books Obasan brings her, past and present blend. They amalgamate in her 'hospital dream' (158), a nightmare of a baby with 'fried-egg eyes', his scalp a 'wet wound', his excrement 'soft and yellow as corn mush', overseen by a doctor who is 'angry and British' (158).

In vertiginous narrative migrations, Naomi moves from dream to reality, from the past to the present, as she attempts to come to terms with the brutality of the pedagogical lesson she has learned in Slocan, a lesson that tells her why she has been banished from the reality that has so far nurtured her. There is no trace here of the dialogic corporeality within which she felt 'supremely safe'. Her hospital stay, coupled with her hospital dream, suggests a different kind of corporeality, which forces her to reconceive her body in pathological terms. What impels her narrative in this chapter is self-loathing disguised as hatred: 'I hate school. I hate running the gauntlet of white kids in the woods close to home. I hate, now, walking through the field where the chicken was killed. And I hate walking past the outhouse where the kitten died. At least it should be dead now' (157). If she marks as white the boys who persecute her and Stephen, it is because she has been shown to be coloured herself. No longer 'secret[s]', racialization and racism are out of the closet of her historical unconscious. Now she experiences her subjectivity as the violent representation of Japanese Canadian identity imposed from the outside.

'What is this thing about chickens?' she wonders early in this chapter. 'When they are babies, they are yellow. Yellow like daffodils. Like Goldilock's yellow hair. Like the yellow Easter chicks I lost somewhere. Yellow like the yellow pawns in the Yellow Peril game' (152). The paratactic structure of her rationalization parodies the racialist logic according to which body colour determines identity. But her attempt at demystifying the discrimination she experiences is thwarted: yellow can be a sign of pleasure and beauty, of tenderness and vulnerability. But it can also be the colour of impending death, a smear, the colour of hate.

What forces Naomi to confront the ambivalence of colour at this point in the narrative is the racialist lesson she learns through 'Yellow Peril', the Canadian-manufactured board game Stephen is given as a gift that Christmas in Slocan:

> On the red and blue box cover is a picture of soldiers with bayonets and fists raised high looking out over a sea full of burning ships and a sky full of planes. A game about war. Over a map of Japan are the words:
>
> > *The game that shows how*
> > *a few brave defenders*
> > *can withstand a very*
> > *great number of enemies.* (152)

What stands out for me as one of the most disturbing elements in this passage is the unnamed source of this gift to a Japanese Canadian boy who is already interned and whose entire community is under persecution. Most likely, the game was a gift of 'charity', perhaps given by one of the teachers or missionaries who lived alongside the Japanese Canadian community in Slocan. Equally puzzling is why Obasan and Uncle let Stephen and Naomi keep and play such a game. It is, then, to the nature of this gift and the intentions behind it that I wish to turn.

Conventionally, gift-giving is an act of grace bestowed upon the taker. But if, in the anthropology of exchange, gift-giving belongs to a 'peculiar noncapitalist economics of exchange', a general economy, it is also a gesture that 'composes an impossible marriage between self-interest and altruism, between calculated giving and spontaneous generosity' (Taussig 93 and 94), one that may well involve some of the mechanisms of a restricted economy. The gift of Yellow Peril, though, taunts the reader with its lack of grace; and it is completely without ambivalence.

Instead this gift, packaged in the colours of nationalist fervour, is named for what the Canadian nation considers to be the colour of its enemies. The act of giving it is thus an act of thieving, of taking away. It belongs to the *bildung* apparatus of a nation in a state of crisis—and by 'crisis' here I refer not merely to the war going on at the time, but to the Canadian state's aberrant behaviour in branding its own citizens as enemy aliens. The rhetoric of 'yellow peril', although construed in the binary terms of inside and outside, signifies a 'danger' already residing within the state. If the family, as already mentioned, is a model of the nation, the intention behind this game is the desire to mould young citizens after the nation's self-image, whose structure here is obscenely reduced to a very specific configuration of the Us and Them paradigm, to white Canadians versus Japanese Canadians.

The game, then, mimics the racialist ideology of the nation. This is mimicry that echoes the ethos of the state. Its objective, annihilation of the enemy, performs the logic of visuality, constitutes the state's law—the Law of the Father. Framed by earth and sky, the game's bellicose iconography produces a landscape that is at once global and claustrophobic, a masculinist imaginary that reflects the nation's gendering, that sets the rules staging the threshold of identity. If '[t]o play a game is to engage in activity directed towards bringing about a specific state of affairs, using only means permitted by rules . . . where such rules are accepted just because they make possible such activity' (Suits 34), then the intention behind Yellow Peril is to produce a visual economy in which the Father is absent yet ubiquitous, god-like, a compelling and threatening figure. The anxiety embedded in the game derives directly from this figure, and encapsulates its pedagogical intent: to instruct on authenticity and inauthenticity, on purity and contamination, on legitimate and non-legitimate origins, and on the values upholding one side of these binary oppositions.

Looking at the yellow pawns and the blue checker kings, Naomi herself becomes a pawn in this game of nationalist intentions. She is confronted with the impossibility of identification: neither as a female child, nor as a Canadian-born citizen, nor as a Japanese Canadian can she place herself within the categories provided by Yellow Peril. Caught as she is within the restricted economy of the nation, she is expected to identify with the blue kings, but her 'knowing' tells her that her ethnic origins and skin colour make that impossible. It is at this moment in her childhood that she finds the linguistic tropes that can articulate her abjec-tion: 'To be yellow in the Yellow Peril game is to be weak and small. Yellow is to be chicken. I am not yellow. I will not cry however much this nurse yanks my hair' (152). Naomi is impelled to become estranged from herself, to reperceive her body as that of an enemy. For a child who has already learned (and mislearned) the codes of survival, non-identification with yellow is not simply an issue of self-surveillance, but a writing-off of her identity. She is not just an Other to the nation; she becomes an other to herself:

> When the yellow chicks grow up they turn white. Chicken Little is a large Yellow Peril puff. One time Uncle stepped on a baby chick. One time, I remem-ber, a white hen pecked yellow chicks to death, to death in our backyard.
> There it is. Death again. Death means stop. (152)

Naomi intuits the method of her abjection; she articulates the logic of the hysteria that in the end has not been kept at bay. The body may be an 'inscriptive surface', as Grosz argues, 'a map correlating social positions with corporeal intensities' (140), but the game's map of Japan forces Naomi to perceive her body as a proscribed entity. Thus the game succeeds in carrying out its makers' intentions.

The words on the box locate the game ideologically; their performative function is accomplished 'through the citing of power' (Butler 1993b, 15). The power of Yellow Peril is to be measured not only by its impact on Naomi, but also by the way it reproduces the law of the nation. Thus the pedagogic intention behind the game reflects the ethos of 'O Canada' and the school anthem sung by the children in this chapter:

> Slocan get on your toes
> We are as everyone knows
> The school with spirit high!
> . . .
> Come on, rise up, and fight
> And never give up hope
> The banner we will hold with pride
> As to victory we stride. (157)

The rhetoric of pride, the patriotism, the ambivalence of the victory hoped for— all are echoed in the Yellow Peril game, but Naomi can identify with none of them; hence she does not sing along (157). Thus her statement 'I am not yellow' is shown to lack efficacy, as it fails to make her what she is not—white, the colour sanctioned by the nation. Yet another set of hen-and-chicks images interspersed between the verses shows that she clearly perceives the lyrics as speech acts that, while luring her with the hope of a collective identification ('to victory *we* stride'), segregate her, promising instead to perpetuate the invasion she has already experienced. In this school scene, she is cast as a bastard: not an outsider, but not one of the 'family' either.

Whereas the speech act as threat 'tends to produce an expectation, the threat of violence destroys the very possibility of expectation: it initiates a temporality in which one expects the destruction of expectation and, hence, cannot expect it at all' (Butler 1997b, 9). This temporality accounts, I think, for the ways in which Naomi, while bedridden in the hospital, meanders in her mind from inner to outer spaces, from living to lived times, traversing all the locations that have stigmatized her as Other. Narratively and structurally, this meandering is not so much an explanation of the stigma she bears as it is a direct result of the bodily and speech acts that threaten her. As Butler says, 'the threat emerges precisely through the act that the body performs in the speaking of the act' (1997b, 11). 'I am not yellow' may be intended to ward off the violence of the threats Naomi experiences, but she knows all too well that the threat promised is already delivered. 'Yellow is to be chicken,' she says, but she is certainly not chicken in the school where she does not join in the singing.

The Book of Absence

Where Naomi is now, how she perceives her reality, and how she is treated both confirm and contradict the reasons behind her non-identification: 'I am in a hospital. Father is in a hospital. A chicken is in a hospital. Father is a chicken is a dream that I am in a hospital where my neck and chin are covered with a thick red stubble of hair and I am reading the careful table of contents of a book that has no contents' (150). This book, its contents named yet undisclosed, its writing erased yet carefully traced, reveals the crisis of language and identification Naomi is going through. As a text where writing is absent, one that resists reading and therefore signals the death of the reader, it becomes an analogue of the law of the nation whose historiography is synonymous with the closing off of meaning. Its absent contents speak of the past that never was, of the future that may never arrive.

The absence represented by this book may seem in sharp contrast to the confidence of purpose displayed by, for example, Emily, who wants to 'get the facts straight' (183), who dedicates her life to making the meaning of history transparent. Still, the unreadable contents of the book are not unlike what Emily's archive becomes after it has been deposited with Obasan and Uncle. Gathering dust, covered by spider webs (24), her documents become a text of silence. But Naomi, who believes that 'the past waits for us to submit, or depart', who keeps 'wondering' 'Why did my mother not return?' (26), never actively searches for an answer to her question, never sees the documents until Obasan gives them to her. Had she found them on her own, though, the meaning of the facts stored in them would still have been inaccessible: they are in Japanese, which Naomi does not read. Until the surviving family members gather together on the occasion of Uncle's death, the event that frames the novel's narrative, Emily's archive is also a book of absence.

The book of absence is the site where the repressed gather before they return, and in this it is a text of radical ambivalence, obscuring what is there while articulating lack. Thus it can be read as representing either a restricted or a general economy of writing: it could prohibit discontinuity or difference, or it could posit itself as 'foreign to difference', as 'transgressing the limit of discursive difference' (Derrida 1978, 263). Since the meaning of this text consists in the disappearing act it performs under the reader's eye, whether it manages or unwrites the materiality of history depends on who reads it, as well as the conditions under which it is read.

The silence of this book, then, announces the death of alterity, and indeed death is a recurring motif in this chapter. But this annulment of alterity is suspended by a disturbing, yet intriguing, series of grotesque images: the father as chicken, emasculated by his helpless situation; the red stubble of hair growing on Naomi's body; the kitten in the outhouse she does not rescue. Nevertheless, within the fractured economy of Naomi's displaced subjectivity, the grotesque introduces an element of excess, of things that cannot be fully assimilated. It thus resists full incorporation into the national imaginary, precisely what it recites, but it also deconstructs the logic of visuality. The very grotesqueness of the dream that ends the chapter in question demonstrates how Naomi both internalizes and repels the dangers to her identity. A dream, Freud tells us, is an excretion of thought that has been stifled (4.79). In this sense, Naomi's dream of the dying kitten and the soiled baby is the psychological and narrative medium through which she vents what is repressed in her, the medium articulating the conundrum she experiences her identity to be.

Dream Scatology and the Scandal of Homogeneity

The kitten in Naomi's dream is a reminder of an earlier encounter with a white girl, which, although brief, seems to have had a lingering impact. When she meets Naomi, the girl 'turns her head away' and 'her nostrils widen', 'as if she has suddenly smelled something bad'. The kitten belongs to her. She unfairly accuses Naomi of having thrown it in the outhouse, and orders her to go 'get' it. Although she feels menaced, Naomi doesn't go. On her way to school she walks by the outhouse where the kitten is trapped, hears it 'mewing', but does nothing about it (158). Her defiance of the white girl is further proof that Naomi is not chicken. Nevertheless, she feels complicit in the kitten's slow dying, and therefore dreams of it.

In her dream the kitten is trapped in the outhouse for days, until it is covered in 'maggots', 'slime and feces' (158). Naomi is disturbed by this; still she does nothing. The abandoned kitten thus becomes an object of pity and disgust, a grotesque reflection of Naomi's own frail and dismissed identity. Out of sight but not out of mind, the kitten materializes the visibility/invisibility trap of racism within which Naomi is caught. This dream, though, is also about threats and guilt, the white girl's unjust accusation as well as Naomi's guilt over not rescuing the kitten. Naomi's guilt must be understood, though, as part of the injury she experiences as a result of the white girl's behaviour; it is a manifestation at once of her vulnerability and of her having internalized the impact of both bodily and speech acts of racism. This kind of guilt may translate into complicity, but it continues to point toward the racist discourse engaged in by the white girl. That a marginalized subject like Naomi can become doubly marginalized when she is the object of hate speech reflects the power of this discourse.[26] On the other hand, the complicitous nature of Naomi's guilt explains why, as an adult, she is inclined to turn her back on history ('turn the page and move on'), why she resists Aunt Emily's activism:

> Crimes of history, I thought to myself, can stay in history. What we need is to concern ourselves with the injustices of today. [. . .] Out loud I said, 'Why not leave the dead to bury the dead?'
> 'Dead?' [Emily] asked. 'I'm not dead. You're not dead. Who's dead?'

'But you can't fight the whole country,' I said.
'We are the country,' she answered. (41-2)

Reread in the context of the dream, this passage suggests that Naomi's complicity is the outcome of the nationalist pedagogy she is, in part, a product of. Yet it also suggests that her way of atoning for her complicity in the kitten's abandonment is to identify with it. In this instance, 'leave the dead to bury the dead' reflects the way 'we sometimes cling to the terms that pain us because, at a minimum, they offer us some form of social and discursive existence' (Butler 1997b, 26).

Naomi's identification with the kitten and the baby also reflects her abandonment by her mother. The absence of a motherly figure in the dream corresponds to the absence of the book's contents; she is inscribed in the dream by her very disappearance, by the conditions that make her presence necessary. Not only must kittens and babies have mothers, but, being forsaken and injured, they need them badly. The absence of Naomi's mother is made even more pronounced by the presence of the doctor, the figure of the Father. His Britishness and his anger show his function to be that of prohibition, of laying down the law; they expose the historical unconscious at work here, the coming together of psychic and political processes in the formation of subjectivity. Not to be confused with the image of the father as chicken, the doctor upholds the symbolic order of power; he represents at once the state turned against its own citizens and the promise of a cure. The doctor's imperial authority is not tempered by the presence of the nurse who continues to comb Naomi's hair, hurting her. Her medical role makes her complicit with the symbolic order the doctor represents; she is a facilitator of the control he exercises.

This control depends, of course, on those who suffer under the system's own unaccommodating order: Naomi at the hospital, the kitten dying in the outhouse, the injured baby in the care of the doctor—'patients'. 'Patient', coming from the Latin *pati*, which in turn comes from the Greek πασχω (as in *Pasch*, Easter), meaning 'to suffer', dramatizes the pathology of these subjects who suffer for being Other, from being othered by the system. Naomi's reference earlier in the chapter to the 'little passover several times a day', to 'the Death angel pass[ing] over at Passover' (153), alludes to the historical Jewish diaspora and its accompanying sacrifice, but also speaks of her own diasporic condition. The angel of Death is not that different from the angel of history: Naomi's dream, then, as it expresses the historical unconscious that marks her body, is about the ways in which discourse 'produce[s] the phenomena that it regulates and constrains' (Butler 1993b, 2).

If the suffering that the dream is about is caused by the symbolic order the doctor represents, this doesn't mean that the dream entirely lacks a maternal element. The feces of the kitten and the baby certainly signify defilement, but they also represent release, the return of the repressed, as it were. If, as many writers have argued, the maternal is the abject, what has to be repressed because it is inescapable, then 'Mother' is the name that cannot be spoken, the name that insists on speaking for heterogeneity. In the dream, the body, the polluting filth and stench of its feces, is both *mater* and matter. As a substance the body expels, excrement defies the logic of prohibition. Since it is something that comes from inside the body, it parodies what the body politic, in the Name of the Father, declares to be excluded. As Kristeva writes, 'Excrement and its equivalents (decay, infection, disease, corpse, etc.) stand for the danger to identity that comes from without: the ego threatened by the non-ego, society threatened by its outside, life by death.' This is why, according to Kristeva, 'Defilement is what is jettisoned from the "*symbolic system*" [,] . . . what escapes that social rationality, that logical order on which a social aggregate is based' (1982, 71 and 65).

The scatological imagery of Naomi's dream, then, signifies excess, the differences that remain undigested by the nation's self-image, what the body politic cannot absorb—not unlike the 'wastage' I discussed in the chapter on Grove. It is in this way that the maternal is present, figuring as the return of what has been repressed. The return of the maternal shows the inability of the law of the Father to entirely eliminate what it prohibits, 'outlining the *weakness of prohibition* and finally the *matrilineal order* . . . that causes the abject to exist' (Kristeva 1982, 65). As represented in her dream, Naomi's abjection reflects her self-alienation, but also the abject itself, 'the price the body must pay if it is to become *clean and proper*', what 'tears me away from the indifferentiated and brings me into subjection to a system' (Kristeva 1982, 108 and 111). Cleanliness is synonymous with the cultural homogeneity that both constructs and rejects Naomi's difference. But as the dream affirms the permeability of the body, so it also affirms the 'weakness' of the system. If homogeneity means complete assimilation, the end of all waste products, the kitten's decaying body and the baby's 'excrement [. . .] soft and yellow as corn mush' show homogeneity to be the real scandal here. The scatological imagery, the kitten's half-dead body complete with maggots and slime, the unsavoury scab on the baby's head, reveal the body to be open to the world; they unsettle the deceptive neatness of the binary inside/outside. Defilement in circulation: impurity is always voided prohibition.

The infantile economy of the dream echoes Freud's interpretation of an infant's feces as 'represent[ing] his first "gift": by producing it he can express his active compliance with his environment and, by withholding it, his disobedience' (7.186). But that gift is the colour of gold. Thus the baby's yellow excrement is Naomi's gift, the Other to Yellow Peril, the residue that is left after her declaration that she is not yellow. It represents the material history of the 'yellow peril', a representation that unsettles the racialist process determining her subjectivity. This gift is also the other to the medicine the doctor administers to his own 'uncomely children' (158), but to no one else in the dream. It is the real *pharmakon*. Excrement as both remedy and poison, as *pharmakon* (like the phantasmic stench that keeps the white girl at some distance from Naomi), is, as Derrida has shown, a figure of ambivalence: its effects being 'visible' and 'invisible', it is 'movement' and 'locus'. It 'also acts like an aggressor or a housebreaker, threatening some internal purity and security' (1981b, 127 and 128). The defecating body and the body from which maggots grow are ultimately bodies that give birth to life, that return the materiality of the missing mother to the abject.

There is, then, a peculiar symmetry in this chapter opening with a book that cannot be read and ending with a dream in which the body resides on the fragile threshold of an identity representing the failure of homogeneity. It is tempting to suggest that the book's contents are those of the dream, since as an adult Naomi attempts to recompose her subjectivity by tracing the script of her history. This history does not resolve conflicts in value, but upsets the polarization of those values. Because she can figure there only as abject—'contaminated, condemned'—the script of that history is marked by 'the fading away of all meaning and all humanity' (Kristeva 1982, 18). Silence as unnameability.

Silence as Archive

In my reading of Chapter Twenty-Two, Naomi's silence is not a unified discourse: it is a marker of her cultural difference, but it is also the kind of silence that does not have to be, or cannot be, overcome. Further, her silence is the archive of her abjection. It comes from the recesses of her consciousness, but the interiority of her subjectivity, like her wounds that never quite close, is already open to the world. So her silence may defy language's will to power, but in its elusiveness it is just as articulate as language, if not more so. It lingers on the threshold of words: neither nothingness nor a complement to language, it perpetually agitates the depths as well as the surface of things.

In some respects, Naomi's silence is like that of Obasan and Uncle; in fact, she has learned from them 'that speech often hides like an animal in a storm' (3). As hidden speech, their silence serves primarily to cover up what has already been said or done. Naomi's silence shares that intent. 'People who talk a lot about their victimization make me uncomfortable,' she admits; 'From my years of teaching I know it's the children who say nothing who are in trouble more than the ones who complain' (34). Silence-as-concealment here resists identity in terms of victimhood, but this silence is also motivated by a double economy of preservation and protection reflected in Uncle's 'Kodomo no tame', 'For the sake of the children' (219)—the attitude that has kept Naomi and Stephen in the dark about their mother's fate in Japan. As Emily reminds Obasan and Uncle, however, this silence-as-archive operates within temporal boundaries: 'But they are not children. They should be told' (219). Nevertheless, the knowledge this silence keeps in store functions like capital: it accumulates value, though not always in the interest of those involved. The silence surrounding her mother's absence traumatizes Naomi, increasing and prolonging her sense of abandonment.

Further, this silence perpetuates Naomi's infantile state. As she herself admits early in the novel, 'Whatever [Uncle] was intending to tell me "some day" has not yet been told. I sometimes wonder if he realizes my age at all. At thirty-six, I'm hardly a child' (3). But as a woman who has internalized the 'rules' of prohibition at the source of her abjection, she is reluctant to defy the taboo that this silence has become. She remains a diffident child, hesitant to probe beyond the surface of things. Silence as the concealment of truth becomes synonymous with lying, balancing between knowing and unknowingness.

Hysteria and 'Racialized Sexuality'

Naomi's silence does not belong only to her. Nor does it contain only the facts withheld by Obasan and Uncle's silence. There is one event that is not included in Emily's archive, an event Naomi never talks about to anyone: her molestation by Old Man Gower, which becomes her 'secret of sex'.

In the same chapter in which Naomi remembers the time her mother prevented hysteria from setting in, she also remembers the trauma most obviously allied with her hysteria. It is up to the reader to establish that hysteria is inscribed in the narrative through a deflecting, and therefore deferring, gesture. 'There is nothing about me that my mother does not know, nothing that is not safe to tell,' Naomi says, concluding the paragraph in which she credits her mother with averting hysteria, a statement we can readily accept since we know of the dialogic corporeality that informs her childhood. Yet the deferral lasts only as long as it takes us to move from that paragraph to the next, where Naomi declares herself a liar. Or, to be less categorical, she revises her statement, thus showing it to be an instance of repression, that is, 'nothing else than the avoidance of unpleasure' (Freud 14.153). And so we read: 'Except there is the one secret thing that emerges even now, curious as an infant fern, a fiddlehead question mark asking with its unformed voice for answers still hidden from me' (61).

In the remaining four-and-a-half pages of the chapter, we find out about Naomi's repeated sexual abuse, which starts in her fourth year. Naomi recollects her molestation through dreams and a diachronically structured narrative, both of which are essential elements in the Freudian understanding of hysteria. Despite the importance of the experience, she offers only a four-page account. As if these recollections were not traumatic enough, when we reach the very end of the chapter we are told that what has caused 'a rift' in 'the centre of [Naomi's] body' (65) is not just this 'one secret thing' (61), Old Man Gower leading her through the shrubs separating their houses into his bedroom or bathroom. 'The secret is this,' Naomi says: 'I go to seek Old Man Gower in his hideaway. I clamber unbidden onto his lap. His hands are frightening and pleasurable' (64-5). The silence that surrounds this double secret, which only the novel's readers are privy to, is of a different order from Naomi's other silences, for it is one that Naomi learns from Old Man Gower: '"Sh," Mr. Gower says. One finger is on his lips and the other hand on my mouth' (64). The silence that follows suggests a narrative symmetry between Obasan's and Uncle's secret and her own, but it also becomes the blind spot in Naomi's family.

Above all, it points to the discursive nature of Naomi's abjection.

The primary cause of hysteria, according to Freud, was a 'passive sexual experience before puberty' (3:152); but as his own revisions and theoretical shifts demonstrate, the origins of hysteria are inextricably linked to power abuse, more specifically to patriarchy and the discursiveness of its hegemonic variants. Interestingly, in trying to come to terms with her abuse, Naomi focuses on what she sees as her own complicity: seeking out, 'unbidden', Old Man Gower. Yet that complicity, if that is what it is, is only a part of what creates her hysteria. That hysteria may be traceable to sexual abuse, but I would like to argue that its real source is the convergence of the 'secret of race' and the 'secret of sex' in her formation as subject.

Her racialization is reinscribed in her memories of molestation in terms of what JanMohamed calls 'racialized sexuality': 'white patriarchy's sexual violation of the racial border' (1992, 104). What distinguishes 'racialized from white bourgeois sexuality,' JanMohamed tells us, 'is its strategic, rather than merely tactical, deployment of a peculiar "silence"' (1992, 103), a silence which speaks of what has always been an 'open secret': a 'common knowledge' about the recurrence of sexual violation along racial lines which 'could not be admitted to the realm of' any kind of public or official discourse 'lest it undermine the socio-political impermeability of that [racial] border' (1992, 104). Racialized sexuality, then, is synonymous with the violation of racial and power borders. In addition, it operates through an 'allegorical structure' (1992, 102) that exposes the double function both of violation and of the silence that sanctions it. As JanMohamed explains:

> racialized sexuality is structured by a set of *allegorical* discourses: silence and repression weave a limited configuration of symbols and desires that are deeply resonant but never available to pseudo-scientific methods. Whereas bourgeois sexuality is a product of an empiricist, analytic, and proliferating discursivity, racialized sexuality is a product of stereotypic, symbolizing, and condensing discursivity: the former is driven by a will to knowledge, the latter by both a will to conceal its mechanisms and its own will to power. (1992, 105-6)

Thus racialized sexuality is the product of master discourses; it shows hegemonic systems to operate as desiring machines in which desire signifies at once libidinal force and administrative intention.

The silence that emerges from Naomi's 'secret of sex' is marked by the fact that Old Man Gower is a white man. And it is important to remember that Old Man Gower is not only her molester, but also, as we read in the following chapter, the man who promises to take care of some of the family's belongings after their forced departure: 'I'll keep them for you, Mark. Sure thing' (69). Not only does he talk to her father in a voice 'unlike the low gurgling sound [she is] used to when he talks to [her] alone', but he also 'acts as if [Naomi is] not here' (69). The duplicity characterizing Old Man Gower, together with the fact that the 'Father's eyes are not at ease' and that 'safety has not returned to him' after Old Man Gower leaves (69), points to the uneven power dynamics that mark this encounter. Needless to say, with a neighbour allegorizing the 'yellow peril' ideology, the family does not get back any of its belongings.

Naomi bemoans her father's inability 'to move aside all the darkness'—a reference both to the enforced 'blackout' (69) at the time, and to the feeling of doom that looms over the family—but it is obvious that there is little, if anything, the father can do under the circumstances. Still, in young Naomi's eyes her father is imaged once again as a chicken, displaced in his own house by Old Man Gower, who 'seems more powerful than Father, larger and more at home even though this is our house' (69). The invasion Naomi experiences when she is stared at is allied here with Old Man Gower's invasion both of her body and of the family house. This doubleness dramatizes the fact that her hysteria is linked with both racialization and corporeality. Present or absent, Old Man Gower exercises sovereign control over Naomi's consciousness; perhaps this is why, apart from the references to him in this chapter, he is barely mentioned. Although his character is scantily developed, it is invested with the ideology and abusive attitudes of Canadian society at the time. In effect, he materializes hegemonic power, which Naomi experiences through racial and sexual abuse. It is in this literal and allegorical way that Old Man Gower haunts Naomi's narrative of hysteria.

The 'Hysterical Cultural Script'

To better understand how Naomi's silence relates to the novel's historical context and also challenges certain assumptions about hysteria, I would like to trace some of the implications of hysteria as a concept. Conventional understandings and applications of psychoanalysis have, for the most part, resisted the significant role that both class and racial determinants play in the disorders often manifested in gendered subjectivity. What is often construed as a psychological disorder is a resistance to the status quo, a radical departure from normative ideas about what informs a healthy—read white/heterosexual/bourgeois—subject. Although the founders of psychoanalysis did not appear to address race, 'the explicit discourse on gender and sexuality . . . was informed by implicit assumptions about racial difference' (Walton 783). In other words, as I have already shown, the absence of racial signifiers does not mean that race is a non-issue; on the contrary, the suppression of racialized experience is often itself a symptom of what afflicts a subject. In early psychoanalysis, '"Race" was blackness, . . . and seemed to have nothing to do with the "civilized" white human subject' (Walton 780).[27] Disorder, then, becomes a matter of reflexivity, for it points as much to what disturbs the inherited ideological values underpinning psychoanalysis as to what troubles subjectivity.

Freud rejected his seduction theory of hysteria,[28] Martha Noel Evans argues, because he was troubled by '[t]he incestuous nature of the sexual trauma at the root of hysteria, especially the culpability of the father' (74). Setting aside the fact that 'seduction', implying persuasion if not consent, was already a misnomer for the sexual injury of young girls, Freud convinced himself that the stories his female hysteric patients had been telling him were figments of their ailing imaginations.[29] There was no real abuse; the trauma had its source in the subject's morally unacceptable desire for a paternal figure. In fact, Freud's replacement of the seduction theory with the theory of the Oedipal complex points to his own seduction 'in the construction of theory itself': 'fathers, as a result of this shift, no longer play the role of sexual pervert but of something coming close to a victim' (Evans 76 and 75). As Evans shows, Freud's Oedipal theory not only releases the father figure from his guilt and accountability, but also replaces the boy with the girl. In this restructured scenario of hysteria, the hysteric woman suffers from the repression of her own desire for the paternal figure, and is denied any corporeal relation with the mother. Imaged as a seducer, she not only lies but is in effect the site producing both her trauma and its symptoms. As Christine Froula puts it, 'The history of the seduction theory shows Freud's genius, but it also shows his seduction by the hysterical cultural script that protects the father's credit' (151). Interestingly, the substitution trope that characterizes Freud's theoretical shifts goes hand in hand with the trope of silence: it is necessary to 'silenc[e] woman's speech when it threatens the father's power' (Froula 141).

We must move, then, beyond a monologic understanding of repression as the burial either of an inadmissible sexual desire or of sexual abuse. Repression is also produced by the silence imposed on women; it has a dialogic structure, as it speaks of the way hysteria is historically and ideologically induced and managed by those in positions of power. Understanding repression in these terms leads us to consider hysterical symptoms and the talking cure as reflexive discourses articulating not only the particularity of trauma, but also the discursive conditions, both ideological and cultural, that historically have inhibited women's self-determination.[30] If the trope of silence in the 'hysterical cultural script' indeed operates dialogically and reflexively, then it does so in the ways in which we have seen Naomi's silence functioning.

Sometimes silence can function as mimesis: in this mimetic discourse, originally defined clinically by Charcot, somatic symptoms mimic both external disorders and, as the symptoms' excessive nature suggests, the paradigms of normative power.[31] Silence is also a discourse of resistance, subverting and as a result exceeding the normative function of mimesis: a sign of hysterical disturbance, but one that questions the negativity of such symptoms as 'stammering' (Freud 2.79) and 'dumb[ness]' (Breuer, in Freud 2.25), for it posits itself as the negative of amnesia, which is seen as a pathological condition (Freud 2.234); that is, instead of signalling the repression of memories, silence may well function as the other side of a hysteric's lies—'a lie, not as in "untruth" but as in fiction' (Mitchell 95), what Naomi's narration performs when we read it historically. Finally, sometimes silence is not the opposite or the deferral of the talking cure, but a discourse that demands a different hermeneutics, the kind that bypasses the mediation of an analyst (or the equivalent) and that takes into account the reflexivity and dialogic nature of the articulation of hysteria.

Understood in this way, the hysteric's silence returns to her some of her lost agency, but also signals the need to revise our understanding of what repression and the desired cure mean.

Hysteria as History

My reading of Naomi's hysteria argues against the assumption that the hysteric woman has no power to change anything because she is part of the problem itself. Contrary to Toril Moi, who argues that hysteria 'is not . . . the incarnation of the revolt of women forced to silence, but rather a declaration of defeat, the realiza-tion that there is no other way out' (1981, 67), I would suggest that Naomi's narrative rewrites the 'hysterical cultural script' in a way that reveals the dialogic and reflexive nature of repression. As a discursive process, repression operates at more than one level; it is for this reason that Naomi refers to hysteria explicitly, but in a double gesture of giving away and withholding.

It is because of this reflexive function of hysteria that Naomi's first-person narrative relates not only her own life story but also her community's history, which in turn exposes hegemonic history as a discourse that exists on the border-line of lies as both fictionality and untruth. 'Hysterics suffer mainly from reminis-cences,' Freud and Breuer argue (2.7), but Freud is, more often than not, too eager to limit the relevance of those memories to the particularities of the hysteric's identity and familial environment.[32] Naomi's narrative works against this Freudian interpretation, attempting to deconstruct the symbolic and, by implication, the hegemonic order of things.

As her narration makes abundantly clear, neither her memories nor her hyste-ria are personal matters to be understood only in relation to herself and Old Man Gower. Far from minimizing the impact of Old Man Gower's abuse, this interpre-tation requires that we see her sexual trauma as part of the continuum of history that victimizes Naomi's community as well as herself. As Catherine Clément states, the hysteric 'resumes and assumes the memories of . . . others' (5). As a hysteric narrator, Naomi, has a 'conservative' (Clément 5) function: in giving 'verbal utter-ance' (Breuer in Freud 2.30) to her story, she preserves not only her own experi-ence, but those of her family and the Japanese Canadian community at large.

In this respect, her hysterical script both supplements and deconstructs the historical archive compiled by Emily. For, while she shows herself to be a meticu-lous historian, Emily focuses on what JanMohamed calls, drawing on Foucault, the 'juridico-discursive' (1992, 97) apparatus of discrimination rather than on what lies behind and what constitutes these socio-political discourses of power in the first place. Instead, Naomi's hysteria preserves, and therefore thematizes, what Emily's history does not include: the way the prohibitive power exercised upon corporeality involves the double 'secret' of race and sex. It is ironic, then, that Emily, the overt political activist in the novel, leaves untouched questions of sexuality, while Naomi, aligned with silence, is the one who exposes the socio-cultural and epistemological apparatuses that construct her subjectivity as an Other.

This explains why Emily offers a monologic reading of Naomi's silence, seeing it as a reflection of her reluctance to engage politically, rather than as a discourse that reveals both the cause and the effect of power relations. Interested in how hegemonic power affects bodies rather than how it can form them, Emily exhibits a similar approach to the materiality of the phenomenal world when she talks about Stephen's limp. She attributes it to an injury that 'never healed properly' (89), in effect removing it from the context of the historical events that she is so concerned with. His limping begins, as Emily records in her diary (89), at the same time that the Japanese Canadian community experiences 'outright race persecution' (85), and becomes worse by the time the family is evacuated, so that Stephen is 'carried on board the train, [with] a white cast up to his thigh' (112). By contrast, Naomi's narrative invites us to see her brother's trauma, like his growing discomfort with things Japanese and his relationship with a French divorcée, as a symptom of hysteria. But while Naomi's hysteria has both a conservative and a subversive function, there are no signs that Stephen's hysteria moves beyond its translation of repression into somatic and societal symptoms.

Naomi's hysteria may be a product of repression, but as an archive it shows repression to be the direct result of hegemonic relations. In her hysterical script, Naomi narrates events that neither official history nor Emily's historicizing includes. Thus her telling demonstrates not only that hegemonic history perpetuates itself by appropriating the body, but that the body can survive that appropriation. It would therefore be a mistake to see the narrativization of Naomi's abjection simply as a matter of record-taking, an attempt to particularize the internment of Japanese Canadians. Rather, the reflexive employment of repression, together with the rewriting of history as a history enmeshed with corporeality, suggests that Naomi's hysteria has the potential 'to work not only a "cure" of her silence in culture but, eventually, a more radical cure of the hysterical cultural text' (Froula 151).

Silence as the Talking Cure

Hysteria—be it conservative or subversive, self-afflicting or contagious—is conventionally seen as a sign of dis-ease, the body speaking on behalf of the afflicted subject; it has to be moved beyond, cured, erased. Yet Naomi does not seek a cure as such. Instead, what Naomi wants is to be written into the very history from which she has been exiled, to revise the scenario that she has been forced to inhabit. Not only is her wish to re-encounter her mother the impetus behind her narrative, as the mother's disappearance is a contributing factor in her hysteria, but when she finally does find her again, it is a disfigured body she sees:

'The skin on your face bubbles like lava and melts from your bones. Mother, I see your face. Do not turn aside' (242). The mother's disfigurement, a result of the atomic bombing of Nagasaki, corresponds to Naomi's self-image as 'a parasite' growing on her mother's body, as the 'other' she 'become[s]' under 'Mr. Gower's hands' (64), but it is undeniably also an image of the ugliness and destructiveness of history.

Far from eliding the complex of causes behind her hysteria, and despite her various acts of evasion, Naomi narrativizes her silence in a way that leads her towards a confrontation with history: a history understood dialogically and diachronically as a series of related as well as seemingly unrelated events in which the private and the collective are intertwined. This history, as Naomi's case demonstrates, does not necessarily comfort her or remedy her anxieties. What it reveals to her is as disquieting as what has already traumatized her. Her mother's disfiguration, her subsequent silence and death, and the memorandum excerpt that closes the novel together restore the missing links in Naomi's repressed memories, and disclose the history of her hysteria to be identical to the history of abuse of power.

Similar to the hysterical symptoms of Dora, Freud's famous patient, Naomi's narrative about silence materializes not the repression of her 'pleasure' in her molestation, but a refusal to maintain her identity as it has been determined for her through race and sexuality (this is precisely the kind of refusal that Freud missed in Dora's case). Naomi's refusal is thematized in her language:

He offers me a toffee. I neither wish nor do not wish to have the candy, but it is more polite to refuse.

'Would you like me to tell you a story?' he asks.
I do not respond. If I am still, I will be safe. (62)

I cannot move. I cannot look at his face. It is unthinkable to be held by force.
He lifts me up saying that my knee has a scratch on it and he will fix it for me. I know this is a lie.

I have never seen his wife. Does she not live here?

He begins to undress me. I do not resist. One does not resist adults. But I know this is unnecessary for my knee. He is only pretending to fix my scratch. (63)

Naomi's use of negative sentence structures and her compliance with the rules of proper behaviour illustrate the various texts (cultural, political, sexual) of her hysteric silence. To read her response as acquiescence or complicity is, in fact, to mistranslate Naomi's learned body language. Vacillating between knowing and unknowing, she says 'no' the only way she knows: by remaining silent. Thus her narrativization of the abuse replicates what happened and at the same time discloses the causes of her hysteria and its menacing power. Her silence is a discourse that cures precisely because it simultaneously mimics and resists.

An example of this discourse that involves both language and the way the hysteric body addresses what afflicts it is evident in Naomi's memory of the disgust exhibited towards her by the white girl in Slocan. Beyond her exchange with the girl about the kitten, Naomi makes no comment about the girl's display of disgust; she simply reports it. Yet as my reading of that passage above and my exploration of hysteric silence illustrate, Naomi is infected by, and internalizes, this disgust, but she also turns it around: what inspires disgust in the dream about the kitten and the baby subverts the ideology expressed by the white girl's racist behaviour. This is a paradigmatic instance of the 'epistemology of disgust' that informs hysteria, which 'is always also the epistemology of movement and of motility', a movement signified by 'the tropological substitutions that describe the language of hysterical speech and of the hysterical body' (Lukacher viii). The reflexive function of Naomi's hysteric silence is to turn her head away from the objects of disgust in her life.

In this context it becomes clear why I am arguing that Naomi's narrativization of her silence functions as a radical cure of her hysteria: its radicalness lies in the paradox that she practises the talking cure but does so in silence. Her hysteria, then, operates as a double trope: it turns towards itself by addressing its causes; and, in so doing, it turns away from what afflicts it—Naomi's most effective way of stating her refusal.

Freud listened to hysteric women's stories of seduction and abuse, the telling of which was to dispel their symptoms. But as Claire Kahane argues, 'the talking cure undermines the image of woman as ear listening to male speech. [. . .] The talking cure evokes the classic image of seduction, the lips whispering into an ear, yet it also raises the question of who is seducing whom' (140). By resisting the imperative of external mediation, by making her readers, rather than any character in the novel, listen to her story, Naomi accomplishes three things: she draws our attention to her body's history; she relates that history to the history and politics of corporeality; and she compels her readers to address their own relation to history. In her telling of hysteria, Naomi thus transforms seduction into pedagogy (a point to which I will return).

To appreciate the significance of Naomi's dispensing with the mediation of a third party, it is important to remember that, although hysteria is conventionally posited as a privileged site of epistemology (the body hysteric fetishized as an object of knowledge to be mastered), the hysteric woman is relegated to a passive role in which she remains subject to someone else's diagnosis.[33] The talking cure, which largely depends on how successfully the hysteric and her analyst speak to one another, overrides the language of her body. The body's discourse is suspended, while the hysteric is reconstituted as a discursive field that exists only insofar as it is interpreted and narrativized by someone else. Thus shown to be an inadequate, even unnecessary, reader of her body's discourse, she loses charge of her own condition. If we insist, then, on considering hysteria as a symptom that externalizes the trauma inducing it, the hysteric woman is further removed from agency—a lack she already suffers from. Contrary to this scenario, Naomi's script of silence resists outside interference. Thus she encounters no resistance in her intention to articulate her body's history as history proper. In this sense, we must understand the cure of her narrative as representing not exactly a remedy for what afflicts her, but her will to power, her desire to represent the conditions that define her as Other; it dramatizes the resistant function of her silence.

Both a silent woman and a first-person narrator, she not only takes hold of her body, making it legible in terms determined by her, but she also shows her hysteria to precede the manifestation of its symptoms, to be directly related to the contingencies of her history. Through the silent talking that makes it manifest, her hysteria makes visible, while turning inside out, the visual nature of her racialization and abuse, epistemologies that traditional psychoanalysis is not concerned with. In other words, Naomi discloses completely the 'foreign body' that constitutes her 'memory of trauma' (Freud and Breuer 2.6), a body that invades and contaminates her own.

Interestingly, in the classical Freudian scenario nothing is done to the foreign body that invades the hysteric: it is simply recognized. Putting it into words may break its hold over the hysteric's body, but its discursiveness and the epistemological dynamics that put it in circulation remain intact. By contrast, Naomi's appropriation of the talking cure frees her from the Law of the Father by exposing its various manifestations; in fact, it prevents Naomi from being completely appropriated by that law.

The Triangle of Hysteria

The silence of Naomi's hysteria records her process of writing the self. As her narration of her abuse doubles to become a narration of her separation from her mother, she talks of 'the rift' between them caused by Old Man Gower and his law of silence:

> But here in Mr. Gower's hands I become other—a parasite on her body, no longer of her mind. My arms are vines that strangle the limb to which I cling. I hold so tightly now that arms and leg become one through force. I am a growth that attaches and digs a furrow under the bark of her skin. If I tell my mother about Mr. Gower, the alarm will send a tremor through our bodies and I will be torn from her. But the secret has already separated us. [. . .] His hands are frightening and pleasurable. In the centre of my body is a rift.
>
> . . . My mother is on one side of the rift. I am on the other. We cannot reach each other. My legs are being sawn in half. (64-5)

By recalling here the image of the severed bodies of the oriental women in her recurring dream (61-2), Naomi points to the ideological symmetry that links her sexual abuse with master hegemonic narratives. But she also portrays herself as a hysteric daughter, the result both of the dialogic corporeality through which she identifies with her mother and of the forced separation from her.

In the Freudian scenario of psychic development, as McClintock puts it, 'identification *with* the mother figure is seen as pathological, perverse, the source of fixation, arrest and hysteria' (1995, 91). Although, as McClintock and others show, this theory often eludes confrontation with issues of gender and class construction, it explains why Naomi experiences her abuse by Old Man Gower as a triangular relationship that includes her mother. For the violation Naomi suffers at Old Man Gower's hands entails alienation from her mother. Also evident here is what happens when 'the mother-child dyad', as Potter argues, is 'intercept[ed]/interrupt[ed] . . . by the father, whose set of laws and taboos treat the mother as though she were a source of harm, filth, and incestuous entrapments' (121). But in this triangle of hysteria, the father figure is not Naomi's father. Already absent from the intimate relationship Naomi shares with her mother, her father is displaced by Old Man Gower, who affirms, as we have seen, the white Father's law.

The father is not the only figure that Old Man Gower substitutes for. The most detailed scene of abuse that Naomi narrates takes place in his bathroom where he 'stands' her 'on the bathroom toilet' and 'begins to undress' her on the pretext that he is going to 'fix' a scratch on her knee (63). When Stephen calls her from outside, Old Man Gower locks Naomi in the bathroom and goes out to give Stephen 'a penny to go and buy some candy. My mother,' Naomi says, 'never does this.' '[N]ot permitted to move, to dress, or to cry out,' Naomi is 'flood[ed]' with 'shame' (64). This scene is a grotesque parody of Naomi's memories of bathing bliss with her grandmother and the dialogic corporeality that binds daughter and mother. What determines Naomi's sense of corporeality here is the absence of her mother, whose tender nurturing is replaced by Old Man Gower's menacing gestures. Moreover, the penny he gives Stephen symbolizes the liquidation of Naomi's Japanese Canadian familial economy, symbolizes the fact that some Japanese Canadians, grateful to survive their persecution, did not resist as vigorously as they might have—a fact that Emily's political engagement is partly directed against. Kept a prisoner in the bathroom, forced to remain quiet, Naomi must 'hide in the foliage' and begin to learn how 'the lie grows like a horn' (63).

Naomi's relationship with her mother deconstructs, as I noted earlier, the nature/culture paradigm, but so does her use of organic metaphors to talk about her mother and Old Man Gower. While she thinks of her mother as 'a tree trunk of which I am an offshoot—a young branch attached by right of flesh and blood', she perceives Old Man Gower as 'the forest full of eyes and arms', a 'tree root that trips Snow White' (64). Nature in the novel seems to be a site at once of *jouissance* and surveillance, of identification and violent differentiation, of security and trickery. The 'eye' imagery that defines Old Man Gower here reiterates the fact that Naomi's hysteria is as much a matter of racism as it is of sexual abuse. It becomes obvious, then, that the site mother and daughter inhabit is already contaminated. Naomi, at the apex of the triangle of hysteria, sees herself as the carrier of that infection: the parasite growing on her mother's body, the vine that strangles her. Yet her way of writing the self discloses that it is Old Man Gower who engineers this transformation, who grafts her onto her mother's body as a foreign body.

Her self-image as parasite represents her abjection, reflects the self-loathing instilled in her through racialization, racism, and sexual violation. However, it also shows her hysteria to be a contagious condition affecting her mother's own body. Thus the physical closeness of mother and daughter is replaced by contagion, a plight that Naomi translates into yet another kind of complicity. She keeps the abuse a secret because Old Man Gower tells her to, and also because she wants to protect her mother from that knowledge, but this safe-keeping backfires: Naomi hears the silence of her disappeared mother as an indictment of her complicity with Old Man Gower, and her double secret. First 'strangled' in Naomi's script of hysteria, her mother eventually becomes so utterly disfigured in Nagasaki that her own mother, Naomi's grandmother, fails to recognize her.

This disfiguration and misrecognition posit Naomi's hysteria as prophecy precisely because its narrativization operates diachronically and synchronically: the anachronism that marks the hysteric, the fact that her past supersedes her present, becomes a kind of second sight in that her past pushes forward into the future. This is yet another way in which Naomi's hysteria is symptomatic simultaneously of her racialized sexuality and of her nostalgia for her missing mother, her desire to return to the 'desperate paradise' (Mehlman 25) of her unbroken childhood corporeality. As Freud suggests, an unresolved 'attachment to the mother is . . . intimately related to the aetiology of hysteria' (21.227).

Thus Naomi's corporeality is produced by Old Man Gower's violation and her mother's absence, each to be understood in the cultural and political contexts within which I have read them. That the elements of the maternal and racialized sexuality are brought together in Naomi's hysteria becomes evident in her repeated references to a recurring childhood dream, first in the chapter where she talks of her abuse and again in the chapter where she tries to come to terms with the truth about her mother's absence and death. In this dream a mountain breaks in two, and daughter and mother stand on separate sides of the chasm; Naomi's legs are 'sawn in half'. In the first occurrence, they cannot see each other; in the second, Naomi sees 'bubbles like lava' on her mother's 'melt[ing]' face (65 and 242).

The chasm that separates mother and daughter in this dream is no different from the rifts that create Naomi's abjection. Like the Freudian amnesiac who seeks to remember, Naomi articulates through memories and dreams the complexity of her 'abject longing' (62). But the closer she comes to full expression of what she has repressed, the more she realizes that she cannot afford to forget what has caused that repression. To do so would be tantamount to practising cultural amnesia, forgetting the history of her body and her racialization, collaborating with the appropriating and assimilating strategies of hegemony. This is why, I believe, Naomi's talking cure takes the form of silence. Naomi's silent discourse reflects the liminality of her subjectivity, but it also discloses her reflexive use of repression to be an important political strategy. Thus her narrative 'emerge[s] from the abyss of enunciation where the subject splits, . . . [and] the pedagogical and the performative are agonistically articulated' (Bhabha 1990b, 304). The pedagogical function of Naomi's hysteria, as I have already suggested, lies precisely in the fact that it addresses the reader. Neither a confession to anyone in particular nor a narrative triggered by any overt or singular political cause, her hysteric script is as a subtle manifestation of 'oppositional pedagogy',[34] a pedagogy offered as an answer to Freud's simultaneous confidence in the imperative of education as a guarantor of civilization and his skepticism about the possibility of education in practice (21.5-9 and 51-6).[35] Hers is a pedagogy that destroys the false notion of progress and redefines it in terms of the impossibility of separating the personal from the political, the corporeal from the ideological.

Naomi the Teacher / Sigmund the Student: A Lesson on the Uncanny

The coming together of all these planes of experience both in Naomi's hysteria and in her pedagogical concern with the invasion of the stare can be traced to her role as teacher in Cecil, Alberta. The classroom scene in Chapter Two initiates her politics of reflexive repression, and problematizes epistemology with regard to race, gender, and sexuality. About to embark on a journey that is as important and traumatic as was the family's journey to Slocan, and eventually to Granton, Alberta, Naomi as teacher is at once 'the subject supposed to know' (Lacan 232) and a woman whose discourse slides between conscious and unconscious understanding. Whereas her necessary fall into the past takes place mostly in silence, in the Cecil schoolroom Naomi delivers a lesson, complete with phonics, that is the antecedent of, and the reason for, her silent talking cure.

This school scene precedes the phone call that announces the death of Naomi's uncle, the event that triggers her journey into the past. 'I am standing,' Naomi says, 'in front of my grades five and six class':

> This year there are two Native girls, sisters, twelve and thirteen years old, both adopted. There's also a beautiful half-Japanese, half-European child named Tami. Then there is Sigmund, the freckle-faced redhead. Right from the beginning, I can see that he is trouble. I'm trying to keep an eye on him by putting him at the front of the class. (5)

The legacy of colonialism, hybridity, dislocation, unease about authority—these elements show the classroom to be a field of contestation where Naomi, although nominally a figure of authority and discipline, is not at home. As she admits, 'It usually takes me at least two weeks to feel at home with a new class' (5). What transpires in this classroom, where what teacher and students have in common at the start of the new school year is their difference from each other, has an instructive function for students and teacher, but also for us readers. What does this lesson tell us about Naomi's attempts to deal with the spectator consciousness, the epistemology of visuality that has mobilized her racialization and the racism suffered by her community?

We could begin to answer this question by noticing the first thing Naomi herself articulates about her spatial relation in regard to the class: her discomfort about the traditional pedagogical situation of observer and observed. Although as teacher she stands in front of her students, in her perception both teacher and students are at once observers and observed. That she stands in front of the students 'defending' herself speaks volumes on her self-definition as a teacher. Naomi's pedagogical perspective is filtered through her history, which has taught her that she does not occupy a privileged position. Indeed, contrary to the conventional assumption that the teacher is a master of truth and of discipline, Naomi as a Japanese Canadian woman knows otherwise: there is no ideological difference between the City Fathers who, mobilized by their 'yellow peril' ideology, planned her family's evacuation, and traditional pedagogy, with its 'apostolic function . . . [which] synchronizes its own temporality with the transcendent temporality of' an 'original truth' (Radhakrishnan 1996, 99 and 98). Her own schooling experience in Slocan taught her that much.

Naomi's act of 'defending' herself may not be a pedagogical technique as such, but what brings it about certainly informs her pedagogy. Even before she has to face a student's impertinence, she knows that as teacher she is already positioned by her students and read as one of the texts in the class. If she conveys any privileged knowledge to the class, it is her awareness that 'knowledge [is] structure rather than content' (Freedman 181). The actual practice of her teaching, then, must be understood as a manifestation of the materiality of her history.

The historical and pedagogical dynamic of this class episode is also indicated by Naomi's acts of identification and nomination: she identifies by race those students who, like herself, are racialized, and names only one white child, Sigmund. If naming is often intended to confer a certain honour on the person named, Sigmund deserves the distinction because she identifies him as a troublemaker. He is the student whose hand is always up, not 'calmly but shak[ing] . . . frantically like a leaf in the wind' (6). Not a sign of the eagerness the student-as-nerd displays, his raised hand draws attention to himself as he assumes the role of a subject presumed to know. It is, then, no surprise that the lesson in question is occasioned by Sigmund's desire to undermine his teacher's authority and instead establish his own control over the class.

The lesson begins when Sigmund names the teacher, revealing for the first time in the novel the narrator's name:

> Sigmund's hand is up, as it usually is.
> 'Yes, Sigmund.'
> 'Miss Nah Canny,' he says.
> 'Not Nah Canny,' I tell him, printing my name on the blackboard. NAKANE.
> 'The a's are short as in "among"—Na Ka Neh—and not as in 'apron' or 'hat.' (5-6)

Sigmund's naming act is simultaneously an act of unnaming. In addressing her as 'Miss Nah Canny', Sigmund parodies, while acknowledging, Naomi's cultural specificity and pedagogical authority. Yet by misappropriating her name, by declaring in effect that she is *uncanny*, Sigmund of Cecil, Alberta, signs himself as Sigmund of Vienna, father of psychoanalysis, and Naomi 'Nah Canny' is inscribed as a woman whose alterity is distorted and restrained.

In keeping with her characteristic use of language, Naomi responds to 'Miss Nah Canny' with negative statements meant to be corrective. Yet they also affirm the point Sigmund unwittingly makes: that she is not '"*heimlich*" ["homely"]' or '"*heimisch*" ["native"]' (Freud 16.220). In fact she has already stated, through her description of the other students in the class, who is 'native' and who is not. Thus Sigmund's mispronunciation of her Japanese name illustrates that what is at stake in the pedagogical situation that has already begun is the way Naomi's identity as a racialized woman is experienced by herself and her students. She is the Canadian uncanny: Canadian-born and 'foreign' at the same time.

According to Freud, 'the uncanny is that class of the frightening which leads back to what is known of old and long familiar', a process revealing 'in what circumstances the familiar can become uncanny and frightening' (16.220). This definition could serve as a summation of the way *Obasan* explores the materiality of history, especially if we remind ourselves of Freud's research into the linguistic usage of the opposite of the uncanny. The word *heimlich*, he discovered, is so ambiguous in its range of applications that in at least one of its usages it has come to mean its opposite: 'on the one hand it means what is familiar and agreeable, and on the other, what is concealed and kept out of sight' (16.224-5). Freud surmised that what constitutes 'the secret nature of the uncanny' is that, 'in reality', there is 'nothing new or alien' about it, 'but something which is familiar and old-established in the mind and which has become alienated from it only through the process of repression' (16.241). His conclusion: 'the prefix "*un*" ["un-"] is the token of repression' (16.245).

Sigmund's un-naming act, then, does more than demonstrate the uncanny way in which Naomi's gender, race, and ethnicity are intertwined; it also leads to a pedagogical incident that I see as initiating Naomi's reflexive strategy of repression. That it is a white male student who occasions this turn of events is entirely fitting, for it illustrates the double function of Naomi's hysteria as a means of articulating repression that at once addresses the factors that repress her and reduces the risk of transference that is inherent in analysis.

Sigmund's language and attitude invite Naomi to deal with the way transference and countertransference[36] operate in the classroom. 'The student,' Constance Penley remarks, 'like the child with the parent, is almost *clairvoyant* when it comes to understanding the desire of the Other and how best narcissistically to mirror what the Other desires' (133). By chance, the clairvoyance of Sigmund the student is surpassed by the insight of the Sigmund he unwittingly becomes. Freud's abiding preoccupation with the efficacy of education, together with his skepticism about the ability of psychoanalysis to heal, dramatizes the meaning of the uncanny; it also helps us to understand how Naomi experiences the (counter)transference that determines her scene of instruction. A concise version of what Naomi intuits through the mediation of young Sigmund can be found in Freedman's personification of psychoanalysis: 'Psychoanalysis proclaims: "I am that which by definition does not have a place; hence I am always in two places at once. Because I am that which is denied a place, my identity is that which is repressed but will return; my place is a process of displacement"' (181).

Sigmund's resistance to Naomi's pedagogic authority both initiates and facilitates her coming to terms with what she has repressed. Naomi discovers, along with the reader, that teaching is like analysis, and vice versa: it 'deal[s] not so much with *lack* of knowledge as with *resistances* to knowledge' (Felman 1982, 30). Obliged to confront Sigmund's resistance to her, Naomi begins to decipher her own resistances and abjection. Her exchange with Sigmund, then, marks the beginning of her talking cure. If Naomi is a speechless speaker throughout the greater part of the novel, her exchange with Sigmund in this early chapter explains why she needs to displace from her narrative another possible Sigmund-like spectator, an interrogator who will not simply listen but will also attempt to place her in the position of the uncanny. Therefore Naomi opts for a 'third ear',[37] that of the reader.

A Spinster and a Matchmaker Discourse on Love

What is it about Sigmund's interrogation that turns the first class of the year into a lesson on Naomi's abjection?

'Have you ever been in love, Miss Nakane?' (6), Sigmund asks Naomi, after the pronunciation of her name is established. The impertinence of the question reflects his being white and male, but this display of his power, designed to jolt the teacher, is immediately curtailed by Naomi's response. She does not discipline Sigmund; instead, she reacts in a manner that is ironic and ambiguous, even comical: 'In love? Why do you suppose we use the preposition "in" when we talk about love?' I ask evasively. 'What does it mean to be "in" something?' (6). Naomi's evasiveness is not just a part of her pedagogy, as we have seen. Turning 'this ridiculous discussion' (8) into a lesson on prepositions enables her to answer a question with a meta-question. Her emphasis on the preposition 'in' restates the uncanny; through her enunciatory behaviour, she slides towards an unconscious acknowledgement that Sigmund's facile question is in reality a question that concerns her history. Her pedagogical reflexivity—analogous to, if not symptomatic of, the reflexivity of her repression and hysteria—initiates a double lesson on the way knowledge and ignorance constantly displace each other. This lesson begins by showing that even the teacher does not always know what she is supposed to know. Not fully aware of this, Naomi concedes that Sigmund's question is about desire, desire as what shapes representation historically and ideologically. If '[t]o ask a question is always to want something' (Martusewicz 100), Naomi's own question in lieu of an answer also recognizes desire both as lack and as the impetus that leads to the revelation of her historical unconscious.

Sigmund may be impertinent in asking her if she has ever been in love, but Naomi herself has asked some impertinent questions[38] in her own fashion. Sigmund does not volunteer any knowledge as to what it means to be '"in" something', yet it is his initial question and now his fleeting silence that invite Naomi to open a narrative parenthesis, to remember a scene that both answers and further complicates her own question: 'I am thinking of the time when I was a child and asked Uncle if he and Obasan were "in love". My question was out of place. "In ruv? What that?" Uncle asked. I've never once seen them caressing' (6). In the tradition of the talking cure, it is Sigmund's initiative that facilitates this release of memory.

Naomi's interior dialogue executes a number of intriguing reversals, an instance of how transference and countertransference function in pedagogy. In her memory she assumes Sigmund's questioning role while her Uncle takes on Naomi's role, asking, 'In ruv? What that?' The interchange of positions establishes the connection between the scene of instruction and Naomi's history. It shows that the classroom is a theatre of historical relations, but it also reveals Naomi's lesson to have an unconscious. In both the classroom and the remembered scene, desire is simultaneously present and absent, articulating the conflictual site that engenders Naomi's subjectivity. That she cannot remember ever seeing Obasan and Uncle embracing not only raises questions about the codes of love and physical behaviour she has internalized; it also points to Obasan's and Uncle's surrogate parenthood, to her missing mother, indeed to the entire complex of events that inform Naomi's life. What it means 'to be "in" something' is never answered directly by either Naomi or Sigmund. Instead, the question is reiterated, as we have seen, by Naomi's hysteric script: it is asked over and over again, and in its different guises it serves to articulate the liminality of Naomi's subjectivity.

We do know, though, the answer to Sigmund's question: Naomi is not in love; she has never been in love. And as Sigmund knows, she is not married either. In fact, to the delight of the students who gasp and titter (6 and 7), he asks Naomi if she is 'going to get married' (6), and soon thereafter comes his declaration that Naomi is 'a spinster' (7). It is at this point that the plot of this learning scene thickens.

Sigmund double-speaks. On one hand, he repeats what his mother has told him, that Naomi does not 'look old enough to be a teacher' (6). 'That's odd,' Naomi thinks, taken by surprise: 'It must be my size . [. . .] there were some surprised looks when parents came to the classroom door. Was it my youthfulness or my oriental face: I never learned which' (6). Naomi represses the question of her racialization, but the position in which she is situated leaves no doubt that the problem lies in the way what she is supposed to represent as a teacher is read through her body. Sigmund's reiteration of his mother's observation serves to highlight his role as interrogator: he situates Naomi by displacing her. In doing so, Sigmund articulates Freud's belief that, as Susan Katz persuasively shows, 'marriage [is] a standard for mental health': 'The equation of marriage with health and, conversely, spinsterhood with illness, was part of the cultural and literary mythology of Freud's time' (297).[39] In this scenario, hysteria and spinsterhood are synonymous. On the other hand, Sigmund (like Freud) attempts to remedy the situation. 'My friend,' he states unabashedly, 'wants to ask you for a date' (6).

Naomi's sagacious answer to these questions is that 'there are many questions I don't have answers for' (7). Far from trying simply to deflect Sigmund's mischievousness, or rendering herself vulnerable as an ill-equipped teacher, she practises a reflexive pedagogy. On one hand, she expresses the incompleteness of knowledge, the error the subject who is presumed to know can make in assuming that knowledge can be totalized, and therefore commodified and circulated as product. On the other, her acknowledgement of not knowing articulates the ignorance revealed by her pedagogical unconscious. Felman argues that ignorance is not '*opposed* to knowledge: it is itself a radical condition, an integral part of the very *structure* of knowledge'. Ignorance, then, is 'a kind of forgetting—of forgetfulness: while learning is obviously, among other things, remembering and memorizing . . . , ignorance is linked to what is *not remembered*, what will not be memorized. But what will not be memorized is tied up with repression, with the imperative to forget—the imperative to exclude from consciousness, to not admit to knowledge' (1982, 29). Naomi admits that the label 'spinster' and its cognates 'old maid' and 'bachelor lady' 'certainly apply' in her case (8)—'At thirty-six, I'm no bargain in the marriage market' (8); she acknowledges what she is, and that it is consistent with her socialization. Nevertheless, at this stage of the novel, she remains ignorant of what she has repressed, namely her racialization and sexual abuse. She is truly a subject *supposed* to know, for we see Naomi knowing but also needing to learn.

At this point in her narration, Naomi's hysteria is indicated only by her spinsterhood, but her pedagogical unconscious already points to the genealogy of her abjection. 'I suppose I am an old maid,' is her reply to Sigmund, but she goes on to say that her 'aunt in Toronto' is one too (8). Sigmund instigates Naomi's recognition of a 'crone-prone syndrome' in the family. 'Must be something in the blood' (8), she says. As her hysteric script demonstrates, though, there is nothing wrong with the family's 'blood' except insofar as it is pronounced tainted by the dominant society. The reflexivity of her pedagogy, as well as that of her repression, posits itself as a political strategy, 'a rejection of the cultural norms of femininity, marriage, and family life' (Katz 303). As match-maker Sigmund adopts Freud's standard of health, but Naomi rejects the cure: her 'spinsterhood' may be a sign of her repression, but it is also the conduit through which her 'unmeant knowledge' is articulated.

Her unmarried status, then, works against the phallic pedagogy that declares Naomi not to be a 'bargain in the marriage market'. It thus has an ambivalent instructive function manifested in the way she turns Sigmund the student into Sigmund the master of psychoanalysis. Naomi's spinsterhood is a sign of her refusal to be coerced into living a life written for her by others, a life with a discernible telos. The lesson of her spinsterhood is addressed to the Freudian blind spot about hysteria. The talking cure can never fully erase the causes of hysteric symptoms. It seems that, for Freud, remembering the past suggests a clean break with it; but in *Obasan* this kind of remembering would amount to ignorance, 'an active dynamic of negation, an active refusal' (Felman 1982, 30). This is the why the novel 'closes', as Miki reminds us, not with Naomi's telling but with an excerpt from a memorandum submitted to the House and Senate of Canada in 1946 by three white Canadians in defence of Japanese Canadians' rights.

Although she appears to have internalized the logic of the hegemonic phallic pedagogy, Naomi teaches us precisely what Freud resisted hearing in his hysteric women's stories. The socio-political terrain that her repressed memories point to is, as we have seen, so heavily inscribed on her body and psyche that simply composing a memory document out of it cannot dislocate the fierce logic that has kept it in place for so long. The lesson here is that we cannot forfeit the knowledge we decipher from Naomi's silent script.

Ending without Resolution

Naomi's narrative of remembering makes us witnesses; but her story also reminds us that a witness is an observer whose gaze is, more often than not, trained to objectify, to implement the logic of visuality. Witnesses who do not resist what they see, who do not shift from their position of observation, perpetuate the very ideology that discriminates against Naomi and others like her. If at the end of the novel Naomi can let her 'loved ones . . . rest' in peace (246), it is because she has done all *she* can for those who have passed away, writing them into history. There is no doubt that Naomi embraces the body of 'Love', that of 'familiar lost' ones (246), at the end of the novel. Obviously this embrace is not meant as a revised answer to Sigmund's question as to whether she is 'in' love; but neither is it an answer to the host of political questions her narrative raises—although this is what most critics argue. The political efficacy of Naomi's hysteria has nothing to do with this kind of cure.

There is a gap at the novel's conclusion, I would argue, between Naomi's cognition and her speaking knowledge. We may endorse the Love she experiences as her resolution of what she has been afflicted by, but we should also read it against her intention, and through the lessons her pedagogical unconscious and hysteric script have taught us: that a progressivist view of history reproduces the transcendental values and truths that posit homogeneity as normative. As a result of her abjection, Naomi personalizes history. Nevertheless, her affirmation of Love represses what her speaking knowledge discloses, the interrelated factors that determine (her) history. The allegory she employs at the end of her narrative depersonalizes that history, but she remains lodged within the blueprint of the very same ideology that inscribes a telos on historical contradictions in the name of progress. Naomi errs because she embraces a Love that compels her to close the page of history she has opened. To borrow words from Radhakrishnan, she conserves the past; she does not deauthorize it (1996, 21).

The Love she is flooded with is overwhelmed by her Grief,[40] a bizarre allegorical figure that I believe Naomi misreads:

> Grief wails like a scarecrow in the wild night, beckoning the wind to clothe his gaunt shell. With his outstretched arms he is gathering eyes for his disguise. I had not known that Grief had such gentle eyes—eyes reflecting my uncle's eyes, my mother's eyes, all the familiar lost eyes of Love that are not his and that he dons as a mask and a mockery. (245-6)

Naomi is seduced by Grief's eyes. If, as many readers claim, she reaches a resolution at the end of her narration, it is one marked by both blindness and insight, for she still represses some of her knowledge. She ignores her own insight that Grief's eyes are not his but those of her lost and loved ones. Her allegorization and masculine impersonation of Grief do little to rehabilitate history, to thwart hegemonic ideology. Although stirred emotionally, she is fixed by those eyes. She is held 'in' place, politically immobilized.

What Grief disguises is precisely what is spoken by the reflexivity of Naomi's repression and her pedagogical unconscious. Interestingly, the imagery she uses to talk about Grief echoes the imagery with which she talks about the other 'spinster' in the family, Emily: 'Has Aunt Emily ever, I wonder, been in love? Love no doubt is in her. Love, like the coulee wind, rushing through her mind, whirring along the tips of her imagination. Love like a coyote, howling into a "love 'em and leave 'em" wind' (8). If Emily's love is like a howling coyote, it must also share some of the unpredictability that comes with the coyote's cunning and ingenuity. But in this scene, as at the end of the novel, Naomi teases the reader with a resolution based on what she knows, a resolution, though, that is belied by what is still repressed within her. She may be an anti-pedagogue, as we have seen, but she is also a product of the kind of pedagogy that aspires to reconciliation for the sake of the presumed comfort that comes with imposing a telos on things.

Naomi's ignorance here is not ignorance as knowing what we do not know, but as not knowing what we already know.

That at the end of the novel 'Japanese Canadians are still *spoken for*' (Miki 1995, 144) is a reminder of how knowledge is structured, of the need to read *Obasan*, as well as ourselves, through a personalized and depersonalized view of history, synchronically and diachronically. Because Naomi's narration both exposes and disavows the politics of visuality, she inhabits a social space that is infused with undecidability.

> The only thing I carry in my wallet is my driver's licence. I should have something with my picture on it and a statement below that tells who I am. Megumi Naomi Nakane. Born June 18, 1936, Vancouver, British Columbia. Marital status: Old maid. Health: Fine, I suppose. Occupation: School teacher. I'm bored to death with teaching and ready to retire. What else would anyone want to know? Personality: Tense. Is that past or present tense? It's perpetual tense. I have the social graces of a common housefly. That's self-denigrating, isn't it? (7)

Naomi devises this self-portrait in the course of her exchange with Sigmund. Mimicking an official identity description, it is her ironic response to the pressure she experiences under Sigmund's interrogation, only he does not hear it. Instead, it inaugurates her hysteric script of silence; it opens up history for the reader to see why Naomi is 'self-denigrating'.

It is disappointing, then, that Naomi ends her narrative on a note of nostalgia that takes us back to the novel's opening: 'Umi no yo,' she remembers her now dead Uncle saying about the movement of the prairie grass; 'It's like the sea' (1 and 247). Naomi finds consolation in that elegant movement, but the repetition of this memory demands that the novel reach the kind of resolution that comes from a circular structure. Naomi's consolation suggests a repression of Uncle's own nostalgia, a forgetting of the intransigent order of things that kept him away from the sea. Her nostalgia is an invitation to revisit history twice over, and thus it functions against her own pedagogical unconscious. If Naomi is 'perpetually tense', it is because she has not fully learned what she already knows. By the end of her narrative, the skeletons of history are decidedly out of the closet. Also brought to light, however, is the double imperative not only to expose the contents of history, but also to change history's shape.

Notes

Critical Correspondences

1. Said attributes the 'politics of blame' to postcolonial critics, but the theoretical and political context in which he uses the term is similar to the one in question here.

2. Sara Suleri views the different discourses and fields of practice that pit 'the "academy" against the "real world"' as 'a simplistic binarism', a 'most tedious dichotomy' (756). Despite the vexing questions raised by this opposition, dismissing this binarism as tedious does nothing to address either its lived reality or the factors that have constructed the academy-vs-reality dichotomy in the first place. See 'Women Skin Deep: Feminism and the Postcolonial Condition', *Critical Inquiry* 18 (Summer 1992): 756–69.

3. On the concepts of restricted and general economy, see Georges Bataille, *Inner Experience*, trans. Leslie Anne Boldt (Albany: State University of New York Press, 1988) and 'The Notion of Expenditure' in *Visions of Excess: Selected Writings 1927–1939*, ed. and with an Introduction by Allan Stoekl, trans. Allan Stoekl, with Carl R. Lovitt and Donald M. Leslie, Jr (Minneapolis: University of Minnesota Press, 1985), 116–29.

4. Benjamin bought Paul Klee's watercolour *Angelus Novus* in Munich in the spring of 1921; see Momme Brodersen, *Walter Benjamin: A Biography*, trans. Malcolm R. Green and Ingrida Ligers, ed. Martina Dervis (London and New York: Verso, 1996), 120. See also Benjamin's essay 'Theses on the Philosophy of History' (1969).

5. This quotation, as well as the next one from Bhabha, is from his essay 'Anxious Nations, Nervous States', published in Joan Copjec, ed., *Supposing the Subject* (London and New York: Verso, 1994); my citation is from the manuscript version of the essay that Bhabha read at the University of Victoria in 1994. Parts of this essay are also included in Bhabha 1995.

6. The film's title in German is *Der Himmel über Berlin* ('The Sky over Berlin'). Its script was co-written by Wenders and the Austrian writer Peter Handke. The two had collaborated before in the film *Falsche Bewegung*, translated into English as *Wrong Move* (1974). The lead roles in *Wings of Desire* are played by Bruno Ganz (Damiel) and Otto Sander (Cassiel); Marion is played by Solveig Dommartin; Homer is Curt Bois, 'an actor who worked with Max Reinhardt and Bertolt Brecht and fled Nazi Germany in 1933' (Paneth 2); Peter Falk plays Peter Falk—with a

difference. The cinematographer is Henri Alekan, who was the cinematographer for Jean Cocteau's 1946 *Beauty and the Beast. Wings of Desire* won numerous awards, including Best Director at Cannes.

7. Since then I have come across an essay on *Wings of Desire* by Roger Cook, who also refers to Benjamin's inscription in the film; Cook's main argument centres on the film's relation to history.

8. As Charles H. Helmetag points out, the lines echo 1 Corinthians 13:11: 'When I was a child, I spake as a child, I understood as a child, I thought as a child: but when I became a man, I put away childish things.'

9. Thomas F. Barry's interpretation of the function of writing in the film, that it 'signals the presence of an author figure', specifically Wenders' co-writer Peter Handke, is appropriate; studying Handke's work in German and the film's German script, Barry argues that the writing in the film echoes 'in both style and content' Handke's own published journals (54). My interpretation of writing here, although it doesn't contradict Barry, points in a different direction. See Barry, 'The Weight of Angels: Peter Handke and *Der Himmel über Berlin*', *Modern Austrian Literature* 23, 3/4 (1990): 53–63.

10. This is from Wenders' *Die Logik der Bilder* (1988), but I am relying here on Cook's abbreviated translation.

11. Wenders said about his choice of the location where the angels would live: 'Since angels are not really linked between people and God anymore we could not do a church [sic], so we tried for another place.' He found his inspiration in one of his favourite films, Truffaut's *Fahrenheit 451*, where 'everybody represents a book that they have learned by heart because books are persecuted and burned; and to me that was really a vision of paradise . . . I thought this is a heavenly place, a library' (Paneth 6).

12. Cassiel is also tempted to fall, but postpones his plunge into humanity until *Far Away, So Close*, the sequel to *Wings of Desire*.

13. According to Wenders, behind this kind of innovative camera movement was the desire to 'create a benevolent look (*einen liebevollen Blick*) for the eye of the camera' (Cook 36).

14. 'Companiero' is the expression Falk uses consistently every time he addresses the angels he feels (he points to his stomach by way of emphasizing his gut feeling) but can no longer see.

15. Working both with and against the obvious metaphysical level of the film are the various historical signs inscribed in it, ranging from the Berlin Wall (on both sides of which the angels move) and the documentary footage of Berlin being bombed during the Second World War, to the Kaiser Wilhelm Gedächtniskirche, the Siegessäule, Potsdamer Platz, and the Esplanade. Wenders' choice of easily identifiable locations is important in that it stresses the historical layers that his characters have to traverse in their present. For example, the Esplanade, a building located on one side of Potsdamer Platz, the underground location of Hitler's bunker, was the gathering place of the Nazi elite but was, until recently,

abandoned and in a state of ruin.

16. Barry points out that Marion's reflections 'are virtually direct quotes from [Handke's] *Das Gewicht der Welt*' (55). Although Rodowski's point that Marion is given 'ready-made linguistic material' is interesting, I don't necessarily agree with him that this 'implies that Handke and Wenders make little effort to find specific forms of expressing female subjectivity' (406). To isolate her interior monologues as a sign of her co-opted female subjectivity is reductive; not only does she deliver the longest monologue in the film, but she stresses her 'decision' to choose to love Damiel. On a different note, it is interesting that her inner voice also recites the lines of the poem about the child spoken for the first time by Damiel.

17. Paneth's interview was obviously conducted before the collapse of the Berlin Wall.

18. This strategy, in which a native tongue and its (in this case) English translation have different impacts depending on the viewers' linguistic knowledge, is also employed by Atom Egoyan in his film *Calendar*.

19. These historical layers of the city are directly thematized in the film's sequel, *Far Away, So Close*, in which there are many flashbacks set in the Nazi period.

20. I am indebted to Roger Cook for this reference.

21. See my discussion of the Janus-faced figure in the chapter on Grove, 53–7.

22. My point here about the need to negotiate diasporic subjectivity and nationalism, as well as the need to be cautious about globalism, certainly requires elaboration, but this is not the place for it. On the various aspects of diasporic and cosmopolitan identities, and their relation to different manifestations of global development, see the recent collection of essays edited by Pheng Cheah and Bruce Robbins, *Cosmopolitics: Thinking and Feeling Beyond the Nation*, (Minneapolis and London: University of Minnesota Press, 1998).

23. It is not my intention here is to collapse the complex differences among these theorists and teachers, but rather to draw attention to what I perceive as their common concern, the need to question the means in which we disseminate knowledge and the kind of knowledge taught. See Paulo Freire, *Pedagogy of the Oppressed* (New York: Continuum, 1995), and Robert Con Davies, 'A Manifesto for Oppositional Pedagogy: Freire, Bourdieu, Merod, and Graff', in Bruce Henricksen and Thaïs E. Morgan, eds, *Reorientations: Critical Theories and Pedagogies* (Urbana and Chicago: University of Illinois Press, 1990). References to the other critics can be found in the bibliography.

Chapter 1

1. This diary, transcribed and edited by Paul Hjartarson, is published in *A Stranger to My Time* (301–42).

2. See, for example, Hjartarson's editorial comments in *A Stranger to My Time* (specifically those preceding Grove's essays), as well as his essay 'Design and Truth' (1981).

3. Interestingly, Grove's letter was written shortly after Bothwell's review of *Settlers of the Marsh* appeared (14 Nov. 1925). While positive on the whole, Bothwell's review begins by establishing 'an instant comparison' with Ostenso's novel and finding Grove's, 'though melodramatic enough, . . . not so well adapted to the movies as is Miss Ostenso's' (Pacey 1970, 108).

4. Grove made liberal use of ellipses in his writing; to differentiate them from my own, the latter will be enclosed in square brackets. Citations from Grove not followed by a date are from *Settlers of the Marsh*.

5. Most of the reviews of *Settlers of the Marsh* excerpted in Pacey's *Frederick Philip Grove* (1970) compare Grove's novel to Ostenso's; some also refer to Salverson's *The Viking Heart*.

6. This essay is one of the lectures Grove presented on three national tours sponsored by the Association of Canadian Clubs: February-April 1928; September-November 1928; January-March 1929 (Pacey 1976, xxviii).

7. For another critical response to the New Canadian Library, see the fifth chapter in Robert Lecker's *Making It Real*. Also, *Imagining Canadian Literature: The Selected Letters of Jack McClelland*, ed. Sam Solecki (Toronto: Key Porter Books, 1998), includes a number of letters that shed light on the founding vision of the New Canadian Library.

8. I say 'true origins' here only with respect to the bare facts about Grove's birth. Grove's own fabrication of many 'events' in his life, as well as the various constructions about him that emerge both from his writing and from studies about him, remains a fertile field for exploration. Two such studies, Klaus Martens' *Felix Paul Greves Karriere: Frederick Philip Grove in Deutschland* (St. Ingbert: Röhvig Universitäts Verlag, 1997) and Richard Cavell's 'Felix Paul Greve, the Eulenburg Scandal, and Frederick Paul Grove', *Essays on Canadian Writing* 62 (Fall 1997): 12–45, offer valuable new information.

9. See, for instance, the studies of Lawrence Ricou, *Vertical Man / Horizontal World: Man and Landscape in Canadian Prairie Fiction* (Vancouver: University of British Columbia Press, 1973), and Dick Harrison's *Unnamed Country: The Struggle for a Canadian Prairie Fiction* (Edmonton: University of Alberta Press, 1977).

10. See, for example, the section 'Connecting Empire to Secular Interpretation' in Said's *Culture and Imperialism*. Vassilis Lampropoulos' *The Rise of Eurocentrism* deals specifically with the theological, philosophical, and philological courses that have marked modernity as it relates to nationalism and other such Eurocentric movements. As Lampropoulos says, 'The national and the cultural, as they are still understood today, were produced together, verifying and supporting each other. It is in Germany that culture becomes a conscious project, a means of resistance as well as legitimation, of national differentiation as well as superiority' (58–9).

11. On this point see Leon Surette's essay 'Creating the Canadian Canon', in *Canadian Canons* (Lecker 1991).

12. Cavell's reading of Grove in Germany's 'homosocial' and homosexual context at the time suggests other possible reasons for Grove's departure. See note 8 above.

13. This interpretation of Grove's Canadian content is echoed by J.J. Healy's 'Grove and the Matter of Germany: The Warkentin Letters and the Art of Liminal Disengagement' (Hjartarson, ed. 1986).

14. See the recent volume *Comparative Literature in the Age of Multiculturalism* (Bernheimer 1995), which brings together 'the Bernheimer Report' on comparative literature as a discipline and responses by such authors as Chow, Apter, K. Anthony Appiah, Mary Louise Pratt, and Françoise Lionnet. As Apter writes, postcolonialism has 'usurped the disciplinary space that European literature and criticism had reserved for themselves' (86). Despite some of the differences between comparative literature as it was traditionally defined and practised and postcolonial theory and criticism, historical events and exile inform both, though in different ways. 'The current generation of exilic critics'—Bhabha, Spivak, Chow, and Suleri would be some examples—'is often, as might be expected, deeply antithetical to their Eurocentric counterparts'; yet the critical project of this generation of critics also resembles 'its European antecedents' because of its 'cultural ambivalence' and 'confusion induced by "worlding" or global transference' (Apter 90).

15. Consider, for example, Arun Mukherjee's criticism of Michael Ondaatje's *Running in the Family* in her *Oppositional Aesthetics*, or Marlene Nourbese Philip's critique of Neil Bissoondath's *A Casual Brutality* in her *Frontiers*. Both essays offer rigorous critiques of the universalist assumptions of Western discourse, and both reveal a homogenizing impulse in what they find lacking in Ondaatje's and Bissoondath's works respectively.

16. See Hayden White (20–1).

17. For an example of an argument that questions the progressivist implications of certain kinds of postcoloniality, see Anne McClintock, 'The Angel of Progress: Pitfalls of the Term "Post-Colonialism",' *Social Text* 31–32 (1992): 84–98 (also included in McClintock 1995). As she says, 'The United States, South Africa, Australia, Canada, and New Zealand, remain, in my view, breakaway settler colonies that have not undergone decolonization, nor, with the exception of South Africa, are they likely to in the near future' (89).

18. The Scandinavians' positive image is pervasive in many studies of that period. As Donald Avery observes in his book *'Dangerous Foreigners': European Immigrant Workers and Labour Radicalism in Canada 1896–1932* (Toronto: McClelland and Stewart 1979; rpt 1983), 'Scandinavians and Germans were a special case; many native English-speaking Canadians regarded them as close cultural relatives. . . . [They] fitted in easily; other Eastern and Central Europeans did not, whether the differences lay with themselves or their host society' (14). Jorgen Dahlie, though, argues that this positive image 'is an interpretation that has had a ready acceptance rather than careful scrutiny based on solid historical evidence'. Thus he proceeds to take 'into account the perceptions of those on the "inside"' (102).

19. Benjamin discusses this concept in his 'Theses on the Philosophy of History' (1969). Although I am influenced by his work, my use of the term here is not,

strictly speaking, Benjaminian.

20. On the author 'outside' the text and the author 'inside' the text see the chapter 'The Female Authorial Voice' in Kaja Silverman's *The Acoustic Mirror* (187–234). As she says in *Male Subjectivity at the Margins*: 'The author "outside" the text can perhaps best be described as an "origin under erasure"—as a site which is simultaneously productive of desire, and devoid of authorial "substance" or presence. He or she in some sense "gives rise" to the author "inside" the text, but is at the same time constituted as authorial subject only through that construct' (161).

21. See the reviews of the novel selected in Pacey 1970 (105–17); for a somewhat different perspective on the issue, see 'Spokesman of a Race?', Edward A. McCourt's chapter on Grove in his *The Canadian West in Fiction* (Toronto: Ryerson, 1949).

22. Nowhere in the novel's third-person narrative is there a gender reference to the narrator. However, for the sake of simplicity and because of the connections I am drawing between the narrator and Niels and the former and Grove, I will refer to the narrator as 'he'.

23. I would also include in these narratives his letters, for the Grove I am talking about here is the product of the various discourses (writerly and non-writerly) that he produced.

24. See Benjamin's essay 'The Task of the Translator' in *Illuminations*, 69–82.

25. See Ryerson, *Elements of Political Economy* (Toronto: Copp, Clark, 1877) and Wayland, *Elements of Political Economy* (Boston: Gould and Lincoln, 1870). Although it is more likely that Grove had Ryerson in mind, the lack of further evidence in the novel makes it impossible to ascertain which of the two identical titles Grove alludes to. Interestingly, Wayland's influential book, originally published in 1840, is included among the 'most authoritative works on Political Economy' that Ryerson credits, works from which he borrowed 'the phraseology' and 'the materials' he 'compiled and condensed' ('Prefatory Notice').

26. For an in-depth study of Sifton and his policies see D.J. Hall.

27. This is one of the most frequently cited comments of Sifton both in immigration studies of his time and in later historical books. As the novelist Vera Lysenko says, in her socio-historical study *Men in Sheepskin Coats: A Study in Assimilation* (Toronto: Ryerson, 1947), 'The phrase would be repeated many times, sometimes questioningly, sometimes scornfully, as the end of the nineteenth and the beginning of the twentieth centuries saw trainloads of new-comers hurled at the Canadian prairies. . . . As they surged through the station at Montreal and the great immigration sheds of the west, their foreign appearance aroused the greatest curiosity: . . . 'Sifton's Sheepskins!' they jeered. Would such sheepskins ever become Canadians?' (6–7).

28. This business-like approach to immigrants is also reflected in an 1872 paper on immigration by Thomas White, Jr (Minister of the Interior in 1887), in which he talked about the 'inexhaustible' 'supply of immigrants' and favoured, as Sifton did, American immigrants (cited in Magrath 37). All the early Canadian studies of

immigration I have consulted, including those cited in this chapter, talk about immigrants in terms of supply and demand; this clearly suggests that the construction of immigrants, be they British settlers or minoritized Others, should be examined in the context not only of postcolonialism but of capitalism and the relations between labour and nationalism.

29. The published material of the 1910s and 1920s on which I rely here offers poignant descriptions of the discrimination suffered by many groups of European and Asian immigrants, although discrimination in these studies figures as normative, hence honourable and patriotic, behaviour. For an account of such discriminatory practices see Morris Davis and J.F. Krauter, *Minority Canadians: Ethnic Groups* (Toronto: Methuen, 1978).

30. Superintendent of the Methodist All Peoples' Mission in Winnipeg, and later the first leader of the Co-operative Commonwealth Federation (CCF), Woodsworth 'has been described as an "untypical Canadian"' (Barber, 'Introduction', Woodsworth x) and, as John Porter says, 'was later to be called the saint of Canadian politics' (65). While his saintly image reflects the compassion of some of his views about immigrants, which show him to be, at least to some extent, ahead of his time, his study exemplifies the racist stereotyping that was rampant in his day. See also Kenneth McNaught's *J.S. Woodsworth* (Don Mills, Ont.: Fitzhenry and Whiteside, 1980), and Allen Mills' *Fool for Christ: The Political Thought of J.S. Woodsworth* (Toronto: University of Toronto Press, 1991).

31. On this point see also Grove's essay 'Assimilation' in Hjartarson, ed.

32. According to Woodsworth, Dr Allan McLaughlin was 'of the U.S. Marine Hospital Service', and published 'a comprehensive series on "Immigration"' in the *Popular Science Monthly* between 1903 and 1905 (10).

33. On some of the implications of Woodsworth's 'social gospel' see Marilyn Barber, 'Nationalism, Nativism and the Social Gospel', in Richard Allen, ed., *The Social Gospel in Canada* (Ottawa, 1975): 186–226.

34. See, for example, Pacey's references to their relationship in his annotations in Grove's Letters 1976, (96, 101, 296, 311). Based on 'Grove's letters elsewhere [Pacey does not specify what or where these letters are], it appears that he knew' Woodsworth 'rather intimately' (311). In another annotation (14), Pacey draws attention to the fact that in 1943 Grove ran unsuccessfully as a candidate for the CCF, which was founded and led by Woodsworth himself.

35. As Hjartarson points out in his introduction to these essays, with their publication Grove 'entered a debate on immigration fuelled by such works as J.S. Woodsworth's *Strangers Within Our Gates*' (1986, 177). All references to these essays in the discussion that follows will be to Hjartarson's collection.

36. It is relevant to mention here that Grove's intimate knowledge of Flaubert's work was not limited only to his fiction. Grove was involved in the editing of Flaubert's letters, many of which were written, as Grove remarks in his annotated comments, while on his 'great Orient journey with Maxime Ducamp [. . .] The journey, which lasted one and a half years, goes from Marseilles over Malta to

Egypt. From there via Syria, Rhodes, Asia Minor, Constantinople, Greece, Italy and back to France' (*Gustave Flauberts Gesammelte Werke*, Bd. 7 *Briefe uber seine Werke*. Ausgewahlt, eingeleitet und mit Anmerkungen versehen von F.P. Greve. Minden: J.C.C. Bruns' Verlag, 1904, p. 24). The familiarity of Grove/Greve with Flaubert's work is just one indication that we might read some of the former's work in an orientalist context, but I will leave discussion of this issue for another occasion. My thanks to Heike Härting for her translation from German into English, and for her help with locating relevant material in Germany.

37. Grove uses this expression in both 'Canadians Old and New' and 'Assimilation' without any specific ethnic or national overtones (Hjartarson, ed. 175 and 183 respectively).

38. I am borrowing here from '*Alias* Grove: Variations in Disguise', the title of Blodgett's essay (1982).

39. As the phallus in Lacanian theory is neither the penis nor a symbol but a signifier, a function of language that has value and meaning only in relation to other terms, so the terms 'Law of the Father' and 'Name of the Father' do not refer to an individual male subject; rather, they relate to the symbolic order of things—in other words, to the law of patriarchy. Because the symbolic order is the effect of linguistic functions, the Law of the Father determines the subject—libidinally, culturally, and socially. In this regard, the Law of the Father is a sign that speaks of the prohibition, on pain of castration, of incest with the mother, thus alienating the male child from his mother while rewarding him with a symbolic association with the Name of the Father. It is in this sense that I continue to employ in this study the Law of the Father and the Name of the Father as signs of authority. For example, in Niels's case, the Name of the Father alludes not to *his* father, but to the way the *figure* of his father is allegorized in the text as a manifestation of the Law of the Father. For a full elaboration of these theoretical issues see Lacan, *Écrits: A Selection*, trans. Alan Sheridan (New York and London: W.W. Norton, 1977), Lacan (1979), and *Feminine Sexuality: Jacques Lacan and the École Freudienne*, ed. Juliet Mitchell and Jacqueline Rose, trans. Jacqueline Rose (New York and London: W.W. Norton, 1982).

40. What I call Niels's cross-gendering incites and is supplemented by the cross-gendering elements of Ellen's character. Here, though, I am referring not to what Lorraine McMullen has called an 'androgynous society' in Grove's work (75)—which suggests a balancing of sexual differences—but rather to cross-gendering as a means of disruption. See McMullen, 'Women in Grove's Novels', in John Nause, ed., *The Grove Symposium* (Ottawa: University of Ottawa Press, 1974), 67–76.

41. See 'Phantasy (or Fantasy)', in Laplanche and Pontalis; see also Zizek (1989) and Chow (1998), 156–7 and 76 respectively.

42. Although my reading of Niels's dreams or visions is largely informed by Freudian concepts, I use the terms 'fantasy' and 'dream' interchangeably, since my primary goal here is not to test psychoanalytic theories about fantasy but rather to understand the various levels of materiality (including that of psychic reality) underly-

ing the function of Niels's dreams.

43. I am referring to Roland Barthes, *The Pleasure of the Text*, trans. Richard Miller, with a note on the text by Richard Howard (New York: Farrar, Straus and Giroux, 1975). The text of 'pleasure' is predictable—it 'bores me' (4)—because it 'comes from culture and does not break with it, is linked to a *comfortable* practice of reading'. The text of 'bliss' or *jouissance* is a 'text that imposes a state of loss, the text that discomforts' (14).

44. Among the projects that Bedson initiated were 'educational classes for Indians and other inmates who were unable to read' (J.T.L. James 38). For historical and critical accounts of the Canadian penal system at the time see D. Owen Carrigan, *Crime and Punishment in Canada: A History* (Toronto: McClelland and Stewart, 1991), 349–50. On the state of federal penitentiaries and the changes they underwent, see also C.W. Topping, *Canadian Penal Institutions* (Toronto: Ryerson, 1929), and John Kidman, *The Canadian Prison: The Story of a Tragedy* (Toronto: Ryerson, 1947).

45. The question I would have liked to explore here, if this chapter were not already long enough, is why anarchy and degeneracy are represented in the novel by a European woman, and what this situation entails in relation to 'wastage', gender, corporeality, and the construction of whiteness.

Chapter 2

1. Stam identifies four major factors in negative responses to multiculturalism: the misperceptions of multiculturalism as 'anti-European'; as a movement that threatens to 'disunit[e] America'; as a 'therapy for minorities'; and as a form of 'new puritanism'. Although his article analyzes multiculturalism in the United States, I find its critical perspective relevant to the Canadian situation. For an account of the various interpretations of Canadian multiculturalism, see, for example, Evelyn Kallen. For a brief overview, see my 'Introduction' to *Making a Difference: Canadian Multicultural Literature* (Toronto: Oxford University Press, 1996), especially 10–13.

2. Valpy, 'Is multiculturalism a threat to the status quo?' *The Globe and Mail*, 2 July 1994: D1 and D5.

3. For a discussion of media representation and minorities in Canada see Augie Fleras, 'Media and Minorities in a Post-Multicultural Society: Overview and Appraisal', in J.W. Berry and J.A. Laponce, eds, *Ethnicity and Culture in Canada* (Toronto: University of Toronto Press, 1994), 267–92.

4. While 'media discourse' does not refer exclusively to newspapers, I use *The Globe and Mail* as my chief example not only because what appears in its pages often becomes a central element in multicultural debates, but also because newspapers, especially those assuming a 'national voice', traditionally function as registers of national consciousness. See, for example, Benedict Anderson, *Imagined Communities* (33).

5. For the sake of simplicity, unless an article appears on more than one page, I do not provide page references to the newspaper articles discussed in this section.

6. See, for example, Kirk Makin's article 'Benefiting from Diversity—Multicultural grants: Just about every ethnic minority as well as filmmakers and business organizations receive money', *The Globe*, 30 June 1994: A1, A2.

7. A member of the audience at a conference where I presented this argument told me that Gina Mallet is an immigrant from the United States. Whether this information is accurate or not, her immigrant status does not change the dominant perspective inscribed in her article.

8. Ross's fairy-tale motif, as I read it, relies not only on Ricci's literary success, but also on what she calls the 'fantastic and the fabulous' elements in Ricci's romance with his wife. His wife is the writer Erika de Vasconcelos, whose first novel, *My Darling Dead Ones* (Toronto: Knopf, 1997), was, according to Ross, 'a highlight of the spring publishing season'. It goes without saying, of course, that my reading here is concerned with Ross's mode of writing and not Ricci's.

9. See *The Globe and Mail* (1989): 'Charges of Racism Spark Protest at Writers' Congress', 26 Sept.: A19; '"All Aboard!" Writers' Express Heads for Montreal', 28 Sept.: C11; 'PEN Organizers Stress the Positive', 2 Oct.: C7. See also Marlene Nourbese Philip, especially 148–67.

10. The major controversies that surrounded this exhibit, curated by Jeanne Cannizzo, were widely reported in the Canadian press. See, for example, *The Globe and Mail*: 'A revealing journey through space and time' (17 Nov. 1989); 'Eight ROM protesters arrested' (4 June 1990); 'Museum wins injunction restraining demonstrators' (12 May 1990); 'ROM Coalition to talk' (20 June 1990); 'Controversial show to be changed' (4 Aug. 1990); 'U.S. museums cancel Africa exhibit—ROM may lose $100,000 after demise of North American tour' (29 Nov. 1990); and 'ROM resolves backlash over exhibit' (6 June 1991). See also *The Toronto Star*: 'African exhibits inspire awe and anger' (7 May 1990) and 'Chanting group pickets ROM but respects court injunctions' (13 May 1990). See also Cannizzo's Introduction to ROM's *Into the Heart of Africa* catalogue (1989, 10–12), her interview with Hazel A. Da Breo, 'Royal Spoils: the museum confronts its colonial past', *Fuse* (Winter 1989–90): 28–37, and her article 'Exhibiting Cultures: "Into the Heart of Africa",' *Visual Anthropology Review* 7, 1 (1991): 150–60. Linda Hutcheon's chapter 'The End(s) of Irony: The politics of appropriateness' (1994, 176–204) also deals with the exhibit.

11. See, for example, Lee Maracle, 'Native Myths: *Trickster Alive and Crowing*', in Scheier et al. (182–7); and Daiva Stasiulis, '"Authentic Voice": Anti-racist politics in Canadian feminist publishing and literary production', in Sneja Gunew and Anna Yeatman, eds, *Feminism and the Politics of Difference* (St. Leonards, NSW, Australia: Allen and Unwin, 1993), 35–60.

12. Kostash, 9 May 1994: A19; Drainie, 16 April 1994: E1; Miki, 7 April 1994: A17.

13. Editorial, 9 April 1994, D6; Fulford, 30 March 1994: C1. For other examples of responses to the conference see, in *The Globe*, Evelyn Lau, 'Why I didn't attend the

Writing Thru "Race" conference', 9 July 1994: D3, in *The Vancouver Sun*, the editorial 'Victim-writers meeting the stuff of great art', 9 April 1994: A22, and in *The Toronto Star*, Gerry Shikatani, 'Writing Thru Race a step toward shaping a vision', 9 July 1994: G6.

14. The program of events defines the mandate of the conference as follows: 'One goal of the conference planning committee was to create a publicly funded space that valued First Nations people and people of colour gathering on *our own*. Writing Thru Race recognizes that private gatherings of this sort take place every day in homes, on the street, in workplaces, in meetings—and the conference is an affirmation of their important contribution to the cultures of this land *throughout history*.

    Writing Thru Race celebrates the positive impact that First Nations writers and writers of colour continue to have through the recovery of histories, writing for children, screenwriting, editing, theorizing and making clear the real power inequalities due to racism in this country.

    Writing Thru Race recognizes the need for individuals and community groups writing in Canada to strategically work together to fight these power imbalances and forge a more accessible space for listening and the telling of stories (program 2).

15. Michel Dupuy, Minister of Canadian Heritage at the time, withdrew the promised $22,500, but the conference received support from many individuals as well as the Canada Council, the City of Vancouver, the Humanities Institute (Simon Fraser University), the Japanese Canadian Studies Society, the BC Ministry of Small Business, Tourism and Culture, the Ontario Arts Council, and the Writers' Union of Canada (Writing Thru Race program 8).

16. Moore, 'Will Ayatollah's curse turn multicultural dream into nightmare?' *The Globe and Mail*, 4 March 1989: C1.

17. See, for example, Sourayan Mookerjea, 'Some Special Times and Remarkable Spaces of Reading and Writing thru "Race"', *West Coast Line* 28, 3 (Winter 1994–95): 117–29.

18. Consider, for example, Neil Bissoondath's *Selling Illusions: The Cult of Multiculturalism in Canada* (Toronto: Penguin, 1994).

19. See, for example, Michael Keefer, *Lunar Perspectives: Field Notes from the Culture Wars* (Toronto: Anansi, 1996), and John Fekete, *Moral Panic* (Montreal: R. Davies, 1995).

20. On this point see E.D. Blodgett, 'Ethnic Writing in Canadian Literature as Paratext', *Signature* 3 (Summer 1990): 13–27.

21. The government document I am quoting from has no page numbers.

22. In *A Guide for Canadians: The Canadian Multiculturalism Act* (Multiculturalism and Citizenship Canada, 1990), this exclusion is explained as follows: 'The Yukon and the Northwest Territories, as well as Indian bands and band councils, are excluded from the application of the Act in compliance with the ongoing process of delegation of powers by the Government of Canada' (9). This and other such

statements, the *Guide* warns, 'are for explanatory purposes only, and should not be taken as legal interpretations of the provisions of the Act' (inside cover copy).

23. See Stanley Fish, 'Fish v. Fiss', in *Doing What Comes Naturally: Change, Rhetoric, and the Practice of Theory in Literary and Legal Studies* (Durham, NC: Duke University Press, 1989), especially 135. Also relevant are John Michael, 'Fish Shticks: Rhetorical Questions in Stanley Fish's *Doing What Comes Naturally'*, *Diacritics* 20, 2 (Summer 1990): 54–74; and Paul Brest and Drucilla Cornell.

24. 'Bounded objectivity,' for Fiss, 'is bounded by the existence of a community that recognizes and adheres to the disciplining rules used by the interpreter and that is defined by its recognition of those rules' (745).

25. See, for example, John Edwards' attempt to render this contradition as 'the great difficulty in the reconciliation of charter dualism and ethnocultural pluralism' (183) in his *Multilingualism* (London and New York: Routledge, 1994); Rezno Viero, 'Ethnic Groups in Quebec: Participation or Solitude', in *'Multiculturalism: Canadian Reality': A Report of the Canadian Conference on Multiculturalism* (Ottawa: Minister of State, 1978), 35; and Himani Bannerji's critique of the Canadian media and legal institutions with regard to multiculturalism (1996).

26. This speech was the government's response to Book IV of the *Report of the Royal Commission on Bilingualism and Biculturalism*. 'Trudeau's pronouncement', Robert F. Harney notes, was 'his first and last parliamentary utterance on the issue' (Harney 72). Interestingly, between the White Paper in 1971 and the Multiculturalism Act in 1988 there was no enabling legislation of any kind about multiculturalism or ethnic group rights.

27. For an example of critical analysis of the White Paper, see Manoly R. Lupul.

28. Here I'm conflating the positions of Fiss and Brest in their critical dialogue about law as interpretation and the interpretation of law, but a detailed consideration of the subtleties of those positions would be tangential to my argument at this point.

29. On this point I agree with Judith Butler's reading of Althusser: 'Although [Althusser] refers to the possibility of "bad subjects", he does not consider the range of *disobedience* that such an interpellating law might produce' (1997a, 382).

30. This term, first used by Mary Louise Pratt, refers to 'the space of colonial encounters, the space in which peoples geographically and historically separated come into contact with each other and establish ongoing relations, usually involving conditions of coercion, radical inequality, and intractable conflict. . . . A "contact" perspective emphasizes how subjects are constituted in and by their relations to each other. [It stresses] copresence, interaction, interlocking understandings and practices, often within radically asymmetrical relations of power' (6–7). See also James Clifford's use of the concept (1997).

31. See Warner Sollors, *Beyond Ethnicity* (New York and Oxford: Oxford University Press, 1986).

32. For an analysis of the relations between folklore and multiculturalism that is contrary to my interpretation here, see Carole Carpenter, 'Folklore and Government in Canada', in Kenneth S. Goldstein, ed., *Canadian Folkloric*

Perspectives (St John's: Memorial University Press, 1978), 53–68, and 'Folklore as a Tool of Multiculturalism', in Stella Hryniuk, ed., *20 Years of Multiculturalism: Successes and Failures* (Winnipeg: St John's College Press, 1992), 149–60. Because of her almost exclusive concern with the object of folklore learning, as opposed to how this learning is achieved and under what conditions, Carpenter allows for a too easy identification of folklore with ethnic culture.

33. Gibbon, a much praised employee of the Canadian Pacific Railway, could be seen as the father of heritage festivals, the first of which he organized in 1926 at the Banff Springs Hotel. See his *Canadian Mosaic: The Making of a Northern Nation* (Toronto: McClelland and Stewart, 1938).

34. As Christian Zervos writes in the Foreword to the English translation of Stratou's book *The Greek Dances: Our Living Link with Antiquity*, trans. Amy Mims-Argyrakis (Athens: Dora Stratou, 1966), 'The spectacle Dora Stratou has offered us these past many years embraces only those dances whose authenticity is absolutely guaranteed. . . . And the tremendous value of Dora Stratou is that she has succeeded in showing us this choreography absolutely unaltered, with all its archaic elements intact' (cited in Pizanias 53n.29).

35. See, for example, Jane K. Cowan's *Dance and the Body Politic in Northern Greece* (Princeton: Princeton University Press, 1991).

36. Desh Pradesh, first coordinated in 1990 by writer Ian Iqbal Rashid, takes place in Toronto. For reflections on the first four years of its operation, see 'Dear Desh . . .' a compilation of letters by various South Asian artists compiled by Rashid, in *Rungh* 2, 4 (1994): 16–18.

37. 'Self Not Whole' was a month-long (2–30 Nov. 1991) exhibition of installation, video, painting, and photo-based work accompanied by readings, performances, workshops, and panel discussions. See the exhibition's catalogue (in English and Chinese) of the same title, published by the Chinese Cultural Centre, 1991; see also Henry Tsang (one of the curating and participating artists), '"Self Not Whole": In Search of Cultural Space with the Chinese Cultural Centre in Vancouver', *Rungh* 2, 4 (1994): 12–15. Similarly, the multidisciplinary exhibition 'Racy Sexy' (26 Nov.–11 Dec 1993), organized by Karin Lee and Henry Tsang, branched out to include artists of diverse backgrounds from across Canada.

38. The pagination of Taylor's essay is exactly the same in both the 1992 and 1994 editions of the book. Unless dates of his other publications are given, all references to him are to 'The Politics of Recognition'.

39. In my discussion of Taylor's argument about 'the other' in this section, I follow his lower-case spelling of the term.

40. Here I am appropriating the title of Alfonso Lingis's book *The Community of Those Who Have Nothing in Common* (Bloomington and Indianapolis: Indiana University Press, 1994), which, although not directly related to my concerns here, offers interesting insights into how we constitute the other through its focus on mortality as one condition that brings together people who may seem to share nothing. Lingis's title, together with his focus on mortality, echoes Georges Bataille. See

also Nancy.

41. The fact that Taylor examines the same philosophical traditions in 'The Politics of Recognition' and *The Malaise of Modernity* and *Reconciling the Solitudes* is not the only substantial overlap in content.

42. See, for example, the chapter 'Concerning Violence' in *The Wretched of the Earth*, especially 66.

43. For a discussion of various views of Fanon's notion of violence see Ato Sekyi-Otu, *Fanon's Dialectic of Experience* (Cambridge, Mass., and London: Harvard University Press, 1996).

44. On the way Sartre revised his own notion of humanism in his preface see Robert Young's discussion in 'Disorienting Orientalism' (1990, 119–29).

45. See 'Foucault on Freedom and Truth', *Philosophy and the Human Sciences: Philosophical Paper 2* (Cambridge: Cambridge University Press, 1985), 152–84, and his *Sources of the Self* (Cambridge, Mass.: Harvard University Press, 1989). For a critique of Taylor's treatment and misreading of Foucault see Réal Robert Fillion, 'Foucault *contra* Taylor: Whose Sources? Whose Self?', *Dialogue* XXXIV (1995): 663–74, and William Connolly, 'Foucault and Otherness', *Political Theory* (August 1985): 365–76.

46. Bruce M. Landesman (untitled review, *Ethics* 104, 2 [January 1994]: 386) and Bannerji (1996) make the same point.

47. Perhaps it was comments of this nature that prompted editor Amy Gutmann to include essays by Jürgen Habermas and Appiah in the volume's second edition (1994). It should be mentioned, though, as Dumm also notes, that Susan Wolf's 'Comment' (75–85) is the only response to Taylor's essay in the original edition that displays a concrete awareness of multicultural debates.

48. In addition to Dumm, and Wolf and Appiah (in Taylor 1994), see Seshadri-Crooks; Linda Nicholson, 'To Be or Not To Be: Charles Taylor and the Politics of Recognition', *Constellations* 3, 1 (1966): 1–16; and Amelie Oksenberg Rorty, 'The Hidden Politics of Cultural Identification', *Political Theory* 22, 1 (February 1994): 152–66; and in the Canadian context Ian Angus (147–54).

49. Although Taylor credits Bakhtin's *Problems of Dostoyevsky's Poetics* and Michael Holquist's and Katerina Clark's *Mikhail Bakhtin* (Cambridge, Mass., and London: Belknap Press of Harvard University Press, 1984) for his concept of dialogism (33), his use of it can only be seen as a misreading of Bakthin. As Holquist and Clark point out, for Bakhtin dialogism 'encompass[es] differences in a simultane-ity. He conceives the old problem of identity along the lines not of "the same as" but of "simultaneous with". He is thus led to meditate on the interaction of forces that are conceived by others to be mutually exclusive. How, for example, can . . . an individual self be unique and yet also incorporate so much that is shared with others?' (9–10). Taylor, as I am trying to show through my reading of Herder, holds virtually the opposite view.

50. Taylor has a special attachment to Herder; as he says with reference to his student years in Europe, 'I was able to understand him [Herder] from the situation I had

experienced outside school, outside university, and I was able to engage with his thought, internalize it, and (I hope) make something interesting out of it' (1993, xii).

51. On this point see Kant's review (1785) of Herder's book, reprinted in part in Emmanuel Chukwudi Eze, ed., *Race and the Enlightenment: A Reader* (Cambridge, Mass.: Blackwell, 1997), 66–70.

52. On the ambivalences characterizing some of Herder's views on cultural and racial differences, see Robert Young (1995, 36–43).

53. See, for example, his chapter 'Concluding Remarks on the Opposition between Genesis and Climate' (184–7).

54. Taylor's position in relation to the First Nations peoples is unclear. While there are instances when the 'Québécois and aboriginals' are grouped together in juxtaposition to the Charter of Rights that 'guarant[ees] equality between individuals' (1993, 194), neither in 'The Politics of Recognition' nor in *Reconciling the Solitudes* does Taylor attempt to negotiate how aboriginal people would be regarded within a 'distinct' or sovereign Quebec.

Chapter 3

1. Cited in Momme Brodersen, *Walter Benjamin: A Biography*, trans. Malcolm R. Green and Ingrida Ligers, ed. Matina Dervis (London and New York: Verso, 1996), 12.

2. Barbara Christian makes a similar argument about anthologies 'in this age of official multiculturalism' (244).

3. On the structure and politics of mainstream anthologies, see Alan Knight, 'Growing Hegemonies: Preparing the Ground for Official Anthologies of Canadian Poetry', *Prefaces and Literary Manifestoes / Préfaces et manifestes littéraires*, eds E.D. Blodgett and A.G. Purdy, in collaboration with S. Tötösy de Zepetnek (Edmonton: Research Institute for Comparative Literature, University of Alberta, 1990), 146–57; see also Charles Steele, 'Canada's New Critical Anthologies', *Ariel* 18, 3 (July 1987): 77–85, and Lien Chao, 'Anthologizing the Collective: The Epic Struggles to Establish Chinese Canadian Literature in English', *Essays on Canadian Writing* 57 (Winter 1995): 145–70.

4. For example, most ethnic anthologies that I have come across in my research appeared after 1971, the year when multiculturalism was introduced.

5. Without exception, all the editors of the ethnic anthologies I have studied would agree with Di Cicco's preference for the Canadian mosaic approach to ethnicity, as opposed to the American melting pot.

6. On the concept and political implications of cosmopolitanism as an answer to national and cultural differences see, for example, Tim Brennan, 'Cosmopolitans and celebrities', *Race and Class* 31, 1 (1989): 1–19. See also Pheah Cheah and Bruce Robbins, eds, *Cosmopolitics: Thinking and Feeling Beyond the Nation*

(Minneapolis and London: University of Minnesota Press, 1998), which appeared too late for full consideration in my study.

7. Here and elsewhere in this study, I use the word 'experience' as it has been defined by Teresa de Lauretis: 'an ongoing process by which subjectivity is constructed semiotically and historically', or 'more accurately as a complex of habits resulting from the semiotic interaction of "outer world" and "inner world", the continuous engagement of a self or subject in social reality' (*Alice Doesn't: Feminism, Semiotics, Cinema* [Bloomington: Indiana University Press, 1984], 182).

8. See, for example, Elizabeth Grosz's *Volatile Bodies*. See also my discussion of corporeality and racialization in the next chapter.

9. On the various ways in which race and sex are related, see Lewis R. Gordon, 'Race, Sex, and Matrices of Desire in an Antiblack World' (117–32), and Naomi Zack, 'The American Sexualization of Race' (145–55), both in Naomi Zack, ed., *Race/Sex: Their Sameness, Difference, and Interplay* (New York, London: Routledge, 1997). See also Andrew Parker et al., eds, *Nationalisms and Sexualities* (New York and London: Routledge, 1992), and Verena Stolcke, 'Is Sex to Gender as Race is to Ethnicity?' in Teresa del Valle, ed., *Gendered Anthropology* (New York and London: Routledge, 1993), 17–37.

10. In all the ethnic anthologies I have consulted, the convention of mentioning the author's birthplace in biographical notes assumes a heavier weight than usual. With very few exceptions, contributors' notes always include precise information about the authors' diasporic movements. In the case of Canadian-born authors, the editors make a point of referring to the authors' genealogy.

11. See also Elliott's introduction to his *Literary Writing by Blacks in Canada* (1988).

12. On how some of these Chilean Canadian writers, including Nómez, fit within both the Canadian and the Chilean literary traditions, see Lake Sagaris, 'Countries Like Drawbridges: Chilean-Canadian Writing Today' (12–20), and Hugh Hazelton, 'Quebec Hispánico: Themes of Exile and Integration in the Writing of Latin Americans Living in Quebec' (120–35), both in *Canadian Literature* 142/143 (Fall/Winter 1994).

13. One might push this point a bit further by asking whether Pivato is suggesting here that a distinction should be made between, say, the Italian immigrants and those other immigrants whose ancestors had no role to play in the 'discovery', exploration, and founding of Canada. Antonio D'Alfonso's *In Italics: In Defense of Ethnicity* (Toronto, New York, Lancaster: Guernica, 1996) puts forward one of the most complex and intriguing arguments on these issues articulated by a Canadian ethnic writer.

14. This may be hyperbole, for it is not clear what publications by other ethnic women Cromwell has in mind. *One Out of Many* preceded the other ethnic anthologies I have encountered in my research.

15. See Diane McGifford and Judith Kearns, eds, *Shakti's Words: An Anthology of South Asian Canadian Women's Poetry* (Toronto: TSAR, 1990); Ann Wallace, ed., *Daughters of the Sun, Women of the Moon* (Stratford, Ont.: Williams-Wallace, 1991);

George Elliott Clarke, ed., *Fire on the Water: An Anthology of Black Nova Scotian Writing*, vols I (1991) and II (1992) (Lawrencetown Beach, NS: Pottersfield Press); Ayanna Black, ed., *Voices: Canadian Writers of African Descent* (Toronto: HarperCollins, 1992); Makeda Silvera, ed., *Piece of my Heart: A Lesbian of Colour Anthology* (Toronto: Sister Vision, 1991); Diane McGifford, ed., *The Geography of Voice: Canadian Literature of the South Asian Diaspora* (Toronto: TSAR, 1992); Eva C. Karpinski and Ian Lea, eds, *Pens of Many Colours: A Canadian Reader* (Toronto: Harcourt Brace Jovanovich, 1993); Ayanna Black, ed., *Fiery Spirits: Canadian Writers of African Descent* (Toronto: HarperPerennial, 1994); Makeda Silvera, ed., *The Other Woman: Women of Colour in Contemporary Canadian Literature* (Toronto: Sister Vision, 1995); and *Making a Difference: Canadian Multicultural Literature* (Toronto: Oxford University Press, 1996), edited by myself.

16. See the critical exchange between Lecker and Davey: Lecker, 'The Canonization of Canadian Literature: An Inquiry Into Value' (656–71); Davey, 'Canadian Canons' (672–81); Lecker, 'Response to Frank Davey' (682–9), all in *Critical Inquiry* 16, 3 (Spring 1990); Lecker, 'A Country without a Canon? Canadian Literature and the Esthetics of Idealism', *Mosaic*, 26, 3 (Summer 1993): 1–19, and *Making It Real: The Canonization of English-Canadian Literature* (Toronto: Anansi, 1995); Davey, *Canadian Literary Power* (Edmonton: NeWest, 1994), and *Post-National Arguments: The Politics of the Anglophone-Canadian Novel since 1967* (Toronto: University of Toronto Press, 1993). See also the essay by Tracy Ware, 'A Little Self-Consciousness Is a Dangerous Thing: A Response to Robert Lecker', *English Studies in Canada* XVII, 4 (December 1991): 481–93.

17. The contributors include Jeannette Armstrong, Lee Maracle, Sky Lee, Joy Kogawa, Betsy Warland, Vancouver Sath, Barbara Herringer, and Louise Profeit-LeBlanc. Other conference participants did not wish to be included in the book.

18. To make documentation less cumbersome in this section, all references to this anthology, including Hutcheon's introduction, will be followed by page numbers only. Page numbers accompanied by dates refer to other works.

19. Hutcheon's 'Multicultural Furor: The Reception of *Other Solitudes*' (1996) is a revised version of 'The Multicultural Debate: The Reception of *Other Solitudes*' (1992). I will be citing from the revised publication.

20. For a sampling of the reviews the anthology received, see Lisette Bioly, 'Multiculturalism and Its Discontents', *Toronto South Asian Review* (Spring 1991): 77–87; W.H. New, 'Other Relations', *Books in Canada* (November 1990): 29–30; and Joshua Mostow, 'Family Resemblance', *Canadian Literature* 134 (Autumn 1992): 134–5. For a recent and more balanced review of the anthology see Lorna Marie Irvine, 'Pluralism, Diversity, Heterogeneity: Continuing the Debate', 'Idols of Otherness: The Rhetoric and Reality of Multiculturalism', special issue of *Mosaic*, 29, 3 (September 1996): 141–53.

21. Lest I seem to unduly stress the use of parentheses and the alliance of 'ex-centric' identities, I should mention that, with very few exceptions, in *A Poetics of Postmodernism* ethnicity appears in similar parenthetical and paratactic structures.

22. See, for example, Hutcheon's introduction to *Splitting Images*, and *Irony's Edge*, especially 44–56.

23. Hutcheon addresses the differences between postmodernism and postmodernity —see, for example, 'Postmodernity, postmodernism, and modernism' (1989, 23–9)—but, if I read her stress on postmodernism's double-coding strategies correctly, she tends either to privilege the former or to conflate the two.

Chapter 4

1. Unless otherwise noted, all page references not accompanied by author or title are to Kogawa's *Obasan*.

2. The epigraph, which is also used in *Itsuka*, is from Revelation 2:17.

3. For two examples of critics who see the novel in terms of, respectively, 'synthesis' and 'resolution of puzzles', see P. Merivale, 'Framed Voices: The Polyphonic Elegies of Hébert and Kogawa', *Canadian Literature* 116 (Spring 1988): 68–82, and Erika Gottlieb, 'The Riddle of Concentric Worlds in "Obasan"', *Canadian Literature* 109 (Summer 1988): 34–53. For an interpretation of Naomi's silence in terms of Japanese aesthetics, see Teruyo Ueki.

4. In this, as well as in the earlier quotation in the same paragraph, Buck-Morss is citing from Benjamin's *Passagen-Werk* (The Arcades Project).

5. All references to Freud are to *The Standard Edition* of his work, and are by volume and page number.

6. See Emile Benveniste, *Problems in General Linguistics* (Miami Linguistics Series #8), trans. Mary Elizabeth Meek (Coral Gables, Fla.: University of Miami Press, 1971).

7. For an extension of Butler's argument about speech acts and their relation to the body, see her essay 'Performativity's Social Magic' (in Schatzki and Natter).

8. Robin Potter also discusses the significance of the bathing scenes in the novel (129–33). Although here and elsewhere in her article, there is some overlap with my general theoretical framework and certain of my textual concerns, Potter—I suppose because her article focuses as much on Kristeva as on Kogawa—tends to look for similarities between the two rather than ways in which Kogawa departs from some of Kristeva's psychoanalytic formulations.

9. The concept of attentiveness is crucial to Cheung's reading of the novel. It comes, she says, from Gayle K. Fujita's term 'attendance', 'a non-verbal mode of apprehension', but Cheung resists Fujita's tendency to 'subsume' 'several forms of reticence under the rubric "attendance"' (128). See Fujita, 'To Attend the Sound of Stone: The Sensibility of Silence in *Obasan*', *MELUS* 12, 3 (1985): 33–42.

10. This is not to say that Stephen is a gregarious child, or a forthcoming adolescent; rather, his silence is of a different order from Naomi's. See Cheung's discussion of the differences between Japanese Canadian women and men in the novel with regard to silence (140–3). On the impact of diasporic experience on Asian American men see Lisa Lowe.

11. 'Issei', 'Nisei', and 'Sansei' are Japanese words referring to, respectively, first-, second- and third-generation Japanese Canadians.

12. Mason Harris is one critic who thematizes the diversities internal to the Japanese Canadian community; see his 'Broken Generations in "Obasan": Inner Conflict and the Destruction of Community', *Canadian Literature* 127 (Winter 1990): 41–57. For a historical perspective on some of these differences, see Forest E. La Violette, *The Canadian Japanese and World War II: A Sociological and Psychological Account* (Toronto: University of Toronto Press, 1948) and, more recently, Cassandra Kobayashi and Roy Miki, eds, *Spirit of Redress: Japanese Canadians in Conference* (Vancouver: JC Publications, 1989), and Kirsten Emiko McAllister, 'Confronting Official History With Our Own Eyes', in Miki and Wah (66–84).

13. For an analysis of the kinds of languages and linguistic registers employed in Japanese American households, see Dorinne Kondo, 'The Narrative Production of "Home," Community, and Political Identity in Asian American Theater', in Smadar Lavie and Ted Swedenburg, eds, *Displacement, Diaspora, and Geographies of Identity* (Durham and London: Duke University Press, 1996), 97–117.

14. See, for example, Donald C. Goellnicht, 'Minority History as Metafiction: Joy Kogawa's *Obasan*', *Tulsa Studies in Women's Literature* 8, 2 (Fall 1989): 287–306, and Manina Jones, 'The Avenues of Speech and Silence: Telling Difference in Joy Kogawa's *Obasan*', in Martin Kreiswirth and Mark A. Cheetham, eds, *Theory Between the Disciplines: Authority/Vision/Politics* (Ann Arbor: University of Michigan Press, 1990), 213–29.

15. On the political, economic, and diplomatic implications of the 'Oriental Problem' as it was viewed before and immediately after the Second World War, see A.R.M. Lower, *Canada and the Far East—1940* (New York: The Haddon Craftsman, Inc., 1940) and H.F. Angus, *Canada and the Far East: 1940–1953* (Toronto: University of Toronto Press, 1953).

16. There is no consensus about who first used the term 'yellow peril'. Richard Austin Thompson, in *The Yellow Peril, 1890–1924* (New York: Arno Press, 1978), offers three possibilities: first, according to a Chinese writer, 'the phrase originated in the European newspapers in China during the Boxer Rebellion of 1900'; second, according to various sources, Kaiser William II was the first to use the phrase, in 1895; third, 'no one really knew who invented the term yellow peril. It was certain, however, that the Kaiser popularized it' (4). Thompson is inclined to accept the third possibility as the most credible. The reference to the Kaiser is interesting, especially because of the visual element it involves. As Thompson explains, the Kaiser commissioned a painting, copies of which he sent as gifts to some of his fellow rulers in Europe, as well as to US President McKinley. The painting, 'one of the most talked-about political illustrations of the late nineteenth century' (1), depicted the following allegorical scene. In the foreground stood, high upon a rock, France, Germany, Russia, Austria, England, and Italy, portrayed as 'mail-clad Valkyries beneath the sign of a radiant cross. The Archangel Gabriel stood before them, sword in one hand while pointing with the other towards a horrible spectacle in the East. High in the smoke of the burning cities of Europe a

Chinese dragon, symbolic of destruction, emerged bearing a seated Buddha upon its back. Beneath the picture the Kaiser placed the words, "Nations of Europe! Join in Defense of Your Faith and Your Home!"' (1–2).

A more recent project radically questioning the visuality of 'yellow peril' epistemology is *Yellow Peril Reconsidered*, an exhibit of video, art, and photo work by twenty-five Asian Canadians that travelled across Canada between fall 1990 and summer 1991. The accompanying publication of the same title (Vancouver: On Edge, 1990), edited by Paul Wong, suggests that the same epistemology remains operative in present-day reactions to, for example, the 'invasion' of Canada by Japanese money and Hong Kong 'yacht people'.

See also Phil Hammond, ed., *Cultural Difference, Media Memories: Anglo-American Images of Japan* (London and Washington: Cassell, 1997), especially Gina Owens' contribution, 'The Making of the Yellow Peril: Pre-War Western Views of Japan' (25–47).

17. Kogawa, as she acknowledges in the novel, borrowed liberally from Kitagawa's letters and essays (among other sources). However, Emily's character should not be taken to be a literary incarnation of Muriel. Although many critics, following Kogawa's note, acknowledge Kitagawa's letters, no critic to my knowledge has examined them. My brief discussion of Kitagawa's writing is meant to establish not character similarities, but the historical chain of ideas and ideologies that Emily's position represents.

18. It is not my intention to dismiss the historical need for revision of traditional gender roles in Japanese culture. Rather, I am interested in the way ideological values travel from one culture to another without taking into account cultural particularity. In this context, see Minamoto Junko's 'Buddhism and the Historical Construction of Sexuality in Japan', *U.S.-Japan Women's Journal* (English Supplement) 5 (1993): 87–115, which argues that 'Japanese sexual culture cannot be analyzed or explained according to the principles of Western feminism' (89) but also concedes, as Kitagawa does, that 'Western feminism is more progressive' (90).

19. Robert Young's chapter 'The Complicity of Culture: Arnold's Ethnographic Politics' (1995) is an excellent discussion of the politics and history of racialization; see especially page 65 on the use of the family as a key metaphor in this process.

20. Hakujin is 'Japanese for "Caucasians", literally "white men"' (ed. note, Kitagawa 72).

21. As Kogawa writes in her Foreword to Keibo Oiwa, ed., *Stone Voices* (Montreal: Véhicule, 1991): 'Within the Canadian patchwork quilt is a bright little square reserved for Japanese Canadians. Interestingly enough, every single thread in that patch, like every other thread in every other human patch, is made of an infinite mix of shadings and colours' (6).

22. For example, the anonymous interviewees in Dionne Brand and Krisantha Sri Bhaggiyadatta, eds, *Rivers Have Sources, Trees Have Roots: Speaking on Racism*, (Toronto: Cross Cultural Communications Center, 1985) invariably define racist

behaviour in terms of a 'look'.

23. It is important not to collapse these two functions of the look into one another. Despite the difficulty of exploring them separately, since they are so tightly interwoven, this is precisely what I am trying to do, to articulate how gender and race operate in the novel.

24. I call the man's wink approving because it is most likely playful, an acknowledgement of her success in pulling the streetcar cord for the next stop. This positive interpretation, far from cancelling out my point regarding Naomi's racialization, illustrates that racialization operates even when racism is not overtly an issue.

25. Diggs builds on Foucault's premise that the discourse of sexuality developed through various narratives of 'secrecy and disclosure' (15). On the relationship of Foucault's theory of sexuality to race, see also Stoler (1997a).

26. I am indebted for this point to Butler; see her chapter 'On Linguistic Vulnerability' (1997b), especially page 26.

27. Here is an example of a casual reference to 'race' in Freud's history of Frau Emmy von N.: 'the way in which she stretched her hands in front of her with her fingers spread out and crooked expressed horror, and similarly her facial play. This, of course, was a more lively and uninhibited way of expressing her emotions than was usual with women of her education and race' (2.91).

28. See his letter to Fliess, 21 Sept. 1897, in *The Complete Letters of Sigmund Freud to Wilhelm Fliess, 1887–1904*, trans. and ed. Jeffrey Moussaieff Masson (Cambridge, Mass.: Belknap Press of Harvard University Press, 1985).

29. There has been intense discussion of Freud's rejection of his seduction theory. See, for example, Jeffrey Moussaieff Masson, *The Assault on Truth: Freud's Suppression of the Seduction Theory* (New York: Farrar, Straus, and Giroux, 1983) and William J. McGrath, *Freud's Discovery of Psychoanalysis: The Politics of Hysteria* (Ithaca and London: Cornell University Press, 1986), especially chapter 6. Both studies consider the change in Freud's theory of hysteria in the context both of his personal and professional life and of the political climate at the time.

30. This formulation may be my own, but I certainly am not alone in arguing this general point. The literature on hysteria is so vast that it would be virtually impossible to credit specifically all the material that has helped me over time reach my own understanding of hysteria, and its relation to silence, in this context.

31. See Luce Irigaray, *Speculum of the Other Woman*, trans. Gillian C. Gill, and *This Sex Which Is Not One*, trans. Catherine Porter (both Ithaca: Cornell University Press, 1985).

32. Notably, a number of studies of Freud's theories of hysteria and sexuality deal not only with the histories of Freud's individual cases, but also with the historical context of the rise of psychoanalysis. See, for example, Arnold Davidson, 'How to Do the History of Psychoanalysis: A Reading of Freud's "Three Essays on the Theory of Sexuality"', *Critical Inquiry* 13, 2 (1987): 252–77, and Steven Marcus, 'Freud and Dora: Story, History, Case History', in Charles Benheimer and Claire Kahane. eds, *In Dora's Case: Freud-Hysteria-Feminism*, (New York: Columbia

University Press, 1985), 56–91.

33. See Jerre Collins, J. Ray Green, Mary Lydon, Mark Sachner, and Eleanor Honig Skoller, 'Questioning the Unconscious: the Dora Archive', *Diacritics* 13 (Spring 1983): 37–42, for a critique that both questions and thematizes the 'privileged position' of the analyst.

34. I say 'subtle' because oppositional pedagogy, as developed by, among others, Paulo Freire in *Pedagogy of the Oppressed* (New York: Continuum, 1982) and *The Politics of Education* (South Hadley, Mass.: Bergin and Garvey, 1985), has a strongly articulated political agenda that Naomi's pedagogy lacks.

35. As Freud writes, 'there are three impossible professions—educating, healing, governing—and I was already fully occupied with the second of them' (19.273); he states the same point elsewhere: 'It almost looks as if analysis were the third of those "impossible" professions in which one can be sure beforehand of achieving unsatisfactory results. The other two, which have been known much longer, are education and government' (23.248).

36. On how transference and countertransference function both in psychoanalysis and in pedagogy see, for example, Felman (1982), Freedman, and Jay Gregory, 'The Subject of Pedagogy: Lessons in Psychoanalysis and Politics', *College English* 49, 7 (November 1987): 785–800.

37. As Freedman says, 'If, as Lacan maintains, "elements do not answer in the place where they are interrogated," then we must develop what Lacan champions as the third ear of the symbolic from which a dual relation is apprehended; when the unspeakable conversation unfolds in the presence of a third party, it is no longer the same' (182).

38. This reference to 'impertinent questions' is intended to be read, partly, in the context of Jane Gallop's chapter 'Impertinent Questions' in *The Daughter's Seduction: Feminism and Psychoanalysis* (Ithaca: Cornell University Press, 1982), where she discusses Irigaray's reading of Freud through Lacan. See also Gallop's 'Im-personation: A Reading in the Guise of an Introduction', in Gallop, ed., *Pedagogy: The Question of Impersonation* (Bloomington and Indianapolis: Indiana University Press, 1995), in which she addresses 'impertinent question[s]' in a pedagogical context (3).

39. Katz reads Freud's cases of Dora, Elizabeth von R. and Anna O. in terms of the literary device of narrative closure. She argues: 'As the originators of a new science, Breuer and Freud depended on the structure of novels to make accessible (and acceptable) to their audience their probing into psychological and sexual places the Victorian novel rarely dared to go' (298–99). She shows that Freud responded to the stories told by his hysteric patients as if they were Victorian novels.

40. I should say here that this passage about 'Love' and 'Grief' is one that has always troubled me. Together with the text that precedes the novel proper, it seems to register Kogawa's authorial intentions. Kogawa has said that 'we have within us the Aunt Emily and the Naomi. We have within us the political person and at

times I think that person is yanked out of silence to speak' (Redekop 15–6); yet no character in the novel seems to be torn by this double impulse. Moreover, when Kogawa is asked to speak on the novel, she often does so in religious terms that cannot, I believe, be adequately understood by reference to her bicultural Buddhist-cum-Christian upbringing alone, as some critics argue. Kogawa summons us to 'discover for ourselves the secret key to divine abandonment, that is, God [who] has abandoned divine power completely and utterly into the human condition [so] that we might not abandon one another' (cited in Ueki 17). This declaration of faith may help us to understand that, in the novel, the 'mother's absence is the prime analogy for the experience of divine abandonment' (Kogawa cited in Redekop 17), but the author's statements on her faith do not suffice, I think, to explain Naomi's silence. A full examination of the political implications of the authorial intentions, though, would require yet another chapter.

Works Cited

Abu-Laban, Yasmeen, and Daiva Stasiulis. 1992. 'Ethnic Pluralism under Siege: Popular and Partisan Opposition to Multiculturalism'. *Canadian Public Policy— Analyse de Politiques* XVIII, 4: 365–86.

Adachi, Ken. 1991. *The Enemy That Never Was: A History of the Japanese Canadians*. Intr. Timothy Findley. Afterword Roger Daniels. Toronto: McClelland and Stewart.

Adorno, Theodor W. 1973. *The Jargon of Authenticity*. Trans. Knut Tarnowski and Frederic Will. Foreword by Trent Schroyer. Evanston: Northwestern University Press.

Ahmad, Aijaj. 1992. *In Theory: Classes, Nations, Literatures*. London: Verso; Bombay: Oxford University Press.

Alcoff, Linda. 1991–92. 'The Problem of Speaking for Others'. *Cultural Critique* (Winter): 5–32.

Althusser, Louis. 1994 (1970). 'Ideology and Ideological State Apparatuses (Notes towards an Investigation)'. Pp. 100–40 in Slavoj Žižek, ed. *Mapping Ideology*. London and New York: Verso.

Anderson, Benedict. 1991. *Imagined Communities*. London and New York: Verso.

Angus, Ian. 1997. *A Border Within: National Identity, Cultural Plurality, and Wilderness*. Montreal and Kingston: McGill-Queen's University Press.

Appiah, K. Anthony. 1997. 'Is the "Post-" in "Postcolonial" the "Post-" in "Postmodern"?' Pp. 420–44 in McClintock et al., eds.

———. 1993. '"No Bad Nigger": Blacks as the Ethical Principle in the Movies'. Pp. 77–90 in Marjorie Garber, Jann Matlock, and Rebecca L. Walkowitz, eds. *Media Spectacles*. New York and London: Routledge.

———. 1992. *In My Father's House*. Cambridge, Mass.: Harvard University Press.

———. 1991. 'Is the Post- in Postmodernism the Post- in Postcolonial?' *Critical Inquiry* 17, 2 (Winter): 336–57.

Apter, Emily. 1995. 'Comparative Exile: Competing Margins in the History of Comparative Literature'. Pp. 86–96 in Bernheimer, ed.

Arac, Jonathan. 1987. *Critical Genealogies: Historical Situations for Postmodern Literary Studies*. New York: Columbia University Press.

Bakhtin, Mikhail. 1981. *The Dialogic Imagination: Four Essays*. Ed. Michael Holquist. Trans. Caryl Emerson. Austin: University of Texas Press.

Balan, Jars, and Yuri Klynovy, eds. 1987. *Yarmarok: Ukrainian Writing in Canada since the Second World War*. Edmonton: Canadian Institute of Ukrainian Studies,

University of Alberta.

Bannerji, Himani. 1996. 'On the Dark Side of the Nation: Politics of Multiculturalism and the State of Canada'. *Journal of Canadian Studies*, 31, 3 (Fall): 103–28.

———, ed. 1993. *Returning the Gaze: Essays on Racism, Feminism and Politics*. Toronto: Sister Vision.

Bauman, Zygmunt. 1991. *Modernity and Ambivalence*. Cambridge: Polity.

Behdad, Ali. 1994. *Belated Travelers: Orientalism in the Age of Colonial Dissolution*. Durham and London: Duke University Press.

Benjamin, Walter. 1977. *The Origin of German Tragic Drama*. Trans. John Osborne. London: NLB and Verso.

———. 1969. *Illuminations*. Ed. and with an Introduction by Hannah Arendt. Trans. Harry Zohn. New York: Schocken.

Bennett, Donna. 1993–4. 'English Canada's Postcolonial Complexities'. *Essays on Canadian Writing* 51–52 (Winter–Spring): 164–210.

Bernheimer, Charles. 1995. 'The Bernheimer Report, 1993. Comparative Literature at the Turn of the Century'. Pp. 39–48 in Bernheimer, ed.

———, ed. 1995. *Comparative Literature in the Age of Multiculturalism*. Baltimore and London: The Johns Hopkins University Press.

Bhabha, Homi K. 1995. 'Are You a Man or a Mouse?' Pp. 57–65 in Maurice Berger, Brian Wallis, and Simon Watson, eds. *Constructing Masculinity*. New York and London: Routledge.

———. 1994. *The Location of Culture*. London and New York: Routledge.

———. 1992. 'Postcolonial Authority and Postmodern Guilt'. Pp. 56–66 in Grossberg et al., eds.

———. 1990a. 'Introduction: Narrating the Nation'. Pp. 1–7 in Homi Bhabha, ed. *Nation and Narration*. London and New York: Routledge.

———. 1990b. 'DissemiNation: time, narrative, and the margins of the modern nation'. Pp. 291–322 in *Nation and Narration*.

———. 1982. 'The other question: difference, discrimination and the discourse of colonialism'. Pp. 148–72 in Francis Barker, Peter Hulme, Margaret Iversen, and Diana Loxley, eds. *Literature, Politics and Theory: Papers from the Essex Conference 1976–84*. London and New York: Methuen.

Black, Ayanna, ed. *Voices: Canadian Writers of African Descent*. Toronto: HarperCollins, 1992.

Blodgett, E.D. 1982. *Configurations: Essays on the Canadian Literatures*. Downsview, Ont.: ECW.

Brest, Paul. 1982. 'Interpretation and Interest'. *Stanford Law Review* 34 (April): 765–73.

Brooks, Peter. 1984. *Reading for the Plot: Design and Intention in Narrative*. New York: Vintage.

Brydon, Diana. 1987. 'Discovering "Ethnicity": Joy Kogawa's *Obasan* and Mena Abdullah's *Time of the Peacock*'. Pp. 94–110 in Russell McDougall and Gillian Whitlock, eds. *Australian/Canadian Literatures in English: Comparative Perspectives*. Melbourne: Methuen.

Buck-Morss, Susan. 1993. *The Dialectics of Seeing: Walter Benjamin and the Arcades Project*. Cambridge, Mass., and London: MIT Press.

Burroughs, Catherine B., and Jeffrey David Ehrenreich. 1993. 'Introduction: Reading the Social Body'. Pp. 1–14 in Catherine Burroughs and Jeffrey David Ehrenreich, eds. *Reading the Social Body*. Iowa City: University of Iowa Press.

Butler, Judith. 1997a. 'Gender is Burning: Questions of Appropriation and Subversion'. Pp. 381–95 in McClintock et al., eds.

———. 1997b. *Excitable Speech: A Politics of the Performative*. New York and London: Routledge.

———. 1993a. 'Poststructuralism and Postmodernism'. *Diacritics* 23, 4 (Winter): 3–11.

———. 1993b. *Bodies that Matter: On the Discursive Limit of 'Sex'*. New York and London: Routledge.

———. 1991. 'Imitation and Gender Insubordination'. Pp. 13–31 in Diana Fuss, ed. *Inside/Out: Lesbian Theories, Gay Theories*. New York and London: Routledge.

Caillois, Roger. 1984. 'Mimicry and Legendary Psychasthenia'. *October* 31 (Winter): 17–32.

Caldwell, David, and Paul W. Rea. 1991. 'Handke's and Wenders's *Wings of Desire*: Transcending Postmodernism'. *The German Quarterly* 64, 1: 46–54.

Canadian Multiculturalism Act. Second Session, Thirty-third Parliament, 35–36–37 Elizabeth II, 1986–97–88. As Passed by the House of Commons, July 12, 1988. Ottawa: Canadian Government Publishing Centre.

Chambers, Ross. 1997. 'The Unexamined'. Pp. 187–203 in Mike Hill, ed. *Whiteness: A Critical Reader*. New York and London: New York University Press.

Cheah, Pheng. 1998. 'Given Culture: Rethinking Cosmopolitical Freedom in Transnationalism'. Pp. 290–328 in Pheng Cheah and Bruce Robbins, eds. *Cosmopolitics: Thinking and Feeling Beyond the Nation*. Minneapolis and London: University of Minnesota Press.

Cheung, King-kok. 1993. *Articulate Silences: Hisaye Yamamoto, Maxine Hong Kingston, Joy Kogawa*. Ithaca: Cornell University Press.

Chicago Cultural Studies Group. 1992. 'Critical Multiculturalism'. *Critical Inquiry* 18, 3 (Spring): 530–55.

Chow, Rey. 1998. *Ethics after Idealism: Theory-Culture-Ethnicity-Reading*. Bloomington and Indianapolis: Indiana University Press.

———. 1995a. *Primitive Passions. Visuality, Sexuality, Ethnography, and Contemporary Chinese Cinema*. New York: Columbia University Press.

———. 1995b. 'In the Name of Comparative Literature'. Pp. 107–16 in Bernheimer, ed.

————. 1993a. *Writing Diaspora: Tactics of Intervention in Contemporary Cultural Studies*. Bloomington and Indianapolis: Indiana University Press.

————. 1993b. 'Ethics after Idealism'. *Diacritics* 23, 1 (Spring): 3–22.

Christian, Barbara. 1995. 'A Rough Terrain: The Case of Shaping an Anthology of Caribbean Women Writers'. In Pp. 241–59 in David Palumbo-Liu, ed. *The Ethnic Canon: Histories, Institutions and Interventions*. Minneapolis, London: University of Minnesota Press.

Clément, Catherine. 1975. 'The Guilty One'. Pp. 1–59 in Hélène Cixous and Clément, *The Newly Born Woman*. Trans. Betsy Wing. Intr. Sandra M. Gilbert. Minneapolis: University of Minnesota Press.

Clifford, James. 1997. *Routes: Travel and Translation in the Late Twentieth Century*. Cambridge, Mass.: Harvard University Press.

————. 1992. 'Traveling Cultures'. Pp. 96–112 in Grossberg et al., eds.

————. 1988. *The Predicament of Culture: Twentieth-Century Ethnography, Literature, and Art*. Cambridge, Mass., and London: Harvard University Press.

Cook, Roger. 1991. 'Angels, Fiction and History in Berlin: Wim Wenders' *Wings of Desire*'. *The Germanic Review* 56, 1 (Winter): 34–47.

Cornell, Drucilla L. 1988. 'Institutionalization of Meaning, Recollective Imagination and the Potential for Transformative Legal Interpretation'. *University of Pennsylvania Law Review* 136, 4 (April): 1135–1229.

Crewe, Jonathan. 1991. 'Defining Marginality?' *Tulsa Studies in Women's Literature* 10, 1 (Spring): 121–30.

Cromwell, Liz, ed. 1975. *One Out of Many: A Collection of Writings by 21 Black Women in Ontario*. Toronto: Wacacro.

Dabydeen, Cyril, ed. 1987. *A Shapely Fire: Changing the Literary Landscape*. Oakville, Ont.: Mosaic.

Dahlie, Hallvard. 1993. *Isolation and Commitment: Frederick Philip Grove's* Settlers of the Marsh. Toronto: ECW Press.

Dahlie, Jorgen. 1977. 'Scandinavian Experiences on the Prairies, 1890–1920: The Frederiksens of Nokomis'. Pp. 102–13 in Palmer, ed.

Davies, Carole Boyce. 1992. 'Collaboration and the Ordering Imperative in Life Story Production'. Pp. 3–19 in Sidonie Smith and Julia Watson, eds. *De/Colonizing the Subject: The Politics of Gender in Women's Autobiography*. Minneapolis: University of Minnesota Press.

de Certeau, Michel. 1986. *Heterologies: Discourse on the Other*. Trans. Brian Massumi. Foreword Wlad Godzich. Minneapolis: University of Minnesota Press.

De Fehr, William, ed. 1974. *Harvest: Anthology of Mennonite Writing in Canada*. Winnipeg: Centennial Committee of the Mennonite Historical Society of Manitoba.

Deleuze, Gilles, and Félix Guattari. 1986. *Kafka: Toward a Minor Literature*. Trans. Dana Polan. Minneapolis: University of Minnesota Press.

———. 1983. *Anti-Oedipus: Capitalism and Schizophrenia*. Preface Michel Foucault. Trans. Robert Hurley, Mark Seem and Helen R. Lane. Minneapolis: University of Minnesota Press.

Deleuze, Gilles, and Claire Parnet. 1987. *Dialogues*. Trans. Hugh Tomlinson and Barbara Habberjam. New York: Columbia University Press.

de Man, Paul. 1986. *Resistance to Theory*. Foreword by Wlad Godzich. Minneapolis: University of Minnesota Press.

Dench, Geoff. 1986. *Minorities in the Open Society: Prisoners of Ambivalence*. London and New York: Routledge and Kegan Paul.

Derrida, Jacques. 1992. 'Before the Law'. Pp. 181–220 in Derek Artridge, ed. *Jacques Derrida: Acts of Literature*. New York and London: Routledge.

———. 1987. *The Post Card: From Socrates to Freud and Beyond*. Trans. Alan Bass. Chicago and London: University of Chicago Press.

———. 1985. *The Ear of the Other: Otobiography, Transference, Translation. Texts and Discussions with Jacques Derrida*. Trans. Peggy Kamuf ('Otobiographies' trans. Avital Ronell). Ed. Christie V. McDonald. New York: Schocken.

———. 1981a. *Positions*. Trans. Alan Bass. Chicago: Chicago University Press.

———. 1981b. *Dissemination*. Trans. and Intr. Barbara Johnson. Chicago: University of Chicago Press.

———. 1978. *Writing and Difference*. Trans, Intr., and Additional Notes, Alan Bass. Chicago: Univesity of Chicago Press.

Di Cicco, Pier Giorgio, ed. 1978. *Roman Candles: An Anthology of Poems by Seventeen Italo-Canadian Poets*. Toronto: Hounslow.

Diggs, Marylynne. 1994. 'Surveying the Intersection: Pathology, Secrecy, and the Discourses of Racial and Sexual Identity'. *Journal of Homosexuality* 26, 2/3: 1–19.

DiGiovanni, Caroline Morgan, ed. 1984. *Italian-Canadian Voices: An Anthology of Poetry and Prose (1946–1983)*. Oakville, Ont.: Mosaic.

Douglas, Mary. 1975. *Implicit Meanings: Essays in Anthropology*. London and Boston: Routledge and Kegan Paul.

Dumm, Thomas L. 1994. 'Strangers and Liberals'. *Political Theory* 22, 1 (February): 167–75.

Eagleton, Terry. 1991. *Ideology: An Introduction*. London and New York: Verso.

Elliott, Lorris. 1990. 'Black Writing in Canada: The Problems of Anthologizing and Documenting'. Pp. 167–73 in Joseph Pivato, in collaboration with Steven Tötötsy de Zepetnek and Milan V. Dimic, eds. *Literatures of Lesser Diffusion/Les littératures de moindre diffusion*. Edmonton: Research Institute for Comparative Literature, University of Alberta.

———. 1988. *Literary Writing by Blacks in Canada: A Preliminary Study*. Ottawa: Department of the Secretary of State, Multicultural Sector.

———, ed. 1985. *Other Voices: Writing by Blacks in Canada*. Toronto: Williams-Wallace.

El-Malh, Youssef. 1989. 'Jumping in Air'. Pp. 22–3 in Kamal A. Rostom, ed. *Arab-Canadian Writing: Stories, Memoirs, and Reminiscences*. Fredericton, NB: York Press.

Evans, Martha Noel. 1989. 'Hysteria and the Seduction Theory'. Pp. 73–85 in Dianne Hunter, ed. *Seduction and Theory: Readings of Gender, Representation, and Rhetoric*. Urbana and Chicago: University of Illinois Press.

Ewald, François. 1990. 'Norms, Discipline, and the Law'. *Representations* 30 (Spring): 138–61.

Fanon, Frantz. 1967. *The Wretched of the Earth*. Preface by Jean-Paul Sartre. Trans. Constance Ferrington. London: Penguin.

———. 1963. *Black Skin, White Masks*. Trans. Charles Lam Markmann. New York: Grove Press.

Felman, Shoshana. 1983. *The Literary Speech Act: Don Juan with J.L. Austin, or Seduction in Two Languages*. Trans. Catherine Porter. Ithaca: Cornell University Press.

———. 1982. 'Psychoanalysis and Education: Teaching Terminable and Interminable'. *Yale French Studies* 63: 21–44.

Fiss, Owen M. 1982. 'Objectivity and Interpretation'. *Stanford Law Review* 34 (April): 739–63.

Foucault, Michel. 1980. *Power/Knowledge: Selected Interviews and Other Writings 1972–1977*. Ed. Colin Gordon. New York: Pantheon.

Freedman, Barbara. 1990. 'Pedagogy, Psychoanalysis, Theatre: Interrogating the Scene of Learning'. *Shakespeare Quarterly* 41, 2 (Summer): 174–86.

Freud, Sigmund. 1953–74. *The Standard Edition of the Complete Psychological Works of Sigmund Freud*. Trans. and ed. James Strachey. London: Hogarth Press. Vols 1–24.

Friesen, Gerald. 1984. *The Canadian Prairies: A History*. Toronto: University of Toronto Press.

Froula, Christine. 1986. 'The Daughter's Seduction: Sexual Violence and Literary History'. Pp. 139–62 in Micheline R. Malson, Jean F. O'Barr, Sarah Westphal-Wihl, and Mary Wyer, eds. *Feminist Theory in Practice and Process*. Chicago and London: University of Chicago Press.

Fujita, Gayle K. 1985. 'To Attend the Sound of Stone: The Sensibility of Silence in *Obasan*'. *MELUS* 12, 3: 33–42.

Gilroy, Paul. 1993. *Small Acts: Thoughts on the Politics of Black Cultures*. London: Serpent's Tail.

———. 1992. 'Cultural Studies and Ethnic Absolutism'. Pp. 187–98 in Grossberg et al, eds.

Giroux, Henry. 1994. 'Living Dangerously: Identity Politics and the New Cultural Racism'. Pp. 29–55 in Henry Giroux and Peter McLaren, eds. *Beyond Borders: Pedagogy and the Politics of Cultural Studies*. New York and London: Routledge.

Golding, Alan C. 1984. 'A History of American Literature and the Canon'. Pp. 279–307 in Robert von Hallberg, ed. *Canons*. Chicago: University of Chicago Press.

Grossberg, Lawrence. 1994. 'Introduction: Bringin' It All Back Home—Pedagogy and Cultural Studies'. Pp. 1–25 in Henry Giroux and Peter McLaren, eds. *Between Borders: Pedagogy and the Politics of Cultural Studies*. New York and London: Routledge.

———, Cary Nelson, and Paula Treichler, eds. 1992. *Cultural Studies*. New York and London: Routledge.

Grosz, Elizabeth. 1994. *Volatile Bodies: Toward a Corporeal Feminism*. Bloomington and Indianapolis: Indiana University Press.

Grove, Frederick Philip. 1991 (1927). *A Search for America*. Afterword W.H. New, 461–68. Toronto: McClelland and Stewart (New Canadian Library).

———. 1989 (1925). *Settlers of the Marsh*. Afterword Kristjana Gunnars, 267–75. Toronto: McClelland and Stewart (New Canadian Library).

———. 1982 (1929). *It Needs to Be Said . . .* Intr. by W.J. Keith, vii–xiii. Ottawa: Tecumseh.

———. 1957. *Over Prairie Trails*. Intr. Malcolm Ross, v–x. Toronto: McClelland and Stewart (New Canadian Library).

———. 1946. *In Search of Myself*. Toronto: Macmillan.

Guillory, John. 1993. *Cultural Capital: The Problem of Literary Canon Formation*. Chicago and London: University of Chicago Press.

Gunew, Sneja. 1993. 'Feminism and the politics of irreducible differences: Multiculturalism/ethnicity/race'. Pp. 1–19 in Gunew and Anna Yeatman, eds. *Feminism and the Politics of Difference*. St Leonards, Australia: Allen and Unwin.

Gutmann, Amy. 1993. 'The Challenge of Multiculturalism in Political Ethics'. *Philosophy and Public Affairs* 22, 3 (Summer): 171–206.

Hall, D.J. 1985a. *Clifford Sifton*. Vol. II: *A Lonely Eminence 1901–1929*. Vancouver and London: University of British Columbia Press.

———. 1985b. 'Clifford Sifton: Immigration and Settlement Policy, 1896–1905'. Pp. 281–308 in R. Douglas Francis and Howard Palmer, eds. *The Prairie West: Historical Readings*. Edmonton: Pica Pica Press (Textbook Division of the University of Alberta Press).

Hall, Stuart. 1997. 'The Local and the Global: Globalization and Ethnicity'. Pp. 173–84 in McClintock et al., eds.

———. 1996. 'For Allon White: metaphors of transformation'. Pp. 287–305 in David Morley and Kuan-Hsing Chen, eds. *Stuart Hall: Critical Dialogues in Cultural Studies*. London and New York: Routledge.

———. 1992. 'New Ethnicities'. Pp. 252–60 in J. Donald and A. Rattansi, eds. *'Race', Culture and Difference*. London: Sage.

———. 1990. 'Cultural Identity and Diaspora'. Pp. 222–37 in Jonathan Rutherford, ed. *Identity: Community, Culture, Difference*. London: Lawrence and Wishart.

————. 1981. 'The White in Their Eyes: Racist Ideologies and the Media'. Pp. 28–52 in George Bridges and Rosalind Brunt, eds. *Silver Linings: Sane Strategies for the Eighties*. London: Lawrence and Wishart.

Harney, Robert F. 1988. '"So Great a Heritage as Ours." Immigration and the Survival of the Canadian Polity'. *Daedalus* 117, 4 (Fall): 51–97.

Hartsock, Nancy. 1990. 'Foucault on Power: A Theory for Women?' Pp. 157–75 in Linda J. Nicholson, ed. *Feminism/Postmodernism*. New York and London: Routledge.

Hays, Michael. 1992. Foreword: 'The Scene and the Unseen of the Critic's Discourse'. Pp. vii–xxvii in Michael Hays, ed. *Critical Conditions: Regarding the Historical Moment*. Minneapolis: University of Minnesota Press.

Helmetag, Charles H. 1990. '". . . Of Men and of Angels": Literary Allusions in Wim Wenders's "Wings of Desire"'. *Film Literature Quarterly* 18, 4: 251–3.

Herder, Johann Gottfried. [1784–91] 1800. *Outlines of a Philosophy of the History of Man*. Trans. T. Churchill. New York: Bergman Publishers.

Hill, Mike. 1997. 'Introduction: Vipers in Shangri-la: Whiteness, Writing, and Other Ordinary Terrors'. Pp. 1–18 in Mike Hill, ed. *Whiteness: A Critical Reader*. New York and London: New York University Press.

Hjartarson, Paul. 1981. 'Design and Truth in Grove's "In Search of Myself"'. *Canadian Literature* 90 (Autumn): 73–90.

————, ed. 1986. *A Stranger to My Time: Essays by and about Frederick Philip Grove*. Edmonton: NeWest.

Hutcheon, Linda. 1996. 'Multicultural Furor: The Reception of *Other Solitudes*'. Pp. 10–17 in Winfried Siemerling and Katrin Schwenk, eds. *Cultural Difference and the Literary Text: Pluralism and the Limits of Authenticity in North American Literatures*. Iowa City: University of Iowa Press.

————. 1994. *Irony's Edge: The Theory and Politics of Irony*. London and New York: Routledge.

————. 1992. 'The Multicultural Debate: The Reception of *Other Solitudes*'. *Italian Canadiana* 8: 7–14.

————. 1991. *Splitting Images: Contemporary Canadian Ironies*. Toronto: Oxford University Press.

————. 1989. *The Politics of Postmodernism*. London and New York: Routledge.

————. 1988. *A Poetics of Postmodernism: History, Theory, Fiction*. New York and London: Routledge.

————, and Marion Richmond, eds. 1990. *Other Solitudes: Canadian Multicultural Fictions*. Toronto: Oxford University Press. Introduction by Hutcheon: 1–16.

Inglis, Fred. 1990. *Media Theory: An Introduction*. Oxford: Basil Blackwell.

James, J.T.L. 1978–79. 'Gaols and their Goals in Manitoba 1870–1970'. *Canadian Journal of Criminology* 20–21: 34–42.

Jameson, Fredric. 1991. *Postmodernism, or, The Cultural Logic of Late Capitalism.* Durham: Duke University Press.

JanMohamed, Abdul R. 1992. 'Sexuality on/of the Racial Border: Foucault, Wright, and the Articulation of "Racialized Sexuality"'. Pp. 94–116 in Domna C. Stanton, ed. *Discourses of Sexuality: From Aristotle to AIDS.* Ann Arbor: University of Michigan Press.

———. 1983. *Manichean Aesthetics: The Politics of Literature in Colonial Africa.* Amherst: University of Massachusetts Press.

———, and David Lloyd. 1990. 'Introduction: Toward a Theory of Minority Discourse: What Is To Be Done?' Pp. 1–16 in Abdul JanMohamed and David Lloyd, eds. *The Nature and Context of Minority Discourse.* New York: Oxford University Press.

Johnson, Barbara. 1985. 'Taking Fidelity Philosophically'. Pp. 142–8 in Joseph F. Graham, ed. *Difference in Translation.* Ithaca and London: Cornell University Press.

———. 1982. 'Teaching Ignorance: *L'Ecole des Femmes'*. *Yale French Studies* 63: 165–82.

Kahane, Claire. 1989. 'Seduction and the Voice of the Text: *Heart of Darkness* and *The Good Soldier'*. Pp. 135–53 in Dianne Hunter, ed. *Seduction and Theory: Readings of Gender, Representation, and Rhetoric.* Urbana and Chicago: University of Illinois Press.

Kallen, Evelyn. 1982. 'Multiculturalism: Ideology, Policy and Reality'. *Journal of Canadian Studies/Revue d'études canadiennes* 17, 1 (Spring): 51–63.

Katz, Susan. 1987. 'Speaking out against the "Talking Cure": Unmarried Women in Freud's Early Case Studies'. *Women's Studies* 13: 297–324.

Kitagawa, Muriel. 1985. *This is My Own: Letters to Wes and Other Writings on Japanese Canadians, 1941–1948.* Ed. Roy Miki. Vancouver: Talonbooks.

Kogawa, Joy. 1983 (1981). *Obasan.* Markham, Ont.: Penguin.

Kristeva, Julia. 1993. *Nations Without Nationalism.* Trans. Leon S. Roudiez. New York: Columbia University Press.

———. 1991. *Strangers to Ourselves.* Trans. Leon S. Roudiez. New York: Columbia University Press.

———. 1982. *Powers of Horror: An Essay on Abjection.* Trans. Leon S. Roudiez. New York: Columbia University Press.

Kroetsch, Robert. 1995. 'I Wanted to Write a Manifesto'. Pp. 41–64 in Kroetsch *A Likely Story: The Writing Life.* Red Deer, Alberta: Red Deer College Press.

———. 1989. 'The Grammar of Silence'. Pp. 84–94 in Kroetsch. *The Lovely Treachery of Words.* Toronto: Oxford University Press.

Krönagel, Alex. 1991. 'Frederick Philip Grove and the Problem of a Canadian National Literature'. *Neophilologus* 75: 470–9.

Lacan, Jacques. 1979. *The Four Fundamental Concepts of Psycho-analysis.* Ed. Jacques-

Allain Miller. Trans. Alan Sheridan. Harmondsworth, England: Penguin.

Lagos-Pope, Maria-Ines. 1988. *Exile in Literature*. Lewisburg: Bucknell University Press.

Lamer, Antonio. 1992. 'How the Charter changes justice'. *The Globe and Mail*. 17 April: A17.

Lang, Berel. 1997. 'Metaphysical Racism (Or: Biological Warfare by Other Means)'. Pp. 17–27 in Naomi Zack, ed. *Race/Sex: Their Sameness, Difference, and Interplay*. New York and London: Routledge.

Laplanche, J., and J.-B. Pontalis. 1973. *The Language of Psychoanalysis*. Trans. Donald Nicholson-Smith. New York: W.W. Norton.

Lawson, Alan. 1995. 'Postcolonial Theory and the "Settler" Subject'. *Essays on Canadian Writing* 56 (Fall): 20–36.

Lecker, Robert, ed. 1991. *Canadian Canons: Essays in Literary Value*. Toronto, Buffalo, and London: University of Toronto Press.

Levinas, Emmanuel. 1986. 'The Trace of the Other'. Pp. 345–59 in Mark C. Taylor, ed. *Deconstruction in Context: Literature and Philosophy*. Chicago: University of Chicago Press.

Lingis, Alfonso. 1994. *The Community of Those Who Have Nothing in Common*. Bloomington and Indianapolis: Indiana University Press.

Lloyd, David. 1994. 'Adulteration and the Nation: Monologic Nationalism and the Colonial Hybrid'. Pp. 53–92 in Alfred Arteaga, ed. *An Other Tongue: Nation and Ethnicity in the Linguistic Borderlands*. Durham and London: Duke University Press.

Loriggio, Francesco. 1987. 'The Question of the Corpus: Ethnicity and Canadian Literature'. Pp. 53–68 in John Moss, ed. *Future Indicative: Literary Theory and Canadian Literature*. Ottawa: University of Ottawa Press.

Lowe, Lisa. 1996. *Immigrant Acts: On Asian American Cultural Politics*. Durham and London: Duke University Press.

Lubiano, Wahneema. 1997. 'Shuckin' Off the African-American Native Other: What's "Po-Mo" Got to Do with It?' Pp. 204–29 in McClintock et al., eds.

Lukacher, Ned. 1989. 'The Epistemology of Disgust'. Foreword (vii–xxi) to Monique David-Ménard. *Hysteria from Freud to Lacan: Body and Language in Psychoanalysis*. Ithaca and New York: Cornell University Press.

Lupul, Manoly R. 1982. 'The Political Implementation of Multiculturalism'. *Journal of Canadian Studies/ Revue d'études canadiennes* 17, 1 (Spring): 93–102.

McCallum, Pamela. 1992. 'The Construction of Knowledge and Epistemologies of Marked Subjectivities'. *University of Toronto Quarterly* 61, 4 (Summer): 430–6.

McCarthy, Dermot. 1991. 'Early Canadian Literary Histories and the Function of a Canon'. Pp. 30–45 in Lecker, ed.

McClintock, Anne. 1997. '"No Longer in a Future Heaven": Gender, Race and Nationalism'. Pp. 89–112 in McClintock et al., eds.

———. 1995. *Imperial Leather: Race, Gender and Sexuality in the Colonial Context.* New York and London: Routledge.

———, Aamir Mufti, and Ella Shohat, eds. 1997. *Dangerous Liaisons: Gender, Nation, and Postcolonial Perspectives.* Minneapolis and London: University of Minnesota Press.

Magrath, C.A. 1910. *Canada's Growth and Some Problems Affecting It.* Ottawa: Mortimer.

Mallet, Gina. 1997. 'Multiculturalism: Has diversity gone too far?' *The Globe and Mail.* 15 March: D1, D2.

Mandel, Eli. 1977. 'Ethnic Voice in Canadian Writing'. Pp. 91–102 in Mandel *Another Time.* Erin, Ont.: Porcepic.

Maracle, Lee. 1992. 'The Post-Colonial Imagination'. *Fuse* 16 (Fall): 12–15.

Martusewicz, Rebecca A. 1997. 'Say Me to Me: Desire and Education'. Pp. 97–113 in Sharon Todd, ed. *Learning Desire: Perspectives on Pedagogy, Culture, and the Unsaid.* New York and London: Routledge.

Mehlman, Jeffrey. 1974. *A Structural Study of Autobiography.* Ithaca: Cornell University Press.

Miki, Roy. 1995. 'Asiancy: Making Space for Asian Canadian Writing'. Pp. 135–51 in Gary Y. Okihino, Marilyn Alguizola, Dorothy Fujita Rong, and K. Scott Wong, eds. *Privileging Positions: The Sites of Asian American Studies.* Pullman, Washington: Washington State University Press.

———. 1994. 'Why we're holding the Vancouver conference'. *The Globe and Mail.* 7 April: A17.

———, and Fred Wah. 1994. Preface to special issue, 'Colour. An Issue', eds Miki and Wah. *West Coast Line* 13/14 (Spring/Fall): 5–6.

Miles, Kevin Thomas. 1997. 'Body Badges: Race and Sex'. Pp. 133–43 in Naomi Zack, ed. *Race/Sex: Their Sameness, Difference, and Interplay.* New York and London: Routledge.

Mitchell, Juliet. 1992. 'From King Lear to Anna O and Beyond: Some Speculative Theses on Hysteria and the Traditionless Self'. *The Yale Journal of Criticism* 5, 2: 91–107.

Moi, Toril. 1981. 'Representation of Patriarchy: Sexuality and Epistemology in Freud's Dora'. *Feminist Review* 9 (October): 60–74.

Mulvey, Laura. 1989. *Visual and Other Pleasures.* Bloomington and Indianapolis: Indiana University Press.

Nancy, Jean-Luc. 1991. *The Inoperative Community.* Ed. Peter Connor. Trans. Peter Connor, Lisa Garbus, Michael Holland and Simona Sawhney. Foreword by Christopher Fynsk (vii–xxxv). Minneapolis and Oxford: University of Minnesota Press.

Nida, Eugene A., and Charles R. Taber. 1974. *The Theory and Practice of Translation.* Leiden, Netherlands: E.J. Brill.

Nómez, Naín, ed. 1982. *Chilean Literature in Canada/Literatura Chilena en Canada*. Ottawa: Ediciones Cordillera.

Pacey, Desmond. 1945. *Frederick Philip Grove*. Toronto: Ryerson.

——, ed. 1976. *The Letters of Frederick Philip Grove*. Toronto and Buffalo: University of Toronto Press.

——, ed. 1970. *Frederick Philip Grove*. Toronto: Ryerson.

Pache, Walter. 1986. 'Frederick Philip Grove: Comparative Perspectives'. Pp. 11–20 in Hjartarson, ed.

Padolsky, Enoch. 1994. 'Canadian Ethnic Minority Literature in English'. Pp. 361–86 in J.W. Berry and J.A. Laponce, eds. *Ethnicity and Culture in Canada: The Research Landscape*. Toronto: University of Toronto Press.

Pagden, Anthony. 1995. 'The Effacement of Difference: Colonialism and the Origins of Nationalism in Diderot and Herder'. Pp. 129–52 in Gyan Prakash, ed. *After Colonialism: Imperial Histories and Postcolonial Displacements*. Princeton, NJ: Princeton University Press.

Palmer, Howard, ed. 1977. *The Settlement of the West*. Calgary: University of Calgary Press.

Paneth, Ira. 1988. 'Wim and His Wings'. An interview with Wim Wenders. *Film Quarterly* XLII, 1 (Fall): 2–8.

Penley, Constance. 1986. 'Teaching in Your Sleep: Feminism and Psychoanalysis'. Pp. 129–48 in Cary Nelson, ed. *Theory in the Classroom*. Urbana: Illinois University Press.

Pivato, Joseph. 'Preface'. Pp. 13–15 in DiGiovanni, ed.

Pizanias, Caterina. 1996. '(Re)thinking the Ethnic Body: Performing "Greekness" in Canada'. *Journal of the Hellenic Diaspora* 22, 1: 7–60.

Porter, John. 1965. *The Vertical Mosaic: An Analysis of Social Class and Power in Canada*. Toronto, Buffalo, London: University of Toronto Press.

Potter, Robin. 1990. 'Moral—In Whose Sense? Joy Kogawa's *Obasan* and Julia Kristeva's *Powers of Horror*'. *Studies in Canadian Literature* 15 (1): 117–39.

Pratt, Mary Louise. 1992. *Imperial Eyes: Travel Writing and Transculturation*. London and New York: Routledge.

Radhakrishnan, R. 1996. *Diasporic Mediations: Between Home and Location*. Minneapolis: University of Minnesota Press.

——. 1992. 'Nationalism, Gender, and the Narrative of Identity'. Pp. 77–95 in Andrew Parker, Mary Russo, Doris Sommer, and Patricia Yaeger, eds. *Nationalisms and Sexualities*. New York and London: Routledge.

——. 1990. 'Ethnic Identity and Post-Structuralist Differance'. Pp. 50–71 in JanMohamed and Lloyd, eds.

Rapport, Nigel. 1995. 'Migrant Selves and Stereotypes: Personal Context in a Postmodern World'. Pp. 267–82 in Steve Pile and Nigel Thrift, eds. *Mapping the Subject: Geographies of Cultural Transformation*. London and New York:

Routledge.

Report of the Royal Commission on Bilingualism and Biculturalism. 1967–70. Books I–IV. Ottawa: Queen's Printer.

Rogowski, Christian. 1993. '"*Der liebevolle Blick*?" The Problem of Perception in Wim Wenders's *Wings of Desire'*. *Seminar* 29, 4 (November): 398–409.

Roman, Leslie G. 1993. 'White is a Color! White Defensiveness, Postmodernism, and Anti-Racist Pedagogy'. Pp. 71–88 in Cameron McCarthy and Warren Crichlow, eds. *Race, Identity and Representation in Education*. New York and London: Routledge.

Rose, Marilyn Russell. 1988. 'Politics into Art: Kogawa's *Obasan* and the Rhetoric of Fiction'. *Mosaic* 21 (Spring): 215–26.

———. 1987. 'Hawthorne's "Custom House", Said's *Orientalism* and Kogawa's *Obasan*: An Intertextual Reading of an Historical Fiction'. *Dalhousie Review* 67, 2/3 (Summer/Fall): 286–96.

Ross, Chambers. 1997. 'The Unexamined'. Pp. 187–203 in Hill, ed.

Ross, Valerie. 1997. 'Laying to rest "this whole immigrant thing"'. *The Globe and Mail*. 13 Sept.: C4.

Ruger, Hendrika, ed. 1989. *Dutch Voices: A Collection of Stories and Poems by Dutch-Canadians*. Windsor, Ont.: Netherlandic.

———, ed. 1988. *Transplanted Lives: Dutch-Canadian Stories and Poems*. Windsor, Ont.: Netherlandic.

———, ed. 1987. *Distant Kin: Dutch-Canadian Stories and Poems*. Windsor, Ont.: Netherlandic.

Ryan, Michael. 1989. *Politics and Culture: Working Hypotheses for a Post-Revolutionary Society*. Baltimore: Johns Hopkins University Press.

Said, Edward. 1993. *Culture and Imperialism*. New York: Knopf.

———. 1986. 'Intellectuals in the Post-Colonial World'. *Salgamundi* 70–71 (Spring-Summer): 44–81.

———. 1983. *The World, The Text and the Critic*. Cambridge, Mass.: Harvard University Press.

Schatzki, Theodore R., and Wolfgang Natter. 1996. 'Sociocultural Bodies, Bodies Sociopolitical'. Pp. 1–25 in Theodor R. Schatzki and Wolfgang Natter, eds. *The Social and Political Body*. New York and London: Guilford Press.

Scheier, Libby, Sarah Sheard, and Eleanor Wachtel, eds. 1990. *Language in Her Eye: Writing and Gender*. Toronto: Coach House.

Scott, Joan W. 1992. 'Multiculturalism and the Politics of Identity'. *October* 61 (Summer): 12–19.

Serres, Michel. 1982. *The Parasite*. Trans. Lawrence R. Schehr. Baltimore: Johns Hopkins University Press.

Seshadri-Crooks, Kalpana. 1995. 'At the Margins of Postcolonial Studies'. *Ariel* 26, 3 (July): 47–71.

Shohat, Ella. 1991. 'Ethnicities-in-Relation: Toward a Multicultural Reading of American Cinema'. Pp. 215–50 in Lester D. Friedman, ed. *Unspeakable Images: Ethnicity and the American Cinema*. Urbana and Chicago: University of Illinois Press.

————, and Robert Stam. 1994. *Unthinking Eurocentrism: Multiculturalism and the Media*. London and New York: Routledge.

Silverman, Kaja. 1992. *Male Subjectivity at the Margins*. New York and London: Routledge.

————. 1988. *The Acoustic Mirror: The Female Voice in Psychoanalysis and Cinema*. Bloomington and Indianapolis: Indiana University Press.

Simon, Sherry. 1991. 'Culture and Its Values: Critical Revisionism in Quebec in the 1980s'. Pp. 167–79 in Lecker, ed.

Skinner, Shirley, Otto Driedger, and Brian Grainger. 1981. *Corrections: A Historical Perspective of the Saskatchewan Experience*. Regina: Canadian Plains Research Center, University of Regina.

Smith, Paul. 1995. 'Eastwood Bound'. Pp. 77–97 in Maurice Berger, Brian Wallis, and Simon Watson, eds. *Constructing Masculinity*. New York and London: Routledge.

Smith, W.G. 1920. *A Study in Canadian Immigration*. Toronto: Ryerson.

Snow, Robert P. 1983. *Creating Media Culture*. Beverly Hills, London, New Delhi: Sage.

Spanos, William. 1997. 'Rethinking the Postmodernity of the Discourse of Postmodernism'. Pp. 65–74 in Hans Bertens and Douwe Fokkema, eds. *International Postmodernism: Theory and Literary Practice*. Amsterdam, The Netherlands; Philadelphia, PA: John Benjamins.

Spettigue, Douglas O. 1969. *Frederick Philip Grove*. Toronto: Copp Clark.

Spivak, Gayatri Chakravorty. 1997. 'Teaching for the Times'. Pp. 468–90 in McClintock et al., eds.

————. 1994. 'Responsibility'. *Boundary 2* 21, 3 (Fall): 19–64.

————. 1993. 'Marginality in the Teaching Machine'. Pp. 53–76 in Spivak. *Outside in the Teaching Machine*. New York and London: Routledge.

————. 1990. 'The Post-modern Condition: The End of Politics?' A dialogue with Geoffrey Hawthorn, Ron Aronson, and John Dunn. Pp. 17–34 in Sarah Harasym, ed. *The Post-colonial Critic: Interviews, Strategies, Dialogues*. New York and London: Routledge.

————. 1985. 'Scattered Speculations on the Question of Value'. *Diacritics* 15, 4 (Winter): 73–93.

Srivastava, Aruna. 1993. 'Re-Imaging Racism: South Asian Canadian Women Writers'. Pp. 103–21 in Bannerji, ed.

Stafford, James. 1992. 'The Impact of the New Immigrant Policy on Racism in Canada'. Pp. 69–91 in Vic Satzewich, ed. *Deconstructing a Nation: Immigration,*

Multiculturalism and Racism in '90s Canada. Halifax, NS: Fernwood Publishing and Social Research Unit, Department of Sociology, University of Saskatchewan.

Stalybrass, Peter, and Allon White. 1986. *The Politics and Poetics of Transgression*. London: Methuen.

Stam, Robert. 1997. 'Multiculturalism and the Neoconservatives'. Pp. 173–203 in McClintock et al., eds.

———. 1991. 'Bakhtin, Polyphony, and Ethnic/Racial Representation'. Pp. 251–76 in Lester D. Friedman, ed. *Unspeakable Images: Ethnicity and the American Cinema*. Urbana: University of Illinois Press.

Stoler, Ann Laura. 1997a. *Race and the Education of Desire: Foucault's* History of Sexuality *and the Colonial Order of Things*. Durham and London: Duke University Press.

———. 1997b. 'Sexual Affronts and Racial Frontiers: European Identities and the Cultural Politics of Exclusion in Colonial Souteast Asia'. Pp. 198–237 in Frederick Cooper and Ann Laura Stoler, eds. *Tensions of Empire: Colonial Cultures in a Bourgeois World*. Berkeley, Los Angeles, London: University of California Press.

Suits, Bernard. 1978. *The Grasshopper: Games, Life and Utopia*. Toronto: University of Toronto Press.

Takaki, Ronald. 1989. *Strangers from a Different Shore: A History of Asian Americans*. Boston, Toronto, London: Little, Brown and Co.

Taussig, Michael. 1993. *Mimesis and Alterity: A Peculiar History of the Senses*. New York and London: Routledge.

Taylor, Charles. 1993. *Reconciling the Solitudes: Essays on Canadian Federalism and Nationalism*. Ed. Guy Laforest. Montreal and Kingston, London and Buffalo: McGill-Queen's University Press.

———. 1992. *Multiculturalism and 'The Politics of Recognition'*. An Essay by Charles Taylor with commentary by Amy Gutmann, Steven C. Rockfeller, Michael Walzer, and Susan Wolf. Ed. Amy Gutmann (15–73). Princeton, NJ: Princeton University Press. Rpt in 1994 as *Multiculturalism: Examining the Politics of Recognition*. Ed. and Intr. Amy Gutmann, with additional commentary by Jürgen Habermas and Anthony K. Appiah. Princeton: Princeton University Press.

———. 1991. *The Malaise of Modernity*. Toronto: Anansi.

Taylor, Mark C. 1987. *Altarity*. Chicago and London: University of Chicago Press.

The Telling It Book Collective (Sky Lee, Lee Maracle, Daphne Marlatt and Betsy Warland). 1990. *Telling It: Women and Language Across Cultures (the transformation of a conference)*. Intr., 'Meeting on Fractured Margins', Daphne Marlatt (9–18). Vancouver: Press Gang.

Trudeau, P.E. 1968. *Federalism and the French Canadians*. Toronto: Macmillan.

Turner, Margaret. 1995. *Imagining Culture: New World Narrative and the Writing of*

Canada. Montreal and Kingston, London, Buffalo: McGill-Queen's University Press.

Ueki, Teruyo. 1993. '*Obasan*: Revelations in a Paradoxical Silence'. *MELUS* 18, 4 (Winter): 5–20.

Varadharajan, Asha. 1995. *Exotic Parodies: Subjectivity in Adorno, Said and Spivak*. Minneapolis and London: University of Minnesota Press.

Vierhaus, Rudolph. 1996. 'Progress: Ideas, Skepticism, and Critique—The Heritage of the Enlightenment'. Pp. 330–41 in James Schmidt, ed. *What Is Enlightenment? Eighteenth-Century Answers and Twentieth-Century Questions*. Berkeley, Los Angeles, London: University of California Press.

Wallerstein, Emmanuel. 1991. 'The Construction of Peoplehood: Racism, Nationalism, Ethnicity'. Pp. 71–85 in Etienne Balibar and Immanuel Wallerstein, *Race, Nation, Class: Ambiguous Identities*. London and New York: Verson.

Walton, Jean. 1995. 'Re-Placing Race in (White) Psychoanalytic Discourse: Founding Narratives of Feminism'. *Critical Inquiry* 21 (Summer): 775–804.

Weber, Samuel. 1991. *Return to Freud: Jacques Lacan's Dislocation of Psychoanalysis*. Trans. Michael Levine. Cambridge: Cambridge University Press.

Wenders, Wim. 1992. 'Wim Wenders's Guilty Pleasures'. *Film Comment* 28 (January/February): 74–7.

———. 1987. *Wings of Desire*. Script by Wim Wenders and Peter Handke.

White, Hayden. 1987. *The Content of The Form: Narrative Discourse and Historical Representation*. Baltimore and London: Johns Hopkins University Press.

White Paper. Announcement of Implementation of Policy of Multiculturalism within Bilingual Framework. House of Commons, Canada. Friday, 8 Oct. 1971.

Woodsworth, James S. 1972 (1909). *Strangers within Our Gates: or Coming Canadians*. Intr. Marilyn Barber. Toronto: University of Toronto Press.

Young, Iris Marion. 1990. 'The Ideal of Community and the Politics of Difference'. Pp. 300–23 in Linda J. Nicholson, ed. *Feminism/Postmodernism*. New York and London: Routledge.

Young, Robert J.C. 1995. *Colonial Desire: Hybridity in Theory, Culture and Race*. London and New York: Routledge.

———. 1990. *White Mythologies: Writing, History and the West*. London and New York: Routledge.

Žižek, Slavoj. 1989. *The Sublime Object of Ideology*. London, New York: Verso.

Zubrycki, Richard M. 1980. *The Establishment of Canada's Penitentiary System: Federal Correctional Policy 1867–1900*. Toronto: University of Toronto Press.

Index

Abjection, 73, 141, 195, 199–200, 201–2, 203, 212, 216, 218, 220
Adachi, Ken, 186
Adorno, Theodor W., 20, 22
Agency, 1, 14, 55, 67, 70, 104, 110, 117, 129, 134, 143, 157, 158, 161, 178, 206, 210
Ahmad, Aijaz, 66, 170
Alcoff, Linda, 5
Althusser, Louis, 54, 104, 105, 121
Anderson, Benedict, 7
Angus, Ian, 84
Anti-Semitism, 51
Appiah, K. Anthony, 89, 142, 169
Apter, Emily, 35, 37
Arac, Jonathan, 168
Aránguiz, Manuel, 149–50
Atwood, Margaret, 85, 133, 162, 164
Authenticity, 4, 39, 40, 147, 158, 161, 195; and 'heritage', 106, 107, 110; 'jargon of', 22, 56; in Taylor, 115, 116, 120, 121, 122, 124–5, 127, 128; in *Wings of Desire*, 8, 16– 17, 8, 20, 21

Bakhtin, Mikhail, 98, 115, 122
Balan, Jars, and Yuri Klynovy, *Yarmarok: Ukrainian Wriitng in Canada since the Second World War,* 133, 150–1
Bannerji, Himani, 88, 113, 131, 160, 163
Bauman, Zygmunt, 175
Bedson, Samuel Lawrence, 69–70
Begamudré, Ven, 144
'Benetton effect', 169, 176
Benjamin, Walter, 1, 6, 7, 8, 15, 20, 25, 28, 46, 96, 97, 98, 132, 170, 176
Bennett, Donna, 38–40, 43, 134
Bernheimer, Charles, 36
Bhabha, Homi K., 3, 7–8, 22, 55, 60, 100, 110–11, 139, 156, 161, 213

Biculturalism, 126, 136
Bilingualism, official, 95, 96, 97, 103, 126; *see also* Official Languages Act

Bill C-93. *See* Canadian Multiculturalism Act
Bissoondath, Neil, 154, 164
Black, Ayanna, *Voices: Canadian Writers of African Descent,* 133, 148
Blodgett, E.D., 28–9, 40–1
Body, 90; discourse/language, 179–80, 182, 184, 208; materiality of, 12; and mind, 77; maternal, 146, 147, 177; and nation, 3, 79; in *Obasan*, x, 176, 177, 178, 190, 218; permeability of, 180, 185, 187, 200; as representational economy, 89–90; social, 3, 4; term, ix; *see also* Corporeality
Brand, Dionne, 88, 163, 164
Brest, Paul, 99
Breuer, Joseph, 205, 206
Brooks, Peter, viii
Brown, Russell, and Donna Bennett, 134
Brydon, Diana, 177
Buck-Morss, Susan, 176
Burroughs, Catherine B., and Jeffrey David Ehrenreich, 3
Butler, Judith, 4, 9, 93, 104, 130, 179, 180, 196, 199

Caillois, Roger, 111
Caldwell, David, and Paul W. Rea, 14, 19
Canada: Constitution, 93, 95, 99; 'founding/heritage nations', 93, 95, 98, 163–4; history, 89, 100, 101, 164; pan-Canadianism, 101, 104, 106
Canadian Charter of Rights and Freedoms, 82, 93, 101, 127, 128; 'notwithstanding' clause, 125

Canadian Human Rights Act, 99
Canadian Multiculturalism Act, 82,
    95–103, 126, 126, 135, 137, 163,
    165–6; 'Implementation' section, 103;
    'Interpretation' section, 96; preambles,
    99; 'preservation and enhancement',
    104, 105–6, 107, 109, 110, 111, 155;
    see also Law; Multiculturalism
Canon, 28, 81, 91, 133, 158, 159–60,
    161, 165; in Hutcheon, 163–4, 166
Chambers, Ross, 191
Charcot, Jean, 205
Cheah, Pheng, 23
Cheetham, Mark, 167
Cheung, King-Kok, 181
Chicago Cultural Studies Group, 169
Chow, Rey, viii, 1, 11, 21, 25, 37, 46, 99,
    147, 185
Choy, Wayson, 51–2
Christian, Barbara, 134
Clarke, Austin, 51–2, 164
Class, 4, 49, 58–9, 121, 144; and gender,
    204; see also Labour
Clément, Catherine, 206
Clifford, James, 17
Cohen, Leonard, 163
Colombo, John Robert, 136–8
Colonialism, vii, 2, 3, 23, 40, 65–6, 70,
    72, 79, 86, 124–5, 136, 214
Commodification, x, 61, 84, 88, 109, 150,
    163, 169, 218; of immigrants, 48, 187
Comparative literature, 29, 34–6, 37
Con Davies, Robert, 25
Connor, Ralph, 51–2
Consensus, 93, 171, 174
Contamination, 5, 24, 49–50, 97, 129,
    195, 200–1, 212; in Grove, 52, 75, 79;
    in Herder, 124, 125; and 'heritage', 106;
    and hybridity, 138; and knowledge, 25;
    in Wings of Desire, 13–14, 15, 20
Contestation, 159, 160–1, 214
Cook, Roger, 10
Cornell, Drucilla L., 94, 101
Corporeality, ix, 79, 142, 207, 213;
    dialogic, 180, 191, 202, 211; and
    subjectivity, x; see also Body
Crewe, Jonathan, 164
Criticism: diasporic, 21–3, 24, 26; 'multi-
    cultural critical idiom', 37–8; see also
    Grove
Cromwell, Liz, One Out of Many, 132,

155–7
Cudjoe, Vera, 156–7

Dabydeen, Cyril, 149, 151; A Shapely Fire:
    Changing the Literary Landscape, 132,
    154–5
Dahlie, Jorgen, 42
Darbasie, Nigel, 148
Davey, Frank, 158
David, Jack, 133–4
Davies, Carole Boyce, 150
Davies, Robertson, 164
de Certeau, Michel, 23–4
De Fehr, William, et al., Harvest: Anthology
    of Mennonite Writing in Canada
    1874–1974, 132
Deleuze, Gilles: and Félix Guattari, 26, 62;
    and Claire Parnet, 64
de Man, Paul, 97
Dench, Geoff, 190
Derrida, Jacques, 6, 23, 47, 104, 117, 118,
    197, 200–1
de Shields, Andrea, 156
Desh Pradesh, 109
Diaspora, vii, viii, 2, 3, 4, 13, 23, 60; and
    dissemination, 38, 58; politics of, 8; in
    Taylor, 128; see also Criticism; Ethnicity;
    Immigration
Di Cicco, Pier Giorgio, Roman Candles,
    132, 135, 136
Diggs, Marylynne, 192
DiGiovanni, Caroline Morgan, Italian-
    Canadian Voices, 132–3, 135–6, 137,
    153, 155
Disciplinary gestures, 79, 80, 97, 102,
    103, 130, 174, 184, 186; see also Gaze;
    State
Diversity: containment of, 82; demoniza-
    tion of, 83; in Taylor, 119; and use
    value, 88; see also Ethnicity;
    Multiculturalism
Douglas, Mary, 3–4
Drainie, Bronwyn, 90
Dumm, Thomas L., 117, 120

Eagleton, Terry, 104–5
Economy: domestic, 60, 163; general, 101,
    103; libidinal, 56, 57, 61, 62–3, 65, 67,
    73, 79; representational, 89–90, 129;
    restricted, 5, 61, 104, 194, 195; of
    visibility, 173

Education, 50, 213, 216; *see also* Pedagogy
Elliott, Lorris, 151; *Other Voices: Writings by Blacks in Canada*, 132
El-Malh, Youssef, 140–3
Enlightenment, 71, 86, 118, 122, 173
Epistemology, 9, 138–40, 143, 144, 147, 156, 187, 209, 213, 214; epistemological anxiety, 59, 136, 146, 147, 148, 152, 158, 182
Essentialism, 17, 18, 27, 37, 49, 102, 107, 117, 125, 134, 135, 140, 142, 144, 145, 148, 150, 182
Etcheverry, Jorge, 149
Ethnicity, 2, 3, 83, 143; and absence, 160; as commodity, x, 88, 109, 150, 169; constructed, 21, 37, 138–40, 145–6, 158; as faction/fiction, 135, 147; as fixed identity, 38 (*see also* Essentialism); and gender, 181; in Hutcheon, 163, 168, 172; idealized, viii; and law, vii, viii, x, 94, 106, 148; as malady/threat, 37, 49, 84, 127; overdetermined, 106, 130, 151; and postmodernism, 169; reified, 5; and sovereign identity, 144–5; term, 17; *see also* Diversity; Incommensurability; Law; Media; Multiculturalism; Scandal
Ethnocentrism, 1–2, 97
Eurocentrism, 34, 37, 43
Evans, Martha Noel, 204–5
Ewald, François, 102

Family: and nation, 78, 187, 189, 194–5
Fanon, Frantz, 116–17, 118, 120, 187
Father. *See* Lacan
Felman, Shoshana, 25, 180, 216, 218, 219
Findley, Timothy, 164
First Nations, 40, 88, 96, 127
Fiss, Owen M., 97, 99
Flaubert, Gustave, 51; *Madame Bovary*, 67
Folklore, 107, 109; *see also* 'Heritage'
Foucault, Michel, 11, 12, 28, 117, 118, 186, 206
Freedman, Barbara, 25, 70, 214, 216
Freire, Paulo, 25
Freud, Sigmund, 177, 198, 200, 206, 208, 212, 219; on education, 213, 216; on hysteria, 74, 202, 203, 204–5; on marriage, 218; on 'the uncanny', 215
Froula, Christine, 205, 207
Fulford, Robert, 90

Fynsk, Christopher, 121

Gaze, 10, 15, 44, 60, 109, 111–12, 183; and 'birth' as Other, 139; disciplinary, 110; double, 154; 'look', 42, 191; panoptic, 18; *see also* Visuality
Geddes, Gary, 133
Gender, x, 4, 61, 62, 77, 141, 144; and class, 204; and ethnicity, 181; in Grove, 30; and nation, 189, 195; in *Obasan*, 177, 178; and progress, 188; and race, 156, 177, 178, 204
Gerson, Carole, 160
Gilroy, Paul, 4, 132, 145
Giroux, Henry, 89
Globe and Mail, The, 82, 83–9
Godbout, Jacques, 164
Goddard, Horace, 155
Golding, Alan C., 133
Greece, 108
Grossberg, Lawrence, 70
Grosz, Elizabeth, 180, 195–6
Grove, Frederick Philip, vii, ix–x, 27–79, 176–7; 'The Aim of Art', 44; 'Assimilation', 50, 54–5; as author 'outside'/ 'inside' text, 44, 45–7, 51, 52, 57, 61, 63, 72–3, 79; and 'British readers', 39, 41, 43, 52, 79, 80; on Canada, 43, 45, 46, 53–4; and Canadian literature, 29–30, 32, 56, 62, 64, 66; 'Canadians Old and New', 50, 53–4, 55; critics' views, 27–40; 'Flaubert's Theories of Artistic Existence', 51; 'The Happy Ending', 63; 'mistaken' for an immigrant, 55; 'The Novel', 44; and realism, 40, 44–5, 46, 57, 66–7, 70, 72, 75; 'Realism in Literature', 44; *A Search for America*, 46, 59; *In Search of Myself*, 46, 53, 59; self-image, 29–30, 31–4, 36–7, 45–6, 50–6; 'Thoughts and Reflections', 29, 53; *see also* Niels; *Settlers of the Marsh*; Universalism
Guillén, Claudio, 36
Guillory, John, 92, 159
Gunew, Sneja, 144
Gunnars, Kristjana, 42, 59, 144
Gutmann, Amy, 94, 101–2

Hall, D.J., 48
Hall, Stuart, 2, 4, 83, 94, 105

Harney, Robert F., 102
Harris, Claire, 144, 154
Hartsock, Nancy, 133
Hegel, G.W.F., 115
Helmetag, Charles H., 19
Herder, Johann Gottfried, 115, 191; *Outlines of a Philosophy of the History of Man*, 122–4, 126, 127, 129
'Heritage', multicultural, 106–12; *see also* Canada; Folklore
Heterogeneity, 18, 59, 133, 134, 158, 190, 191, 200; in Hutcheon, 173–4
Highway, Tomson, 164
Hill, Mike, 91
History, viii, x, 2, 19, 23–4, 38, 86, 87, 88; Canadian, 89, 100, 101, 153–4, 160, 164; in ethnic anthologies, 140, 147, 152, 153, 154, 160, 170, 207–8, 221; and 'heritage', 108, 109; in Hutcheon, 166, 168, 169–72; and hysteria, 206–7; materiality of, 174, 187, 214; in *Obasan*, 175–6, 185–7, 198, 201, 207–8, 221; and postmodernism, 167; and progress, 23, 40; 'reified', 105; repetition of, 6–7; representation of, 43; in Taylor, 120; totalized, 99; in *Wings of Desire*, 14, 20, 21; *see also* Realism
Hjartarson, Paul, 37
Homogeneity, 101, 124, 181, 191, 192, 200, 201, 220; in Taylor, 128
Hoogland, Cornelia, 144
Humanism, 24, 33, 34, 52, 69, 70, 115, 117, 119
Hutcheon, Linda, x, 98–9; on 'consensus', 171, 174; and history, 169–72; 'Multicultural Furor: The Reception of *Other Solitudes*', 163, 169, 171; on multiculturalism, 163– 74; on postmodernism, 166–74; (with Marion Richmond) *Other Solitudes: Canadian Multicultural Fictions*, x, 132, 162–9; *Poetics of Postmodernism: History, Theory, Fiction*, 167, 168, 170, 173–4; *Politics of Postmodernism*, 171–3; *Splitting Images*, 172
Hybridity, 3, 5, 14, 17, 21, 22, 23, 40, 55, 56, 59, 93, 100, 138, 155, 156, 157, 182, 183, 190, 214; and gender, 61; in *Wings of Desire*, 13
Hysteria, 74, 90; and history, 206–7; 'hysterical cultural script', 204–6; male,

64; in *Obasan*, 178, 195, 202–3, 204–13; pedagogical function, 213

Immigrants, 14, 49, 127; attitudes towards, x, 73; as commodities, 48, 187; Oriental, 49–50, 51 (*see also Obasan*: 'yellow peril'); as 'parasites', 50; in Quebec, 126; Scandinavian, 42, 49, 52; in Taylor, 128–9
Immigration, 156, 160; policy, 27, 42, 48–9, 161–2
Incommensurability, ix, 2, 5, 28, 37, 94, 101, 105; in Herder, 124
Inglis, Fred, 88
Interpellation, 23, 70, 121, 181, 184; racial, 187; and law, 104–5

Jalink-Wijbrans, Marieke, 150
James, J.T.L., 70
Jameson, Fredric, 169, 170, 172
JanMohamed, Abdul, 152, 203, 206; and David Lloyd, 164, 171
Janus figure, 22, 53, 54, 55
Johnson, Barbara, 25, 46, 80, 95

Kahane, Claire, 209
Katz, Susan, 218, 219
Keith, W.J., 29
Kiriak, Illia, 51–2
Kitagawa, Muriel: *This Is My Own: Letters to Wes and Other Writings on Japanese Canadians, 1941–1948*, 188–90
Klee, Paul, 8
Klein, A.M., 39, 163
Kogawa, Joy, x, 163, 164, 174, 175, 177; *see also* Naomi; *Obasan*
Kostash, Myrna, 90
Kristeva, Julia, 127, 149, 200, 201
Kroetsch, Robert, 1, 135
Krönagel, Alex, 29
Kulyk Keefer, Janice, 164

Labour, 60, 77–8; *see also* Class
Lacan, Jacques, 58, 70, 111, 213; 'Father', 59, 61–2, 63, 64, 65, 73, 200, 210, 211; 'stain', 111–12, 187
Ladha, Yasmin, 144
Lamer, Antonio, 101
Lang, Berel, 142
Laplanche, J., and J.-B. Pontalis, 75
Lau, Evelyn, 81

Laurence, Margaret, 50
Law, 54, 125–6; interpellation ('hailing') by, 104–5; and language, 96; and legitimation of ethnicity, 94–106, 110, 111, 112, 148; 'natural', 127, 186
Lawson, Alan, 41
Layton, Irving, 163
'Learner', 25–6
Lecker, Robert, 158; *Canadian Canons: Essays in Literary Value*, 158, 159–60, 161; and Jack David, 133–4
Lee, Sky, 158
Levinas, Emmanuel, 112
Liberalism, 4, 49, 88, 157, 188, 190; 'difference-blind', 127; 'nonprocedural', 114, 117, 126; 'of rights', 115; and tolerance, 170; *see also* Pluralism
Lingis, Alfonso, 162
Loriggio, Francesco, 28
Lowe, Lisa, 185
Lubiano, Wahneema, 168
Lukacher, Ned, 209
Lupul, Manoly, 98

McCallum, Pamela, 158
McCarthy, Dermot, 160
McClintock, Anne, 7, 43, 71, 74, 78, 189, 190, 211
McLaughlin, Allan, 49
MacLennan, Hugh, 164
Magrath, C.A., 48–9
Maharaj, Rabindranath, 51–2
Mallet, Gina, 84–6
Mandel, Eli, 41, 163
Maracle, Lee, 40, 158
Margins, 58, 65–6, 85, 132; marginality, 4, 18, 164 167–8, 172; marginalization, 16, 38, 148–9, 155, 158, 159, 161, 163, 164, 198
Marlatt, Daphne, 158, 159
Martusewicz, Rebecca A., 217
Materialism, 13
Materiality, 12, 13, 159, 174, 176, 180
Media, x, 6, 82–93; 'disavowal' of ethnicity/multiculturalism, 83, 84–5, 86, 88, 110; 'scandal', 83
Meech Lake Accord, 125
Mehlman, Jeffrey, 212
Miki, Roy, 90, 175, 219, 221; and Fred Wah, 183
Miles, Kevin Thomas, 142–3

Millán, Gonzalo, 153
Mimicry, 2, 31, 37, 101, 138, 156, 195, 205; diasporic, 110–12
Mistry, Rohinton, 81, 163, 164, 165
Mitchell, Juliet, 205
Mobility, 18, 20
Moi, Toril, 206
Montesquieu, 115
Moore, Mavor, 91–2
Mukherjee, Bharati, 140
Mulhallen, Karen, 164
Mulroney, Brian, 98
Multiculturalism, 157; as anarchy, 86; and biculturalism, 126; and Canadian/Western culture, 82, 85–6, 91–2, 100; as counternarrative, 93; dehistorized, 84; 'functional', 92; in Hutcheon, 163–74; as 'ideal', 98–9;; 'multicultural fatigue', 83, 95; 'multicultural gothic', 84–6; 'official', *see* Multiculturalism policy; 'politics of', 113; and postmodernism, 170–1, 173; 'residual', 86, 92; in *Wings of Desire*, 21; *see also* 'Scandal'
Multiculturalism policy, vii, viii, 145, 148, 154; and containment of ethnicity, 82, 163; criticism of, 166; funding, 84, 89, 90, 91, 107, 109–10, 134–5; and marginalization, 163; as reactive gesture, 98; as redundant, 87, 90; White Paper on (1971), 97–8, 103; *see also* Canadian Multiculturalism Act; 'Heritage'; Law; Taylor
Mulvey, Laura, 10

Nairn, Tom, 3, 7
Nancy, Jean-Luc, 121
Naomi: hospital dream, 197–8, 199; hysteria, 178, 195, 202–3, 204–13, 215–16, 219; as 'montage', 176; racialization, 185–8, 189–95, 202–4, 218; repression, 177, 178, 218–19; sexual abuse, 202–4, 210–12, 218; as spinster, 217–18, 220; as teacher, 191, 213–19
Nation: and bodies, 3, 79; and difference, 190; and family, 78, 187, 189, 194–5; and gender, 195; as narrative, 100; pedagogy of, 190, 194–6, 199
Nationalism, x, 5, 7, 8, 23, 108, 111, 125, 145, 174, 185, 194; and literature, 29, 32, 34–5
New Canadian Library, 32

Nida, Eugene A., and Charles R. Taber, 95
Niels: inarticulacy, 45, 46; 'moral
    masochism', 65, 72; 'new dream', 63,
    64, 65, 72; 'old dream', 57–8, 60–1, 63,
    64, 73; in prison, 68–71, 72–6; self-
    image, 40–2, 52, 63; as 'settler/
    colonizer', 41, 71; 'superiority', 57, 63
Nietzsche, Friedrich, 29, 117, 118; neo-
    Nietzscheans, 119, 129
Nómez, Naín: Chilean Literature in Canada,
    133, 149, 151–3
Nostalgia, 9, 16, 20, 41, 58, 61, 72, 107,
    140, 149, 152; in Obasan, 212, 221

Obasan, 174–221; body imagery, 176, 190,
    192, 218; Emily, 182, 186, 187, 188
    197, 198– 9, 207, 220; end (govern-
    ment document), 175–6; father, 204;
    'Grief', 220; history, 175–6, 185–6, 187,
    198, 201, 214; 'Love', 175, 176, 219;
    Naomi's mother, 177, 178–9, 199,
    207–8, 210–12; nostalgia, 221; Old
    Man Gower, 193, 202–4, 210, 211–12;
    'resolution', 175, 220–1; Sigmund, 213,
    214–19, 221; silence, 177, 178–9, 181,
    201–3, 207–10; the stare, 182, 183–4,
    188, 191–2, 213; Stephen, 181, 182;
    'yellow peril', 186, 194–6, 200, 204,
    214; see also Kogawa; Naomi
Official Languages Act, 93, 95, 97, 136
Ondaatje, Michael, 163, 164
Origin(s), 1, 8, 9, 16, 28, 37, 60, 102,
    103, 105, 134 138, 140, 147, 148 152,
    158, 195; 'cult of', 149; originality
    (Taylor), 122, 127, 129
Ostenso, Martha, 28, 30, 39
Othering, 4, 9, 11, 14

Pache, Walter, 27, 28–30, 31–7
Paci, Frank, 51–2
Padolsky, Enoch, vii
Pagden, Anthony, 124
Pedagogy, ix, 3, 6, 79–80, 102, 108, 113,
    115, 161, 183, 191, 195, 214, 216–17,
    219; familial, 183, 184, 190; multicul-
    tural, 129; national, 190, 194–6, 199;
    negative, 25–6; 'oppositional', 213;
    positivist, 70, 73–5; reflexive, 193, 217,
    218, 219; and seduction, 209
PEN conference (1989), 88
Penley, Constance, 216

Phelps, Anthony, 154
Philip, Marlene Nourbese, 154
Pivato, Joseph, 153–4
Pizanias, Caterina, 106–9
Pluralism, 8, 18, 171, 172; liberal, 22, 90,
    93; see also Liberalism
Politics, 'sedative', 82, 104, 109–10, 162
Porter, John, 172
Positivism, 18, 21, 52, 70, 130, 145; legal,
    101, 104
Postcolonialism, 40
Postmodernism, x, 99, 166; and complic-
    ity, 171–2; and history, 167; and
    marginality, 167–8; and multicultural-
    ism, 173; and postmodernity, 169–70;
    and 're-presentation', 173; see also
    Hutcheon
Poststructuralism, 117–18, 119
Potter, Robin, 211
Progress, 20, 23, 71, 173, 213; and gender,
    188; myth of, 175; progressivism, 19,
    24, 39, 40, 79
Psychoanalysis, 216; see also Freud

Quebec, 114, 115, 120, 121, 122, 125–6,
    128, 160; 'heritage' status, 126–7

Race, x, 2, 4, 5, 141, 154; and gender,
    156, 177, 178, 204; and sexuality,
    142–3, 192, 203, 207; and visibility,
    183; see also Racialization; Racism
Racialization, 83, 90, 142–3; in Obasan,
    185–7, 188, 192–3, 212, 214, 218; and
    visuality, 189, 210; see also Race; Racism
Racism, 3, 51, 90, 103, 141, 142, 193,
    214; and hysteria, 212; 'racist' (term),
    85; state, 181, 182; and visibility, 185,
    187, 198; see also Race; Racialization
Racy Sexy: Race, Culture & Sexuality, 109
Radhakrishnan, R., 24–5, 26, 101, 156,
    174, 214, 220
Ranke, Leopold von, 6
Rapport, Nigel, 143
Realism, 15, 39, 43; 'libidinal', 57, 74; and
    reality, x, 6, 7, 10, 11, 13, 14, 16, 18, 19,
    21, 40, 51, 66–7, 70, 75; 'selective', 51
Reflexivity, 3, 5, 15, 25, 204, 205, 217;
    and postmodernism, 168
Relativism, ix, 22; cultural, 23, 101–2, 129
Representation, ix, 2–3, 4, 10, 17, 21, 28,
    37, 55, 66, 104, 109, 135, 217; of

history, 43; limits of, 11; and postmodernism, 173; self-, 157; *see also* Media; Mimicry; Realism

Repression, 44, 57, 58, 61, 70, 77, 167; in *Obasan*, 177, 178, 198, 199–200, 202, 203, 205, 207, 208, 212–13, 215–16, 218; reflexive, 213; social, 72

Ricci, Nino, 40, 81, 86–8, 164, 165

Richler, Mordecai, 163

Richmond, Marion, 162

Ricou, Laurie, 57

Rogowski, Christian, 13, 15, 16

Roman, Leslie G., 1

Rose, Marilyn Russell, 176

Ross, Malcolm, 32–3

Ross, Val, 86–8

Rostom, Kamal A., *Arab-Canadian Writing: Stories, Memoirs, and Reminiscences*, 132, 141

Rousseau, Jean-Jacques, 115, 125

Royal Ontario Museum, 88

Ruger, Hendrika, 144–6; *Distant Kin*, 144; *Transplanted Lives*, 132, 150

Ryan, Michael, 94

Said, Edward, 1, 6, 24, 34, 35, 36, 86, 157

Salverson, Laura Goodman, 28, 39

Sartre, Jean-Paul, 117

'Scandal', ix, 72, 83, 88, 89, 180

Schepers, Ine, 146–7

Schroyer, Trent, 22

Scott, Joan, 112

Self Not Whole: Cultural Identity and Chinese-Canadian Artists, 109

Self-location, 1, 2, 4, 5–6, 22, 25, 158

Serres, Michel, 1, 42, 44, 50, 81, 114

Seshadri-Crooks, Kalpana, 113, 125

Settlers of the Marsh, 37; anti-Semitism, 51; Canada/Sweden comparisons, 41, 58, 62; Clara, 58, 67, 70–3, 73, 75, 76–8, 79; 'counter-discourse' of ethnicity, 47; dominant society in, 51–2; Ellen, 63, 64, 67, 79; father figure, 57, 58, 59–60, 61–6, 73, 79 (*see also* Lacan); mother figure, 57, 58, 59–60, 61, 74, 78–9; 'real books', 75, 80; 'riff-raff', 53, 55–7; Sigurdsen, 76–7, 78–9; 'special race', 42, 60; warden, 68–9, 70, 79; 'wastage', 41–2, 47, 48–9, 51, 52, 55–6, 57, 66, 210; *see also* Grove; Niels

Sexuality, x, 71, 141, 144; and labour, 77–8; and race, 142–3, 177, 178, 192, 203, 206, 207

Shohat, Ella, 17; and Robert Stam, 161, 169

Sifton, Clifford, 48, 61

Silence, 5, 9, 17, 192–3, 197; as discourse, 205–6; and repression, 205; and resistance, 205, 210; as talking cure, 207–10, 213

Silverman, Kaja, 44, 65

Simon, Sherry, 160

Skinner, Shirley, et al., 69

Skvorecky, Josef, 163

Smith, Paul, 63, 64, 65

Smith, W.G., 49

Snow, Robert P. , 89

Spanos, William, 168, 170

'Spectacularity', 185

Spectatorship, 10, 60, 214

Spettigue, D.O., 33

Spivak, Gayatri, 24, 25, 26, 92, 105, 130, 153, 168

Srivastava, Aruna, 139–40

Stafford, James, 161

'Stain'. *See* Lacan

Stalybrass, Peter, and Allon White, 72

Stam, Robert, 17, 67, 82, 89

Stare, 182, 183–4, 187, 188, 189, 191–2; *see also* Gaze

State: 'bio-regulation', 186; 'desire-machine', 3, 26; disciplinary methods, 26; neurosis 3; racism, 181, 182; *see also* Nation

Stereotypes, 51, 89, 110, 130, 143, 186; internalized, 87

Stoler, Ann Laura, 70, 74, 78, 186

Stratou, Dora, 108

Suits, Bernard, 195

Surveillance, 110; -self, 192–3, 195

Takaki, Ronald, 186

Taussig, Michael, 194

Taylor, Charles, x, 92, 113–28; dialogism, 115, 120, 121, 122, 127, 129; *Ethics of Authenticity*, 115; and Herder, 122–5; *Malaise of Modernity*, 115, 118; *Multiculturalism*, 120; 'The Politics of Recognition', 113–29; *Reconciling the Solitudes*, 115, 126, 128; *Sources of the Self*, 115; 'study of the other', 113, 117, 120

Taylor, Mark, 27
Telling It Book Collective, 158–9, 160
Temporality, 2, 7, 105, 140, 147, 154, 172, 196; disjunctive, 3; 'post-Ethnic', 174
Ternar, Yeshim, 164
'Third Space', 55
'Third Force', 97
Time, 'homogeneous', 15, 19, 58, 100, 106, 174
Totalization, 99–100, 105–6, 108, 112, 117, 127, 144, 169, 172–3, 174, 218
Translation, 13, 17–18, 24, 46, 95–6, 98
Trilling, Lionel, 115
Trudeau, Pierre Elliott, 97–8
Turner, Margaret, 30–1, 32, 36

Ueki, Teruyo, 181
'Uncanny, the', 63, 215, 216
Universalism, x, 17, 20, 24, 33, 34, 36, 37, 38, 59, 92, 155, 165, 175, 176; in Grove, 28, 40, 43, 44–5, 56, 58, 60, 70, 75

Valpy, Michael, 82
Van Tighem, Kevin, 145
Varadharajan, Asha, 4–5
Vassanji, M.J., 81
Vico, G.B., 6
Vierhaus, Rudolph, 23
Visibility, 11, 15, 110 111, 167, 183, economy of, 173; and invisibility, 10, 52, 56–7, 60, 91, 131, 200–1; and racism, 198; and vulnerability, 12; see also Visuality
Visuality, 21; epistemology of, 214; 'logic of', 11, 185, 190, 191, 195, 219; and power, 12; and racialization, 187–8, 189, 210; and transparency, 8; see also Gaze; Spectatorship; Stare; Surveillance; Visibility; Voyeurism
Vlassie, Katherine, 164
Voyeurism, 10, 110

Wallace, W.S., 48
Wallerstein, Immanuel, 2
Walton, Jean, 204
Warfare, 2, 5
Warland, Betsy, 158
'Wastage', 41–2, 47, 48–9, 51, 52, 56, 57, 66, 210
Weber, Samuel, 59
Weier, John, 145
Weir, Lorraine, 160
Wenders, Wim, 17; see also Wings of Desire
White, Hayden, 39
Whiteness, 4, 90–1, 138, 141, 190, 191, 196
Wings of Desire, ix, 8–21; Berlin, 8, 14, 18; Damiel's fall, 12; history, 14, 20, 21; Homer, 19–20; language in, 9, 10 14, 16; reality and realism, 10, 11, 13, 14; visuality in, 10–11
Women's Press, 88
Woodworth, J.S., 42, 49, 50, 52
Writing, 9, 11, 18; and efficacy, 24; materiality of, 57; see also Translation
Writing Thru Race conference (1994), 6, 90, 91, 92

Young, Robert, 78, 105, 172, 174, 181
Young, Iris Marion, 112
Yuzyk, Paul, 97

Žižek, Slavoj, 99
Zubrycki, Richard M., 69